Y0-AHQ-566

DISCARDED BY MASLAND LRC

The Long Day of Joshua and Six Other Catastrophes

THE LONG DAY OF JOSHUA AND SIX OTHER CATASTROPHES

A UNIFIED THEORY OF CATASTROPHISM

By
DONALD W. PATTEN,
RONALD R. HATCH and
LOREN C. STEINHAUER

PACIFIC MERIDIAN PUBLISHING CO.
SEATTLE   1973

*All rights in this book are reserved.
No reproduction in any form of this book,
in whole or in part (except for brief
quotations in critical articles or reviews),
may be made without written authorization
from the publisher.*

Copyright 1973 by

PACIFIC MERIDIAN PUBLISHING CO.

13540 39th Ave. N.E.

Seattle, Washington 98125

Library of Congress Catalog Card No. 73-85828

PRINTED IN THE UNITED STATES OF AMERICA

FIRST EDITION 1973

To our parents

Richard V. Hatch
E. Lottie Hatch
Eugene P. Patten
Ella D. Patten
Kenneth W. Steinhauer
Evangeline G. Steinhauer

The year 1973 has been designated Copernican Year in honor of 500th anniversary of the birth of Copernicus in 1473. In keeping with this commemoration, this book is presented.

Acknowledgements

THIS IS TO EXPRESS OUR THANKS to those friends who have given so much help and encouragement with this book. We owe much to:

Dennis W. Burrowes, secretary of the Evolution Protest Movement, North America, in literary consultation in this production.

Ralph T. Chang, consultant in mathematics and computer programming for research on the behavior of planet orbits under catastrophic conditions.

C. W. DeCeault, physicist and mathematician, consultant in celestial mechanics.

Leslie Garcia, artist for the jacket cover artwork.

Charles McDowell, geographer and historian, consultant in the intermesh of catastrophism with archaeological and historical materials.

William I. Thompson III, astrogeophysicist and science librarian, in consultation regarding current technical science publications pertaining to catastrophism.

Emma G. Hale, editor of the Chieftain Press and technical production consultant in this production.

Maureen J. Wesseler, literary consultant in this project.

Historian's Foreword

The Long Day of Joshua and Six Other Catastrophes

Patten, Hatch and Steinhauer's work on catastrophism comes to the market place in an age when the accepted ideas of cosmology (astronomical history of the solar system) have been exposed as being partially unsound. Increasingly, as data is gathered by the space age probes and research of the Moon, Venus, Mars and other planets, evidence is mounting that the inner part of the solar system has been exposed to interplanetary catastrophes. It has not had a history of unbroken celestial peace, or functional isolation.

Authorities now quarrel about the meaning of the new data. Everyone should be encouraged. Historically, similar periods of dissension allowed real academic progress by permitting new thinkers and new thoughts to supply the requirements for a new balance of ideas.

Ours is a period of academic flux with innumerable breaches in the established systems of thought. Patten, Hatch and Steinhauer have provided a theoretical framework by which we are able to approach the reconstruction of past events.

We have been conditioned to believe that we can-

not know the truth in the natural realm unless we can compare an idea with the most exact experience which can be observed today. These three authors, however, compare the observable in nature today, and the scars of the solar system from the past, with what was observed, experienced and reported by ancient man. In this methodology, a new validity is given to historical observations. I venture to say that in a decade, this methodology will be widespread.

        Charles McDowell
        Ph.D — Semitic Studies
        Chairman, Department of Geography
        History and Political Science,
        Western Campus
        Cuyahoga Community College
        Parma, Ohio
        July 1973

Astrogeophysicist's Foreword

The Long Day of Joshua and Six Other Catastrophes

THE LONG DAY OF JOSHUA AND SIX OTHER CATASTROPHES should become a landmark in fields such as ancient history, biblical exegesis, cosmology, geophysics and solar system astrophysics. In the following pages, a panoramic picture of seven astronomical cataclysms, which besieged the Earth in the era 2500 B.C.- 701 B.C., will be explained.

The authors consider the historical, physical and religious contexts during which the Earth underwent major upheavals caused by the planet Mars—a Mars in a different orbit from its present-day orbit. The eight events considered in detail are:

The Noachian Flood ....(circa 2500 B.C.)
The Tower of Babel Catastrophe...(1930 B.C.)
The Sodom-Gomorrah Catastrophe (1877 B.C.)
The Exodus Catastrophe ....(1447 B.C.)
The Long Day of Joshua ....(1404 B.C.)

The Greater Davidic
    Catastrophe .... *(972 B.C.)*
The Joel-Amos Catastrophe .... *(756 B.C.)*
The Isaiahic Catastrophe .... *(701 B.C.)*

It is postulated that each of these events, with the exception of the Noachian Flood, was caused by a close approach, or fly-by, by the planet Mars which was in a resonant orbit with the Earth.

Resonance phenomena in planetary orbits have only been recently discovered. Basically the motions of two planets or satellites can couple together so that the ratio of their orbital periods has the value of p/q where p and q are small integers. This kind of coupling also occurs between the spin of one body and the orbital motion of another. Two examples of resonance are the orbital coupling between Neptune and Pluto, and the capture resonance of the Asteroid 1685 Toro and Earth. In the present book, a mode of an ancient orbital relationship between Mars and the Earth is developed which postulates a 2:1 resonance orbit for Mars' orbit and Earth's orbit.

The many facets of these catastrophes included: depopulation, crustal tides and Earth shocks, oceanic and magma tides, renewed vulcanism, incoming meteors and bolides, orbital shifts (resulting in calendaric problems) and spin axis shifts (resulting in shifts in latitude and tilt). Among the historical and literary results were cosmic imagery in ancient literatures, origins of astrology, the Atlantis story of Plato, and interest in planet deities.

Several major conclusions are derived from this work:

1. *The planet Mars was in a former 1:2 resonance with Earth's orbit.*

2. *The origin of the asteroids and several planetary moons of Jupiter and Mars is considered to have come about from the shattering of a small former planet (Electra) during a very close encounter with Mars.*

3. *The heavily cratered surfaces of Mars and the moon can be explained, at least in part, from the present model as well as the ancient polar migrations recently in evidence on Mars.*

4. *The ancients, in both profane and sacred literature, were describing actual events, albeit in various manners and degrees of accuracy.*

5. *The insights and outworkings of these ancient planet relationships in space and time supply a key to understanding the cosmologies—not just the mythologies—of many ancient people.*

6. *The evolutionary-uniformitarian view of Earth history, i.e. the present is the key to the past, is totally unable to predict or reconstruct these catastrophic events.*

In view of the above, I believe that this book presents the basis for a Unified Astrogeophysical History for the Earth and its environs.

However, it should be emphasized that THE LONG DAY OF JOSHUA AND SIX OTHER CATASTROPHES describes only a limited amount of historical, physical and spiritual truth. It is the authors' desire that this book be an aid to the seeker after truth to discover an intimate and vital relationship with the one who said, "I am the way, the truth and the life: no man cometh unto the Father, but by me."

> *William I. Thompson, III*
> *M.S. - Astrogeophysics*
> *U.S. Department of Transportation*
> *Cambridge, Massachusetts*
> *June 1973*

Prefatory Note

CATASTROPHISM has experienced a 100 year period of hard times as the evolutionary-uniformitarian view rapidly assumed command in the philosophy of natural history. It is like a forest, having experienced a forest fire, with the fauna and flora almost being obliterated. But in sufficient time in the forest, a new and perhaps slightly different regime sprouts forth and prospers. So it is with catastrophism. A decade ago, dozens of writers were beginning to assert the catastrophic philosophy in an authoritative manner. In this decade, hundreds of authors and lecturers are following suit in a variety of ways. During the next decade, this will expand to thousands, possibly tens of thousands of authors, lecturers and teachers.

Authors and lecturers approach catastrophism from a wide variety of ways. Some are closely related to the Biblical faith, and some are not. Some are based on ancient literary or archaeological sources for data. Some are based on geographical or geological data. Some approaches are based on astronomical or physical data for principles. Variety in catastrophism is healthy, but can be unstructured. Catastrophism can be seen as a cohesion of a series of spectacular ancient events. Or it can be presented as a series of very interesting, but isolated and unrelated events.

In this work, after considerable research in team effort, we present a UNIFIED THEORY OF ANCIENT CATASTROPHISM. In biology, the whole is considered more than the sum of the parts. Our understanding is to present a cohesiveness between the series of ancient upheavals, a unified theory. We believe we have succeeded.

THE AUTHORS

Donald W. Patten

Donald W. Patten was born in Conrad, Montana, in 1929. He attended the University of Montana (1947-1950) and the University of Washington (1950-1952, 1961-1962). He holds the B.A. (1952) and M.A. (1962) degrees in Geography at the University of Washington. His minor was in history.

He is an author, editor and lecturer. His first and major work was "The Biblical Flood and the Ice Epoch" (1966) for which the work in hand is a sequel. He is the editor of the Symposium on Creation series for Baker Book House. Among his essays are "The Noachian Flood and Mountain Uplifts" and "The Ice Epoch" in "Symposium on Creation I" and "The Greenhouse Effect" in "Symposium on Creation II." He is a lecturer on themes relating to catastrophism, and his most successful lecture has been reproduced in the filmstrip "Cataclysm From Space 2800 B.C." by American Media. This was based on a slide-illustrated lecture given at the New England Rally for God, Family and Country, July 4, 1970, in Boston.

He is married and has seven children. He is the owner of a successful microfilm service bureau in Seattle. Among his hobbies are umpiring Little League baseball, "one-on-one" basketball and chess. He is a member of the Evergreen Baptist Church in Seattle.

Ronald R. Hatch

Ronald R. Hatch was born in Freedom, Oklahoma, in 1938. His early schooling was in western Kansas and Oklahoma, and at Sunnyside, Washington. He received a B.S. in Physics and Mathematics from Seattle Pacific College (1962). He directed the operations of the Satellite Tracking Exhibit, located in the U.S. Science Pavilion at the Seattle World's Fair. He has taken graduate work in mathematics at the University of Maryland.

Mr. Hatch has been employed as an associate physicist at the Applied Physics Laboratory of Johns Hopkins University (1963-1965), where he participated in the development of computer programs required in the Navy Navigational Satellite System. He was employed as a senior engineer in the Space Division of the Boeing Company (1965-1970) where his duties included orbital analysis. He is currently employed as a software supervisor with the Magnavox Research Laboratories, Los Angeles, where his duties include computer program development for satellite-based navigation equipment.

He is married and has six children. His hobbies include chess and tennis. He is a member of the University Bible Church, Los Angeles, California.

Loren. C. Steinhauer

Loren C. Steinhauer was born in Eugene, Oregon, in 1944. He holds a B.S. (1966), M.S. (1967) and Ph.D. (1970) in Aeronautics and Astronautics from the University of Washington.

He is employed as a theorist at Mathematical Sciences Northwest, Inc. of Seattle. He has served as Acting Assistant Professor at the University of Washington, and Instructor at both Massachusetts Institute of Technology and Harvard University, having taught courses in aerodynamics, orbital mechanics and applied mathematics. His primary research thrust has been on laser interaction with plasmas, in which he has a half dozen technical publications.

Since 1970 he has devoted considerable study to catastrophic themes, primarily from the viewpoint of gravitational and orbital mechanics. Among his publications are "Out of Whose Womb Came the Ice?", in "Symposium on Creation IV"; "Tracing the Past—Is Uniformity Meaningful" and "The Case For Global Catastrophism", both scheduled for "Symposium on Creation V", for 1974.

Dr. Steinhauer and his family reside in Seattle where he has served as Sunday school superintendent at Evergreen Baptist Church. His hobbies include chess and mountain climbing.

Contents

HISTORIAN'S FOREWORD	vii
ASTROGEOPHYSICIST'S FOREWORD	ix
PREFATORY NOTE	xii
BIOGRAPHIES OF THE AUTHORS	xiii
I. EIGHTEEN HUNDRED YEARS OF CATASTROPHISM	1
II. ANCIENT COSMOLOGIES OF NON-HEBREW CIVILIZATIONS	9
The Decline of the Planetary Deities	9
Teutonic and Celtic Cosmologies	12
Roman Cosmology	16
Romulus	20
Numa's Role in Roman Cosmology	22
Indo-Aryan Cosmology from India	26
Calendaric Correlations	28
Maori (Polynesian) Cosmology of New Zealand	29
III. THE ISAIAHIC CATASTROPHE AND HISTORY	32
The Historic Situation in 701 B.C.	32
Rabshakeh	34
Sennacherib	36
Shebna	38
Micah	41
Habakkuk	42
Hezekiah	47
Manasseh	53
Isaiah	55
Isaiah as a Historian	55
Isaiah as a Cosmologist	56
Isaiah's Historical Impact	63
Short Range Impact	63
Medium Range Impact	64
Long Range Impact	64

IV. THE ISAIAHIC CATASTROPHE AND SCIENCE 66

Mars' Ancient Orbit 67
A General Theory of Orbital Resonance 71
    Current Examples 71
        The Merry-Go-Round 72
        Alinda, An Asteroid in the Hestia Gap 73
            The Teeter-Totter 75
        The Hecuba Gap and Its Three Asteroids 77
            The Pendulum 78
    Similarities Between the Hecuba-Jupiter
        and Earth-Mars Resonances 81
    Differences Between the Hecuba-Jupiter
        and the Ancient Earth-Mars Resonances 82
        Superior Conjuctions and Inferior Conjuctions 84
        Hestia and Hecuba in Greek Mythology 84
Conjunction Patterns Within the Resonant Orbit 86
    The 54-Year and 108-Year Cycles 86
A General Theory of Fragmentation 88
    Mars and Its Ancient Mars-Asteroids 88
    The Fragmentation of Electra 90
Bolides and Meteors 92
    Bolides and Meteors in Roman Literature 92
    Bolides and Meteors in Greek Literature 93
    Bolides and Meteors in Hebrew Literature 94
The Geometry of the Mars Fly-By,
    March 20-21, 701 B.C. 96
    Closeness of Approach 97
    Geometry of Approach 98
    Relative Speed of the Two Planets 99
    Perturbation of Earth's Orbit 103
    Perturbation of the Martian Orbit 105
    On Difficulties With Model: Post-
        Resonance Orbital Decay 108
    The Effect of the Martian Fly-Bys on Earth's
        Geomagnetic Field 109
    The Canals of Mars 109
The Tidal Effects Caused by the Fly-By 111
    Tidal Effects on Earth's Crust 111
    The Tidal Effect on Mars' Crust 112

       Tidal Effects on Earth's Oceans,
           Atmosphere and Ionosphere 113
A General Theory of Spin Axis Precession 113
   The Precession of Earth's Spin Axis 113
      Gravity Gradient 114
      Earth Oblateness 116
      Gyroscopic Effect 119
      A Change in the Spin Axis 119
      The Sun Dial of Ahaz 122
   A Spin Axis Precession For Mars 123
On Plutarch 126
Conclusion 128

V. THE JOEL-AMOS CATASTROPHE 130

Naming the Catastrophe 130
Dating the Catastrophe 131
   By the Model 131
   By Amos 133
   By Jonah 135
   By Josephus 136
   By The Talmud 138
A Historical Frame of Reference for
      Cosmic Catastrophism 138
The Joel-Amos Catastrophe
   As Forecast and Described by Amos 139
   As Described and Forecast by Joel 142
   As Described and Forecast by Nahum 143
The Geometries of the Catastrophies 145
   Case One 145
   Case Two 145

VI. CATASTROPHES OF THE DAVIDIC ERA 152

The Elijahic Catastrophe 864 B.C. 153
   The Setting 155
   The Dating 158
   The Fire 158
The Greater Davidic Catastrophe 972 B.C. 159

CONTENTS   xix

    The Dating 160
    Depopulation 161
    Homer's *Iliad* 163
    The Lesser Davidic Catastrophe
        Estimated 1025 B.C. 165
    The Samuelic Catastrophe
        Estimated 1080 B.C. 166
        On Schliemann and Archaeology 169
    The Deborah Debacle Estimated 1188 B.C. 169

VII. THE LONG DAY OF JOSHUA 172

    Dating The Catastrophe 173
        Dating by The Resonant Orbit Model 173
        Dating by Scriptural Chronologies 175
        Dating by The Works Of Josephus 176
        Centuries of Double Catastrophes 176
    Characteristics Of The Long Day of Joshua 178
        Dating by Day and Month 178
        Meteoritic and Bolidic Materials 179
        Earthquakes and Earth-Shakings 179
        The Lengthening of the Day 183
        Descriptive Cosmic Movements 184
    The Geographical Scene Of This Catastrophe 185
    On Cosmology in Western Civilization 186
    The Historical Scene of The Long Day of Joshua .. 191
    Cosmic Intervention in History 194
    Conclusion 197

VIII. THE EXODUS CATASTROPHE 199

    The Job Catastrophe Estimated 1663 B.C. 200
    The Book of Job—A Cosmological Reference
        for the Hebrews 203
    The Ten Plagues in Egypt, March 1447 B.C. 208
        The Timing Difficulty of the Ten Plagues ... 214
    Comparisons Between the Exodus Catastrophe
        and the Isaiahic Catastrophe 215
    Dating the Exodus Catastrophe 219

Ramifications of the Exodus Catastrophe	219
Depopulation of Egypt—The Plague of Death	220
On Crustal Tides and Earth Shocks—	
The Plague of Death	221
Solid Earth Distortion by Mars	221
Renewed Vulcanism—The Darkness Plague	224
On Iron Dust—A Red Snow	225
On Meteors and Bolides—The Plague of	
Hail Mingled With Fire	226
On Orbital Shift—Resulting in	
Calendaric Changes	227
The Ancient Hebrew Calendar	230
On Spin Axis Shift—A Change in Latitude	232
On Cosmic Scenery	234
On Cosmic Imagery—The Golden Calf	235
On Astrology	237
On Ancient Catastrophism in the Aegean	238
Thera	239
The Atlantis Story by Plato	245
Vestiges of Ancient Cosmic Catastrophes	
in Current Life	248

IX. THE SODOM-GOMORRAH CATASTROPHE — 251

Dating the Sodom-Gomorrah Catastrophe	252
By Ancient Literatures	252
By Model	254
Bolides and Meteorites	256
Earthquakes and Earth-Shakings	257
The Great Rift Valley	258
Continental Drift Theory Versus	
Spin Axis Shift Theory	261
Descriptive Cosmic Scenery	263
Stonehenge, An Ancient Astronomical Temple	264

X. THE TOWER OF BABEL CATASTROPHE — 268

Dating—Short Term	268
Dating—Long Term	269

CONTENTS xxi

    A Grand Cycle of Catastrophism Theory 272
    Jupiter In Resonance 274
    Saturn In Resonance 276
    On Models 278
    On Gambling and Dominoes 279
    On Saturn 281
    Earthquakes and/or Earth-Shakings 282
    Bolides and Meteorites 283
    Descriptive Cosmic Scenery 286
    The Structure and Purpose of the Tower of Babel 286
    The Peleg Catastrophe—Estimated 2146 B.C. 290

XI. THE TWO MYSTERIOUS MOONS OF MARS:
      DEIMOS AND PHOBOS 292

    Part I—The Existence of Deimos and Phobos 293
    Part II—Swift and the Laputan Astronomers 297
    Part III—How and When Deimos and Phobos
            Were First Sighted 303
    Conclusion 303

XII. THE FLOOD CATASTROPHE 306

    Dating by Calendaric Day and Month 307
    Dating the Year According to the Julian Calendar 309
        By Scripture 309
        By Josephus 309
        By The Book Of Jasher 309
        By Model 310
        By Transient Decay Curve 311
    Earthquakes and Earth-Shakings 311
        Earthquakes 311
        Earth-Shakings (Spin Axis Shifts) 313
    Meteors and Bolides 314
    Descriptive Cosmic Scenery 315
    Other More Ancient Catastrophes 316

BIBLIOGRAPHY 319

INDEX 324

List of Figures

Fig. 1	The 2:1 Resonance Orbit	3
Fig. 2	The Geometry of the Isaiahic Catastrophe	68
Fig. 3	Mars' Older and Newer Orbits	70
Fig. 4	Asteroids Swept Out of 2:1 Gap Peak At 1:88 Of Jupiter's Orbital Period	74
Fig. 5	Asteroid-Jupiter Geometry Conjunctions in the Hestia Gap (Alinda-Jupiter 3:1 Resonance)	76
Fig. 6	Asteroid-Jupiter Geometry Conjunctions in the Hecuba Gap	79
Fig. 7	Combined Conjunction Patterns (Hecuba and Hestia)	85
Fig. 8	Earth-Mars-Sun Geometry March 20/21, 701 B.C.	100
Fig. 9	Isaiahic Catastrophe Approach and Retreat March of 701 B.C.	101
Fig. 10	Mars' Postcatastrophe Mean Distance	106
Fig. 11	Mars' Postcatastrophe Periheilon	107
Fig. 12	Gravitational Forces Acting on a Dumbbell-Shaped Satellite	115
Fig. 13	"Rotation" and "Pulling Apart" Forces	117
Fig. 14	Gravity Gradient Effect of Mars on Earth	118
Fig. 15	Gyroscopic Precession Three Dimensional Diagram	120
Fig. 16	Pre and Postcatastrophe Spin Vectors of the Earth	121
Fig. 17	The Shadow of Ahaz' Sun Dial	124
Fig. 18	The Geometry of the Joel-Amos Catastrophe	132
Fig. 19	Case 1 Trajectories and Case 2 Trajectories	146
Fig. 20	Case 1 Velocities and Case 2 Velocities	147
Fig. 21	The Great Rift Valley of Mars	148
Fig. 22	The South Polar Region and Frost Plates on Mars	149
Fig. 23	The Geometry of the Catastrophe Locations Of The Davidic Era	154
Fig. 24	The Geometry of the Long Day of Joshua Catastrophe	174

LIST OF FIGURES

Fig. 25 A Closeup of the Battle Site of the
       Long Day of Joshua 187
Fig. 26 The Geometry of the Exodus Catastrophe (I) 216
Fig. 27 The Geometry of the Exodus Catastrophe (II) 217
Fig. 28 Effects of the Krakatoa Eruption in 1883 222
Fig. 29 Three Egyptian Obelisks 229
Fig. 30 The Exodus Route From Goshen
       Through the Sea of Reeds 236
Fig. 31 The Eruption and Collapse of a Typical Caldera 240
Fig. 32 The Eastern Mediterranean Sea 241
Fig. 33 The Metropolis of Atlantis According to Plato 247
Fig. 34 The Geometry of the
       20th Century B.C. Catastrophes 253
Fig. 35 The Great Rift Valley of Africa 260
Fig. 36 Stonehenge 265
Fig. 37 Master Time Line Chart 273
Fig. 38 Jupiter-Mars-Earth in 1:6:12 Resonance 275
Fig. 39 Saturn-Jupiter-Mars-Earth in 2:5:30:60 Resonance .. 277
Fig. 40 Helios Driving the Solar Chariot on a Normal Day .. 284
Fig. 41 Phaethon Driving the Solar Chariot on a
       Catastrophic Day 285
Fig. 42 Mars, Deimos and Phobos 296
Fig. 43 Two Great Circle Patterns of Mountain Uplifts:
       Recent Deformation (The Circum-Pacific
       Cycle and the Alpine-Himalayan Cycle) 312

List of Tables

Table I	Major and Minor Catastrophes 756 to 1404 B.C.	5
Table II	Teutonic Days and Teutonic Deities	14
Table III	Comparing The Ancient And Current Orbits of Mars	69
Table IV	Mars' Biennial Approaches To Earth 756 B.C. to 701 B.C.	97
Table V	Timetable of Approach And Retreat of Mars, March 701 B.C.	103
Table VI	Case One And Case Two Geometries	150
Table VII	Comparison of the Exodus and the Isaiahic Catastrophes	218
Table VIII	Solid Earth Distortion By Mars	224
Table IX	The Laputan Measurements of Mars' Two Satellites Versus Recent Measurements	298

chapter **I**

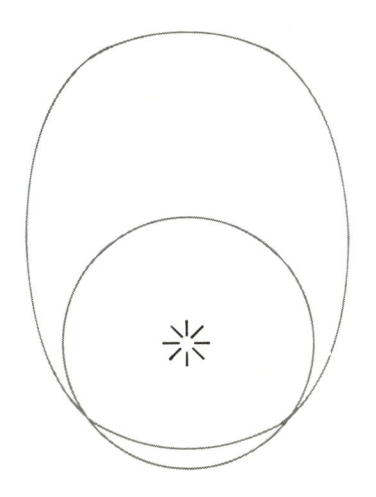

Eighteen Hundred Years of Catastrophism

THIS BOOK, *The Long Day of Joshua and Six Other Catastrophes* is a work analyzing an era of astronomical cataclysms which the Earth encountered in ancient times. The era begins circa 2500 B.C., the time of the Deluge, or Biblical Flood, and it ends on the night of March 20/21, 701 B.C., the date of the last of the seven major catastrophes.

The cause of the catastrophes was Mars—Mars in another orbit, a Mars surrounded by orbiting meteoritic debris (like asteroidal material), Mars feared by many ancient peoples as the deity of "war." The war was, of course, a cosmic warfare rather than a political warfare. Later, when Mars settled down into a non-catastrophic orbit, it continued to be the god of war for the Romans, as was Indra (Mars) in Indian folklore, and Tyr[1] (Mars) in ancient Teutonic mythology. For the pantheistic Romans, all of the five known planets were deities.

Those 1800 years of planetary warfare between Mars and

---

[1]The word *Tyr* in its genitive form is Tiewes, giving us our "Tiewes-daeg," the third day of the week after "Sun-day" and "Moon-day." Tiewes is derived from the Sanskrit word *devas*, from which the Romans derived their word *deus* or "deity." *Encyclopaedia Brittanica*, Chicago: William Benton, Publisher, 1958, Vol. 22, p. 652.

the Earth-Moon system are the concern of this volume. We propose that the orbits of Earth and Mars had a particular, a peculiar relationship. They were in RESONANCE.[2] Surprisingly, resonance can and does occur with some orbits. Although there are several different ratios of resonance, this orbital resonance-ratio was 2:1. The insights and outworking of this ancient planetary relationship shall supply the key to *understanding* the cosmologies, as well as the mythologies, of many ancient peoples.

Figure 1 illustrates what is meant by a *resonance orbit*. This relationship will help us understand why ancient peoples were so interested in planetary movements, in eclipses, in the wrath of planetary deities, in zodiacs, in sun-dials, sun caves, gnomons, obelisks, sun-temples, planet-temples, astrologies and other astronomy-related phenomena. Ancients were inveterate (and sometimes panic-gripped) planet-watchers.

During the period 2500 B.C. to 701 B.C., ancient Carthaginians, Etruscans, Hebrews, Greeks, Phoenicians, Teutons and others carefully measured the paths of the planets in the sky and mapped the zodiac in which they moved. The zodiac was given twelve sectors or "signs" to correspond with the twelve months of the year. In the technical sense, each "sign" is 30 degrees counting from the position of the sun at the vernal equinox.[3] This concept of astronomical geography is as old as Chaldea itself, where it originated.

A careful analysis of Hebrew historical records, primarily the Bible, but also including the works of Josephus, the *Talmud*, and their commentaries will yield a description of seven major catastrophes and several minor ones. Three of these seven major

---

[2]In *physics*, the reinforced vibration of a body exposed to the vibration at about the same frequency of another body. *Webster's New World Dictionary*, Cleveland: World Publishing Co., 1962, p. 1239.

[3]Figure 1 illustrates that one of the frequent dates of ancient astronomical peril for the Earth was March 20/21, the vernal equinox (the first day of spring). The vernal equinox is the point at which the Sun's path, the ecliptic plane, crosses the equator from south to north. From ancient times, March 21 has been known as the first point of Aries, or Mars. What is not widely realized is that the first point of Aries dates back to the era of the resonant orbit when Mars crossed Earth's orbit at that location. Even earlier, March 21 is the orbital location for Earth where the second cycle of the Flood Catastrophe occurred. The ancient veneration for March 21 reflects the degree to which astrology and astronomy were intermixed, indeed often were one and the same thing to the ancient star-watcher.

EIGHTEEN HUNDRED YEARS OF CATASTROPHISM 3

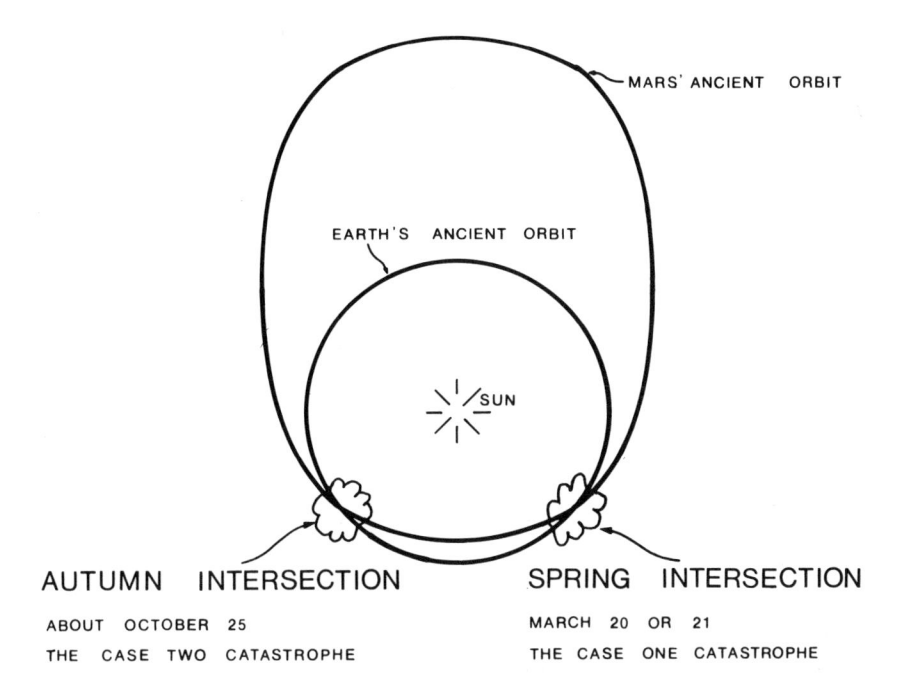

MARS' ANCIENT ORBIT

EARTH'S ANCIENT ORBIT

SUN

AUTUMN INTERSECTION
ABOUT OCTOBER 25
THE CASE TWO CATASTROPHE

SPRING INTERSECTION
MARCH 20 OR 21
THE CASE ONE CATASTROPHE

THE 2:1 RESONANCE ORBIT

EARTH'S ORBIT AVERAGES 360 DAYS	2
MARTIAN ORBIT AVERAGES 720 DAYS	1

FIGURE 1
The model of the orbits of Earth and Mars in 2:1 resonance. Mars crosses Earth's orbit in late October and mid-March. Occasionally the Earth is at the scene as Mars crosses, and these occasions which are catastrophes are seen to be cyclic in timing.

holocausts occurred on or about March 20/21.[4] This repeating pattern suggests that this particular day was a location of much peril for Earth in its orbital travel. The four other major catastrophes all are believed to have occurred at the other intersection, that of the week of October 25 (according to our current calendars).[5]

Does it surprise the reader that these seven catastrophes can be dated, and that from these dates (and including dates of several minor catastrophes)[6] a cyclic pattern unfolds? This, however surprising, is correct. This cyclic pattern indicates that the catastrophes were somewhat *predictable* to the ancients, were repetitive, and were prophesied by oracles, seers, augurs and prophets. They were quite visible in their approach, and were closely watched.

To most readers, particular numeric patterns in years are not easily apparent from Footnotes 4, 5 and 6. One pattern which should be noted is the following:

Two major catastrophes occurred in the 8th century B.C.

Two major catastrophes occurred in the 15th century B.C.

Two major catastrophes occurred in the 20th century B.C.[7]

---

[4]The three spring or vernal equinox catastrophes are dated as follows:
    March 20/21, 1877 B.C.   The Sodom-Gomorrah Catastrophe
    March 20/21, 1447 B.C.   The Exodus Catastrophe
    March 20/21, 701 B.C.   The Isaiahic Catastrophe
The recorders, or chief recorders, of these three events were Abraham, Moses and Isaiah. Micah and Habakkuk add to the Isaiahic account.

[5]The four autumn catastrophies of the fire and brimstone era are dated as follows:
    October 25, 1930 B.C.   The Tower of Babel Catastrophe
    October 25, 1404 B.C.   The Long Day of Joshua Catastrophe
    October 25, 972 B.C.   The Greater Davidic Catastrophe
    October 25, 756 B.C.   The Joel-Amos Catastrophe
Among the viewers and recorders of these events were Joel, Amos, Isaiah and the author of the book of Joshua. It must be kept in mind that in the Scriptures we have preserved eye-witness observations of these events.

[6]Two minor catastrophes occurred in or about 1080 B.C. and in 864 B.C. The former one of 1080 B.C. is named "The Samuelic Catastrophe" and the latter one of 864 B.C. is named "The Elijahic Catastrophe." Each will be studied and discussed in later chapters.

[7]In the book by Donald Wesley Patten, *The Biblical Flood and the Ice Epoch* (Seattle: Pacific Meridian Publishing Co., 1966, p. 146), it was demontrated that there were two cycles of astronomical catastrophism during the Deluge, with about a 140 day interval. In that book, this event was dated

This list therefore suggests that heavy catastrophes frequently occurred in pairs per century (when they occurred), and generally about every five or six centuries. This is to begin seeing *part* of the pattern.[8]

A minor catastrophe occurred on or about October 25, 864 B.C. and yet another occurred about October 25, 1080 B.C. Data describing these minor catastrophes will be presented in a later chapter. The first overall pattern was major catastrophes every five or six centuries, in pairs. The second overall pattern is shown in Table I.

TABLE I
MAJOR AND MINOR CATASTROPHES
756 B.C. to 1404 B.C.

The Name of the Catastrophe*	The Date	The Interval
THE JOEL-AMOS CATASTROPHE	756 B.C.	add 108 years
The Elijahic Catastrophe	864 B.C.	add 108 years
THE DAVIDIC CATASTROPHE	972 B.C.	add 108 years
The Samuelic Catastrophe	1080 B.C.	add 324 years**
THE LONG DAY OF JOSHUA	1404 B.C.	

* Major catastrophes are in capitals, minor catastrophes are in lower case.
** Note that 324 is a multiple of the 108 year interval.

This table indicates that there was a period of 108 years, probably to the day, between the first four listed catastrophes.

at about 2800 B.C. plus or minus 400 years. Current research leads us to believe it was closer to 2500 B.C. But significantly, the onset of the Flood Catastrophe occurred during the first week of November, and it ended after the second cycle of astronomical catastrophism, during the last week of March. Here again, these same two dates or orbital locations of Earth in space are prominent in catastrophic history.

If we include the two cycles of the Flood Catastrophe, the catastrophes occurred in pairs per century, about every five centuries. Specifically we refer to the 8th, the 15th, the 20th and the 25th centuries B.C.

[8]It should be observed and correlated that the 8th, 15th, 20th and 25th centuries B.C. coincide with the lives of Isaiah, Moses, Abraham and Noah, respectively. It is as if the centuries of catastrophism coincided with the emergence of great spiritual leaders who could lead their people through the crisis, and in the aftermath establish a new society or a new life style for the nation, for a battered group of people who survived. Each of these leaders predicted catastrophism. Noah built the ark. Abraham avoided Sodom-Gomorrah. Moses led his people out of the holocaust in Egypt. Isaiah advised his king brilliantly and prophetically on the outcome of the 701 B.C. event, enabling the nation to survive.

It also indicates they were of varying intensities, but of cyclic or regular schedule. The resonant orbit model (to be presented in a later chapter) will present data showing why these periods of planetary interaction were *cyclic* rather than random across the centuries, and were also faithful to the week of October 25th.

This work is written to edify the average reader, the historian, the astronomer, the cosmologist, the geologist, the archaeologist and the theologian. As a result of this study, some of these people may begin thinking of Earth history (and the ancient history of man) within a new framework. This book has been written for the scientist as well as the layman. It contains concepts which are orbital, i.e. revolutionary.

Revolutionary catastrophic research, coupled with orbital analysis, reveals that the Bible contains some very excellent history. Compared to other sources of Assyrian, Greek, Egyptian, Indo-Aryan, Phoenician, Roman or Teutonic origin, it is far superior. This is not to infer that these other records lack in significance; they too are important.

This study does not advocate disregarding the celestial mechanics as established by Isaac Newton. They help in understanding the suddenness, the complexity and the source direction of these ancient holocausts. Some writers analyzing these ancient events would suggest celestial mechanics be set aside or challenged. This is a mistake.

This study does have a point of departure with "popular" theory. Specifically, our departure is from the nebular hypothesis of Kant as the theory for the origin of our solar system. With his general theory, Kant speculated that the solar system had been a vast gaseous nebula or filament 5 billion years ago.[9] In his theory, most of the gaseous material condensed into the Sun; some did not. The remaining gases formed globules elsewhere. These smaller globules eventually cooled off and (somehow) formed planets and satellites, and (somehow) acquired spin axes. Kant's work was entitled *The General History of Nature and Theory of the Heavens* (1755).

---

[9]Kant's theory is sacrosanct and essential to the evolutionary world view. He made "chance" and "time" the heroes of history. If Kant's view were correct, this book would be heresy. If our cosmology is correct, Kant's view of solar system origin is unfounded and unworkable. This establishes a basis for realizing that *the entire evolutionary world view is contrary to scientific experience and principles.*

Kant[10] has been taken for a scientist; in reality, he was a philosopher. Kant's view, widely accepted today, does not explain such *basic* issues as:

1. Why the nine planets have different densities, some *very* different. (For instance, Saturn with a mean density of 0.71 would float easily in water.)
2. Why some planets have more rapid spin rates than others. (Jupiter the giant rotates in forward motion in less than 10 hours; Venus rotates in backward motion in 242 days, and its backward rotation is nearly in resonance with Earth's orbit.)
3. Why planets, condensing out of gaseous globules, have spin rates at all.
4. Why the tilts of the spin axes are angularly diverse (except for Earth and Mars which "happen" to have similar tilts of $23\frac{1}{2}°$ and $24°$ respectively).
5. Why some planets have satellites and others do not.
6. Why the shapes (or eccentricities) of the orbits vary so widely.
7. Why the direction of the semi-major axes of the orbits also varies so widely.
8. Why eight of the nine planets (Pluto excepted) are on the same ecliptic plane.
9. Why Pluto is in 3:2 orbital resonance with Neptune.
10. Why the planets contain 98% of the angular momentum whereas the Sun contains 99.8% of all the mass of the solar system.

As the reader persists through the next 300 pages, he may begin to wonder why the modern estimate of ancient catastrophic times has been so unclear and so unresourceful. Why has *all* of the cosmological discussion of the ancients been relegated to the classification of mythology, simplistically and *a priori*? Was

---

[10]Kant was a geographer and a mathematics teacher. He later became a philosopher, and was the leading exponent of "rationalism." Kant's theory provided the basis for Feuerbach's and Marx's atheism. Hence, views on cosmology "can" relate to how man believes and behaves.

there no core of truth in it, or was there, indeed, a very substantial core of truth overlooked?

Jonathan Swift, the Irish satirist, said some 250 years ago that it is good for society to be challenged with basic new ideas every couple of centuries, or else society might go to seed. We are going to challenge some popular theories, theories often arising out of the German rationalism and the followers of Kant, which include such men as Hegel, Feuerbach, Goethe, Marx, Hutton and Lyell. With reference to ancient history, to ancient literature and to historical cosmology, we shall require from our readers *a new framework of thought for ancient history and for cosmology.*

This work is written with specificity and with seeming boldness. The boldness should not imply rashness, since the material herein has been in consideration and study for almost twenty years, and in the writing for five years. Team thinking has been gathered to analyze, corroborate, dispute and revise key and secondary issues. A model of the catastrophic era is presented, with the belief that it is essentially correct, but also with the realization that some of the details eventually may require revision. The model is presented because models graphically identify *assumptions,* the all-important area of consideration.

This book is not for those who are entirely satisfied with prevailing explanations, often evolutionary explanations, for ancient times. The Hebrew word *shaoq* means shock, and earth-shocks were literally a part of the ancient scene. Soon literary shocks may be generated in this modern scene some 33 centuries later. Our challenge as authors and yours as readers is embraced in the Latin phrase, *sapere aude,* dare to think, and a complimentary principle, dare to challenge.

> Many new ideas vanish as soon as they appear unless a particular effort is made to focus attention on them long enough to fix them in the memory.—W. Platt

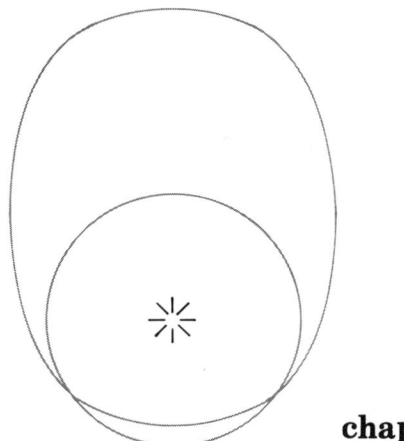

chapter **II**

Ancient Cosmologies of Non-Hebrew Civilizations

The purpose of this chapter is to sketch the astronomical orientation of various ancient peoples. The parallels between these peoples' cosmologies will be considered as general substantiation for our thesis of the Earth-Mars interactions, even though these cosmologies are general rather than specific, and their historicity has been partly lost with the passage of time, and with the ravaging of ancient libraries and societies.

This chapter will also show both the astronomical origin of, and the parallelism between, these ancient cosmologies. These incomplete records from Greece, Rome and the Teutons will by comparison show the care and tenacity of the Hebrew nation as historians.

The Decline of the Planetary Deities

AFTER the year 701 B.C., Mars was sufficiently "bumped" or perturbed in its orbit by Earth to throw its orbit out of 2:1 resonance. It subsequently arrived into its current orbit, which is 1.88 in its period compared to Earth's orbital period. This change will be discussed later. Here, it is sufficient to note that the heavens then "settled down." Astronomical peace came to our planet. This is reflected in several ways in the histories of the ancients.

IN GREECE. The mathematician Thales (640?-546 B.C.) occupied himself with the analysis of the Earth scheme, the new latitude of Greece, the new number of days in the calendar, the new apparent solar path, the new lunar period, the periodicity of eclipses and so forth. Meanwhile later Greek philosophers, such as Socrates, began to doubt the import or the veracity of the Olympic deities. The Olympic deities included Ares (Mars), Aphrodite (Venus), Zeus (Jupiter), Apollo (originally Mars, but later the Sun), Hermes (Mercury), Cronos (Saturn), and Poseidon, god of earthquakes and tidal waves.

Ares was less and less feared and honored; Zeus (Ares' celestial "father") became less and less significant, as did Aphrodite. With the cessation of planetary catastrophes, Greek civilization flowered after 700 B.C. Its pantheon of planets declined in import, not because Greek thinkers had become more intelligent, but rather because, with astronomical peace, civilization was disrupted no more. The study of astronomy-astrology as a "science" and the role of the augurs and seers predicting catastrophes was no longer critical to their national survival.

IN ROME. This same tendency is observable in the history of the republican state of Rome, founded about 750 B.C. Originally, Rome as a state was dedicated to the celestial war-god Mars, with annual Mars festivals, a fraternity of astronomical augurs or priests, celestially-related icons or symbols, planet deities and cosmological lore in abundance.[1] The first month of the year of the Roman republic was originally "Martius' month,"[2] or in the shortened English version, March.

---

[1] In Graeco-Roman astrology, the first point of Aries is the vernal equinox or March 21, the point at which the sun's path crosses the equator from south to north. This is also the historical point in the former era where the catastrophic Martian orbit intersected Earth's orbit. Thus the zodiacal first point of Aries (or Ares) is just another vestige of the ancient astronomical scene. Admittedly the source of the Roman astrology was Graeco-Phoenician, and their source was Chaldean, but it also is to be kept in mind that Chaldea was the original source of migration of peoples as well as ideas.

[2] The next three months, Aprilla, Maius and Juno were named after other observable planets, namely Venus, Mercury and Jupiter. After Juno, the fourth month, originally the next eight months were named after the ordinal numbers up to twelve. (*Encyclopaedia Britannica,* Chicago: William Benton, publisher, 1958, Vol. 4, p. 579.)

Three centuries later (by 364 B.C.) the original astronomical events such as the periodic holocausts of the vernal equinox became so vague that the Roman calendar was reorganized. No longer was March 21 the New Year day, celebrating the passover of Mars, but rather January 1, celebrating the winter solstice when the Sun began to return northward. January, after Janus, became the first month; originally, it had been the eleventh. Still later, by the time of Augustus (63 B.C.-14 A.D.), only two ancient temples dedicated to Mars were left in the imperial city. Time was revising the ancient cosmic-oriented traditions, lores, and religious rites. The change reflects the settling down of Mars in the solar system after going out of orbital resonance with Earth.

IN TEUTONIC LANDS. The cosmological deities also reigned supreme in Northern Europe in the second millenium and first half of the first millenium B.C. The Teutonic planet-deities were originally not considered dormant deities; they were deities of either action or interaction. Like the planet-deities of the Greeks and Romans, they occasionally intervened in human affairs to the advantage or disadvantage of one dynasty or another, one settlement or another, one person or another.

By way of interaction, Freyia, or Frigga (Venus) was considered the "wife" of Odin (Mercury). (We have suggested Mercury interacted with the Earth-Moon system about 2500 B.C. causing the Deluge catastrophe; it went into an inner orbit and interacted with Venus before achieving its current intra-Venus orbit.)

Even as in ancient times Mercury interacted with Venus and the two were considered to be related, so Mars in its orbit appeared to go out into the remote heavens and "meet" Jupiter in a lineup every two years. Hence it is not surprising that the Teutons considered Tyr (Mars)[3] the deity of cosmic battle, nor is it surprising that Tyr was considered the "son" of Thor (Jupiter). In Graeco-Roman mythology Mars was considered a brother of Venus, both being offspring of Jupiter.

---

[3]Our word "deity" comes from the root word *divas* in Sanskrit, from which *Tiwes* comes, merely a genitive form of *Tyr*. The word *Zeus* in Greek and *dyaus* in Hindu are also forms of this same root word, as is the Latin *deus* and the Norse *tivar*. (*Encyclopaedia Britannica*, 1958, Vol. 22, p. 652.)

The Teutonic tribes were converted to (or conquered by) Christendom variously between 400 A.D. and 1300 A.D., roughly 1,000 years after the end of the cosmic wars with Mars. As Christendom absorbed or conquered these fiercely independent peoples of the northern forests, the literatures of the Teutons (along with their traditions, lores, locations of worship, rites of worship and pagan priesthoods) were largely obliterated. Sketchy remains of their ancient cosmologies survive in various languages, such as our English names for the days of the week: "Sun-daeg" or Sunday; "Moon-daeg" or Monday; "Tiwes-daeg" (Mars'-day) or Tuesday; "Odens-daeg" (Mercury's-day) or Wednesday; "Thors-daeg" (Jupiter's-day) or Thursday; "Freyia-daeg" (Venus'-day) or Friday; and Saturn's-day or Saturday.

In Norwegian ancient lore, the royal house claimed ancestry from Odin, or Mercury. On the surface this may be considered fanciful genealogy. However, bear in mind our thesis that Mercury, in heavy interaction with the Earth, caused the Deluge. (See Patten, *The Biblical Flood and the Ice Epoch*, p. 143.) Bear in mind also the lineage from Noah to the ancestors of the Teutons passed through Noah, Japheth, Gomer and Ashkenazy. Gomer is the root word for "Germanica" and "Germany" whereas Ashkenazy is the root word for "Saxony" and "Scandinavia." Hence, the tradition that Mercury or Oden was involved in the establishment of the house of Norway is not without a core of truth. Similarly Mars-Tyr, son of Thor, periodically marauded the earth. For an ancient German hero-figure (Balder) to reportedly be descended from Thor is also not without a core of truth. These are vestiges of the era when there was cosmic warfare in the heavens.

Teutonic and Celtic Cosmologies

Our analysis indicates that Njord was considered the keeper of the cosmos, the gates of heaven (and from this root word comes our "north" and "Norway"). Perhaps Njord had something to do with the region of the several polar stars of ancient times.[4] That planetary deities were in a place of preeminence in

---

[4] It is believed that in five of these ancient catastrophes there occurred a change in both tilt and polar location. Hence there are believed to have been several "Polarises" or polar stars in ancient times. Egyptian lore suggests one of the stars in the Big Dipper was "Polaris" during one of these eras.

ANCIENT COSMOLOGIES OF NON-HEBREW CIVILIZATIONS

Teutonic lore is unquestionable; the examples of the naming of the days of the week and the reported celestial relationship with ancient Teutonic houses has already been mentioned.

In England, an astronomical temple at Stonehenge was built on the Salisbury plain near Southampton. It was probably built between 1900 B.C. and 1600 B.C., and was probably a response to the two catastrophes of the twentieth century B.C. It was built to help the ancient priesthood to augur the new era, to predict not only eclipses of the Moon but eclipses and close fly-bys of Mars in its ancient orbit.[5] See figure 36, p. 265.

Like the Olympic deities in Greece and the planetary pantheon in Rome, later generations in England forgot the ancient catastrophic scene. Now, the druid rites of astrology and augury are gone. The royal houses claiming celestial relationships in their origin are either gone, or have neglected their ancient celestial traditions, but Stonehenge remains.

Another remnant of the ancient catastrophic scene is our English "week" (originally *wicon* or *wicu*). As has been previously mentioned, its elements are named after the planets even as the elements of the Roman calendar, the months, were named after the planets. Table II reflects this. (See Page 14)

Today perhaps only one person in 100 can find Mars in the nocturnal heavens, even in our age of space exploration. This is because its location may be interesting but is inconsequential. Perhaps one in 1,000 can find Jupiter, and perhaps one in 10,000 can locate the dim Saturn. Planet prominence must have been great in Teutonic thought since not only the days of the week,

---

[5]Stonehenge was one of some 500 astronomical temples erected in Great Britain during this era, and the most well known. In his definitive work, *Stonehenge Decoded,* astronomer Gerald S. Hawkins offers the educated estimate that at least 1.5 million man-days of physical labor was involved in its construction and planning. He also calculates it took three centuries to build, or ten generations. "For generations the work on Salisbury Plain must have absorbed most of the energies—physical, mental, spiritual—and most of the material resources of a whole people." (Gerald S. Hawkins, *Stonehenge decoded,* New York: Dell Publishing Co., 1965, p. 73.) It is commonly supposed, and Hawkins concluded, that Stonehenge and other astronomical temples sight on the summer and winter solstices at dawn (in the case of Stonehenge) or at eventide (in other temples). In addition it is commonly supposed Earth's spin rate, axial tilt and polar location were identical in the second millenium B.C. as today. We suggest analysis be made assuming (1) a markedly relocated geographical pole, (2) some shift in spin axis tilt, and (3) that the sightings were made on Mars, the marauding planet in its dreaded approach rather than on the serene solstices.

but also children and even dynasties were attributed to, or named in honor of, certain planets.

TABLE II
TEUTONIC DAYS AND TEUTONIC DEITIES

English Day	Teutonic Deity	Corresponding Luminary
1. Sunday	Sun	Sun
2. Monday	Moon	Moon
3. Tuesday	Tyr (genitive Tiwes)	Mars
4. Wednesday	Oden (Woden, Wuotan)	Mercury
5. Thursday	Thor (Thunor)	Jupiter
6. Friday	Freyia (Frigga)	Venus
7. Saturday	Ullr	Saturn*

*Our research indicates Saturday was named after the Roman planet-deity, Saturn rather than the Teutonic counterpart, Ullr. The reason for this we do not know.

Of the theology of druidism, Caesar tells us that the Gauls, following the druidic teaching, claimed descent from a god corresponding with Dis[6] in the Latin pantheon, and it is possible that they regarded him as a Supreme Being; he also adds that they worshipped Mercury, Apollo, Mars, Jupiter and Minerva [*Venus*], and HAD MUCH THE SAME NOTION ABOUT THESE DEITIES AS THE REST OF THE WORLD.[7] (Italics ours, capitalization for emphasis.)

Why did these planets play such an important role? In our resonance orbit model, Mars in its ancient orbit crossed or intersected Earth's orbit twice. The final intersection was on the day March 20/21, the current and the ancient vernal equinox. This was the catastrophic day the Romans under Numa chose for their New Year Day. The other location of orbital intersection or celestial peril was on or about October 25. Some ancient peoples selected this day of catastrophism (or perhaps more correctly, the day after the catastrophe) as their New Year day.

[6]Caesar's "Dis" corresponds to the Celtic "Tiwes," a form of Tyr, their Mars.

[7]*Encyclopaedia Britannica*, 1958, Vol. 7, p. 679.

ANCIENT COSMOLOGIES OF NON-HEBREW CIVILIZATIONS 15

The Long Day of Joshua Catastrophe and the earlier Tower of Babel Catastrophe were among the panic-filled episodes of ancient times which fell on the October date. The Romans chose the March date for their New Year Day; some ancient peoples chose the October date. The Celtics were among the latter group.

> In Latin countries the evening of October 31 is observed only as a religious occasion, but in Great Britain, Ireland and the United States, ancient Halloween folk customs persist alongside the ecclesiastical observance. Evidence that Halloween reflects influences from the festival of Pomona is scanty, but the occasion shows clear connections with the religion of the Druids in pre-Christian Ireland and Scotland. The Celtic year ended on October 31, the eve of Samhain, and was celebrated with both religious and agrarian rites. For the Druids, Samhain was both the "end of summer" and a festival of the dead. . . . Divination and auguries for the new year were practiced at Samhain. . . . It was also an occasion when fairies, witches and goblins terrified the populace. . . . Bonfires were lighted on hilltops on the eve of Samhain.[8]

There is a long and deep tradition of Halloween[9] as the time of bad luck, black cats, witches flying on broomsticks in the sky, astrologies, auguries, cosmic rites and so forth. (The Druid rituals in our judgment are interrelated with Baal and Ashtoreth worship by the Phoenicians. Baal, as we shall demonstrate, was the Phoenician deity for Mars; Ashtoreth was the deity for Venus.)

It is well established that medieval Christian clergymen endeavored to eradicate these rites and traditions with varying degrees of success in various locales. What is not so well known is our thesis that *real cosmic warfare* antedated the seventh century B.C. and is the basis for the ancient astrologies. Half of the ancient catastrophes occurred or threatened on or about October 25, the same time as the Celtic Samhain. The witch-

---

[8]*Encyclopaedia Britannica*, 1958, Vol. 11, pp. 106B-107.

[9]*Webster's New World Dictionary*, Cleveland: World Publishing Co., 1962, p. 654. [Contraction of *all hallow even*, in which *hallow* is from the Anglo-Saxon *halga*, the definite form of *halif* (see HOLY) in sense "holy person, hence saint"], the evening of October 31, which is followed by All Saints' Day. . . .

and-broomstick theme is merely another vestige of ancient times wherein Mars was visible with its tiny satellites and former meteor streams, some of which shot into Earth's atmosphere during these cosmic crises in dramatic displays and sometimes deadly destruction.

On one or two occasions of the Mars fly-bys, Mars was as close as 70,000 miles from Earth, and at such a distance would appear 50 times as large as the Moon, would reflect 100 times as much sunlight as the Moon (since its albedo or reflectivity is 15% compared to the lunar 7%). Mars at that distance would create tidal effects possibly as much as 350 times as intense as the average lunar tides experienced today.[10] Thus earthquakes plus blizzards of meteors were experienced. Under such circumstances ancient Teutons might well implore Thor to control his "celestial son" Tyr or Tiwes.

Roman Cosmology

In the Roman planetary pantheon, the three supreme deities were Jupiter, Mars and Quirinus. Mars was the "son" of Jupiter, and Quirinus is the phonetic equivalent of the Greek Chronos (Saturn,) but identification is not certain. Mars was the deity of celestial warfare in Rome, and so it also became the god of military warfare on Earth, through the peculiar and martial circumstances of Rome's early history. (Much of Roman cosmology originates from the earlier Etruscan cosmology.) March 21 was the traditional day of Martian peril (and the day of the catastrophe of 701 B.C.). Therefore, on March 21, military leaders would gather in the temple of Mars and inquire of the astrological icons and augurs whether they should undertake war during the coming summer season. If so, war would be undertaken in the name of Mars. (Our word "martial" is a derivative of Mars [other forms, *martis, marspiter, mavors*], which is related to the era of planetary rather than political warfare.)

As a war cult, Mars had its warrior priests, called *flamens,* who had various kinds of religious hardware such as the *ancilia* or "sacred shields," *hasta* or "sacred spears or thunderbolts," and

---

[10]Crustal tides vary according to the *inverse cube principle* as will be discussed in a later chapter. This is according to principles of spherical distortion.

other emblems representing Mars or its assaults on Earth. One of the rites was to have a race among pairs of horses. One member of the winning pair would be sacrificed at the altar of Mars on March 21, the festival called *tubulustrium*. The second of the annual festivals for Mars, *armilustrium,* occurred in the third week of October, very close to the time of the most severe of the ancient orbital intersections about October 25.

In addition, the Roman *lapides sileces* are believed to represent the Martian meteors or meteor streams. These pieces of divine hardware, possibly thunderbolts, also helped the Romans to divine or augur whether or not to go to war for the summer season. The *lapides sileces* were consulted during the March 21 festival, *tubulustrium,* a military holiday.

The circumstances surrounding Rome's founding are important in understanding Rome's official self-dedication to the deity Mars. Rome was founded about 750 B.C.[11] Within a generation, by 720 B.C., the founder (Romulus) had fortified the town, supervised the building and dedication of temples to at least the planets Jupiter, Mars and Saturn. The temple dedicated to the dim Saturn became the Roman treasury; the temple dedicated to Jupiter became the political capitol (Capitoline hill), and the temple dedicated to Mars, located in *Campus Martius,* on a grassy plain, became the military headquarters. It would be an interesting survey as to how many educated Romans of the twentieth century could locate the dim Saturn, Jupiter or even Mars in the nocturnal heavens. Yet the ancient Romans thought these celestials sufficiently important and feared them enough to sight them, track them, build temples to them, and even to center the rites of state around them.

Rome, being founded circa 750 B.C., was founded *between* the last two Mars catastrophes, and perhaps just six years after the dreadful Joel-Amos Catastrophe of October 25, 756 B.C. Details of how this catastrophe was feared and experienced in Palestine are reserved for Chapter V. We will preview that

---

[11]Immanuel Velikovsky, *Worlds in Collision,* New York: Doubleday & Co., 1950, p. 239. "According to the calculation of Fabius Pictor, Rome was founded in the latter half of the first year of the eighth Olympiad, or the year -747; other Roman authorities differ by a few years only. . . . Polybius dated the foundation of Rome in the second year of the seventh Olympiad (-750); Porcius Cato . . . (-751); Verrius Flaccus . . . (-752); Terentius Varro . . . (-753); Censorinus followed Varro."

chapter by saying that those catastrophic times included meteoric streams or blizzards falling across large portions of Earth, and very intense earthquakes in Italy, Palestine and elsewhere.

Why should Rome be founded 15 miles inland and upstream on the Tiber instead of on the seacoast where more commerce could be generated? This inland location would make sense if indeed earlier catastrophes generated tidal waves of 50, 100 or even 200 feet high on the Mediterranean Sea, inundating and destroying coasts and seaport cities. We shall see in a later chapter that at least one such event actually did occur in the eastern Mediterranean,[12] and other lesser tidal waves during other catastrophes also probably occurred.

The Tyrrhenian Sea, the sea between Italy, Sardinia, Sicily and Corsica, the sea into which the Tiber empties, does contain such volcanic islands as Lipari, Stromboli and Vulcano. Lipari is where the legendary Aeolus kept winds confined in caves. Vulcano last erupted in 1890. Stromboli is still active. Marine volcanic activity during a close Martian fly-by would be certain, and marine volcanic activity can create enormous tidal waves.

The founding of Rome upstream from the seacoast is to be noted, but even more important, why should Rome be founded at all? A powerful, successful Etruscan civilization existed in Italy in the eighth century B.C. It was centered in the Arno River Valley area, the Florence-Leghorn-Pisa area, but it extended substantially into Northern and Southern Italy. Why should that government or civilization allow a rival city, a militaristic province, to exist on its southern fringe?

The leading city of the southern portion of the Etruscan civilization was a city known as *Volsinium*. Today it is known as Bolsena. It is about 60 miles north of Rome. Bolsena is on the shore of the present Lake Volsinium (Lago di Bolsena), a shallow, elliptical-shaped or oval-shaped lake seven by nine miles. Its oval shape is unusual. The lake is also unusual in that the bottom of the lake abounds with lava and volcanic ash; yet there

---

[12] A volcanic island, Thera, erupted during the Mars fly-by of 1447 B.C. The planetary interaction resulted in tidal waves that some experts have estimated to have been as high as 600 feet above sea level. This destroyed the Minoan Civilization on Crete and neighboring regions in the Aegean and Mediterranean coasts. This will be discussed in greater detail in Chapter VIII.

ANCIENT COSMOLOGIES OF NON-HEBREW CIVILIZATIONS   19

is no talus of a volcano to suggest a source of the recent ash and lava deposits.

We theorize that during the Joel-Amos Catastrophe October 25, 756 B.C., a meteor perhaps one-third mile in diameter hit Central Italy, leaving a seven to nine mile crater from its impact. It hit the ancient Volsinium, and destroyed it in a matter of seconds, if not less.[13]

> Pliny says also that a bolt from Mars fell on Bolsena, "the richest town in Tuscany," and the city was entirely burned up by this bolt. He refers to Tuscan writings as the source of his information. By Tuscan writings are meant Etruscan books.[14]

> The catastrophes of that century brought the great Etruscan civilization into sudden decline and launched the migrations of newcomers to Italy leading to the founding of Rome. The Etruscans, as cited by Censorinus and quoted in the Section on "The World Ages," thought that celestial prodigies augured the end of each age. "The Etruscans were versed in the science of the stars, and after having observed the prodigies with attention, they recorded these observations in their books."[15]

Velikovsky suggested an interplanetary electrical discharge as the basis for the sudden destruction. We believe the basis was a large meteor and its resultant astrobleme, or crater, the present Lake Volsinium. If this is a correct conclusion, then there is no question that at least the southern part of the Etruscan Empire was in shambles, and perhaps the northern part also. (The Hebrew prophets, Joel and Amos, describe this same catastrophe of 756 B.C. in terms of earthquakes, meteor streams and significant depopulation in Palestine; this subject will be discussed in Chapter V.)

---

[13] Another crater lake in Central Italy is Lake Trasimene, scene of Hannibal's greatest victory over Rome in 217 B.C. This lake also appears to be meteoric in origin, although it likely dates to another, earlier fire and brimstone catastrophe, perhaps the Long Day of Joshua.

[14] Velikovsky, *op. cit.*, p. 273.

[15] *Ibid.*

Romulus

About 810 B.C. prior to the founding of Rome, Amilius was a local chief of the region which became Rome. He expelled his older brother, Numidor, and seized the office by conspiracy and force. He slayed his nephews, who were potential rivals, but he dealt more leniently with his niece, Rhea Silvia. She was allowed to become a vestal virgin.

> . . . under pretence of doing honor to his brother's daughter, Rhea Silvia, having made her a Vestal, by a vow of perpetual virginity he deprives her of all hope of issue.[16]

However, the unforeseen occurred here, unforeseen at least by Amilius. The vestal Rhea was "deflowered by force."

> But, in my opinion, the origin of so great a city, and the first establishment of an empire, in greatness next to the kingdom of the gods, was due to the fates. The Vestal Rhea, being deflowered by force, when she had brought forth twins, declares MARS to be the father of her doubtful offspring, either because she really thought so, or because a god was a more creditable author of her transgression.[17]

Romulus and Remus were the twin baby boys, and Romulus, in opposition to Amilius, was to found the great city and give it his own name. In what way could Mars indeed be the "father" of her twin boys? This undoubtedly was a source of humor to the ancient Romans, which Livy indicates. However, to dismiss the story in rowdy jest may be something less than adequate.

In the Hebrew *Talmud*, it is noted that another important baby boy was born during another night of severe astronomical phenomena, very likely another close pass of Mars. (This was Abraham, born circa 2030 B.C., quite possibly the night of another ancient fly-by or Passover.)[18] If Mars were passing close

---

[16]Titus Livius (Livy), translated by Rev. I. W. Bieber, *Annals of the Roman People,* Philadelphia: David McKay Co., 1872, Book I, p. 19.

[17]*Ibid.*

[18]Louis Ginzberg, *The Legends of the Jews,* Philadelphia: Jewish Publication Society of America, 1909, Vol. I, pp. 186 ff.

to Earth the night of the birth of the twin boys, it might have been as close as 120,000 miles. At this distance, Mars would cause tidal distortion about 70 times the normal intensity of the lunar tidal effect. Anxieties would be extreme and we suspect such anxieties produced a rush of births among near-term pregnant women.

Tides would have occurred in the *oceans* where they may have risen from 15 to 150 feet above normal high tide. Tides would have occurred in the *ionosphere* where the plasma may have stretched hundreds of kilometers. Tides of abnormal proportions would have occurred in Earth's inner and outer *core,* and in its *crust.* Major tides would have occurred in the fluid magma, effecting Earth's thin crust. See Table VIII, page 224.

If such anxieties were the case, Mars (in a fly-by over Earth) might be correlated not with the conception but rather with the delivery of the two baby boys. Perhaps Rhea was providing a correlation with the day of her boys' births, and not just trying to divert attention from the conception. This kind of phenomenon is also indicated in one of the Psalms which describes catastrophism, Psalm 29.

> The voice of the Lord is upon the waters,
> The God of glory thundereth . . .
> The voice of the Lord is powerful . . .
> The voice of the Lord breaketh the cedars . . .
> The voice of the Lord divideth the flames of fire.
> The voice of the Lord shaketh the wilderness . . .
> THE VOICE OF THE LORD MAKETH THE HINDS [*the heifers*] TO CALVE . . .
> The Lord sitteth upon the FLOOD[19] . . .
> (Psalm 29:3-10, King James[20])

---

[19]"Flood" is from the Hebrew word *mabbuwl* which comes from the prime root *yabal,* meaning to bring, to bring forth, to carry, to lead forth, and *mabbuwl* means especially the sense of flowing or movement. (Patten and authors believe the movements described here are astronomical rather than oceanographic.) James Strong, *The Exhaustive Concordance of the Bible,* New York: Abingdon Press, 1970.

All Hebrew word studies in this volume are taken from this concordance.

[20]Throughout this volume, all Biblical quotations are taken from the King James Version, unless otherwise noted.

Within all quotations in this volume, capitalization of complete words is done by the authors for emphasis. Italicized words in brackets are the authors' added for clarity.

Amilius, the power-hungry conspirator, was upset with the birth of the children who were potential rivals. He did not order their immediate execution; yet he displayed a jealous reaction similar to that of Nimrod who was upset over the birth of Abraham, and of Herod, upset over the birth of the Christ-child. Amilius caused the baby boys to be left to the elements, exposed to the weather and the forest fauna on the bank of a river which was expected to flood. Subsequently the survival of the two baby boys was ascribed variously to the wolf star Lupus Martius, to a female wolf (*Canis lupus*), and/or to Faustulus, a lonely shepherd. How seriously Romulus took his alleged ancestry is difficult to determine. (However, we should note the parallel to Teutonic sagas such as the house of Norway, its origin allegedly ascribed to Mercury-Odin, and the house of the Germanic Balder, allegedly originated from Thor-Jupiter.) Later, when Romulus won various military victories over the neighboring tribes, he frequently celebrated by leading the dedication of yet another temple to Mars or another luminary.

This discussion is given in order to help understand the era of Rome's founding, an era of catastrophism, an era of tides and earthquakes, of planet worship and astrological auguries. This is all evidence for the forthcoming model of the resonance orbit. It is also evidence that at least one planetary orbit, that of Mars, was either in disorder or in another cyclic order.

Numa's Role in Roman Cosmology

Romulus, the first king of Rome, was a sort of brigand. He was succeeded by the more literate, academic Numa Pompilius, who reigned during the Isaiahic Catastrophe of 701 B.C., of which more will be said in Chapters III and IV. Numa's talents lay in the direction of statesmanship. He formalized the religious motifs, largely from Etruscan culture. He established the triad of celestial, or planetary, deities. He appointed the astrological priesthood, the *flamens* for these celestial cults. He organized the religious hardwares or icons and possibly helped design the *lapides sileces*, thought to represent falling meteors or "thunderbolts" from Mars. He consulted with the *ancilia* also on whether or not to make war in the name of Mars each new spring season.

During Numa's reign, another important function, the calendar, required reorganization. As a result of the Isaiahic Catastrophe, Earth's spin rate changed and Earth's orbit expanded ever so slightly. The net result was that, after the cosmic holocaust of 701 B.C., 365¼ days were required for one orbit-year, whereas previously 360 completed an orbit-year. Numa had to reorganize the calendar either by adding five days each year, or one month every six years, or one day about every second month, or some other intercalary adjustment.

> The ancient Romans also reckoned 360 days to the year. Plutarch wrote in his *Life of Numa* that in the time of Romulus, in the eighth century, the Romans had a year of 360 days only. Various Latin authors say that the ancient month was composed of thirty days.[21]

> In his *Isis and Osiris* Plutarch describes by means of an allegory the change in the length of the year: "Hermes playing at draughts with the moon, won from her the seventieth part of each of her periods of illumination, and from all the winnings he composed five days, and intercalated them as an addition to the 360 days." Plutarch informs us also that one of these epagomena days was regarded as inauspicious; no business was transacted on that day, and even kings "would not attend to their bodies until nightfall."[22]

Numa did what we might consider the most logical adjustment; he added five days per year. As we shall see, his contemporary, King Hezekiah of Jerusalem, made a different kind of adjustment. He added one month every six years, an adjustment which later rabbis have recorded and then pondered.[23, 24]

---

[21] Velikovsky, *op. cit.*, p. 339.

[22] Velikovsky, *op. cit.*, p. 337.

[23] The later rabbis pondered why Hezekiah doubled the first month instead of the twelfth which they considered far more logical. What they neglected to consider was (1) why he needed to add any days or months at all—that is to say why the successful 360 day calendar suddenly went out of style—and (2) whether the archangel of the Lord which passed over Palestine that fearful catastrophic night might have been the governor of a planet, controller of a luminary. The rabbis were asking questions, but they were asking the wrong questions.

[24] Two relics of ancient Teutonic or Celtic calendar systems are found in medieval England and France. In England, March was considered the first month of the legal year up until as recently as 1752. The Anglo-Saxons described March as *Lencten-monath*, lengthened month. (A modern deriv-

At this point, another parallelism should be observed. The Celts in Great Britain in ancient times considered one catastrophic day (October 25) to be New Year Day while the Romans under Numa considered the other catastrophic day (March 21) to be New Year Day. This is a difference in date but a similarity in purpose. The Celtic Samhain or New Year Day may well date back to the end of October of 1930 B.C., the day we estimate the Tower of Babel was engulfed in meteorites and earthquakes; or it may possibly correlate with the Long Day of Joshua, another October 25 date of ancient catastrophism, the latter in 1404 B.C. Naturally, Celtic cosmologists or augurs would favor the last week of October for their New Year Day if one of these October catastrophies preceded the time when they recalculated or reformed the calendar in Britain.

By the same logic, Numa would naturally prefer the March 21 day, since he was living and ruling in 701 B.C. during the March 21 catastrophe of that year. (Actually the dreaded day was March 20, the day preceding the New Year Day, and it was a day of apprehension, fasting and mourning. This is yet another parallel to the Celtic dread of the evening of Samhain, or Halloween.) It would appear that in their thinking, the ancients felt that once this critical day had passed, a new year or perhaps even a new era of astronomical peace could be expected or forecast.

In Rome, Numa named the first four months after planets beginning with Mars (March or Mars' month), followed by Aphrodite (April or Aprilla's month), Mercury (May or Maius' month), and Jupiter (June or Juno's month). Why Saturn was not similarly honored with the fifth month is a moot question. However, these names are another indication of the cosmic veneration in the eighth century B.C.

---

ative is "lent.") This suggests the Teutonic calendar venerated March 21 as the New Year Day and the calendar revision time.

We have just suggested that during the catastrophe of 701 B.C., 5 or 5¼ days had to be added somewhere in the calendar, and Numa did it in the month of March, just preceding the vernal equinox, March 21. It was indeed a "lengthened month" and some ancient peoples gave it 35 or 36 days, keeping the rest of the months at the traditional 30 days. In Scotland, January replaced March as the first month in 1599 A.D. In France, March was reckoned the first month until 1564 when Charles IX by edict decreed January the first month instead of March.

ANCIENT COSMOLOGIES OF NON-HEBREW CIVILIZATIONS

Ovid, a later Roman poet, described the era of the founding of Rome poetically. His descriptions also contain a substantial core of cosmological truth.

> And Phaethon, his ruddy hair on fire, falls streaming down the long trails of the air. A star, sometimes, falls from clear heaven. . . .[25] [*Echoes of Volsinium*]
>
> After Saturn was driven to the shadowy land of death, and the world was under Jove [*Jupiter*], the Age of Silver came in, lower than gold, better than bronze. Jove MADE THE SPRINGTIME SHORTER, ADDED WINTER. . . . [*Echoes of the lengthened March*]
>
> Heaven was no safer. Giants attacked the very throne of Heaven . . . mountain on mountain, up to the very stars. Jove struck them down with thunderbolts. . . .
>
> He was about to hurl his thunderbolts at the whole world, but halted, fearing Heaven would burn from fire so vast, and pole to pole break out in flame and smoke. . . .
>
> And Jove was witness from his lofty throne. In awful indignation he SUMMONED THEM TO COUNCIL [*a conjunction or line-up of planets?*]. No one dawdled. Easily seen when the night skies are clear, the Milky Way shines white. Along this road the gods move toward the palace of the thunderer.[26]

It is more important to realize that the Celts and Teutons, the Romans and the Greeks, the Phoenicians and the Egyptians experienced war in the heavens on cyclic occasions for more than 1,500 years. Rites, traditions, lores, calendars, architectures and astrologies have persisted down to the present in various forms. It is also important to realize that Rome was founded between the twin catastrophes of the eighth century B.C., even as it is important to realize that Israel was founded between the twin

---

[25]Ovid, translated by Rolfe Humphries, *Metamorphoses*, Bloomington, Indiana: Indiana University Press, 1958, Book II, p. 38.

[26]Ovid, *op. cit.*, pp. 6, 7, 10-11 and 8, respectively.

catastrophes of the fifteenth century B.C.[27] Under these conditions it is easier to understand why Romans venerated Mars and other planets so much. Also it is easier to understand why other ancients looked heavenward in panic and fear for themselves, and yet sometimes in hope, that is hope that their enemies or rivals would be consumed. Within this system of thought, it should be no surprise that ancient architectures, calendars, religious themes and even military campaigns were all centered around this repeating cosmic drama.

Indo - Aryan Cosmology from India

This development on Indo-Aryan cosmology will be brief, not because the data is lacking, but partly because our space in this book is limited, and partly because an author of East Indian origin will be far more competent to develop the theme in depth relative to ancient Indian literature, architecture, calendars, folklore, rites, astrologies, word studies, and so forth. It is hardly necessary to recall that surviving even today in Hinduism are astrologies, fears of eclipses, venerations of zodiacs, adoration of planets, mountains, rivers, wind systems and other prominent natural phenomena.

The Indo-Aryan word for our Jupiter is *Dyaus Pitar,* father of the gods. This corresponds to the Greek *Zeus-pater* or Zeus in its shortened form. This same root word has led to the Latin *deus* for divinity, to the Lithuanian *devas* and the Teutonic *tiwes* for Mars.[28] (Indeed these words suggest a common origin of all of these European languages. The root language, we suspect, is Sanskrit, which may well have been at least similar to the language spoken on the Ark by the eight survivors of the ante-

---

[27]The two fifteenth century B.C. catastrophes were The Exodus Catastrophe, 1447 B.C., and The Long Day of Joshua, 1404 B.C. It is the Joshuaic Catastrophe so spectacular if inexplicable in Biblical literature, that has given its name to various literary works. One example is *Sun Stand Thou Still,* a biography of Copernicus.

[28]The Teutonic *Thor* for Jupiter seems to be a derivative of the Indo-Aryan *pitar,* a word connoting father-influence or origin. The modest discussion of word roots and word relationships in ancient cosmologies illustrates the thought of one of our readers, which is that the system of catastrophic thought set forth in this work could easily generate a hundred doctoral theses. Some of the theses might well be in the study of origin or derivation of words.

ANCIENT COSMOLOGIES OF NON-HEBREW CIVILIZATIONS 27

diluvian age.) Planet worship developed early in Egypt, England, France, Germany, Greece, India, Ireland, Italy, Persia, Philistia and other locations, by peoples who migrated out of the Ararat-Urartu area a few generations after the Flood Catastrophe.

Europa in Greek mythology gave her name to the continent of Europe. Europa was a Phoenician beauty. She excited Zeus, who in his fired love carried her from Phoenicia to Crete where she became the mother of Minos and matriarch of the Minoan Kingdom. Similarly the subcontinent of India has a name also of astral origin, for *Indra* corresponds to Mars, *Agni* corresponds to Venus or Aphrodite, *Mitra* to the Sun or Helios.

Indra is represented with four arms and hands. Two hands hold spears, two others hold cosmic thunderbolts (which recall the *lapides sileces* and the *hasta* of the Roman cosmic religion). The four arms may possibly picture the ancient scene of multiple auroras, wing-like auras, because planetary geomagnetic sheaths were not just passing by, but were deeply clashing.

Sometimes Indra is depicted with 1,000 eyes. This depicts the era, circa 2000 B.C. when thousands of Mars-asteroids or meteors circled the red planet. These ancient meteors are themselves vestiges of when Mars, in a former orbit nearer to Jupiter, encountered a smaller planet which fragmented. Some of these fragments revolved around Mars and assaulted Earth cyclically. These fragments were called *Maruts* in India. Most of these fragments revolve around the Sun and remain there today as asteroids. Thus the *Maruts* of India must be considered in relation to meteors and the fire and brimstone, the pestilence and the hot hail falling from the skies reported in the Biblical accounts of those catastrophic scenes.[29]

---

[29]At least 15 Psalms are concerned with catastrophic themes. This is 10% of the Psalms. These include Psalms 18, 29, 46, 50, 66, 68, 74, 77, 78, 91, 104, 105, 106, 114, 135 and 136.

In the *Rig Veda* (one of the more ancient sacred works of India), Mars being Indra, is the theme of some 300 hymns, or 25% of the total.

One of the catastrophic Psalms, Psalm 46, specifically *describes* the catastrophe of 701 B.C. and its aftermath. Several specifically *describe* the Exodus holocaust. This is when the children of Israel left Egypt amid signs and wonders in the heavens, a pillar of fire by night which was a cloud by day, earthquakes, fiery meteorites, volcanic eruptions and tidal waves.

Calendaric Correlations

We cannot say definitely how ancient the 360 day calendar is, but its usefulness terminated in 701 B.C. Its usefulness may have originated as a consequence of the twin catastrophes of the fifteenth century B.C.

INDIA The texts of the *Veda* period know a year of only 360 days. "All Veda texts speak uniformly and exclusively of a year of 360 days. Passages in which this length of the year is directly stated are found in all the Brahmanas." It is striking that the Vedas nowhere mention an intercalary period.[30]

Here is a passage from the *Aryabhatiya,* an old Indian work on mathematics and astronomy: "A year consists of twelve months. A month consists of 30 days. A day consists of 60 nadis. A nadi consists of 60 vinadikas."[31]

PERSIA The ancient Persian year was composed of 360 days or twelve months of thirty days each. In the seventh century five *Gatha* days were added to the calendar.[32]

CHALDEA The astronomical tablets from the period antedating the Neo-Babylonian Empire compute the year at so many days, without mention of additional days. That the ancient Babylonian year had only 360 days was known before the cuneiform script was deciphered: Ctesias wrote that the walls of Babylon were 360 fur-

---

[30] Velikovsky, op. cit., p. 330. The subsequent quotes are also taken from Dr. Velikovsky, and we consider his research in this area brilliant and sound. It is not to say that others need not pursue research in this area, for that too is important.

[31] Velikovsky, op cit., p. 331.

[32] Velikovsky, op. cit., p. 332.

longs in compass, "as many as there had been days in the year."[33]

ASSYRIA   The Assyrian year consisted of 360 days; a decade was called a *sarus;* a *sarus* consisted of 3600 days.[34]

EGYPT   In the fifth century Herodotus wrote: "The Egyptians, reckoning thirty days to each of the twelve months, add five days in every year over and above the number, and so the completed circle of seasons is made to agree with the calendar."[35]

The number 360 shows up in other interesting ways, for instance in architectures. There were 360 icons in the gnostic genii, 360 gods in the theology of the Greek Orpheus, 360 idols in the palace of Dairi in Japan, 360 statues surrounding Hobal[36] in ancient Arabia. In geometry, the 360° circle is another vestige of the former era, this particular vestige in mathematics, being of Chaldean origin, of the era of 2000 B.C.

Maori (Polynesian) Cosmology of New Zealand

Both the eastern and the western hemispheres contain peoples who had fire and brimstone cosmologies. The Maoris, a branch of the Polynesian race, thought to have been long isolated, also have a fire and brimstone cosmology in their remote Southern Hemisphere location. The story of Maui bears resemblances to the daytime catastrophes of the Bible such as the Long Day of Joshua or Sodom-Gomorrah. However, daytime in

---

[33]Velikovsky, *op. cit.,* p. 333.

[34]Velikovsky, *op. cit.,* p. 334.

[35]Velikovsky, *op. cit.,* pp. 336-337.

[36]Hobal is likely a derivative of the Chaldean Bel and the Phoenician-Canaanite Baal, so fiercely opposed by the prophets of Israel. As we shall show later, Mars is Baal even as Ashtoreth symbolizes Venus. Here we have a suggestion that the worship of Baal, the celestial marauder, was set in an astronomical motif, and the motif illustrated the number of days in a year in the former age.

Palestine is nighttime in New Zealand. Therefore, the evening or midnight catastrophes of the Bible may well describe the daytime Maui story. The Exodus Catastrophe, for instance, was about midnight in Palestine, and 3:00 P.M. in New Zealand.

> ... this set Maui to thinking how the days might be made longer. It was his opinion that they were shorter than they needed to be, and that the sun crossed the sky too quickly. So he said to his brothers: 'Let us catch the sun in a noose and make him move more slowly. . . .' His brothers said it was impossible. . . .
>
> And so they waited there in the darkness at the place where the sun rises. At length the day dawned, a chilly gray at first, then flaming red. And the sun came up from his pit, suspecting nothing. His fire spread over the mountains, and the sea was all glittering. . . . He rose out of the pit until his head was through the noose, and then his shoulders. Then Maui shouted, and the ropes were pulled, the noose ran taut. The huge and flaming creature struggled and threshed, and leapt this way and that, and the noose jerked up and down and back and forth; but the more the captive struggled, the more tightly it held.
>
> Then out rushed Maui with his enchanted weapon, and beat the sun about the head, and beat his face most cruelly. The sun screamed out, and groaned and shrieked, and Maui struck him savage blows until the sun was begging for mercy. . . . Then at last when Maui gave the signal they let him go, and the ropes came loose, and the sun crept slowly and feebly on his course that day, and has done ever since. Hence the days are longer than they formerly were.
>
> It was during this struggle with the sun that his second name was learned by man. . . . That was his name, meaning Great Son the Day, which was never known before. After this feat of laming the sun, Maui and his brothers returned to their house and dwelt there.[37]

The Maori story of Maui, coming from the vast reaches of Oceania, is not greatly different from the Greek tradition of Phaethon.

---

[37] Anthony Alpers, *Maori Myths and Tribal Legends,* London: John Murray, 1964, pp. 46-49.

Phaethon, in Greek mythology, was the son of Helios, the sun-god, and the nymph Clymene (Gr., *phaethon,* "shining," "radiant"). He persuaded his father to let him drive the chariot of the sun across the sky, but he lost control of the horses and, driving too near the earth, scorched it. To save the world from utter destruction Zeus killed Phaethon with a thunderbolt. He fell to earth at the mouth of the Eridanus, a river of northern Europe. . . . The story is most fully told in the *Metamorphoses* of Ovid (i, 750, ii, 336, and Nonnus, *Dionysiaca,* xxxviii).[38]

American Indians of both Americas have ancient astronomical lores, traditions and in some cases architectures. The Phoenix-bird story of ancient Egypt is merely one more version of Phaethon-Maui-Long Day of Joshua narrative. The celestial dragon motif of China is yet another example. In Japanese lore, there is the tradition that camphor boats sail into the celestial (not oceanic) deep, bearing deities.

We do not propose that the Maui catastrophe scene is the Long Day of Joshua. Indeed, we presume it is not. It is merely another of the cycles of catastrophism, one which enveloped Oceania in the daytime. The Long Day of Joshua occurred during the late evening or night hours of Oceania.

It is not the purpose of this book to compile an exhaustive list of ancient literatures and lores which reflect astronomical catastrophism, but it should be observed that there is a great harmony of motifs, though the particular story varies in details. Moreover, of more concern than any collection of accompanying facts, is the overall concept of ancient catastrophism. (Filling in the grid with details is a labor and a privilege reserved for future enterprising scholars in their fields of specialty.)

An interesting collection of facts is stimulating and valuable, but a model of the series of ancient astronomical holocausts is essential. Our model of these ancient times is best seen in the Isaiahic Catastrophe, Chapter IV. The model lays the foundation for a long-needed unified theory of catastrophism.

[38]*Encyclopaedia Britannica,* 1958, Vol. 17, p. 687.

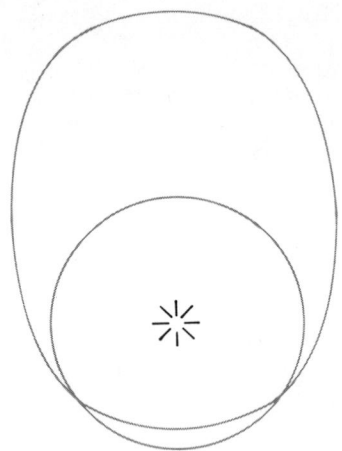

chapter **III**

The Isaiahic Catastrophe and History

March 20/21, 701 B.C.

This chapter is designed to show the kind of actions, leadership and responses which developed in a time of an astronomical holocaust, certainly considered a national crisis. Eight persons will be cited, two of whom perished and a third of whom was injured with cosmic burns. Reactions range from apprehension (Micah), to despair (Shebna), to dismay (Hezekiah), to hope (Isaiah), to cosmic-scheduled battle plans (Sennacherib), and to a casual arrogance (Rabshakeh).

Frequently, events surrounding Judah's experience with catastrophes called forward the best of their leadership, leaders such as Abraham, Amos, Elijah, Joshua, Moses, Isaiah, and (by extension) Noah. In this last of the long series of holocausts, where more literature is extant, we see the stable, stellar figure of Isaiah in the foreground, with a thankful, revitalized Jerusalem and a massive Assyrian graveyard in the background. Isaiah foresaw the coming catastrophe, but also, somehow by Divine guidance, he understood beforehand its outcome.

The Historic Situation In 701 B.C.

THE YEAR 701 B.C. was like the earlier years of dreaded

catastrophism in most respects.[1] It was a year in which attention of numerous peoples of all continents was riveted skyward. The viewing hours of Mars were from about 8 A.M. to 8 P.M. The best viewing hours were just after sunset. This catastrophe was expected to be a crisis much like the earlier ones with meteoritic blizzards, earthquakes, tidal waves in marine regions, vulcanism in various terrestrial regions, and vast auroral displays in the magnetosphere. On each of these six earlier occasions, Mars approached Earth within 150,000 miles, and on one occasion perhaps as close as 60,000 miles.

In 701 B.C., if Mars passed as close as 70,000 miles (an indicated possibility), it would have caused a crustal deformation 350 times greater than the usual 2- to 3-inch lunar-caused, daily crustal deformation. Even if the crustal deformation were only half as great as we have indicated, the walled cities throughout the Middle East, cities such as Jerusalem and Nineveh, stood in considerable danger.

Mars in the sky at a 240,000-mile distance would appear four times as large as the Moon, but since its albedo is twice that of the Moon, it would "shine" eight times greater.[2] Mars, passing on the inside of Earth on this particular occasion, would appear like a silvery slit. Its area in the nocturnal sky would be 50 times greater than the Moon's, and its reflective power would be about 100 times greater than the Moon's reflection. Many of its craters could be seen, as could its two tiny moons, Deimos and Phobos. In addition, there would be a fiery display of Mars-meteors. This would, indeed, be a shocking exhibition. To suggest that the Earth-dwellers of that particular night were uneasy is an understatement. They must have been panic-stricken.

The Joel-Amos Catastrophe had occurred just 54 years and 4½ months earlier, in October of 756 B.C. Of the many children who survived that catastrophe, their eye-witness accounts

---

[1] The earlier years of heavy catastrophism were 1930 B.C., 1877 B.C., 1447 B.C., 1404 B.C., 972 B.C. and 756 B.C. During each of these holocausts, we suspect the Middle East, only one region of the Earth, was depopulated a minimum of 2% and a maximum of 20%.

[2] The Moon reflects 7% of the sunlight that falls on its surface; Mars reflects 14.8%. The reflective ability of a planet is termed its "albedo." Earth's albedo is 39% due largely to its reflective cloud patterns and oceans.

of the 756 B.C. event were frightening.[3] Isaiah was one of the survivors. He had been an impressionable child of perhaps nine or ten years old in 756 B.C. Therefore, he had a frame of reference of solid personal experience, since he had already lived through one dreadful astronomical holocaust. He also had a frame of reference which was historical (for he refers to accounts of the Long Day of Joshua, the Exodus Catastrophe and the Sodom-Gomorrah Catastrophe as three models). In addition, he had a frame of reference which included astronomy, for he was one of the many "watchmen in the night" who frequented Jerusalem's rooftops as observatories.

This chapter shall consider the experiences of eight persons recorded in the Scriptures who lived during this holocaust in the spring of 701 B.C. Six of the eight survived it. Three of the eight were kings; another three were prophets; one was a general and one the king's treasurer. Two were Assyrians and six were Hebrews. The names and positions of the eight are as follows:

1. Rabshakeh — Assyrian general under Sennacherib
2. Sennacherib — Assyrian king and commander-in-chief
3. Shebna — Hebrew official, state treasurer
4. Micah — Hebrew prophet, eighth century B.C.
5. Habakkuk — Hebrew prophet, seventh century B.C.
6. Hezekiah — Hebrew king, 716 B.C. to 686 B.C.
7. Manasseh — Hebrew crown prince and later a king
8. Isaiah — Hebrew prophet and statesman

Rabshakeh

Assyrian armies, in terms of the twentieth century, were something like the panzer divisions of Germany in the early part of World War II. Within the preceding 30 years, 731 B.C. to 701 B.C., the Assyrian armies of Tiglath Pileser, Shalmaneser Sargon, and Sennacherib had conquered some 108 cities throughout the Middle East. This included sites from the Indian Ocean on the south to the Black and Caspian Seas on the north, and

---

[3]Our estimate is that 95% of the populace, at least in Palestine, survived the 756 B.C. catastrophe, and thusly Isaiah described: "Your country is desolate, your cities are burned with fire: your land, strangers devour it in your presence, and it is desolate, as overthrown by strangers." (Isaiah 1:7)

from Persia on the east to the Mediterranean Sea on the west. Often the capture was by surrender, sometimes by siege. The Assyrian armies were strangers to defeat.

When the Assyrian troops approached a city, they usually gave an ultimatum to surrender or to be totally destroyed. If the populace chose surrender, they would be deported to a foreign province, and cultural destruction (a grave threat for a Hebrew) would be the consequence.[4] The other alternative was resistance, capture and destruction, razing of the city structures. If this course were chosen and the city were defeated, it would be levelled, and the males of the city who survived siege would become pawns of the Assyrian soldiers. The soldiers would often flay the captives, peel the skin off their backs with swords or knives while the captives were tied to the ground, and then would bet which one would live the longest. Thus resistance was also a hopeless alternative for a surrounded city. Jerusalem found itself in this situation in February 701 B.C. The Assyrian invaders surrounded the ill-fated city, and rapidly were bringing up siege equipment and supplies.

City after city had fallen to the onslaughts of the Assyrian war machine. Arphad, Babylon, Carchemish, Damascus, Hamath, Lachish, Samaria, Sepharvaim, Sidon, Tyre and some 100 others had fallen, more often through surrender than slaughter. Jerusalem was one of only three cities left in Palestine which had not capitulated. It was a city swollen with refugees, apprehensive, bewildered and hungry, for the Assyrian armies had moved so fast that there had been little opportunity to gather the vast food supplies from the countryside which the populace required for a long siege.

Would Jerusalem elect to surrender, or fight and risk annihilation. Sennacherib was not sure. However, his resources were not limited to a blitzkrieg. He also had a propaganda machine of psychological warfare which he began to employ. Rabshakeh was Sennacherib's "mouthpiece." He endeavored to foster confusion and betrayal within the threatened city. The extensive

---

[4]Sargon, Sennacherib's grandfather, had recently achieved the destruction of Samaria and the Northern Israelite state in 721 B.C. through siege, famine and sword, he slew several hundred thousand persons and deported the rest, who became slaves in other Assyrian provinces. These were what are now called the "ten lost tribes."

account is found in Isaiah 36. In brief, Rabshakeh threatened, intimidated, and tempted the populace, fostering dissension and potential traitors.

Rabshakeh's attitude was one of supreme confidence (like the attitudes of Guderian and Rommel in June 1940 on the eve of the fall of Paris). No city had successfully resisted Assyrian assaults in over 30 years. Furthermore, a close fly-by of Nergal (the Assyrian name for Mars) was on schedule for the third week of March. A close fly-by, which was forecast by all the augurs, might very easily include a crustal tide sufficiently strong to breach, if indeed not to crumble, Jerusalem's city walls. Mars-Nergal might indeed make siege equipment such as mounds, catapults or rams unnecessary. Earthquakes might easily create new breaches in the walls of Jerusalem, or reopen old ones. Victory for the Assyrians was certain, one way or the other.

But there were surprises scheduled on that fateful night of the Mars fly-by, the "passover," the night of March 20. True, during this fateful night there were severe earthquakes and breaches created in Jerusalem's defensive walls, in spite of the fact that they were 40 feet thick and 100 feet high. But there was also an incoming bolide, which fell toward the Assyrian army encampment, and exploded above it.

> Then the angel of the Lord went forth, and smote in the camp of the Assyrians a hundred and fourscore and five thousand: and when they [*the Jewish guard*] arose early in the morning, behold, they were all dead corpses. (Isaiah 37:36)

RABSHAKEH		
	1. Who he was	An Assyrian general
	2. His behavior	Arrogance, planet worship
	3. The experience	His sudden destruction

Sennacherib

Sennacherib was not only a king but also an idolater of Nergal (Mars). He believed that Nergal would help Assyria reduce Jerusalem, for Nergal to the Assyrians was as Ares to the Greeks or Mars to the Romans, "king of battle, who brings the

THE ISAIAHIC CATASTROPHE AND HISTORY 37

defeat, who brings the victory."[5] It is entirely possible that Sennacherib offered a prayer of worship to Nergal, a prayer similar to the following eighth century B.C. Babylonian prayer:

> Shine of horror, god Nergal, prince of battle,
> Thy face is glare, they mouth is fire,
> Raging Flame-god, god Nergal.
> Thou art Anguish and Terror,
> Great Sword-god,
> Lord who wanderest in the night,
> Horrible, raging Flame-god . . .
> Whose storming is a storm flood.[6]

Sennacherib's astrologers and augurs may have chanted in expectation hymns similar to the following, recorded by the Hindu poet Kalidasa in *The Birth of the War God:*

> *There fell, with darting flame and blinding flash*
> *Lighting the farthest heavens, from on high*
> *A thunderbolt whose agonizing crash*
> *Brought fear and shuddering from a cloudless sky.*
>
> *There came a pelting rain of blazing coals*
> *With blood and bones of dead men mingled in;*
> *Smoke and weird flashes horrified their souls;*
> *The sky was dusty grey like asses' skin.*
>
> *The elephants stumbled and the horses fell,*
> *The footmen jostled, leaving each his post,*
> *The ground beneath them trembled at the swell*
> *Of ocean, when an earthquake shook the host.*[7]

It was on the fateful night of Friday the thirteenth of Nisanu in the Assyrian calendar, or March 20 in our calendar, that Sennacherib's troops were suddenly destroyed, whether by per-

---

[5]Velikovsky, *Worlds in Collision*, p. 261.

[6]*Ibid.*

[7]Velikovsky *op. cit.* p. 267.

38   THE LONG DAY OF JOSHUA AND SIX OTHER CATASTROPHES

cussion or by radiation (flash-burns). Sennacherib survived, but according to rabbinical sources, he had been badly burned.[8]

SENNACHERIB	1. Who he was	The Assyrian king and commander-in-chief
	2. His behavior	Planet-worship
	3. The experience	He survived, but was badly burned

Shebna

Shebna was the secretary of the national treasury under King Hezekiah. Unofficially, he was the master political manipulator. He had been born heir to a substantial estate, for financial power had been his father's ambition. A lust for money became in Shebna a lust for political power. Through intrigue, he gained control of the department of state in Jerusalem. He was eager for a new era of politics in the Middle East with Jerusalem as its center, and himself as the master-mind.

Shebna was the architect of the revised Egypt policy. Judah, formerly in a state of alliance with and vassalage to Assyria, had experienced peace and moderate prosperity without brutal taxation. Shebna's bold counsel was for Judah to renege on her alliance with Assyria, and enter into an alliance with African powers, primarily Egypt. With such a new policy, a balance-of-

---

[8] Very obscure is the following remark of Aggadat Shir 8.45: At the time Gabriel received the power to annihilate the host of the Assyrians, Leviathan was empowered to "destroy the rivers." From the connection in which this passage is given it becomes evident that the "rivers of fire flowing from before the Shekinah" are meant. [*We propose it could also mean tidal waves sweeping coastlines and estuaries.*] According to Apocalypse of Baruch 63.6, it is the angel Ramael who destroyed the Assyrians. The co-operation of Gabriel and Michael in the destruction of Babylon is maintained in Tosefta-Targum Is. 21.5, and very likely also Aggadat Shir 5.39, where השומרים is to be explained in accordance with ShR. *loc. cit.* Hezekiah and Isaiah were in the Temple when the host of the Assyrians approached Jerusalem; a fire arose from amidst them, which burned Sennacherib and consumed his host. See Tehillim 22, 180. The burning of Sennacherib is not to be taken literally. (*We propose it is to be taken literally, cosmic burns.*) See Ginzberg, *Legends of the Jews*, Vol. VI, pp. 362-363.

power policy, and with expert political manipulation,[9] perhaps Judah could gradually ascend to political dominance of the entire Middle East. Perhaps by such policies, the golden age of David and Solomon could be restored, and Jerusalem would again become the center of culture of the known world.

It was an audacious policy, including calculated risks, to be sure. One hope in the new policy was that Sennacherib and his armies would be distracted on his eastern and northern borders for a few years. The wild Scythians of the north had been an occasional menace. A second hope was that, in event of armed conflict, Egyptian armies together with Judean armies could successfully hold the Assyrian armies to a standstill in Northern Palestine.

Hezekiah wilted under the heavy economic and political pressure applied by the princes of commerce, and in 702 B.C., the new Shebna policy went into effect. Hezekiah acquiesced with reservations, but it was the easiest course to follow. A few isolated but loud voices objected, and predicted the worst. Among these few voices were those of Isaiah and Micah, spokesmen of God. However, since they were not important politically or economically, little attention was paid to their warnings.

In 702 B.C., Sennacherib easily kept his eastern border (Persia) intact; no invasion from the Scythians developed from the north; and he was antagonized by the covert power play of Judah with Egypt. In late 702 B.C. plans for the 701 B.C. campaign were formulated. The plans included conquering and destroying Jerusalem by the middle of spring, and from there to blitz across the Suez into Egypt. By summertime, according to plans, Egyptian armies were to be destroyed. The entire Middle East needed to be taught a lesson, and Jerusalem, (the rebellious city), would furnish the example.

Shebna's "brilliant" foreign policy began to backfire, and quite rapidly. The master political planner had brought down a major disaster upon the whole nation, which threatened to be final disaster. It was true that Egypt and Ethiopia, in alliance,

---

[9]This was exactly the clandestine foreign policy which led to the downfall of Northern Israel in 721 B.C. Prophets such as Hosea, Amos and Isaiah constantly pointed out to Judea that their strength was in their faith in God and the moral fiber derived therefrom. Relying on political alliances repeatedly was their downfall.

had nearly a half million men under arms; but they had decided against undertaking any campaign to relieve Jerusalem. Instead, they dug in along the Sinai Peninsula and sent Hezekiah and Shebna a large supply of sympathy and best wishes.

In January 701 B.C., Assyrian troops advanced rapidly through such vassal states as Syria and Samaria (the region of Galilee). Since they were vassals, there was no resistance. In February, Judah was captured including all the cities except Jerusalem, and Lachish and Libnah (two smaller cities to the southwest). Jerusalem was surrounded. Rabshakeh issued his call to surrender.

If Jerusalem were to surrender, Shebna could be among the first to be flayed. (There was serious discussion of surrender.) He would be separated from his skin and allowed to die by inches, a calamitous reversal of what he had hoped for. On the other hand, if Jerusalem resisted (and with astronomical catastrophism and earthquakes scheduled soon), the best Shebna could hope for would be sudden death in armed conflict, but he was not even a soldier. The entire populace of Jerusalem was terrified. Some of the dispirited people had decided, since they were doomed to die, to "eat, drink and be merry." It was an infectious refrain within the city. Now, Shebna had no master plan, no solution, and no apparent hope. His grand design had turned to total disaster at every turn, both with the Assyrian invasion and with the lack of Egyptian intervention. He was under extreme strain, and in such a pressure situation, he lacked both stability and spiritual resources. Power had been his deity, and now he would lose it.

His decision was to die and to be buried as he had lived—in style. He selected a proper, expensive sepulchre, and an expensive attire, and he (like Hitler) committed suicide. This was the culmination of his political career, the result of his political manipulations.

SHEBNA		
	1. Who he was	Secretary of the Treasury
	2. His behavior	Power lust and political manipulation
	3. His response	Suicide

Micah

Micah was an associate and a confidant of Isaiah, another prophet who advised Hezekiah. Both were dismayed about the lack of executive leadership in Hezekiah, and about the political machinations of Shebna. Micah had a few words for Shebna's complex control of Jerusalem, a control which extended beyond the economic and political scene into the highest religious councils of the nation. Concerning Shebna, the high level manipulator and his powerful associates:

> . . . the prince asketh, and the judge asketh for a reward [*bribe*]; and the great man [*Shebna*], he uttereth his mischievous desire: so they wrap it up. THE BEST OF THEM IS AS A BRIER: the most upright is sharper than a thorn hedge. . . . (Micah 7:3-4)

Neither did the caliber of the populace in general of the holy city measure up, in any reasonable way, to the citizenship of a divine commonwealth.

> The good man is perished out of the earth: and there is none upright among men: they all lie in wait for blood; they hunt every man his brother with a net. (Micah 7:2)

Micah, the prophet, discussed a triple contention. One was against the evil leadership of the land. A second (discussed above) was against the populace in general. A third was against the *land* itself. Micah anticipated astronomical catastrophism.

> For, behold, the Lord cometh forth out of his place, and will come down, and tread upon the high places of the earth. And the mountains shall be MOLTEN under him, and the VALLEYS SHALL BE CLEFT, as wax before the fire, and as the waters that are poured down a steep place. (Micah 1:3-4) [*Micah predicted hard earthquakes and renewed vulcanism including flowing lava.*]

Micah, like Isaiah, had little sympathy for the idolatrous astrologers of Jerusalem.

> Then shall the seers be ashamed, and the diviners confounded: yea, they shall cover their lips. . . . (Micah 3:7)

Nor did Micah spare the sanctimonious clergy.

> Thus saith the Lord concerning the prophets that make my people err, that bite with their teeth, and cry, Peace. . . . (Micah 3:5)

Micah discussed the forthcoming catastrophism in terms of earlier holocausts:

> . . . the day of thy watchmen and thy visitation cometh; now shall be their perplexity. (Micah 7:4)

> Hear ye, O mountains, the Lord's controversy, and ye strong foundations of the earth: for the Lord hath a controversy with his people. . . . (Micah 6:2)

> According to the days of thy coming out of the land of Egypt [*The Exodus Catastrophe*] will I shew unto him marvellous things. (Micah 7:15)

MICAH   1. Who he was   A prophet with an unpopular message
            2. His attitude   Acceptance of catastrophism as coming from God
            3. His response   To emphasize both judgment and hope

Habakkuk

Habakkuk was a watchful youth in the Negev during the Isaiahic Catastrophe.[10] The development of the Isaiahic Catastrophe in 701 B.C., and the miraculous deliverance of Jerusalem

---

[10] The consensus for dating the Book of Habakkuk is 679 B.C. to 648 B.C. as is suggested in *Dake's Annotated Reference Bible*, p. 898. This dating is not based on any reference to the reign of any king for such is not mentioned. The basis for dating is the lone reference to the Chaldean invasion (Habakkuk 1:6). Traditionally, this is equated with the invasions of Nebuchadnezzar the Babylonian circa 600 B.C. We believe that the Chaldean invasion does not refer to the Nebuchadnezzar era, but rather to the Sennacherib era, and the reference to invading Chaldeans is to Sennacherib's Assyrian army, undoubtedly containing a large Chaldean complement. Assyria governed both halves, the northern and the southern, of the Mesopotamian Valley at this time. *Halley's Handbook* dates Habakkuk at 625 B.C. to 606 B.C., which is 75 years later than our dating of Habakkuk. (Henry H. Halley, *Halley's Bible Handbook*, Grand Rapids, Michigan: Zondervan Publishing House, 1965, p. 372.)

THE ISAIAHIC CATASTROPHE AND HISTORY

from the Assyrian armies was now history. The cause of the bolide, the nocturnal "big blast" passover of Mars at 70,000 miles, and the accompanying crustal shocks were now history. Habakkuk's task was to describe in writing the vivid celestial events of that dramatic evening in March 701 B.C. This he does in chapter 3 of the book of Habakkuk.

As Mars approached Earth in that fateful month of March, it was a slit of light overtaking Earth about 22,500 miles per hour, day after day. Upon its outside fly-by, it suddenly blossomed to quarter, to half and to full-moon reflectivity. Its gravitational field entered into, and deeply clashed with Earth's geomagnetic sheath which today extends well out beyond the Moon. Brilliant auroral streams, electrical discharges and huge descending meteors were a part of the dramatic scene.

> God came from Teman [*the south*], and the Holy One from Mount Paran [*again the south*].[11] Selah. His GLORY[12] covered the heavens, and the earth was full of his praise. And his BRIGHTNESS[13] was as the light; he had HORNS[14] coming out of his hand: and there was the HIDING[15] of his power. (Habakkuk 3:3-4)

[11] "Teman" means Edom, to the south. Mount Paran was also in the southern wilderness. This means that Mars was seen to approach from the celestial south from the viewpoint of an observer in the Northern Hemisphere. Viewing the Martian approach from, say, the Cape of Good Hope in South Africa, it would have seemed to approach from the celestial north. Actually Mars was approaching Earth along the planetary ecliptic plane and the tilt of Earth's spin axis is why to Habakkuk it seemed to be from the south, or "from Teman."

[12] "Glory" is from the Hebrew word *howd*, derived from a word meaning grandeur, majesty, beauty, gloriousness. We believe that this occasion triggered vast auroral displays, and Earth's geomagnetic field was disturbed into a renewed brilliance.

[13] "Brightness" is from the Hebrew word *nogahh*, suggesting the brilliance as of the morning. A full Mars at 70,000 miles could be as bright as 100 full moons.

[14] "Horns" is from the Hebrew word *qeren*, a projection as an elephant's tooth, a peak of a mountain, a ray of light, or in this case, the trajectory of a burning meteor.

[15] "Hiding" is from the Hebrew word *chebyown*, from the word *chebown*, to conceal or concealment. The gravitational force of Mars, acting on Earth, affected the geomagnetic field which could be seen, and affected the Earth's crust which could be felt. In addition possible electric discharges and/or volcanic eruptions caused shocks which could be heard. The term "the hiding of his power" could possibly mean the coming and going of gravity gradient of Mars, gravity of course being invisible.

Some of the interacting phenomena were invisible like gravity and the geomagnetic fields. Some were visible with gradual movements like auroral streams. Other phenomena were visible with sudden movements like meteors and bolides.

> Before him went THE PESTILENCE,[16] and BURNING COALS[17] went forth at his feet.[18] (Habakkuk 3:5)

On this night, not only the Earth, but also Mars trembled. Probably vast chasms and rifts were opened in Mars with lava outflows. In addition, Earth-dwellers also trembled from fright.

> He stood, and MEASURED[19] the earth: he beheld, and drove asunder the nations; and the everlasting mountains were scattered, the perpetual hills did bow. . . . (Habakuk 3:6)

> I saw the tents of Cushan, [*the eastern horizon*], in affliction: and the curtains of the land of Midian, [*the southern horizon*] DID TREMBLE. (Habakkuk 3:7)

Habakkuk as a youth, possibly a teenager, may well have been in the Negev, the steppe land to the south of Jerusalem,

---

[16] "Pestilence" is from the Hebrew word *deber*. This word in the Exodus Catastrophe is translated "plague" and "murrain." In fact, there are eighteen different words used by the King James translators for *deber*. This word may represent bolides, since it is used to describe falling fragments catastrophe after catastrophe. It has the connotation of "to destroy."

[17] "Burning coals" is from the Hebrew word *resheph*, suggesting a burning arrow flashing through the air, burning heat, a hot thunderbolt, a spark. It comes from the root word *saraph* meaning to be set on fire or to kindle and is related to the word for seraphim meaning angels or archangels. We believe burning coals or *resheph* is the equivalent to meteors.

[18] "Went forth at his feet" is a phrase describing the downward or Earthward fall of the burning meteors, speeding through the atmosphere. We believe this direction describes both "the pestilence" or the one falling bolide which destroyed Sennacherib's army, and "the burning coals" the shower of meteors.

[19] "Measures" is from the Hebrew word *muwd*, sometimes translated "to measure" but from the root word meaning "to shake." The word here suggests our planet was shaken, not just measured. We believe it was shaken in two ways: one, crustal tides of from 80 to 100 feet were experienced, and two, the Earth's north pole was physically relocated by at least 400 miles. The language used here, contrary to evolutionary-uniformitarians, is literal, not figurative.

THE ISAIAHIC CATASTROPHE AND HISTORY   45

and not in the holy city during this fateful night. His description of the eastern and southern horizons indeed suggests that he was in the Negev. From the Negev, Cushan and Midian form the mountain horizons. Very likely, some of the silhouette peaks, dormant volcanoes, suddenly reactivated during this catastrophic passover.

> Was the Lord displeased against the rivers? was thine anger against the rivers? was thy wrath against the sea, that thou didst ride upon thine horses and thy chariots of salvation? (Habakkuk 3:8)

Habakkuk discussed crustal tides and crustal deformation in the earlier verses. Here he discussed marine tides and oceanic deformation, tidal waves. His use of the terms "riding upon thine horses" and "chariots of salvation" recalls the Phaethon story of Greece where, one day, the heavenly steeds pulling the solar chariot bucked, and the sun wandered crazily across the sky. A sun wandering crazily in the sky merely is the ancient way of describing that our planet wobbled, or its spin axis precessed.

Habakkuk described crustal tides in the previous verses; in verse 8 he is concerned with the hydrosphere. Subterranean earthquakes resulted in sweeping tidal waves, affecting coast lines and river estuaries. Thus both crustal and marine movements are described as in writhing activity. Since we have auroral displays (atmosphere) in verse 4, and crustal distortion (lithosphere) in verse 6, then this verse 8 completes the triad, atmosphere, lithosphere, and hydrosphere, all in disorder.

"Thy bow was made quite naked. . . . Thou didst cleave the earth with rivers." (Habakkuk 3:9) Could it be that the naked bow, the "quite naked" bow suggests that the curve or the trajectory of Mars-meteors ripping through the Earth's atmosphere?

> The mountains saw thee, and they TREMBLED,[20] the overflowing of the water passed by: the DEEP[21] uttered his voice, and lifted up his hands on high. The sun and moon

---

[20]"Trembled" is from the Hebrew word *chiyl* which suggests to twist, to writhe, to dance, to travail.

[21]"Deep" is from the Hebrew word *tehom* suggesting an abyss, a subterranean deep, but also often suggesting the celestial deep, outer space. It is the celestial deep being described in this case.

stood still in their habitation: at the light of thine arrows they went, and at the shining of thy glittering spear. (Habakkuk 3:10-11)

The brilliant arrows, Mars-meteors, and the glittering spears, Mars-bolides, are here again, describing the battering of our planet *during* the wobbling of Earth due to the interaction with Mars. The visible effect of the wobble, the crazy paths taken by the Sun and Moon, would be most apparent at the height of the passover but would continue for some days afterwards.

Chapter 3 of Habakkuk is a magnificent cosmic report by an eye witness. Habakkuk not only described what happened, but why. The reason was to deliver Judea from Assyria.

> Thou didst march through the land in indignation [*wrath*], thou didst thresh the heathen in anger. Thou wentest forth FOR the salvation of THY PEOPLE. . . . (Habakkuk 3:12-13)

It is lamentable that this dramatic deliverance of Israel is ascribed to the wrong period of history by most Bible commentaries. It is the era of Isaiah, Hezekiah and Sennacherib, and the dramatic deliverance of 701 B.C. It is not the Chaldean invasion of the era of Jeremiah, Daniel and Nebuchadnezzar, a time when Jerusalem was *not* delivered, incidentally, but was destroyed.

What is more lamentable is that this magnificent cosmic report by an eye-witness is assumed by historians and Biblical commentators to be colorful *figurative* language. Their perspective is so over-shadowed by evolutionary uniformitarianism that they cannot conceive of the general picture, much less the precision in detail which Isaiah does give, even more so than Habakkuk. It is the Earth-centered approach to ancient history which we refute. Only an Earth-centered, non-catastrophic, uniformitarian rationale could conclude that this language is figurative and fanciful.[22, 23]

---

[22] An Earth-centered outlook is what Ptolemy had, and his error persisted for 1300 years. An Earth-centered outlook is substantially what the Darwinists and Neo-Darwinists, the Lyellians and Neo-Lyellians also have. How long is their error to persist? (It was Charles Lyell who "created" [*ex nihilo*] the millions of years in the geological time column.)

[23] The reader should note that this section of Habakkuk illustrates that the Bible contains good observations. Observation, or reporting, although it is

HABAKKUK   1. Who he was   A youthful observer during the catastrophe
2. His attitude   Wonderment at the cosmic display
3. His response   To vividly record it in writing

Hezekiah

Hezekiah was a king of Judah in the line of David. His father, Ahaz, was an idolater who changed his idols as one nation or another was victorious in battle. Sometimes he worshipped the Phoenician pantheon, sometimes the Egyptian pantheon, and after Tiglath-Pileser's victories, the Assyrian pantheon. Hezekiah was different. Early in his reign, he reopened the temple and rid it of the idolatries imported by his father. He repressed the Baal-Ashtoreth (Mars-Venus) cult with its astrology, witchcraft and child sacrifice. However, later, possibly under Shebna's influence, he relented and allowed the idolatries to flourish. Hezekiah was indeed a vacillating king. (His reign began in 716 B.C. and continued until his death in 686 B.C.[24] Due to his poor health, his son Manasseh became co-regent at the young age of 12, in the year 697 B.C. Manasseh assumed the throne in 686 B.C. at the youthful age of 23.)

About 702 B.C. Hezekiah had bowed to the counsel of his power-hungry advisors, and adopted a pro-Egypt policy, unilaterally revoking his alliance and protective agreement with Assyria.[25] By January of 701 B.C., it became apparent that Shebna's

---

not science per se, is an integral part of both good historical analysis and good scientific analysis.

Since experimentation is the modus operandi of science, and these Mars catastrophes cannot be "rerun" (except on computer programs) at different distances and angles, we are dealing technically with the historical observations of these scientific events. Habakkuk's account is both careful historical recording and valuable for scientific analysis.

[24] Edwin R. Thiele, *The Mysterious Numbers of the Hebrew Kings*, Grand Rapids: Wm. B. Eerdmans Publishing Co., 1965, p. 205.

[25] This is the identical policy which Hoshea, King of Northern Israel adopted in 727 B.C., which policy led to the siege of Samaria, 724 B.C. to 721 B.C., and the destruction of the Northern Kingdom, the so-called ten lost tribes.

new policy was leading the nation to the brink of disaster. Hezekiah began to listen to new counsellors such as Isaiah and Micah. He began to replace leading officials, part of Shebna's machine, with other men who had less power lust and more interest in spiritual values. This included Eliakim, who eventually became Shebna's own replacement.

Isaiah was among those watching the heavens, and the trajectory of the approaching Mars in the evening and early night-time hours in February and March of 701 B.C. as Mars gradually overtook the Earth at a rate of about 22,500 miles per hour.

> . . . He calleth to me out of Seir, Watchman, [*Isaiah*] what of the night? Watchman, what of the night? (Isaiah 21:11)

> . . . What aileth thee, [*all the citizenry of Jerusalem*], that thou art wholly gone up to the housetops, [*in nocturnal Mars-watching*]? (Isaiah 22:1)

Isaiah's advice to Hezekiah, as we shall see in the next section, was to resist the Assyrians, and to wait for the Lord's deliverance. Isaiah's prognostication of severe judgment on Jerusalem was well-known; he had been preaching about it for many years. However, by January of 701 B.C., even while Hezekiah "rebounded" spiritually, Isaiah's message began to shift to the positive. Formerly, it had been a variation of the following:

> Howl, O gate; cry, O city; thou, whole Palestina, art dissolved for there shall come from the north, [*cosmological north*] a smoke, and none shall be alone in his appointed times. (Isaiah 14:31)

> Thou shalt be visited of the Lord of hosts with thunder, and with earthquake, and great noise, with storm and tempest, and the flame of devouring fire. (Isaiah 29:6)

> . . . for I have heard from the Lord God of hosts a consumption, even determined upon the whole earth. (Isaiah 28:22)

With the approach of the catastrophe-causing planet, and the threatening troops of Sennacherib, the more apprehensive Jerusalem became. Ironically, Sennacherib eagerly anticipated the

THE ISAIAHIC CATASTROPHE AND HISTORY

approach of Mars, hoping that with it would come earthquakes and the breaching of Jerusalem's walls. His seers had recommended this as a good year for military conquests in the west.

For thirty years, while citizens of Jerusalem were complacent, Isaiah's predictions had been pessimistic, telling of coming fire and brimstone, earthquake and demolished city walls. Even as the citizens of Jerusalem became increasingly fearful to the point of panic, Isaiah surprisingly shifted toward optimism. When Isaiah, the nightly celestial scanner, was asked for his morning report, or daily projection, he began to announce, at first cautiously, then forcefully, that danger indeed approached. However, he stated that *the danger was to Sennacherib, not to Jerusalem.*[26]

> And Isaiah said unto them . . . Thus saith the Lord, Be not afraid of the words that thou hast heard, wherewith the servants of the King of Assyria have blasphemed me [*Rabshakeh's call to forget Jehovah and surrender*]. Behold, I will send A BLAST UPON HIM, and he shall hear a rumor, and return to his own land; and I will cause him to fall by the sword in his own land. (Isaiah 37:6-7)

First, it is a matter of record that Sennacherib survived the catastrophe, but was burned. Upon returning to Nineveh, he was assassinated by his sons. Second, "blast" is from the Hebrew word *ruwach* suggesting a violent exhalation. It has connotations of air, or anger and of breath. We propose that a bolide exploded above Sennacherib's army encampment, vaporizing some, burning some, and causing death by concussion to others. This is in accord with the meaning of *ruwach* which is also found in Isaiah 25:4.

> . . . a refuge from the storm, a shadow from the heat,

---

[26] There will be discussion as to whether Isaiah's prognostication was by clairvoyance, by Divine inspiration, or by lucky guess. There will be further discussion as to whether the bolide delivering Jerusalem was by chance or by Divine design. Agnostics will in the future, more and more, discount evolutionary uniformitarianism, and will see the validity in the astronomical, catastrophic view of science and ancient history, yet perhaps without the hand of God. We observe that *if* it were by sheer chance, then Isaiah would have called a million-to-one shot. However, he himself claimed foreknowledge from the Word of the Lord. (In a comparable manner, Noah claimed foreknowledge of the Flood Catastrophe, being warned by the Word of God.)

when the BLAST of the terrible ones is as a storm against the wall.

Another description is in Isaiah 37:36.

> Then the angel of the Lord[27] went forth, and smote in the camp of the Assyrians a hundred and fourscore and five thousand: and when they arose early in the morning, behold they were all dead corpses.

This background of Isaiah's changing advice, and changing message helps one to understand why Hezekiah resisted Assyria in 701 B.C. whereas he vacillated in 702 B.C. under Shebna's pressure. Hezekiah's response was something like "fox-hole faith;" he was under great pressure. He accepted Isaiah's counsel. In the day of test, Hezekiah turned to prayer. This was a highly significant decision, because as the national leader, he in turn led the people of his nation to prayer.

> And Hezekiah received the letter from the hand of the messengers, and read it: and Hezekiah went up unto the house of the Lord, and spread it before the Lord. And Hezekiah PRAYED UNTO THE LORD, saying,
>
> O Lord of hosts, God of Israel, that dwellest between the cherubims, thou art the God, even thou alone, of all the kingdoms of the earth: thou hast made heaven and earth. Incline thine ear, O Lord, and hear; open thine eyes, O Lord, and see: and hear all the words of Sennacherib which hath sent to reproach the living God.
>
> Of a truth, Lord, the kings of Assyria have laid waste all the nations, and their countries, and have cast their gods into the fire: for they were no gods, but the work of man's hands, wood and stone: therefore they have destroyed

---

[27] In Hebrew writings and in Talmudic commentaries, archangels are frequently, in fact usually, associated with astronomical phenomena. Some Hebrew sources such as *The Book of Enoch* assign to seven archangels the governorships of the Sun, the Moon and the luminaries, latent with calamities. In some passages, certain archangels are assigned to specific planets. The archangels in Hebrew literature are the corresponding figures to the planet deities of ancient non-Hebrew literatures. In Hebrew theology, the controller of the archangels is God whereas in pagan religions such as the Greek or Chaldean, the planets themselves are deities. The differences in thought are as important to note as are the similarities.

them. Now therefore, O Lord our God, save us from his hand, that all the kingdoms of the earth may know that thou art the Lord, even thou only. (Isaiah 37:14-20)

After the astronomical holocaust and the destruction of Sennacherib's western army corps, Hezekiah's prayer turned to praises. This praise is reflected in Psalm 46, written shortly after the Isaiahic Catastrophe. This was symptomatic of a reversal in national spirit, a general return to divine viewpoint for the nation. The nation for the next 15 years became a God-centered society. Hezekiah became an increasingly spiritual leader of his people, largely due to Isaiah's continuing influence (and due in part to the death of Shebna and the subsequent disorganization of his council).

God is our refuge, a very present help in trouble.	
Therefore will not we fear, though the Earth be removed,	*orbital shift*
and though the mountains be carried into the midst of the sea;	*crustal deformation*
Though the waters thereof roar and be troubled,	*giant tidal waves*
though the mountains shake with the swelling thereof. . . .	*crustal deformation earthquakes*
God is in the midst of her; she shall not be moved:	*divine protection*
God shall help her, and that right early.	
The heathen raged, the kingdoms were moved:	*Rabshakeh*
he uttered his voice, the earth melted. . . .	*vulcanism*
Come, behold the works of the Lord, what desolations he hath made in the earth.	*185,000 to be buried*
He maketh wars to cease . . .	*the Assyrian war*
he breaketh the bow, and cutteth the spear in sunder;	
he burneth the chariot in the FIRE,	*bolidic explosion*
Be still, and know that I am God:	*spiritual awareness*
I will be exalted among the heathen,	

52 THE LONG DAY OF JOSHUA AND SIX OTHER CATASTROPHES

> I will be exalted in the earth.
> The Lord of hosts is with us; the God of Jacob is our refuge.
> (Psalm 46:1-3, 5-6, 8-11)[28]

destiny of the Judeo-Christian heritage

Another of Hezekiah's responses was to adjust the calendar to the new astronomical situation. This condition was not immediately apparent, but became obvious within a few years. We conclude that an expanded orbit, and perhaps a slightly faster spin rate resulted in more days per year. There were now 5¼ extra days per year. With this lengthening of the year, after several years the calendar would be a full month out of order.[29] Sooner or later, the need for a new calendar would become very clear.

Sometime between 695 B.C. and 690 B.C., Hezekiah arbitarily added a special month to the calendar. It is discussed in a careful reading of II Chronicles 30:15-36. The passover, on this occasion, was celebrated in the second month on the fourteenth day rather than on the fourteenth day of the first month. This famous late passover was the most festive and best-attended that Jerusalem had experienced in 250 years, again illustrating the national spirit of thanksgiving.

HEZEKIAH		
	1. Who he was	A king, who like Numa, ruled during a celestial crisis
	2. His behavior	Dismay, vacillation, then prayer, then praise
	3. His responses	A renewed spiritual outlook, a choice of new advisors, a reorganization of the calendar

---

[28]This Psalm, possibly composed by Isaiah, was popular in Jerusalem for almost 15 years. It reflects the dramatic deliverance from military and cosmic calamity of the nation.

[29]With the spin axis precession of this catastrophe, while there was (1) an orbital expansion requiring more days per year, (2) a polar relocation, (3) a possible change in tilt, and (4) a possible increase in spin rate. It may also have been that, in its wobble, the Earth (5) arbitrarily lost several days, even up to a month, which disappeared from a normal time progression.

Manasseh

Manasseh is the seventh person in our list of characters responding to the catastrophe. He was very young at the time of the catastrophe, perhaps only seven or eight years old. His father's (Hezekiah's) health was poor in the years following the 701 B.C. catastrophe, and Hezekiah's sudden death was considered a real possibility at any time. Manasseh became co-regent in either 697 B.C. or 696 B.C. (He was twelve years old, and nominally, a man.) This co-regency was to preclude political problems at the time of Hezekiah's death, and to ease the transfer of power. Manasseh became sole ruler at the age of twenty-two in 687/686 B.C.

During the era of Hezekiah's reign (715 B.C.-686 B.C.), Isaiah the prophet and counsellor had given divinely inspired advice. His political advice had been astute. His foretelling of the bolide and the destruction of the Assyrian armies had been an impressive prophecy in the realm of cosmology. During the ensuing 15 years, Isaiah's counsel guided the nation. The late passover of circa 690 B.C., was the greatest national holiday and day of thanksgiving in 250 years, since the golden age of Solomon.

> So there was great joy in Jerusalem: for since the time of Solomon the son of David, king of Israel there was not the like in Jerusalem. (II Chronicles 30:26)

Divine viewpoint as expressed in the Pentateuch and the Psalms became national viewpoint. God blessed his people with peace, prosperity and national harmony (social harmony). The late Shebna's distorted dream of a golden age was a reality without distortion for the revitalized nation.

However, Manasseh's inner nature rejected Biblical precepts and faith in God. He began to consort with the priests and the priestesses of Baal. He became an apostate. With his accession to the throne, Judah lost its spiritual direction, its national purpose, and in time its moral fabric.

> For he built up again the [*idolatrous and adulterous*] high places which Hezekiah his father had destroyed; and he reared up altars for Baal, and made a grove, as did Ahab, king of Israel; and worshipped all the host of heaven [*Mercury, Venus, Mars, Jupiter and perhaps Saturn, along with the Sun and Moon*], and served them. (II Kings 21:3)

> And they shall spread them, [*human bones*] before the sun, and the moon, and all the host of heaven, whom they have loved, and whom they have served, and after whom they have walked, and whom they have sought, and whom they have worshipped. . . . (Jeremiah 8:2)

It is quite clear by now that a radically different regime assumed power in Jerusalem in 687/686 B.C. Biblical teaching swiftly went out of style. Manasseh burned children in the idolatrous fires. He persecuted orthodox believers and filled Jerusalem with blood. Jewish and Christian tradition both attest that Isaiah was martyred by the new administration within a few years after its accession.[30] Isaiah was disemboweled, or dismembered alive in front of the nation as an example of the religious policy of the new regime.

If Manasseh undertook this dark display of newfound authority only two years after his accession, circa 684 B.C., then Isaiah was close to 82 years old at the time of his martyrdom. Why would Manasseh (or his Baalish priests) want to so mistreat any aged man, much less an elder statesman and a prophet of God? Was it because Isaiah lost his influence in Jerusalem, or was it because Isaiah symbolized a dedication to Jehovah and a fearless non-conformity with and protest against the new pagan style? If the young king felt it was necessary to make an example of Isaiah, was this a measure of Isaiah's failure as a prophet and reformer, or was this a measure of his successful and positive impact on his people when Biblical precepts were falling into times of repression, times of persecution?

From Manasseh's viewpoint, Jerusalem had been delivered by Baal-Mars rather than Jehovah, creator of the heavens and the Earth. Therefore the renewal of the astrological, debauched, Baalish system was perhaps consistent with that form of thinking.

MANASSEH	1. Who he was	A youthful king
	2. His attitude	Adoration of Mars and Venus (Baal and Ashtoreth)

---

[30]This is indicated in the apocryphal book, *The Martyrdom of Isaiah*, and also could be indicated in Hebrews 11:37 where it is reported one prophet was "sawn asunder" in Jerusalem.

3. His response — Repression of the Hebrew faith, martyring of Isaiah

Isaiah

Isaiah's prognosis and diagnosis of the Isaiahic Catastrophe are equally as important as are his recorded observations of it. Isaiah was (1) a historian, (2) a cosmologist, (3) a counsel of state, and (4) a prophet. In his broad role, Isaiah achieved (a) short-range impact on his city, his nation and his generation, (b) medium range impact on the next few generations, and prophets such as Jeremiah, and (c) long-range impact on all successive generations. We shall briefly examine each of these four roles, and each of the three ranges of impact.[31]

Isaiah as a Historian

Isaiah used the historical astronomical crises as themes for his prognosis of the coming day of the Lord. He did it repeatedly and his contemporaries knew what he had in mind, for catastrophic events of the past were well-remembered in general.

> *THE SODOM-GOMORRAH SCENE of 1877 B.C.* Except the Lord of hosts had left unto us a very small remnant, we should have been as Sodom, and we should have been like unto Gomorrah. (Isaiah 1:9)
>
> *THE EXODUS HOLOCAUST of 1447 B.C.* And the Lord of hosts shall stir up a scourge for him . . . so shall he lift it up AFTER THE MANNER OF EGYPT. (Isaiah 10:26)
>
> *THE LONG DAY OF JOSHUA of 1404 B.C.* . . . it shall be a vexation only to understand the report. . . . For the Lord shall rise up as in mount Perazim, [*where Joshua stood on the fateful day*], he shall be wroth as in the Valley

---

[31]This evaluation is keeping in mind that five of the greatest Old Testament figures led their people *through* major astronomical catastrophes with spectacular success. The five are (1) Noah and the Flood Catastrophe of circa 2500 B.C., (2) Abraham and the Sodom-Gomorrah holocaust of 1877 B.C., (3) Moses and the Exodus Catastrophe of 1447 B.C., (4) Joshua and the Long Day of Joshua of 1404 B.C., and (5) Isaiah.

of Gibeon, that he may do his work, HIS STRANGE WORK; and bring to pass his act, HIS STRANGE ACT. . . . for I have heard from the Lord God of hosts a consumption, even determined upon the whole earth. (Isaiah 28:19, 21, 22)

THE ELIJAHIC CATASTROPHE of 864 B.C. and THE JOEL-AMOS CATASTROPHE of 756 B.C. Nevertheless the dimness shall not be such as was in her vexation, when at the first he lightly afflicted the land of Zebulun and the land of Naphtali, [*northern provinces affected during the Elijahic episode*], and afterward [*the Joel-Amos episode*] did more grievously afflict her by the way of the sea. . . .

THE JOEL-AMOS CATASTROPHE of 756 B.C. Therefore is the anger of the Lord kindled against his people, and he hath stretched forth his hand against them, and hath smitten them: and the hills did tremble. . . . (Isaiah 5:25)

With these five brief reference points for analysis, it is seen that Isaiah had some grasp of the historical fact of fire and brimstone catastrophes. He had considerable understanding of the timing of these episodes, and their astronomical dimension. In addition, he had an understanding of God's occasional deliverance of His chosen people *through* or *amidst* these scenes. Species deliverance occurred during the Noachian catastrophe, the Deluge. Political deliverance occurred during the Exodus event. Military deliverance occurred during the Long Day of Joshua as we shall see in a later chapter. A divine demonstration occurred on the evening of the Elijahic Catastrophe, in 864 B.C., a demonstration meteoritic in nature. Each of these earlier catastrophes will be subjects for later chapters of this book. However, to understand the astronomical picture of the Isaiahic Catastrophe *and* to understand the associated deliverance of Jerusalem is to begin to understand the earlier astronomical crises, and their effect on Middle East history.

Isaiah as a Cosmologist

Isaiah's cosmology was precise and vivid. His prognosis of the coming Isaiahic Catastrophe must be considered in the light of his experience in the Joel-Amos event in his childhood. Thus his expectations of the Isaiahic Catastrophe and his observations of it are really separate sides of the same coin.

Whether Isaiah was, technically, using hyperbole in some of his prognostications may be debatable, (as in 24:1 where he describes the world as being turned upside down). The fact remains that in the bolidic destruction in 701 B.C., at least 185,000 people did perish.[32] This may be conservative if there were other destructive blows other than the bolide over suburban Jerusalem, Sennacherib's encampment. Significant depopulation was definitely an expectation with an approaching catastrophe.

About 50 per cent of the verses in the first 38 chapters of Isaiah deal directly with catastrophism in one or another of its several forms. We cannot be exhaustive in a brief chapter, but the following categorical list will illustrate Isaiah's cosmology. Many of the quotations cited refer to other more ancient events, but they clearly give the flavor of Isaiah's cosmological view.

1. ISAIAH ON THE LOCATION OF THE ORIGIN OF CATASTROPHES

Earth's north pole (and Northern Hemisphere) is tilted backwards 23½ degrees in March (and is tilted forward in the autumn) with respect to its orbital path.

> Howl, O gate; cry, O city; thou, whole Palestina, art dissolved: for there shall come FROM THE NORTH a smoke, and none shall be alone in his appointed times. (Isaiah 14:31)[33]

---

[32] In his book *In the Days of the First Temple,* Jacob S. Golub estimates the population of Judea at about 2,000,000. If this is correct, the destruction of 185,000 soldiers would represent somewhere between 7% and 9% of the populace of the province at that time. This may be a conservative estimate since other destructive blows in scattered areas could also have occurred. (Jacob S. Golub, *In The Days of the First Temple,* Cincinnati: Union of American Hebrew Congregations, 1931.)

[33] Isaiah's early prognosis of the next episode of astronomical crisis was that it would come "from the north," just like the Joel-Amos episode. During October of every year, Earth's north pole tilts 23½° forward with respect to its path. During March the north pole tilts backward. With the north pole's forward tilt in 756 B.C., the celestial scenery would include Mars approaching generally from the north. But with the change of locations, and the reversed role of the tilt with respect to orbital path in 701 B.C., Mars appeared in the celestial scene to approach from the south. Habakkuk described the event as he saw the movements in 701 B.C.; Isaiah forecast the event as he saw the 756 B.C. event.

... the Lord of hosts mustereth the host of the battle. They come from a far country, FROM THE END OF HEAVEN ... the weapons of his indignation, to destroy the whole land. (Isaiah 13:4-5)

2. ISAIAH ON THE CELESTIAL SCENE

... and I will sweep it with the BESOM [*broom*] OF DESTRUCTION. ... (Isaiah 14:23)

And all the host of heaven shall be dissolved, and the heavens shall be rolled together as a scroll. ... (Isaiah 34:4)

... the earth is moved exceedingly. (Isaiah 24:19)

The earth shall reel to and fro like a drunkard, and shall be removed. ... (Isaiah 24:20)

... for the windows from on high are open, and the foundations of the earth do shake. (Isaiah 24:18)

Behold, the Lord maketh the earth empty, and maketh it waste, and turneth it upside down. ... (Isaiah 24:1)

3. ISAIAH ON THE VISIBLE ASTRONOMICAL DESTROYER

... like a ROLLING THING before the WHIRLWIND. (Isaiah 17:13)[34]

"Rolling" is from the Hebrew word *galgal,* a rolling thing, a wheel, a rotating thing.

"Thing" is from the Hebrew word *dabar,* similar to *deber* meaning pestilence, meteorites, murrain, plague. Both words are from the verb *dabar* meaning to appoint, to subdue, to destroy.

"Whirlwind" is from the Hebrew word *cuwphah,* a whirlwind, a tempest, a hurricane.

---

[34]Mars rotates with a spin rate almost identical to Earth's spin rate, and had at least two tiny trabants, and perhaps more orbiting astronomical debris at that time.

THE ISAIAHIC CATASTROPHE AND HISTORY

Then the ANGEL OF THE LORD[35] went forth, and smote in the camp of the Assyrians. . . . (Isaiah 37:36)

4. ISAIAH ON METEORS

Whose ARROWS are sharp, and all their BOWS bent, the horses' hoofs shall be counted LIKE FLINT, and their wheels like a whirlwind: (Isaiah 5:28)

. . . his lips are full of indignation, and his tongue as a DEVOURING FIRE: And his breath, as an OVERFLOWING STREAM. . . . (Isaiah 30:27-28)

. . . and shall shew the lighting down of his arm, with the indignation of his anger, and with the FLAME OF A DEVOURING FIRE, with SCATTERING, AND TEMPEST, AND HAILSTONES. (Isaiah 30:30)

. . . the breath of the Lord, like a stream of BRIMSTONE, . . . (Isaiah 30:33)

And the STREAMS thereof shall be turned into pitch, and the dust thereof into BRIMSTONE, and the land thereof shall become burning pitch. (Isaiah 34:9)

. . . when the OVERFLOWING SCOURGE shall pass through. . . . (Isaiah 28:15, see also 28:18)

. . . which as a TEMPEST OF HAIL AND A DESTROYING STORM, as a flood of mighty waters overflowing shall cast DOWN to the earth with the hand. (Isaiah 28:2)

5. ISAIAH ON ORBITAL PERTURBATION OR CHANGE

. . . and the foundations of the earth do shake. (Isaiah 24:18)

. . . the earth is moved exceedingly. (Isaiah 24:19)

Therefore I will shake the heavens, and THE EARTH

---

[35] This is an archangel, and is also described in the eye-witness accounts in Scripture during the Exodus Catastrophe (1447 B.C.) and during the Greater Davidic Catastrophe (972 B.C.). In the apocryphal *Book of Enoch*, chapter 20, there are six archangels listed by name. These include Raguel who "inflicts punishment on the world and the luminaries." The *Talmud* in obscure commentaries associates the archangel Sammael with astronomical holocausts.

SHALL REMOVE OUT OF HER PLACE. . . . (Isaiah 13:13)

6. ISAIAH ON POLAR MIGRATION

. . . for the windows from on high are open, and the foundations of the earth do shake. The earth is utterly broken down, the earth is clean dissolved, the earth is moved exceedingly. THE EARTH SHALL REEL TO AND FRO LIKE A DRUNKARD, and shall be removed like a cottage. . . . Isaiah 24:18-20)

. . . THE MOON SHALL BE CONFOUNDED, AND THE SUN ASHAMED[36]. . . . (Isaiah 24:23)

For it is a day of trouble, and of treading down, and of PERPLEXITY[37] by the Lord God of hosts. . . . (Isaiah 22:5)

"Here," Isaiah replied, "is the sign from Yahweh that he will do what he has said. Look, I shall make the shadow cast by the declining sun go back ten steps on the steps of Ahaz." And the sun went back the TEN STEPS by which it had declined.[38] (Isaiah 38:8) [*The Jerusalem Bible*, Garden City, New York: Doubleday and Co. Inc., 1971.]

7. ISAIAH ON THE HISTORIC BOLIDE

Behold, I will send a BLAST upon him. . . . (Isaiah 37:7)

---

[36]"Ashamed" is from the Hebrew word *buwsh*, meaning to be confounded, to be delayed, to be too long.

[37]"Perplexity" is from the Hebrew word *mebuwkah* meaning to become entangled, as the Earth-Moon system with Mars. "Perplexity" may be a poor word choice by King James translators, but they lacked an astronomical catastrophic world view. Nevertheless it would be "perplexing" to have to design a new world calendar, relocate north on terrestrial maps, perhaps have to redraw the celestial charts, all without telescopes or calculus.

[38]Our estimate of the height of Ahaz' sun dial is 60 feet. The average of the Egyptian obelisks existing today is 80 feet. We believe the Jerusalem obelisk was somewhat smaller than the Egyptian average. When measured at noon, such an obelisk would have cast a shadow 10 English feet longer had Jerusalem's latitude been 38½° N. or had Jerusalem's latitude been 37° N. and Earth's spin axis tilt been 25°. This will be considered in more detail in Chapter IV.

THE ISAIAHIC CATASTROPHE AND HISTORY 61

... a shadow from the heat, when the BLAST[39] OF THE TERRIBLE[40] ONES is as a storm against the wall. (Isaiah 25:4)

... he uttered his voice, the earth melted. Come, behold the works of the Lord, what DESOLATIONS he hath made in the earth. (Psalm 46:6, 8)

8. ISAIAH ON COSMIC AND/OR CRUSTAL NOISE

In August 1883 when Krakatoa, a small volcanic island between Java and Sumatra, blew up, the quaking and thunder were heard 2000 miles distant in such varied locations as Manila, Australia, and Reunion Island in the Western Indian Ocean. Great noise was expected during the Isaiahic Catastrophe. Whether this noise was due to (1) exploding bolides, (2) volcanic upheaval, (3) clashing geomagnetic fields of the two planets, or (4) perhaps all of these, is an open question. Certainly among the great noises was the bolidic explosion.

Thou shalt be visited of the Lord of hosts with THUNDER, and with EARTHQUAKE, and GREAT NOISE, with storm and tempest, and the flame of devouring fire. (Isaiah 29:6)

Their roaring shall be like a lion. . . . (Isaiah 5:29)

For through the voice of the Lord shall the Assyrian be beaten down. . . . (Isaiah 30:31)

9. ISAIAH ON EARTHQUAKES AND CRUSTAL FRACTURES

... when he ariseth to SHAKE TERRIBLY THE EARTH. (Isaiah 2:19, also 2:21)

For it is a day of trouble, and of TREADING DOWN, and

---

[39]"Blast" is from the Hebrew word *ruwach*, meaning a violent exhalation, a wind, a breath, an angry breath; by extension, a region of the sky, an air blast.

[40]"Terrible" is from the Hebrew word *ariyts*, meaning mighty; a great, strong power; terrible; violent.

of perplexity . . . breaking down the walls, and of crying to the mountains. (Isaiah 22:5)

Ye have seen also the breaches of the city of David, that they are many.[41] . . . (Isaiah 22:9)

. . . and he hath stretched forth his hand against them, and hath smitten them: AND THE HILLS DID TREMBLE, . . . (Isaiah 5:25)

Thou shalt be visited of the Lord of hosts with thunder, and with EARTHQUAKE.[42] . . . (Isaiah 29:6)

10. ISAIAH ON THE CATASTROPHIC SCHEDULE, OR APPOINTMENT, OR ASTRONOMICAL RENDEZVOUS

. . . for I have heard from the Lord God of hosts a consumption, even DETERMINED[43] upon the whole earth. (Isaiah 28:22)

And your covenant with death shall be DISANNULLED, and your AGREEMENT with hell shall not stand; when the overflowing scourge shall pass through. . . . (Isaiah 28:18)

(This prophecy is when Isaiah began to be optimistic, advising Hezekiah that the danger approaching would affect the Assyrians, not the Hebrews bottled up in Jerusalem. Isaiah, through insight or revelation, was becoming increasingly optimistic at the very time the general populace of Jerusalem was turned from dismay and despair to panic.)

. . . WHEN he ariseth to shake terribly the earth. (Isaiah 2:19)

---

[41]This refers to damage from the earthquakes of the Joel-Amos Catastrophe of 756 B.C. The walls of Jerusalem were 40 feet thick and 100 feet high in many places, and were breached or cracked. They were repaired when Isaiah was a teenager in Jerusalm, circa 755 to 750 B.C. Isaiah predicts more of the same kind of experience in the offing.

[42]"Earthquake" is from the Hebrew word *raash* meaning earth-shaking, earth-rattling, commotion.

[43]"Determined" is from the Hebrew word *charats* meaning decided, decreed.

For the DAY OF THE LORD of hosts shall be upon everyone. . . . (Isaiah 2:12)

For IT IS A DAY OF TROUBLE, and of treading down, and of perplexity. . . . (Isaiah 22:5)

Isaiah was a cosmologist, one who carefully observed conditions in the heavens and projected what he saw and read into the historic past, and into at least the immediate future. He considered, "The past is the key to the future." Thus he forecast a coming episode by his understanding of the historical holocausts and by his experience as a child in 756 B.C. Eras of catastrophism were expected to repeat in one kind of cycle, or pattern, or another, as they had for at least 1800 years. Then, (suddenly) Mars went out of resonance in 701 B.C., never to bother the planet Earth again. The past was no longer the key to the future for the succeeding centuries.

Compare Isaiah's cosmology in a catastrophic era with the contemporary popular view in our era. It is the uniformitarian view, whose motto is, "The present is the key to the past." Whether the serene (celestially at least) present is or is not the key to the future is uncertain. And it is not the subject to which we address our work. But whether the serene present is the key to the past is very clear. It is clear that such is not the case.

Isaiah's Historical Impact

Short Range Impact

Isaiah's impact on his generation was substantial before the catastrophe. First, King Hezekiah considered his counsel worth asking for. His sermons of coming judgment were fearful, colorful, stirring. His advice proved very sound. His prophecy concerning the bolide which missed Jerusalem, but destroyed the Assyrians' western army corps was amazing. His stand of faith was a measure of his integrity.

When Psalm 46 was composed in the pleasant aftermath of the catastrophe, it became a classic anthem, sung by the populace. If it was penned by Isaiah, perhaps it was "published" at Hezekiah's suggestion. Second, then, Psalm 46 symbolizes the national reform instituted by Hezekiah under Isaiah's counsel.

Yet a third measure is the celebration of the famous late

passover, the gayest and best-attended in two and one-half centuries, a national day of thanksgiving, a day of festivities. These each suggest that Isaiah set a style of appreciation and worship which the nation as a whole followed, however briefly, for about fifteen years.

Medium Range Impact

The importance of Isaiah's impact is reflected in the fact that Manasseh felt Isaiah was a center of opposition, and martyred him in front of the nation to make maximum counter impact of his own. This indicates that Isaiah was a significant person to the entire nation even in his declining years. He was stable, whether during calamity or prosperity, whether during popularity or persecution. Yet another measure of Isaiah's medium range impact is his influence on the reformer king, Josiah, and on the character of later prophets such as Jeremiah and Ezekiel.

Long Range Impact

To measure Isaiah's long range impact is more difficult, especially briefly. Millions of people over the centuries have read the book of Isaiah carefully. This is remarkable "exposure" even though it is certainly not a complete measure of Isaiah's impact.

The literary style of Isaiah reappears in the writings of such prophets as Ezekiel and Zechariah in the Old Testament, Matthew and John in the New Testament.[44] The pattern of the Apocalypse more closely follows that of Moses, but the style is similar to Isaiah's catastrophic word-pictures.[45]

---

[44]In Matthew 24, the apocalyptic teachings of Christ are quite parallel to Isaiah's catastrophism. The same is true in John's apocalypse, or Revelation. Also the ten plagues of Exodus are a sort of catastrophic pattern for the prophetic world holocausts described in Revelation.

[45]Interestingly, Ezekiel in his chapters 38 and 39, makes the prognosis of fire and brimstone catastrophism in the "end times," falling not on Assyrian armies but on Russian armies invading Palestine. Ezekiel is sufficiently specific as to project that 83% (five-sixths) of the invading Russian and allied hordes will be destroyed. This reminds us that one of Isaiah's characteristics as a prophet was specificity; he did not hide behind vague generalities.

In the aforementioned works such as Ezekiel's apocalypse and John's apocalypse, Isaiah's catastrophic message, or at least his catastrophic style, is echoed. Beyond his catastrophic message, Isaiah also had (1) a messianic message, (2) a millenial message, and (3) a moral message, the details of which are to to be excluded from this work.[46]

> We must not fail to keep in mind the length of time and multitude of years in which these things, if they had been good, would certainly not have remained unknown, for almost everything has been found out, though in some cases what is known has not been systematized, and in other cases men do not make use of the knowledge which they have.—Aristotle
>
> Among the Greeks, those who first disclosed the natural causes of thunder and storms to the untrained ears of man were condemned as guilty of impiety towards the gods.—Francis Bacon

---

[46]Isaiah's messianic message is found particularly in Isaiah 52 and 53. We observe that Jesus came in the forecast pattern, died in the forecast pattern, was buried in the forecast pattern and he "bare the sin of many."

Isaiah's millenial message has guided such world religions as Christtianity, Islam, Judaism, and surprisingly, Communism. For instance, in Augustine's *City of God,* basic to the Middle Ages, millenial themes come from the book of Isaiah. A distortion of the millenial message of Isaiah is found in the utopian doctrines of the world socialists. Isaiah forecast that Jerusalem would be the world capitol during the golden age, with all nations coming in homage and worship. World socialists seem to prefer Moscow or New York as their "Mecca."

Isaiah's millenial message suggests a productive Earth, an age of music and justice, with private ownership and universal freedom. The atheistic millenium projects the reverse image, a somber slave state characterized by want, lack of joy, lack of justice, lack of private ownership. This is another measure, however inverted and perverted, of the impact of Isaiah, his millenial message, his messianic message, his catastrophic message, and his shadow across the face of our civilization. It is a long shadow indeed.

chapter **IV**

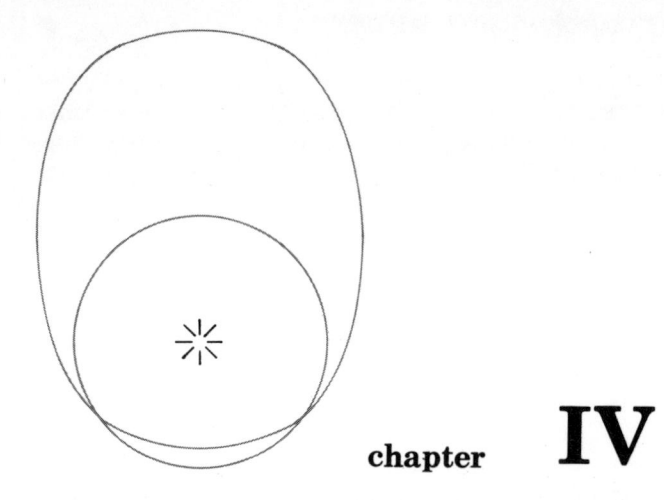

The Isaiahic Catastrophe and Science

March 20/21, 701 B.C.

The Isaiahic Catastrophe was the last of a long series of at least seven major astronomical holocausts spanning some 18 centuries. This last one occurred on the night of March 20/21, 701 B.C. (in the evening, Palestine time). Along with this fly-by of Mars, a falling of meteors and bolides occurred. Mars may have passed as close as 70,000 miles. It was inside Earth's orbit as it lapped the Earth (an inside fly-by). And also it was slightly north of the Earth's ecliptic or orbital plane. With this interaction, Mars broke out of its orbital resonance with Earth's orbit, and proceeded toward its current non-resonant condition.

This chapter shall consider in as basic terms as possible just what happened on the astronomical scene. It will lay a basis for Chapter III, where we discussed the responses and reportings of ancients who lived during this catastrophe. If we can understand what happened on the astronomical scene, then we can understand why ancients worshipped planets, feared catastrophic episodes, and sighted the astronomical marauder. This chapter, then, shall consider the astronomical scene in that catastrophic year, 701 B.C. A model of this catastrophe is presented.[1]

---

[1]The complexities of this chapter are considerable. Some of the detailed discussion in this chapter may be beyond the reader's technical grasp. If the material is too difficult for total comprehension, the reader is urged

The Isaiahic Catastrophe and Science

WHEN THE PLANET MARS made a near fly-by of Earth (as happened on several occasions), five kinds of changes happened to Earth, other than the associated showers of meteors and bolides. These five kinds of changes also happened, to Mars. They were:

1. A perturbation of Earth's orbit (in this case a significant expansion).
2. A reversal of the geomagnetic field.[2]
3. A severe, temporary tide in the Earth's lithosphere (the magma, or lava and the crust).
4. A severe, temporary tide in the Earth's hydrosphere, plus tidal waves.[3]
5. A wobble of the spin axis, technically termed a "precession" of the spin axis.[4]

Mars' Ancient Orbit

Figure 2 on page 68 illustrates the orbit which a planet (or an asteroid) could have, and we believe Mars did have. There are three important features of this proposed orbit. First, the Martian orbit had two intersection locations with Earth's

---

to retain the main points.

A general understanding of the astronomical scene is necessary to understand the catastrophic-oriented thoughts of the ancients. For a more specific understanding of what happened to the Earth, a model of the planetary interaction is necessary. The model of this catastrophe will lay the basis to understand models of the other, more ancient catastrophes, catastrophes in which the themes were similar, but the details differed.

[2] There is a high degree of correlation between magnetic reversals, orogenetic activity and meteoritic activity. Basalt outflows reflect many magnetic field reversals. See J. H. Heirtzler, "Sea-floor Spreading, *Scientific American*, Dec. 1968, p. 60 ff. "A major meteorite (tektite) fall occurred just at the time of the last reversal (see "Tektites and Geomagnetic Reversals" by Billy P. Glass and Bruce C. Heezen; *Scientific American*, July, 1967). Some authors have speculated recently on a relation between mountain-building activity and magnetic reversals; others see a relation between changes in sea-floor spreading and mountain-building.

[3] There were also tides in the atmosphere, and in the plasma contained in the geomagnetic field.

[4] A spin axis precession includes three kinds of phenomena changes, namely (1) a relocation of the two geographical poles on the Earth, (2) a change in tilt, a relocation of the geographical poles with respect to the galaxy, and (3) a possible increase in spin rate itself.

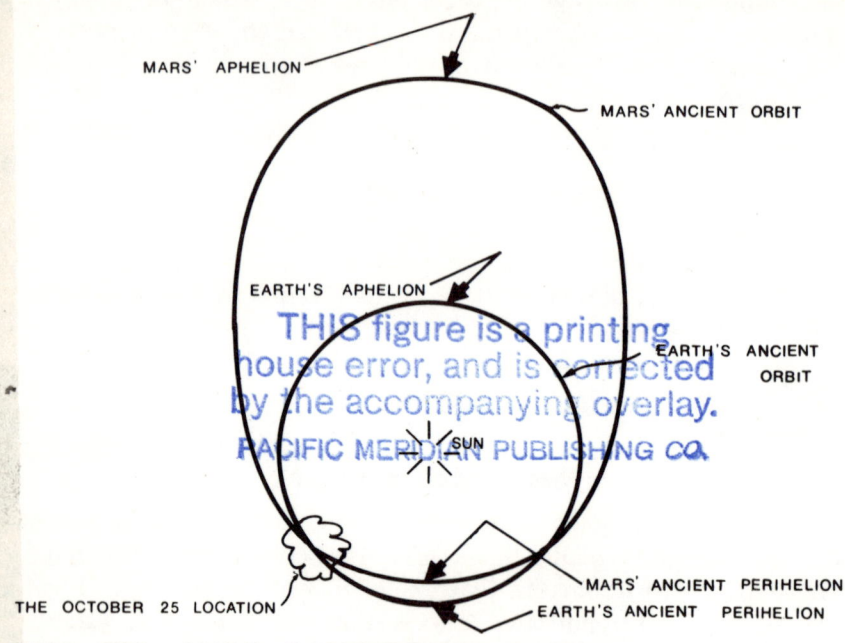

68   THE LONG DAY OF JOSHUA AND SIX OTHER CATASTROPHES

MARS' APHELION
MARS' ANCIENT ORBIT
EARTH'S APHELION
EARTH'S ANCIENT ORBIT
SUN
THIS figure is a printing house error, and is corrected by the accompanying overlay.
PACIFIC MERIDIAN PUBLISHING CO.
THE OCTOBER 25 LOCATION
MARS' ANCIENT PERIHELION
EARTH'S ANCIENT PERIHELION

THE JOEL-AMOS CATASTROPHE REGION
THE CASE TWO LOCATION

THE GEOMETRY OF THE JOEL-AMOS CATASTROPHE

ORBITS AS SEEN FROM POLARIS

FIGURE 2
The geometry of this catastrophe will be repeated in Figures 26 and 34, the Exodus and the Sodom-Gomorrah holocausts both of which also occurred on or about March 20/21.

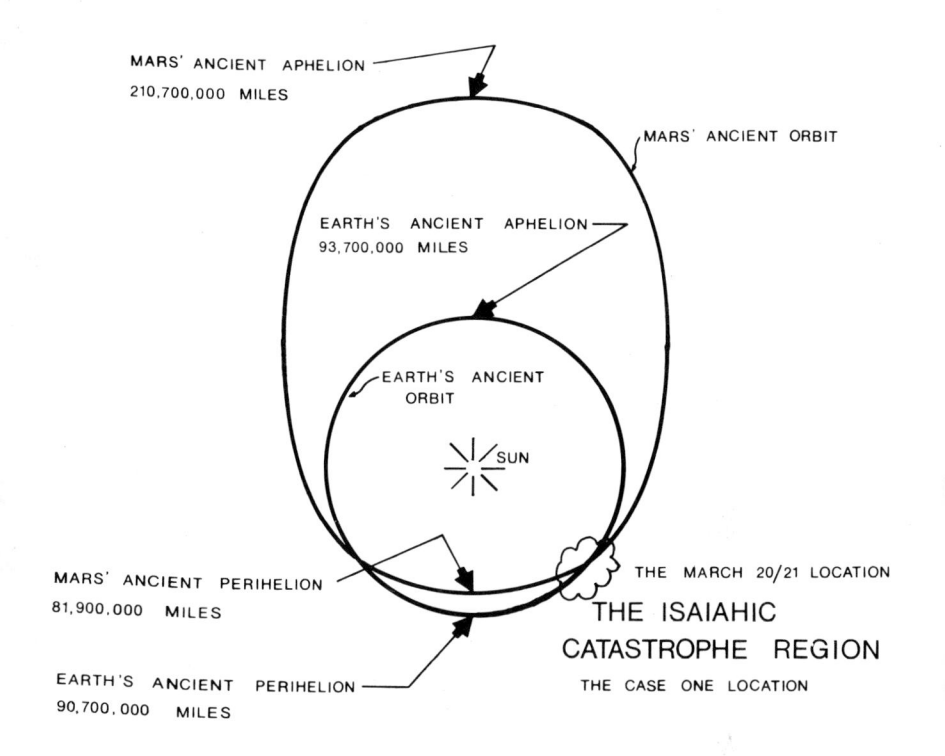

THE LONG DAY OF JOSHUA AND SIX OTHER CATASTROPHES

MARS' ANCIENT APHELION
210,700,000 MILES

MARS' ANCIENT ORBIT

EARTH'S ANCIENT APHELION
93,700,000 MILES

EARTH'S ANCIENT ORBIT

SUN

MARS' ANCIENT PERIHELION
81,900,000 MILES

THE MARCH 20/21 LOCATION

THE ISAIAHIC
CATASTROPHE REGION

EARTH'S ANCIENT PERIHELION
90,700,000 MILES

THE CASE ONE LOCATION

THE GEOMETRY OF THE ISAIAHIC CATASTROPHE
AS SEEN FROM POLARIS

FIGURE 2

The geometry of this catastrophe will be repeated in Figures 26 and 34, the Exodus and the Sodom-Gomorrah holocausts both of which also occurred on or about March 20/21.

orbit, once as it crossed Earth's orbit coming in and once as it crossed going out. According to this geometry, if and when the two planets nearly met, it would have to be at one or the other of the two intersecting locations.

The second important feature of this proposed orbit is that the number of days in the Martian orbit averaged exactly twice as many days as Earth's orbit; that is, it revolved in 720 days to 360 for the Earth, a 2:1 ratio. These two orbits were in a TIMING RESONANCE, just as light rays, ocean waves or sound waves may also be in resonance under certain conditions.

The third feature of the ancient Martian orbit is its unusual approach and retreat from the Sun, its somewhat comet-like orbit. The current Martian orbit has a "perihelion" (closest distance to the Sun) of 128,400,000 miles, and an "aphelion" (farthest distance from the Sun) of 154,900,000 miles. The ancient Martian orbit we propose had a perihelion of just 81,900,000 miles and an aphelion of 210,700,000 miles. Thus the ancient orbit of Mars was shaped differently than its orbit today, more like the orbits of some of the comets. This different shape is illustrated in Figure 3, and it is described in Table III.

TABLE III

COMPARING THE ANCIENT AND CURRENT ORBITS OF MARS

Orbit Characteristic	Ancient Orbit	Current Orbit
Perihelion	81,900,000 miles	128,400,000 miles
Aphelion	210,700,000 miles	154,900,000 miles
Eccentricity	.44	.093
Orbital Period (Current Earth Years)	1.98	1.88
Angle of Orbit's Intersection with Earth's Orbit	101°	No Intersection

ORBITAL VELOCITIES. In the Earth's current orbit, its average speed is about 1,600,000 miles per day. However, when it passes perihelion in early January, its speed is a little faster, about 1,625,000 miles per day. Its speed is correspondingly slower near aphelion. (This same principle is observed in all comets

MARS' OLDER AND NEWER ORBIT

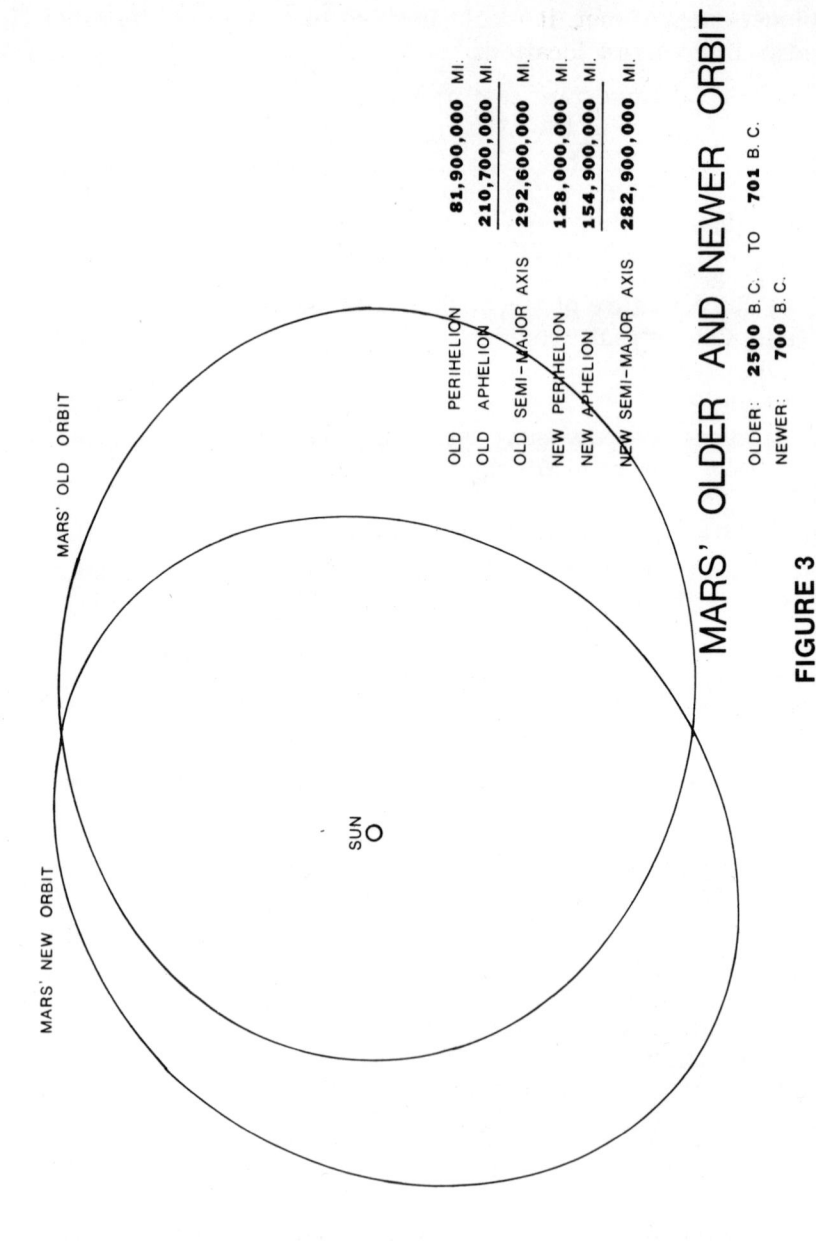

OLD PERIHELION	81,900,000 MI.
OLD APHELION	210,700,000 MI.
OLD SEMI-MAJOR AXIS	292,600,000 MI.
NEW PERIHELION	128,000,000 MI.
NEW APHELION	154,900,000 MI.
NEW SEMI-MAJOR AXIS	282,900,000 MI.

OLDER: 2500 B.C. TO 701 B.C.
NEWER: 700 B.C.

FIGURE 3

The shape of Mars' new orbit differed drastically, but the amount of space swept out by the new orbit varied only slightly (slightly less) from the space swept out by the old orbit.

THE ISAIAHIC CATASTROPHE AND SCIENCE   71

which move more rapidly through perihelion and less rapidly through aphelion). In Mars' ancient orbit, its daily speed was about 1,875,000 miles when it crossed Earth's orbit. That is, Mars' speed was about 270,000 miles per day faster than the Earth's when in the vicinity of the catastrophic intersections.

Therefore, Mars would be approaching the Earth at a rate of about 540,000 miles per day (taking into account Earth's and Mars' vector velocities). Perhaps this is why so many ancients were called stargazers, and the prophet Isaiah was described as a "watchman in the night" (Isaiah 21:11). Other concerned planet-watchers were described as "astrologers, stargazers, monthly prognosticators" (Isaiah 47:13), augers, diviners, seers and so forth.

A GENERAL THEORY OF ORBITAL RESONANCE
Current Examples

An analogy of the former Earth-Mars orbits is the example of two toy cars with intersecting tracks. The toy car labeled Earth travels on a near-circular, flat track. The toy car labeled Mars travels on an oblong track that is inclined. As it goes uphill, away from the crossing of the tracks it loses speed, and the Earth car laps it, going much faster. When the toy car Mars starts coming down the track, it gains rapidly in speed, passing the Earth after the first track crossing, but before the second track crossing.

The size of the Mars track is such that the Earth car makes approximately two laps to one for the Mars car. Obviously this is a dangerous situation, one that would excite a little boy.

In our model of Mars with an ancient orbit in 2:1 resonance with Earth's orbit, Mars sped past the Earth once every two years. Mars at this occasion was closer to the Sun than was the Earth. It passed the Earth when the two planets were in a line-up with the Sun. Such a line-up is termed a "conjunction." When Mars is in the middle, it is termed an "inferior conjunction," that is, when the Earth is on the outside of the line-up. In this position, Mars could (and perhaps occasionally did) cause an eclipse of the Earth just as the Moon sometimes does today.

Mars sped rapidly around its perihelion. In passing beyond the two catastrophic locations, and in approaching aphelion, it began to slow down, ultimately to the relatively slow pace of 795,000 miles per day. Earth sped by Mars, and in a two-year period Earth twice would lap Mars. These line-ups were termed "superior conjunctions" since the Earth was in the middle. Thus there were *three* conjunctions per two year period. One conjunction, the inferior, was the threatening condition, while the other two conjunctions, the superior ones, were serene, as Mars was well out beyond Earth's orbit.

Understanding that there were *three conjunctions* per two year period will make it easier to understand the behavior of this orbital system. In addition, for clarification, we will make analogies to the principles of merry-go-rounds, pendulums and teeter-totters. These analogies will be applied to the proposed Earth-Mars resonance orbits, examples of which can be found currently among the resonant asteroids.

THE MERRY-GO-ROUND. Our first illustration is that of a merry-go-round. The Sun, in a sense, is like a merry-go-round on a 25-day cycle period, which is the period of the Sun's rotation. Sunspots pass the Earth every 25 to 27 days when the Sun is in a period of sunspot activity, just as a child on a merry-go-round would periodically pass his watching parents.

The Earth is another example of a merry-go-round; it has a 24-hour rotational cycle. It is from this merry-go-round vantage point that the ancients observed Mars; however, Mars was moving around, whereas the objects (their parents) which children on a merry-go-round watch are usually standing still. It is from this merry-go-round vantage point that the ancients studied the planets and the stars. The fixed stars in the sky were the immovable background; the planets were the celestial wanderers, the wandering luminaries. Their wanderings or movements concerned the ancients *intensely*.

The ancients not only laid out the Earth's horizon in four divisions (north, south, east and west); they also laid out the immovable stars into divisions numbering twelve, and the source of the number twelve was probably the number of lunar revolutions (months) per year. This twelve-divided celestial region was called the *zodiac* and the 12 zones of the zodiac were calculated, discussed, sometimes personified. The predicted movements of Mercury-Hermes, Venus-Aphrodite, Jupiter-Zeus and especially Mars-Ares were noted, and carefully studied.

Alinda, An Asteroid in the Hestia Gap

Asteroids are scattered between Mars and Jupiter, much as the icy particles comprising Saturn's rings are scattered between Saturn and its innermost moon, Mimas. In the case of Saturn's rings, the inner satellites will "sweep out" a region at a distance from the planet corresponding to a simple fraction of the satellite's period, the time it takes to make one revolution around the planet. For example, the Cassini Division in Saturn's rings is the major open space, and it is at a distance corresponding to half the period of Mimas, simultaneously a third of the period of Enceladus, and a quarter of the period of Tethys.[5]

In the asteroid region too, there are clusters or clumps of asteroids, and empty areas, called "gaps." The gaps are in simple fractional relationships to the period of Jupiter. Taken collectively, the gaps are termed the *Kirkwood Gaps*. The clusters and gaps caused by Jupiter are not visually apparent as in the case of Saturn's rings because of the small number of asteroids with calculated orbits, and the considerable variation in eccentricity and tilt of the asteroidal orbits. But the gaps or clusters become apparent when considering the *distribution of the mean motions* of the asteroids about the Sun. Thus for example a gap at the 3:1 resonance means that no (or very few) asteroids would be found with a mean motion in the neighborhood of three times that of Jupiter. Conversely, a cluster at the 3:1 resonance means that an unusually large number of asteroids would have a mean motion in the neighborhood of three times that of Jupiter. Figure 4 illustrates both the distribution of periods of the asteroids, and the gaps in said distribution.

The clearly identified examples of Kirkwood Gaps have names. At the 3:1 resonance is a gap known as the Hestia Gap, from which all but one asteroid have been swept out. The re-

---

[5]Mimas and Tethys, Saturn's first and third moons, have recently been discovered to be in 2:1 resonance. Enceladus and Dione, the second and fourth satellites, are similarly found to be in 2:1 resonance. Also Titan and Hyperion, its sixth and seventh satellites, are found to be in 4:3 resonance. This is why the icy particles surrounding Saturn are in such a well-defined cluster-and-gap arrangement. See R. R. Allan, "Evolution of Mimas-Tethys Commensurability," *Astronomical Journal*, Vol. 74, No. 3, April 1969, pp. 497 ff.

FIGURE 4

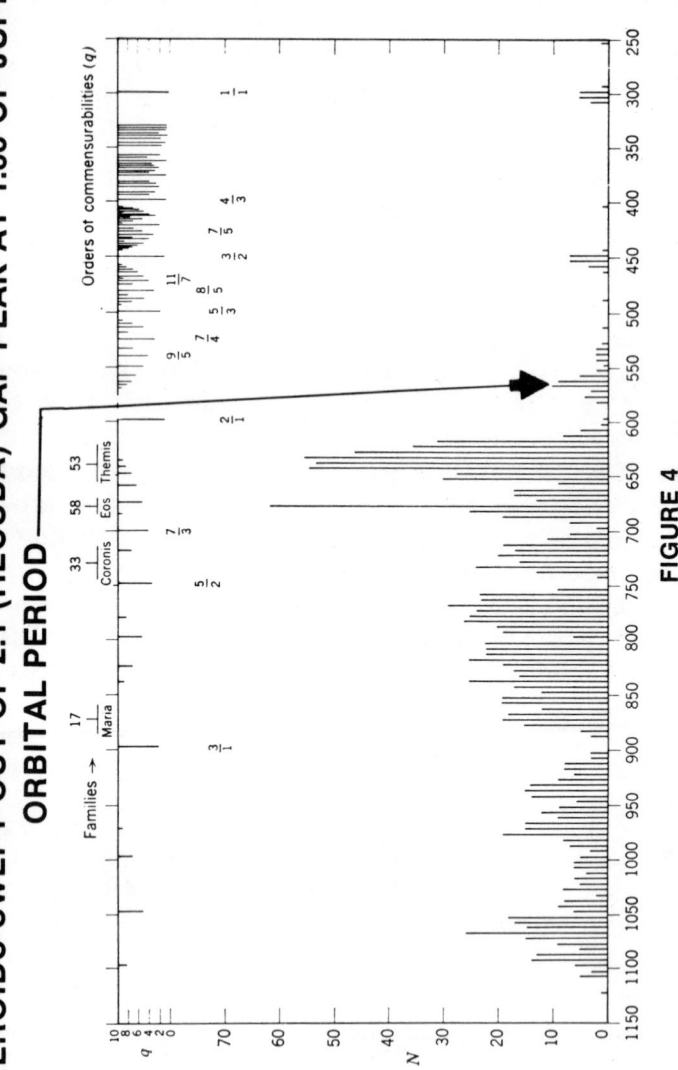

The Hestin Gap is at 900 arc seconds. The Hecuba Gap is at 600 arc seconds. The peak of the asteroids swept out of the Hecuba Gap toward Jupiter compares closely with the shift of the Martian orbit toward Earth in terms of orbital periods. From William M. Kaula, An Introduction to Planetary Physics, New York, John Wiley & Sons, 1968 p. 239. The source of the illustration is Dirk Brouwer, "The Problem of the Kirkwood Gaps in the Asteroid Belt, Astronomical Journal, Vol. 68, 1963, pp. 152-159.

maining one is Alinda (#887). Alinda is in 3:1 resonance with Jupiter. It remains there only because of this very unusual relationship. Because of the particular geometry, Jupiter *first shortens* Alinda's period and then, after this occurs for several Alinda orbits, it *alternately lengthens* Alinda's orbit. This is expected to continue, first one way and then the other, ad infinitum. Figure 5 illustrates this strange "teeter-totter" relationship.

The net result is that three orbits of Alinda *average out* to one orbit for Jupiter. Alinda will make 3,000 orbits while Jupiter makes 1,000, unless unforeseen intrusions occur from more distant regions, such as intrusions by new planets with comet-like orbits. Alinda is not always at exactly the fractional period of Jupiter, for it shifts one way and then the other alternately. But this shift or drift is always corrected and always will be corrected unless Alinda is somehow removed from its resonance with Jupiter.

THE TEETER-TOTTER. The Alinda-Jupiter resonant orbits are much like a teeter-totter. Teeter-totters require four conditions: (1) a "board" connecting two weights, (2) a fulcrum or pivot, (3) one mass at each end of the "board", and (4) an alternating or pulsating spring action at both ends of the "board." Once these four conditions are established, the motion of the teeter-totter will continue until one spring (such as a child's legs) or the other tires. The teeter-totter "board" we shall consider will not be ten feet long nor will it be a wood plank. Instead it will be one billion miles long and it will be invisible. It runs from one end of Jupiter's half billion mile orbit to the other end. The pivot or fulcrum will not be a saw-horse, but rather the Sun, which is nearly at the center of Jupiter's orbit.[6] The two masses we shall consider at either end of the "plank" will be Jupiter-Alinda conjunctions alternating from one part of their orbits to another. The alternating spring action is the gravity of Jupiter as it moves around its orbit.

A conjunction is said to occur whenever the three bodies, Alinda, Jupiter and the Sun are in a straight line. It is this

---

[6]Jupiter's orbit varies in distance from the Sun from 460,200,000 miles at perihelion to 507,100,000 miles at aphelion, with an eccentricity of .048.

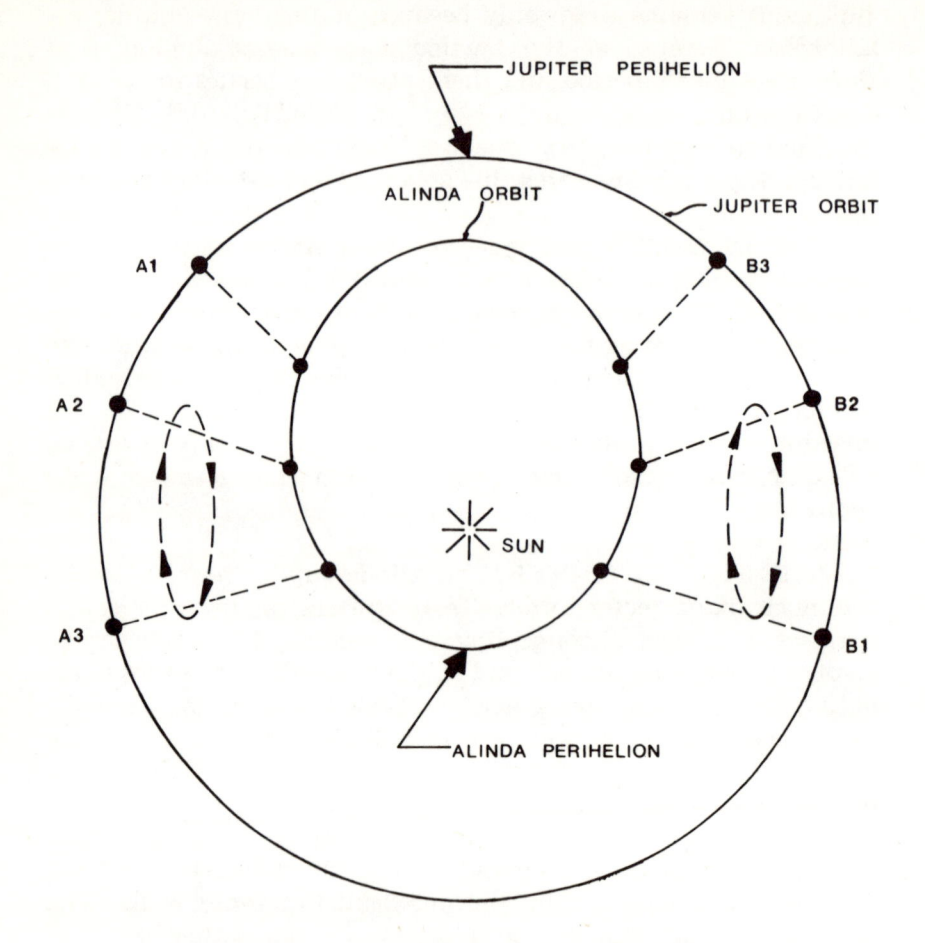

**ASTEROID – JUPITER GEOMETRY
CONJUCTIONS IN THE HESTIA GAP**
ALINDA – JUPITER   3:1   RESONANCE

FIGURE 5
Alinda and its "teeter-totter" geometry. Alinda is the only asteroid in 3:1 resonance, the sole occupant of the Hestice Gap.

pattern of conjunctions to which we now direct our attention. When the A conjunction is up (at position A_1), then the B conjunction is down (at position B_1). Jupiter perturbs Alinda at A_1 more strongly than at B_1 since the two are closer at A_1. This is equivalent to a decrease in weight of a child who is at the bottom of the teeter-totter (child B). The resulting imbalance causes child A to go down and child B to go up. Child B then becomes heavier than Child A; the teeter-totter moves back to its original position, ready to start a new cycle. The sequence of conjunction positions as shown in Figure 5 for Alinda and Jupiter is A_1-B_1, A_2-B_2, then A_3-B_3, A_2-B_2 and back to A_1-B_1 and so forth. Alinda is thus "trapped" in the 3:1 resonance relationship with Jupiter. Alinda is not swept out, because Jupiter alternately sweeps one way and then the other, maintaining the average location of the conjunction points.

The *Hestia Gap* at 3:1 is the second-most prominent of the Kirkwood Gaps. The term "Hestia Gap" has been selected from Greek cosmo-mythology, a popular reservoir for astronomical names.

Hestia was one of 12 celestial deities among the Greeks. When Apollo and Poseidon both became suitors for Hestia's hand, she swore to remain a maiden forever, and Zeus bestowed upon her the honor of presiding over sacrifices. The fact that Apollo (believed to be Mars) and Zeus (clearly Jupiter) influenced the celestial environment is interesting. And it is of further casual interest and coincidence, even a mythological irony, that these two planetary deities courted Hestia even as these two planetary orbits surround the Hestia Gap.

Hestia in the Roman cosmo-mythology becomes Vesta. The vestal virgins of Rome were astrological priestesses in honor of Vesta, or Hestia. Among their duties were astronomical ceremonies including extinguishing the old fire on March 20, the last day of the year, and lighting the new annual fire on March 21 in honor, of course, of Mars.

The Hestia Gap at 3:1 is the second-most prominent of the Kirkwood Gaps. The most prominent of the gaps, as one might expect, is the 2:1 gap.

The Hecuba Gap and Its Three Asteroids

The Hecuba Gap at 2:1, even more than the Hestia Gap,

illustrates our picture of Earth-Mars resonance. Here, there are three asteroids which have not been swept out. They are Clematis (#1101), China (#1125) and Griqua (#1362). Figure 4 illustrates the distribution of the asteroids, of which orbits for some 1,800 have been plotted, in relation to these two gaps.[7] (Other less prominent gaps are at the 5:2 and 7:3 ratios.)

In Figure 4, the Hestia Gap, where Alinda is found, is at 900 arc seconds per day, just three times Jupiter's rate of 300. The Hecuba Gap, where the three asteroids, China, Clematis and Griqua are "trapped," is at the 2:1 zone or 600 arc seconds per day.

THE PENDULUM. Our third illustration of resonance is the pendulum. It, in particular, will apply to the ancient Earth-Mars orbits. In the type of resonance of the Hecuba Gap (2:1), the conjunctions (or line-ups) form a pattern which is like a "pendulum," something different than the "teeter-totter" pattern of Alinda. The pendulum in this case has an arm of about 500,000,000 miles in length. The arm is invisible, the connecting force being gravity rather than a metallic or wooden rod. The fulcrum or pivot is the Sun. On this solar pivot swing the conjunctions of Jupiter and the 2:1 asteroids, to and fro, back and forth. The two masses are Jupiter and any one of the three asteroids. The alternating spring action is Jupiter's cyclic or alternating perturbations of the asteroid, that is, the gravitational field of Jupiter in its various locations as it circles around its orbit.

In a clock, the half stroke of the pendulum is often equivalent to one second. In the case of these three asteroids, a half stroke, meaning the swing of conjunctions from one extreme to the other, averages 34 Jupiter-years (68 asteroid years) or approximately 400 Earth-years. Figure 6 illustrates.

Figure 6 is, of course, a simplification. It shows only five of the series of 34 conjunctions in a half cycle, or stroke. When the asteroid is at positions 1 or 2, its period is shortened several days by Jupiter, and the next conjunction advances to the right,

---

[7] Figure 4 should be kept in mind for future discussion when we turn to the subject of how Mars arrived at its current orbit at a 1.88 orbital ratio to Earth's orbit.

THE ISAIAHIC CATASTROPHE AND SCIENCE

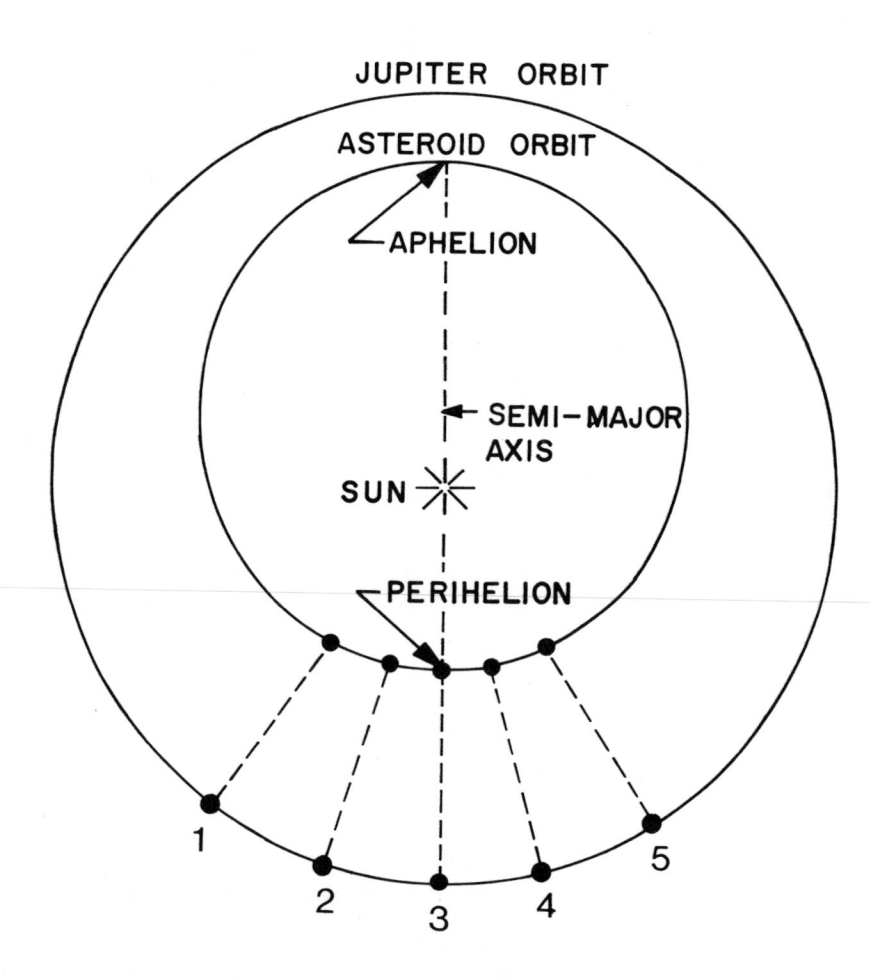

**ASTEROID – JUPITER GEOMETRY
CONJUNCTION IN THE HECUBA GAP**

FIGURE 6
The Hecuba asteroids (Clematis, China and Griqua) and the "pendulum" geometry of their orbits relating to Jupiter.

to positions 3, 4 and 5. Here, Jupiter causes the opposite kinds of perturbations, changes which lengthen the asteroid's orbital period. This causes a reversal of the pattern, the second half of the pendulum stroke. The alternating effects of Jupiter then cause the conjunctions to "librate" or oscillate back and forth, a pattern which is 1, 2, 3, 4, 5, 4, 3, 2, 1, 2 and so forth.[8, 9]. Thus it is seen that there are, in a way, "teeter-totters," "pendulums" and "merry-go-rounds" in space.

Among the 1,800 asteroids for which orbits have been calculated, one is in the 3:1 gap resonating with Jupiter; three are in the 2:1 gap. A cluster exists in the 3:2 condition (450 arc seconds) and yet another cluster is in the 4:3 condition. Among the most interesting of the resonant asteroids are the Trojan asteroids, which is the name given to those asteroids in 1:1 resonance with Jupiter. Their positions always form an equilateral triangle which has the Sun and Jupiter at the other two corners of the triangle. Recent studies have shown that the asteroid, Toro, is in 5:8 resonance with the Earth's orbit. Hence, at least 2% of the asteroids for which orbits are known are in some kind of resonance with Jupiter. This compares to 50% of the planets which are in resonance.[10]

---

[8]The conjunctions of these asteroids oscillate back and forth. They liberate around Jupiter's aphelion and around the asteroids' perihelion. Of comparable interest is a recent finding written by J. G. Williams and G. S. Benson, "Resonances in the Neptune-Pluto System," *The Astronomical Journal*, Vol. 76, No. 2, March, 1971, pp. 167 ff. The orbits of Neptune and Pluto are in 3:2 resonance. One peculiarity of Pluto's orbit is that its perihelion distance is less than that of Neptune. This condition suggests that Neptune and Pluto might make a close approach to one another. However, Pluto's resonance with Neptune is around its aphelion (the opposite of the 2:1 asteroids which resonate around their perihelions).

[9]In the case of the 2:1 resonating asteroids, it requires approximately 34 series of conjunctions for a half stroke, or about 400 Earth-years. In the case of the 3:2 resonating planets, Neptune and Pluto, it requires a series of 40 conjunctions of Pluto and Neptune or 10,000 Earth-years for a half stroke.

[10]Two of the nine planets (Neptune and Pluto) are in orbital resonance. In addition, Mercury's orbit is in 2:3 resonance with its own spin rate. Venus' strange, retrograde spin rate of about 242 days is very close to being in resonance with Earth's orbit, and indeed may have been so in ancient times when Earth's orbit was slightly closer to the Sun, before the 701 B.C. catastrophe.

If we consider the former resonance of the Earth-Moon system with Mars, five planets have been in one kind or another of orbital resonance. It has earlier been mentioned that it is likely that Mars was in 6:1

In Chapter I, Figure 1 (page 3), the model for the ancient Earth-Mars relationship was presented. Of course it was a strange model to most, because this is the first time such a model of planetary catastrophism has ever been introduced.[11] Our model of the ancient scene of Earth-Mars resonance compares in several ways to the Jupiter-Hecuba relationship, that is, Jupiter's relationship to Clematis, China, and Griqua. But there are also contrasts. Thus far, we have shown that resonance can and does occur in the Solar system. Today, 50% of the planets exhibit some kind of resonance, as do 20% of the satellites and 2% of the charted asteroids. By this analogy, we propose that another kind of resonance did occur, a resonance of the 2:1 ratio, and that this analogy best explains the *cyclic patterns* of the ancient Earth-Mars catastrophes.

Similarities Between the Hecuba-Jupiter and Earth-Mars Resonances

1. The Two Weights. The very heavy planet, Jupiter, today causes significant alterations of these three tiny asteroids at distances of 200,000,000 and 300,000,000 miles. Similarly, the heavier Earth accomplished significant alterations or perturbations of Mars' ancient orbit when the two planets were from 5,000,000 miles distant to as close as an estimated 60,000 miles (The Exodus Catastrophe). Several of the catastrophes we believe involved distances of between 75,000 and 150,000 miles for the fly-by. Mars is about one-ninth as massive as the Earth.
2. The Half Cycle. The asteroids are perturbed in a pattern so that approximately 34 conjunctions with Jupiter are

---

resonance with Jupiter while it was in 1:2 resonance with the Earth. Further, Saturn is in 2:5 orbital resonance with Jupiter. So orbital resonance, though only recently discovered, is not rare.

Joachim Schubart first reported cases of commensurability, or resonance among the asteroids in 1968. (See Joachim Schubart, "Long-Period Effects in the Motion of Hilda-Type Planets," *The Astronomical Journal*, Vol. 73, No. 2, Part 1, March, 1968, pp. 99 ff.) Further analysis of the Kirkwood Gaps was reported by Francois Schweizer, "Resonant Asteroids in the Kirkwood Gaps and Statistical Explanations of the Gaps," *The Astronomical Journal*, Vol. 74, No. 6, August, 1969, pp. 779 ff.

[11]This is subject only to the exception of Patten's model of Mercury-Earth interaction (Mercury with a small icy satellite that fragmented forming a deluge of astronomical rain). It is set forth in his work, *The Biblical Flood and the Ice Epoch*, pp. 126 ff.

required to reverse the direction of the conjunctions. Pluto's conjunction pattern with Neptune is reversed about every fortieth orbit. Our study concludes that the ancient Earth-Mars conjunction pattern was reversed, like a half stroke of a pendulum, *on the average*[12] of once every 27 Martian orbits, which was once every 54 Earth orbits. These patterns of 27 orbits, 34 orbits and 40 orbits are of the same order of magnitude.

3. The Perihelion Zone. The three 2:1 asteroids in the Hecuba Gap are near their perihelion when in conjunction with Jupiter. So it was with the ancient Martian orbit. Mars too was near to its perihelion when interacting deeply with the Earth. (This is in contrast with the 3:2 resonance system of Neptune and Pluto where oscillation is around Pluto's aphelion.)

Differences Between the Hecuba-Jupiter and the Ancient Earth - Mars Resonances

Significant differences between the 2:1 analogy with Hecuba and the Earth-Mars relationship exist, and these differences are important to consider.

1. Crossing Orbits. The asteroids of Hecuba *do not cross* Jupiter's orbit, but are entirely within it. Mars *did cross* to the inside of Earth's orbit, the two locations of intersection being the fearful "days of the Lord," days of expected dread in Hebrew cosmology when the world might not survive. These times of appointment were

---

[12]This implies that usually every 54 years (sometimes other close periods, such as 52 or 56 years), astronomical peril *threatened* the Earth and the Moon. Sometimes the peril was merely a threat; on other occasions it was a deadly, traumatic astronomical holocaust which enveloped our tiny rotating sphere. We believe that severe catastrophes developed at least seven times between 2500 B.C. and 701 B.C. This means that of the 33 times the 54-year-cycle pattern was reversed during this 1,800 year period, 7 (or 20%) of these close conjunctions were very severe. Probably another 20% were mildly catastrophic like the ones in 864 B.C. and 1080 B.C., which we shall study. The other 60% of these 33 occasions of celestial appointment were more frightening than deadly.

equally as fearful to the Greeks, Romans, Teutons, Phoenicians and others.[13]

2. Heavy Planet Position. With the Hecuba and Hestia asteroids (Alinda, China, Clematis and Griqua), the *inner orbit* belongs to the light planet or asteroid, and the *outer orbit* belongs to the massive planet, Jupiter in this case. In our resonance model, the *inner orbit* belongs to the heavier Earth and the *outer orbit* belongs to the lighter Mars about one-ninth as massive as our planet.[14]

3. Planet Systems. With the Hecuba and Hestia asteroids, the two controllers are Jupiter and the Sun. There are three controllers of the Pluto resonance, namely, Sun, Neptune and Uranus. Pluto is almost in 3:2:1 resonance with Neptune and Uranus. We believe that Mars *was* in 6:1 resonance with Jupiter *while* it was in 1:2 resonance with the Earth-Moon system. Hence the controllers of Mars were the Sun, Earth, Jupiter and Saturn.[15,16]

---

[13]Most ancient peoples utilized one of the two days, March 21 or circa October 30, as their New Years Day in their calendars. Thus their cyclic experience both looked backward (to the end of the last world age or era) and forward (to the possible reorientation of, or end of, the age in a future holocaust). That they conceived days of scheduled catastrophism as possibly the "end of the world" was not unreasonable. Were similar conditions to recur today, with our astronomical technology, our attentions and concerns would be equally riveted to the heavens if not more so.

[14]Mars is 1/9 as heavy as Earth, and is about 1/3000 as heavy as Jupiter. The heavy planet position of the Earth-Mars resonance in this case compares more favorably to the Neptune-Pluto resonance, where the heavier planet is also on the inside. Pluto is thought to be about 1/500th as massive as Neptune.

[15]The current orbits of Earth, Mars, Jupiter and Saturn are 1.00, 1.88, 11.87 and 29.65 years (current Earth years) respectively. These four planets we believe were in an ancient orbital resonance system where there were periods (in terms of current Earth years) of .99 for Earth, 1.98 for Mars, 11.87 for Jupiter and 29.65 for Saturn. This four-body resonance system then was in a complex 60:30:5:2 resonance.

[16]It is believed that effects caused by the Moon on orbital shifts were so slight as to be insignificant.

Superior Conjunctions and Inferior Conjunctions

The conjunction pattern in the ancient Earth-Mars system contains a further analogy, and point of interest when compared to the conjunctions of the Hecuba-Hestia asteroids. We have already mentioned that Mars in the former orbit experienced one inferior conjunction, (when it was on the inside), and two superior conjunctions, (when it was on the outside), with the Earth each 2-year orbit. The dangerous conjunction was the inferior one; the superior ones were relatively peaceful.

Combining the two resonant models, the Hecuba example of 2:1 and the Hestia example of 3:1, applying both to the Earth-Mars model, it is seen that:

1. The *inferior conjunctions* work like the pendulum (back and forth).
2. The *superior conjunctions* work like the teeter-totter (up and down).
3. The two models are seen to be *working together* to preserve, or to reinforce, resonance. Figure 7 illustrates.

Hestia and Hecuba in Greek Mythology

It has already been mentioned that Hestia was a maiden among the Olympic deities. When Apollo and Poseidon became suiters for her hand, she spurned both, and Zeus bestowed on her the honor of presiding over sacrifices in the Greek cosmo-theology. Ares usually represents Mars in the Greek pantheon. Apollo is usually *assumed* to be the Sun. According to the legend, Apollo was the son of Zeus and Leto (Leto was a titaness, Zeus was Jupiter).

> As to Roscher's derivation of all Apollo's functions from the conception of an original light and sun god it cannot be shown that on Greek soil Apollo originally had the meaning of sun god; in Homer, Aeschylus and Plato, the sun god Helios is distinctly separated from Phoebus Apollo, . . . It is not until the beginning of the 5th century B.C. that the identification makes its appearance. . . . But the fact of the gradual development of Apollo as a god of light and heaven, and his identification with the foreign

THE ISAIAHIC CATASTROPHE AND SCIENCE 85

SUPERIOR CONJUNCTIONS
TEETER-TOTTER PATTERN

SUN

A1
A2
A3

B3
B2
B1

1 2 3 4 5

INFERIOR CONJUNCTIONS
PENDULUM PATTERN

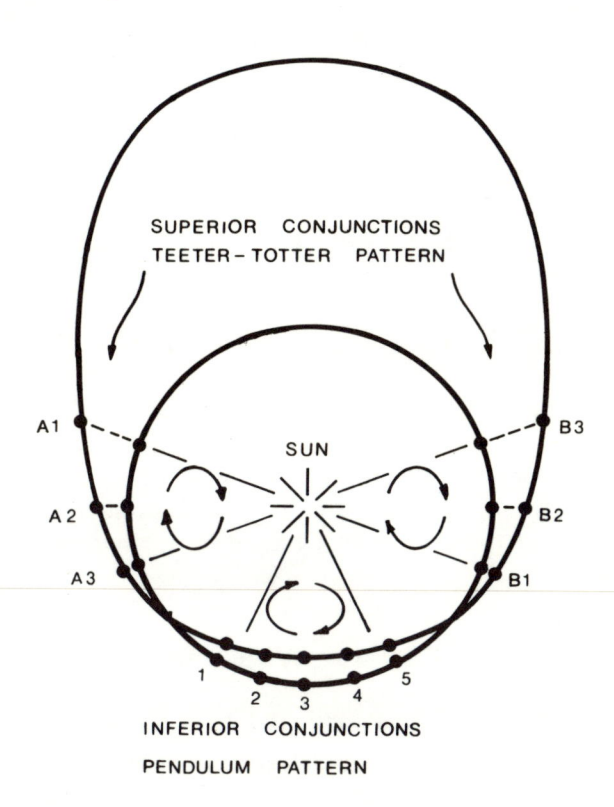

COMBINED CONJUNCTION PATTERNS

PENDULUM TYPE (HECUBA)
TEETER-TOTTER TYPE (HESTIA)

FIGURE 7

The inferior (near) conjuctions worked with the superior (distant) conjunctions to add to the stability of the system. It will also be seen that Jupiter was in 6:1 resonance with Mars, adding another stabilizing factor.

sun gods, is no proof of an original Greek solar conception of him.[17]

The solar deity is actually Helios. Apollo, a celestial, was a war-like deity like the Roman Mars. Apollo is indeed the phonetic equivalent to the Phoenician Baal, and the Chaldean Bel, which Charles McDowell identifies as Mars.[18] Further research needs to be devoted to this matter, and the probability is that Apollo was indeed Mars. It was merely the Helenized version of Baal (Phoenician or Bel (Chaldean) even as Aphrodite was the Helenized version of Ashtoreth (Phoenician) or Ishtar (Chaldean), the Roman Venus.

Hecuba, according to Homer, was the wife of Priam, king of Troy, and the mother of Paris, Paris being the leading abductor of the age. Queen Hecuba then lived during the Greater Davidic Catastrophe of 972 B.C., the era of the Trojan War and of Homer. She has been immortalized by Homer in his poetic saga of the Trojan War, the *Iliad*. This catastrophe shall be studied in Chapter VI and in a future work by Charles McDowell (see footnote 18 this chapter).

The Conjunction Patterns Within the Resonant Orbit

The 54-Year and 108-Year Cycles

In Table I, page 5, it was illustrated that recorded catastrophes of major or minor import occurred during the following years: 756 B.C., 864 B.C., 972 B.C., 1080 B.C. and 1404 B.C. If there were either unreported holocausts or threatening cataclysms in 1188 B.C. and 1296 B.C. it would be a perfect 108 year cyclic pattern (2 x 54 years). Indeed, such astronomical holocausts, we suspect, did threaten Earth at these times (1188 B.C. and 1296 B.C.), and either did not develop into a major disaster, or were not reported, or else the records have been lost.

---

[17]*Encyclopaedia Brittanica*, Chicago: William Benton, Publisher, 1958, Vol. 2, pp. 109, 111.

[18]Charles McDowell, "A History of Middle East Catastrophes, 1500-972 B.C.," an unpublished manuscript. Dr. McDowell is chairman of the department of geography, history and political science, Cuyahoga Community College, Western Campus, Parma, Ohio.

Heavy catastrophes occurred in pairs every five or six centuries. History clearly shows this. The twentieth, the fifteenth and the eighth centuries were the tragic ones in terms of astronomical catastrophism, since each of these centuries contained a *pair* of heavy interactions. There was very likely a third grander cycle of rhythm which will be discussed in Chapter X.

It is noted that the conjunction cycles *averaged* 54 years per half cycle. This is to say that the 54-year cycle was not always exact. For instance, there is ample evidence that the Sodom-Gomorrah event in March of 1877 B.C. was 52 years after the Tower of Babel holocaust, not 54 years.[19] There is evidence that at least one other cycle between 1877 B.C. and 1447 B.C. was 52 rather than 54 years, an item which we shall develop in Chapters VIII and IX. Further, one of the cycles was just 42 years rather than the normal 54. That was the cycle between the Exodus holocaust of 1447 B.C. and the Long Day of Joshua in 1404 B.C. This was considerably shorter because, as we judge from the Biblical text, it was a unique outside fly-by, rather than the usual inside fly-by. Computer testing of the resonant orbit model by Loren Steinhauer and Ralph Chang reveals that resonance will be threatened if not disrupted with an outside fly-by. This shortened cycle is evidence of such a disruption.

In the first third of this chapter we have dealt with the principle of resonance in the solar system. With this established, we are now free to examine the journeys of Mars in its former orbit, swinging in to 81,900,000 miles, and reaching out as far as 210,700,000 miles, far beyond its current orbit. After an examination of the experience of Mars in the former orbit, we shall consider the five kinds of changes which will occur to the Earth,

---

[19]Louis Ginzberg, *Legends of the Jews,* Philadelphia: Jewish Publication Society of America, 1909, Vol. I, p. 253. "For fifty-two years God had warned the godless; He had made mountains to quake and tremble. . . . With nightfall, the fate of Sodom was sealed irrevocably, and the angels arrived there."

On page 255 of this work it states that four of the cities of the plain had been founded 51 years earlier and one (Zoar) 50 years earlier. The indication is that these cities were founded in the first or second year following the Tower of Babel debacle. It may well be that the rifting, or pulling apart of Earth's crust forming the Great Rift Valley, was expanded during that catastrophe. More on this subject will be considered in Chapter IX.

and to Mars, in a close fly-by. These phenomena as previously mentioned are:

1. A perturbation of Earth's orbit.

2. A reversal of the geomagnetic field.

3. A severe, temporary tide in Earth's crust and magma (its lithosphere).

4. A severe, temporary tide in Earth's oceans, atmosphere and plasma in the exosphere, or geomagnetic regions.

5. A wobble, or "precession" of the spin axis, which will take some combination of polar migration, a change in tilt and possibly a change in spin rate.

Once these subjects are studied with some degree of thoroughness, and once the *mechanics* for the Isaiahic Catastrophe of 701 B.C. are established, we will continue our study with the *historcial* account of the earlier holocausts as seen through the eyes and by the pens of the reporters of those earlier ages.

A GENERAL THEORY OF FRAGMENTATION
Mars and Its Ancient Mars-Asteroids

In each of the seven major holocausts we see that severe Earth-shakings, or earthquakes, sometimes along with a spin axis wobble, occurred simultaneously with falling bolides and meteors. The Long Day of Joshua, for instance, is a particularly lucid example. The Bible records that the blizzard of bolides and meteorites (hailstones falling from on high) killed more Canaanite troops than did Hebrew soldiers. It was a day of cosmic slaughter. A massive meteoritic blizzard occurred during the spin axis precession when the apparent paths of the Sun and Moon departed from the normal. From where did these bolides and meteors come?

The blizzard of bolides and meteors, simultaneous with the fly-by, suggests a correlation between the two events. The meteors were probably debris in orbit around Mars.

It is estimated there are 50,000 asteroids, battered fragments of a former planet. Orbits of 1,800 have been calculated, and 90% of them have orbits with either their aphelion or, more often, their perihelion in the vicinity of 200,000,000 miles from the Sun. These fragments are remains of a former planet, possibly one-half the size of our Moon, which fragmented when another, somewhat larger planet (we propose Mars) nearly collided with it.

There is a principle in astronomy describing tidal interaction of two celestial bodies approaching each other. At a certain point, the cohesive force of the smaller body is overcome by the tide-raising force of the larger body, and the smaller body fragments before a direct collision occurs. Edouard Roche, a French astronomer, did considerable research into the nature of the construction of planets and stars. He proved that a liquid satellite of any star will be distorted by the tide-raising forces of the primary star. Moreover, if the two are of equal density and if the satellite were to come as close as 2.44 radii from the primary's center, tide-raising forces would exceed the cohesive gravitational force of such a satellite. Under these conditions, the smaller body would fragment. If it were solid rather than liquid, its fragments would assume multiple orbits around the star in accordance with Kepler's laws.

Roche's analysis, published in 1850, has never been challenged, although it has been recalculated from 2.44 to 2.45 radii. Roche's study applied to stars with a liquid consistency, with satellites having circular orbits. More recently, in 1972, Loren Steinhauer applied this principle to planets (non-liquid bodies) interacting with other planets (assuming non-circular orbits). It was found that if an icy sphere of appropriate size approached Earth, its fragmentation limit would be 2.3 Earth radii.[20] That is, the icy visitor would fragment at some distance (from the center of the Earth) exceeding 2.3 Earth radii.[21] For the case of

---

[20] Loren C. Steinhauer, "Out of Whose Womb Came the Ice?", *Symposium on Creation IV*, Grand Rapids: Baker Book House, 1972, pp. 134 ff.

[21] The modified Roche Limit calculation can be correlated with existing phenomena in the solar system. The leading example is the rings of Saturn. The fragmentation limit for a spherical body composed of water ice approaching Saturn is about 1.17 Saturn radii. That is, the icy body would fragment at some distance beyond 4,500 miles above Saturn's surface (or 40,200 miles from its center). The inner edge of the ring system is 7,000 miles above the surface. This suggests that the modified Roche limit calculation is conservative in that the fragmentation occurs *beyond* the calculated limit. The other correlative examples are the moons of the planets which obviously aren't fragmenting. The moon closest to its mother planet is Phobos, 1.4 radii from the center of Mars: 1.4 exceeds the fragmentation limit of 1.26 for bodies of like density with Mars.

Mars being approached by a smaller body of like density, the fragmentation limit would be 1.26 Mars radii, that is Mars would fragment the visitor at some distance beyond 540 miles above Mars' surface.[22]

The Fragmentation of Electra

Evidence pointing to a fragmentation of a former planet about 200,000,000 miles from the Sun includes:

1. Greek cosmo-mythology.

   Greek cosmo-mythology mentions a former planet, one of the sisters in the heavens, who after amour with Zeus (Jupiter) fled the heavens plucked out her hair, and was changed into a comet. Another record says she lost her brilliancy after a celestial battle. We are proposing that the fragmented planet, the source of the asteroids, was the former planet Electra.[23] (From this word, of course, comes our word "electricity.")

2. The existence of the asteroids, most of which orbit across Mars' ancient orbit.

3. The vast number (estimated at 50,000) and the irregular, fragment-like shape of the asteroids.

4. Two small, irregularly-shaped moons still retained by Mars, apparently captured asteroids.

5. Four irregular-shaped, small asteroid-like outer satellites of Jupiter, apparently captured asteroids.

6. Mars' very numerous craters (astroblemes), as discussed in Chapter II.

7. Indo-Aryan cosmo-mythology: Maruts encircling Indra's head, as discussed in Chapter II.

---

[22] The radius of Mars is 2,070 miles.

[23] The mass of the asteroids collectively has been estimated to equal $\frac{1}{8}$ the mass of the Moon. We believe this is a conservative estimate. This former planet, before fragmenting into asteroids, must have been at least 1,000 miles in diameter. Compare this to the Moon's diameter of 2,160 miles, Mars' diameter of 4,140 miles and Earth's of 7,927 miles. The largest asteroid is 480 miles in diameter.

Saturn's second-largest satellite, Iapetus, has a diameter of an estimated 1,000 miles, and this may well be smaller in size than the former planet which disintegrated.

8. The "fire and brimstone" deposition on Earth as recorded in Hebrew history, such depositions coinciding with Mars' fly-bys.

If Mars did fragment the former planet Electra, then Mars would probably capture some of the fragments, perhaps a few percent. Thus several hundred asteroids of moderate size plus countless micro-asteroids would have remained in an orbit about Mars. The remainder of the fragments would assume orbits around the Sun.[24]

This study proposes that three planets (Earth, Mars and Saturn) have experienced near-collisions, sufficiently near for a fragmentation. Among the effects of these fragmentations were icy rings in two instances, and a cloud of rock-like asteroids in the third. These three episodes were each separate scenes, part of a general play which might be entitled "The Settling Down of the Solar System." The scene involving Mars and the asteroids was, we judge, about 4,000 years ago. The scene involving Earth and an icy fragmentation (and deluge) was about 4,500 years ago. A recent analysis suggests that the formation of Saturn's icy rings also has been within the last 10,000 years. Thus these three scenes are not only dramatic but relatively recent.

We propose that this fragmentation of Electra occurred during the era 2500 B.C. to 2000 B.C. The first recorded dump of fire and brimstone (hot hailstones from above) is in the Tower of Babel holocaust, 1930 B.C. The ancient Greek cosmo-mythology claims to recall the genesis of the event. The proto-Greeks were settling the Achaean peninsula, Macedonia and the Anatolian peninsula during this same era.

---

[24]There are three examples of fragmentation in our solar system; two are extant. They are (1) Saturn's icy rings, (2) the asteroids, and (3) Earth's temporary ice rings formed during the Flood Catastrophe. Of the third, the only remaining area of evidence is the glaciation, the scouring and scraping, which is seen feathering out from the geomagnetic polar regions. This includes erratic boulders, terminal moraines, lateral moraines, striated rocks, lacustrine plains and so forth. For further information, see Patten's *The Biblical Flood and the Ice Epoch*, Chapters VI and VII.

The fact that Deimos and Phobos are in direct motion around Mars would indicate that Electra shattered while passing by Mars on the *outside*. This again suggests that the orbits of Electra and Mars also crossed.

The fact that the four outermost satellites of Jupiter are small irregular shaped rocks in retrograde motion suggests that they too are components of the former planet Electra. The names of these outer satellites of Jupiter are Andastea, Pan, Poisedon and Hades. These satellites vary in size from about 10 to 25 miles in diameter, similar to Deimos and Phobos.

Bolides[25] and Meteors

Fire and Brimstone

As already explained, Mars' seven close appointments with the Earth coincided with heavy meteoritic and bolidic showers on the Earth. On some of these occasions, the Moon also felt the impact of the Mars-asteroids. This is one reason for the high density of craters on the Moon. By 701 B.C., most of the bolides and meteors had been shed off on Earth or Moon or moved into a solar orbit. But a few remained, one which (as we saw in Chapter III) nearly hit Jerusalem. It was called the "Jerusalem Bolide," and was similar to the Tunguska Bolide of 1908.

BOLIDES AND METEORS IN ROMAN LITERATURE. As related in Chapter II, Rome's founding in circa 750 B.C. was related to the fall of a large meteor. At the same time, Volsinium, a large city of southern Etruscany, was destroyed. Only the

---

[25] A *bolide* is a fragment which enters Earth's atmosphere just as does a meteor. The prefix *bolo* in Greek means "to throw." A bolide is a meteor-like body, composed of materials other than iron, nickel and silicon (such as ammonia, carbon or cyanogen). They will ignite upon heating to a high temperature and explode in a vast, chemical explosion causing a concussion and much noise. In the Hebrew records, the word *deber* describes ancient fiery outpourings of Mars, both bolides and meteors. Since the King James translators did not understand the cosmology, they have translated *deber* in 17 different ways, including "pestilence," "murrain," "hot hailstones," "brimstone," "lightning," and "tumults."

Bolides have been known to occur in recent times. A large bolide, (some describe it as a comet), fell into Earth's atmosphere on the night of June 30, 1908. It was estimated to be 400 yards in diameter, and was seen over much of Siberia that night. Its brief journey through Earth's atmosphere resulted in immense friction, triggering a vast chemical explosion equal to the force of a thermonuclear device. It exploded at a point many hundred feet, or perhaps a thousand feet above the ground, near the Tunguska River in uninhabited Northern Siberia. Shock waves were felt and heard for hundreds of miles. Trees were flash-burned for a radius of miles from the point of explosion. This particular bolide (some described it as a comet that hit the Earth) fell in the higher latitudes of the Northern Hemisphere, in unpopulated Siberia and in our century. It could have fallen in a populated region. For example, had it fallen in the *same* latitude but four hours later, St. Petersburg, the modern Leningrad, then a city of 1,500,000 and the capital of Tsarist Russia, would have suffered a fiery fate comparable to the ancient Volsinium, except for the formation of a crater lake.

For further information, see an essay entitled "On The Motion of the Tunguska Meteorite in the Earth's Atmosphere" by L. A. Katasev and N. V. Kulikova, *Solar System Research*, Vol. I, No. 1, Jan-March, 1967.

The word *meteor* comes from a Greek word meaning "something from the air," or in contemporary usage, a shooting star.

crater, together with some associated lava flows, remains as mute evidence. Ovid and Pliny, later Roman historians[26] describe it almost as faithfully as Isaiah and Habakkuk describe their event, and Homer described his catastrophic era.

> Pliny wrote: "Most men are not acquainted with a truth known to the founders of the science from their arduous study of the heavens," namely, that thunderbolts "are the fires of the three upper planets." He differentiated them from lightning caused by the dashing together of two two clouds. Seneca, his contemporary, also distinguished lightnings that "seek houses" or "lesser bolts" and the bolts of Jupiter "by which the threefold mass of mountains fell."[27]

Another picture of bolidic and meteoritic activity is given by Pliny.

> "Heavenly fire is spit forth by the planet as crackling charcoal flies from a burning log." If such a discharge falls on the earth, "it is accompanied by a very great disturbance of the air," produced "by the birth-pangs, so to speak, of the planet in travail."[28]

BOLIDES AND METEORS IN GREEK LITERATURE. Pliny was describing specifically the time of the catastrophe of 756 B.C., the Joel-Amos holocaust. Homer described specifically the catastrophe of 972 B.C., the Greater Davidic Catastrophe, one which was very similar in the Mars fly-by pattern.

> So he went back in anger, and Apollo, who loved him dear-

---

[26] Ovid (Publius Ovidius Naso), 43 B.C.-?17 A.D. Pliny (Gaius Plinius Secundus), "the elder," 23-79 A.D. Pliny wrote in the fields of history and natural science and died while trying to observe closely the eruption of Mt. Vesuvius.
What Pliny described as the ancient "thunderbolts" in former ages were in reality powerful shock waves radiating from the explosion subpoint. K. P. Stanyukovich and V. A. Bronshten, in describing the Tunguska Bolide, pointed out that "shock waves on reaching the earth's surface will produce all of the observed patterns of destruction, while radiation emitted by a powerful shock wave will give rise to flash burn of a number of objects, particularly trees" (as quoted from the aforementioned Katasev and Kulikova).

[27] Immanuel Velikovsky, *Worlds in Collision,* New York: Doubleday and Co., 1950, p. 272.

[28] Velikovsky, *op. cit.,* pp. 272-273.

ly, heard his prayer. Then the god sent A DEADLY DART upon the Argives, and the people died thick on one another, for THE ARROWS WENT everywhither among the wide host of the Achaeans. At last a seer in the fullness of his knowledge declared to us the oracles of Apollo. . . .[29]

"Son of Atreus," said he, "I deem that we should now turn roving home if we would escape destruction, for we are being cut down by war and pestilence at once. Let us ask some priest or prophet, or some reader of dreams (for dreams, too, are of Zeus) who can tell us why Phoebus Apollo is so angry . . . so as to take away the plague from us."[30]

We note the similarities between the deadly darts and the celestial arrows of the Homeric account and the great stones cast down from heaven during the Long Day of Joshua, or the "pestilence" which fell in the days of David, killing a recorded 70,000 men.[31] That such a bolidic rain could be destructive is very possible when it is kept in mind that bolides are believed to be composed of compounds such as ammonia or cyanogen, possibly mixed with iron and silicon, whereas meteors are silica, iron and/or nickel. "Fire" in the fire and brimstone translation of the Hebrew texts, we believe is bolides whereas "brimstone" is meteors, the two occurring simultaneously, but not being identical.

BOLIDES AND METEORS IN HEBREW LITERATURE. The following samplings are from an extensive catastrophic literature of the "fire and brimstone prophets," whose collective

---

[29] Homer, the *Iliad*, translated by Samuel Butler, New York: Walter J. Black, 1942, Book I, p. 16. We have already mentioned that "Apollo" is the phonetic equivalent in Greek of "Baal" in Phoenician and Dr. Charles McDowell in a later publication will be identifying Baal with Mars, even as Ashtoreth (the Greek Aphrodite) is Venus.
Knowledge of the astronomical scene, planet-watching and predictions were the main issue in Book I in the *Iliad*. Did Calchus, the augur or seer, bring the Danaans and Argives in on schedule, or did the personal behavior of Agamemnon so displease Apollo that he altered his celestial visit to plague or decimate the Argives? This is our question which underlies Homer's questions.

[30] Homer, *op. cit.*, pp. 8-9.

[31] II Samuel 24:15-16; see also I Chronicles 21:12-16.

THE ISAIAHIC CATASTROPHE AND SCIENCE   95

"nickname" is most appropriate although seldom understood in its cosmic reality. Illustrations have been taken from five of the fire and brimstone seers of Judah: Nahum, Habakkuk, Isaiah, Joel and Amos.

> Who can stand before his indignation? and who can abide in the fierceness of his anger? HIS FURY is poured out LIKE FIRE, and THE ROCKS are thrown down by him. (Nahum 1:6)

> Before him went THE PESTILENCE, and BURNING COALS went forth at his feet. He stood, and measured the Earth.... (Habakkuk 3:5-6)

> And the Lord shall cause his glorious voice to be heard, and shall shew the lighting down of his arm, with the indignation of his anger, AND WITH THE FLAME OF A DEVOURING FIRE, WITH SCATTERING, AND TEMPEST, AND HAILSTONES. (Isaiah 30:30)

> A fire devoureth THEM; and behind THEM a flame burneth: the land is as the garden of Eden before THEM, and behind THEM a desolate wilderness.... Like the noise of chariots on the tops of mountains shall they leap, like the noise of a FLAME OF FIRE that devoureth the stubble, as a strong people set in battle array. (Joel 2:3, 5)

> I have smitten you WITH BLASTING AND MILDEW.... I have sent among you pestilence after the manner of Egypt.... I have overthrown some of you, as God overthrew Sodom and Gomorrah, and ye were as a firebrand plucked out of the burning.... (Amos 4:9-11)

One of the most dramatic instances of a bolidic explosion is that recorded by Isaiah during the holocaust of March 20, 701 B.C., at a time when Jerusalem was surrounded by the Assyrian army, an army intent on annihilating Jerusalem and all Judea.

> Then the angel of the Lord went forth, and smote in the camp of the Assyrians a hundred and fourscore and five thousand; and when they arose early in the morning, behold, they were all dead corpses. (Isaiah 37:36)

Such an explosion must have been accompanied by a vast blast, or noise, and this is recounted in Psalm 46:

> The heathen raged, the kingdoms were moved; HE UTTERED HIS VOICE, the earth melted. Come, behold the

works of the Lord, what desolations he hath made in the earth. (Psalm 46:6, 8)

The Jerusalem Bolide of 701 B.C. was one of the last remaining Mars-asteroids. It may have been 100 feet in diameter. It left only Deimos and Phobos (diameters estimated to be 5 and 10 miles respectively) as visible clues to that era of catastrophism. However, we do suspect that a considerable amount of finer meteorites and meteoritic dust circling Mars has yet to be discovered.

Resonance of orbits and Mars-meteors are background to our understanding of the geometry of the particular fly-by which occurred in March of 701 B.C., the last of the long and fearful series of Earth-Mars interactions.[32]

The Geometry of the Mars Fly-by, March 20-21, 701 B.C.

How close did Mars come on that catastrophic night of March 20, 701 B.C.? Did it cause any kind of change in the Earth's orbit? Did it cause any kind of change in the tilt of the spin axis? Did it cause any kind of polar migration, and if so, how much and which way? Did Mars pass over on the inside or on the outside of the Earth, and what would be the difference between these two kinds of passes? Did it pass north or south of the Earth's ecliptic, or orbital plane? And what would the difference be? Was there a significant change in polarity, or strength of the geomagnetic field? These are some of the questions which this study shall consider, and we will offer some answers.

---

[32] The total historical model includes the following sub-models:
1. The 2:1 resonant orbit relation of Earth and Mars,
2. The fragmentation of Electra by Mars, resulting in asteroids,
3. The seven major fly-bys between 2500 B.C. and 701 B.C.,
4. The 6:1 resonance between Mars and Jupiter in that era.
5. The 5:2 resonance between Jupiter and Saturn in that era, a resonance which persists into the current era.

Items 1 and 2 are sub-models addressed in this chapter. Item 3 is a sub-model series addressed by the chapters in this work discussing each particular catastrophe. Item 4 is considered in some further detail in Chapter XI, where it will be shown that the line of apsides of Jupiter's orbit was perpendicular to the line of apsides of both Earth and Mars while they were in 12:6:1 resonance. This is to suggest that the influence of Jupiter in this whole system must not be overlooked or minimized.

TABLE IV

MARS' BIENNIAL APPROACHES TO EARTH
756 B.C. TO 710 B.C.[33]

Date of Biennial Approach	Closeness of Approach	
October 25 756 B.C.	120,000 Miles	Year of Catastrophe
November 1 754	1,500,000	
6 752	2,800,000	
11 750	3,900,000	
17 748	4,900,000	
22 746	5,800,000	
27 744	6,600,000	
December 3 742	7,200,000	
8 740	7,800,000	
13 738	8,100,000	
19 736	8,500,000	
24 734	8,700,000	
29 731	8,750,000	
January 5 729	8,800,000	
10 727	8,800,000	
15 725	8,750,000	
21 723	8,700,000	
27 721	8,500,000	
February 2 719	8,100,000	
7 717	7,800,000	
12 715	7,200,000	
17 713	6,600,000	
22 711	5,800,000	
28 709	4,900,000	
March 5 707	3,900,000	
10 705	2,800,000	
15 703	1,500,000	Year of Anxiety
20 701	70,000	Year of Catastrophe

Closeness of Approach

Our conclusion is that Mars approached as close as 70,000 miles to Earth during this last of the ancient fly-bys. The closeness of approach, with a strong alteration of the Martian orbit,

---

[33]This table assumes a perihelion of Mars at 81,900,000 miles and a perihelion of Earth at 90,700,000 miles.

is what is believed to have caused Mars to lose resonance on this occasion.

In the resonant orbit condition, Table V illustrates the shifting dates and shifting distances of Mars' closest approach during the last 54-year cycle. The cyclic coming and going of Mars reflects how ancients could chart its path, estimate its nearness, see its satellites (visible easily when within 1,000,000 miles), and even see its larger craters in particularly close fly-bys.

Geometry of Approach

It is believed that Mars passed on the *inside* of Earth's orbit, at a distance of about 70,000 miles. Mars was slightly to the north of the ecliptic plane, and was visible during the passover primarily in the Northern Hemisphere. An inside fly-by (that is, Mars crosses the intersection point of the two orbits first) will result in the following features.

1. A reduction of the energy of Mars, reducing its orbit between 30 and 45 days.
2. Relocation of the aphelion of Mars, nearer to the Sun, tending to round out the former orbit of Mars.
3. An increase of the energy of the Earth, expanding its orbit between 3 and 4 days.

This interaction was of such a configuration and severity as to break resonance, and to move Mars toward its current orbital position. This is also the kind of adjustment which explains the sudden need for more days per year in ancient calendars, that is the change from 360 to 365 days per year.

Mars was *slightly north* of Earth's ecliptic plane; this kind of fly-by will cause the North Pole to migrate toward Alaska, away from Europe, and lower the latitude of Palestine. When the shadow of the obelisk (or sun-dial) of Ahaz suddenly shortened, this tells us that the *angle of the Sun* at noon became significantly higher, which tells us that the latitude of Jerusalem was shifted southward. Before this catastrophe, we suspect Jerusalem had a latitude of 37° N. like the current latitude of Athens, Greece, and San Jose, California. Today Jerusalem has a latitude of 32° N. like San Diego, California. This polar migration is considered in more detail later in this chapter.

Relative Speed of the Two Planets

Earth in its orbit at perihelion moves about 1,620,000 miles per day. Mars in its ancient orbit sped past its perihelion at a rate of about 1,875,000 miles per day, and slowed to 795,000 miles per day in passing its remote aphelion. As it buzzed Earth, it was approaching our planet at a relative speed of 540,000 miles per day when the vector angles are taken into account.

We will reconstruct the approach of Mars as it was viewed by Palestinians on that fateful day of March 20, 701 B.C. Mars passed over Earth in our model at its closest at about 6:00 P.M., Palestinian time, at about 70,000 miles.

Mars rose in the early morning on March 20, 701 B.C., about two hours later than the Sun, perhaps around 8:00 A.M. It was assaulting the Earth from within Earth's orbit, which is to say from Mars' perihelion, or from "out of the Sun." Hence its dark side was showing primarily toward the Earth, although there was a thin (but extremely bright) crescent showing. Earth-shine undoubtedly illuminated in outline the dark side of Mars even in the daytime sky. As the morning and afternoon progressed, Mars appeared to be overtaking the Sun, though passing to the northward side. In reality it was in the process of making an inside fly-by. Its thin but brilliant crescent was ever narrowing as Mars approached. Simultaneously its size was ever increasing. Its size in the sky at 70,000 miles (at about 6:00 P.M. Palestine time) was such that it covered about 50 times as much area in the sky as does the Moon.[34] Of course it was a day of dread and terror for the ancients.

By 8:00 P.M. (Palestine time) Mars was clearly diminishing in size. As it crossed Earth's orbit ahead of Earth, it moved from an inner to an outer position, and its crescent quickly expanded to a ¾ crescent. Its larger craters and major rift valley were visible as it rotated on its own spin axis. Meanwhile the bolidic and meteoritic showers began suddenly to make their appearance, and rapidly rose to a crescendo. This was amid Earth tremors and quakes as Earth's crust experienced a massive 80-foot crustal

---

[34] Mars has a diameter twice as large as the Moon (4,140 miles to 2,160). At 500,000 miles it would appear as large as the Moon, but it was considerably shinier. Its albedo (reflective power) is 15% compared to the lunar 7%.

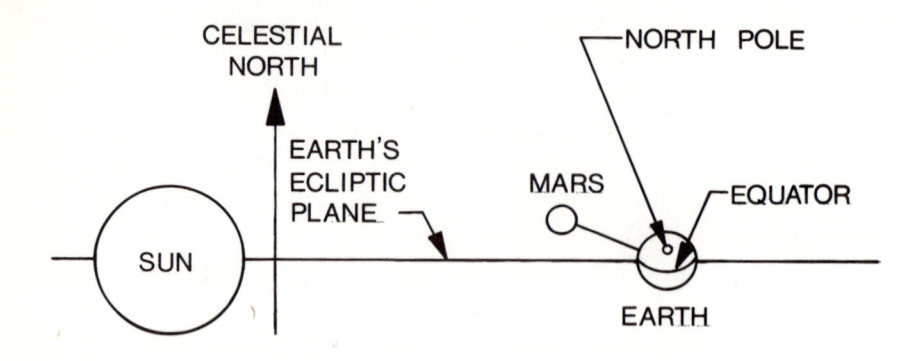

EARTH-MARS-SUN GEOMETRY MARCH 20/21, 701 B.C.

THE EARTH'S ECLIPTIC PLANE AS VIEWED FROM EARTH'S POSITION ON JANUARY 1

FIGURE 8

Mars on an inside fly-by, slightly north of the ecliptic plane. Mars may have passed over Earth nearly over the North Pole.

THE ISAIAHIC CATASTROPHE AND SCIENCE

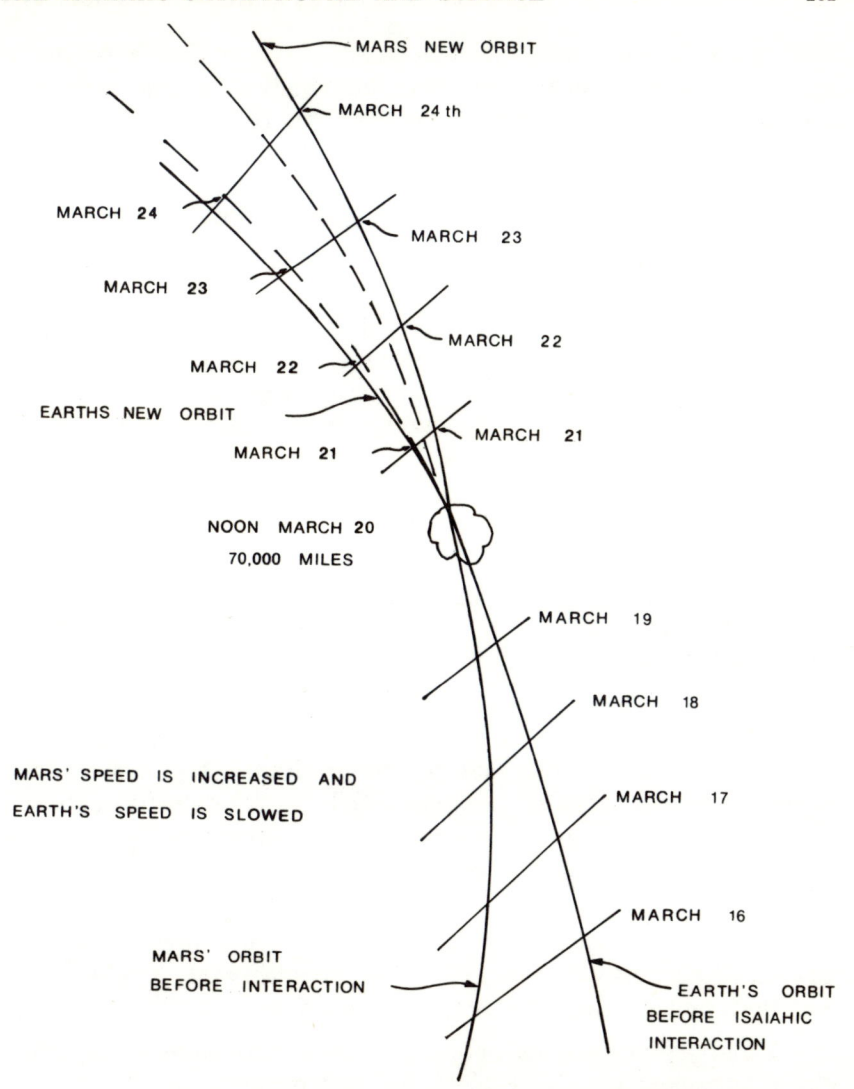

MARS NEW ORBIT
MARCH 24 th
MARCH 24
MARCH 23
MARCH 23
MARCH 22
MARCH 22
EARTHS NEW ORBIT
MARCH 21
MARCH 21
NOON MARCH 20
70,000 MILES
MARCH 19
MARCH 18
MARS' SPEED IS INCREASED AND
EARTH'S SPEED IS SLOWED
MARCH 17
MARCH 16
MARS' ORBIT BEFORE INTERACTION
EARTH'S ORBIT BEFORE ISAIAHIC INTERACTION

ISAIAHIC CATASTROPHE
APPROACH AND RETREAT
MARCH OF 701 B.C.

FIGURE 9
The daily pattern of approach in March, 701 B.C. and the perturbation following the interaction.

tide (plus in some areas, minus in others). As Earth began to experience tidal deformation, simultaneously it began to experience a spin axis precession or wobble. This redirected the apparent lunar and Martian paths, observable in the Americas but not in Palestine for Mars had by now set in the western sky, only to rise again in the eastern sky shortly after midnight.

Then, about 8:00 P.M., the very visible and audible "blast from heaven," the Jerusalem Bolide, made its descent. The speed of its descent was perhaps 33,000 miles per hour, or 9 miles per second. Its visible descent occurred for perhaps 15 or 20 seconds as its ripped through Earth's exosphere, ionosphere, stratosphere and finally, troposphere. Following this crescendo, the bolidic and meteoritic showers quickly diminished and were gone by 9:00 P.M. Mars, now out of orbital resonance with both Earth and Jupiter, was gone as an assaulter of Earth forever.

> And his brightness was as the light; he had horns coming out of his hand: and there was the hiding of his power. (Habakkuk 3:4)

From Table IV it is clear that Mars' closest biennial approach occurred nearer and nearer to Earth and nearer and nearer to March 20 after the year 727 B.C. All eyes were turned skyward to watch every Mars fly-by, to measure, to fear, to hope, and for many astrological religions, to worship out of fear.

By March of 703 B.C. it was evident that each approach was closer, and this year it had been much too close. The next pass in 24 months was a day of cosmic appointment. The question was how bad it might be, not if it would come.

Isaiah reminded his people of the earlier holocausts, especially the ones of 756 B.C. (The Joel-Amos) and the lighter Elijahic Catastrophe of 864 B.C. From these he prognosticated the coming day of appointment:

> Nevertheless THE DIMNESS shall not be such as was in her vexation, when at first [*864 B.C.*] he lightly afflicted the land of Zebulon [*Northern Palestine including Mt. Carmel where Elijah stood*], and the land of Naphtali, and afterward [*756 B.C.*] did more grievously afflict her by the way of the sea. . . . (Isaiah 9:1)

TABLE V

TIMETABLE OF APPROACH AND RETREAT OF MARS, MARCH 701 B.C.

Date in 701 B.C.			Distance of Mars	Viewing The Heavens
Noon	March	10	5,530,000 miles	
"		15	2,840,000	
"		16	2,290,000	
"		17	1,750,000	
"		18	1,215,000	
"		19	680,000	Mars shines as bright as the Moon
3 A.M.		20	345,000	Mars appears as large as the Moon
6 P.M.		20	70,000	Perigee of Mars
8 P.M.		20	83,000	Jerusalem Bolide
Noon		21	410,000	
"		22	945,000	
"		23	1,485,000	

Figure 8 illustrates the geometry of the orbits of the two planets as seen from Earth's January position in space. Figure 9 illustrates the geometries of movements of the two planets during the critical week of catastrophism. Figures 10 and 11 illustrate the changes of the Martian orbit on a near fly-by.

Perturbation of Earth's Orbit

As Mars came closer, the gravitational interaction between the two planets increased. The gravitational force increased according to the inverse square law, leading to orbital shifts proportional to the simple inverse of the perigee. That is, halve the distance and increase the orbital change by two. The tidal deformation of Earth varied according to the inverse of the cube. This effect will apply to crustal tides, oceanic tides, atmospheric tides and plasma tides of the geomagnetic field. Related to tides are spin changes which are proportional to the inverse of the square of the distance of the perigee. This means that as the distance of Mars is reduced by one-half, the spin axis changes of both planets are multiplied by four. And for crustal distortion (tides), as the distance of Mars is reduced by one-half, the increase in the tidal effect is eight, the inverse of the cube.[35]

We believe the Earth gained 5¼ days per year as it left resonance. Of the 5¼ days, opinions are that 70% to 95% of the change was due to orbital expansion, and 5% to 30% was due to a spin rate increase. Conservatively then, we must account for a 3½ to 4 day increase in the calendar due to orbital expansion. This means Earth's orbit expanded from about 92,200,000 miles to the current 92,900,000 miles during this era, a very significant change indeed.

Calculations for this problem have been made, and are summarized below.

The Model Assumptions.

1. The orbits of Earth and Mars were co-planar.[36]

2. The interaction can be treated as three successive two-body problems:
    a. Two planets in independent orbits around the Sun, followed by:
    b. Earth-Mars interaction (two body problem), followed by:
    c. Two planets in independent orbits around the Sun.

3. Before interaction, Earth and Mars had periods of 360 and 720 days respectively.[37]

4. Earth's orbit before interaction was circular.[38]

The results of our calculations are presented in figures 10 and 11.

---

[35] See Sydney Chapman, *The Earth's Magnetism,* London: Methuen and Co. Ltd., 1951, p. 76.

[36] In reality we suspect Mars was somewhat north of the ecliptic plane.

[37] These are the average orbital periods. During the 108-year cycle the number of days per year would oscillate.

[38] Earth's current orbital eccentricity is .0167. Before this catastrophe it may have been slightly greater.

Perturbation of the Martian Orbit

Mars' current orbit has a period of 687 days. In contrast, Mars' ancient period was 720 days, and with a loss of roughly 30 days during the Isaiahic catastrophe, its period immediately following the catastrophe was roughly 690 days. Thus the question arises: how did the 690 day period change to its current 687 day length, and how did the orbit round out to its current shape which doesn't intersect Earth's orbit? The answer lies in a combination of the small perturbing forces of Earth (whose orbit Mars still crossed immediately after the catastrophe) and the distant but giant planet Jupiter. It is believed that secular perturbations by these two planets surrounding Mars as it were, tended to change Mars' period and round out the orbit to its current shape.[39, 40]

In Figure 4, it is illustrated that there are gaps in the asteroid zone based on a distribution of periods. It is apparent that when asteroids were swept out of the 2:1 resonance zone to Jupiter, some were shifted by Jupiter inward (toward the Sun), and some where swept outward (toward Jupiter). Of those which were perturbed or were swept outward toward Jupiter, the peak of their new distribution is at 1.88 of Jupiter's orbital period. This illustrates the magnitude of the effect of secular perturbations, once a body is swept out of resonance. In our illustration, Mars was swept inward, toward the Earth as it left resonance. And in our theory, it was swept inward to a 1.88 orbital zone to Earth, just as in our analogy, asteroids have been swept out to about the 1.88 orbital zone of Jupiter. Thus we can demonstrate that by this particular catastrophe, Mars aphelion shifted inward from its former 210,000,000-mile location, and the entire orbit shifted inward toward the Earth.

---

[39] Current Earth days may be shorter by as much as five minutes (.3%) than the ancient days, due to spin rate changes at the time of the catastrophe.

[40] The Hecuba Gap among the asteroids compares to the Cassini Gap in the rings of Saturn. In the Cassini Gap a peak of icy particles occurs about 1.85 the period of Mimas, the innermost sattelite.

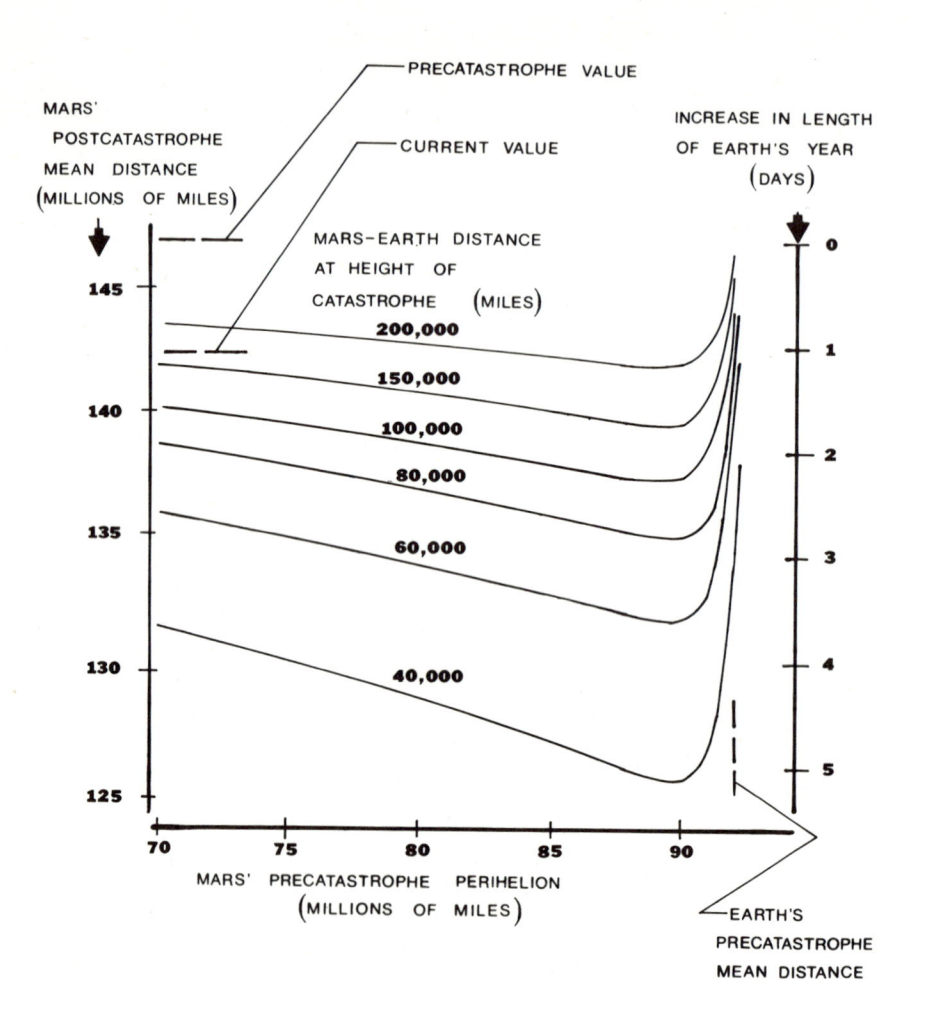

MARS' POSTCATASTROPHE MEAN DISTANCE

FIGURE 10
The closeness of the Martian fly-by and the perturbing of the Martian orbit.

THE ISAIAHIC CATASTROPHE AND SCIENCE

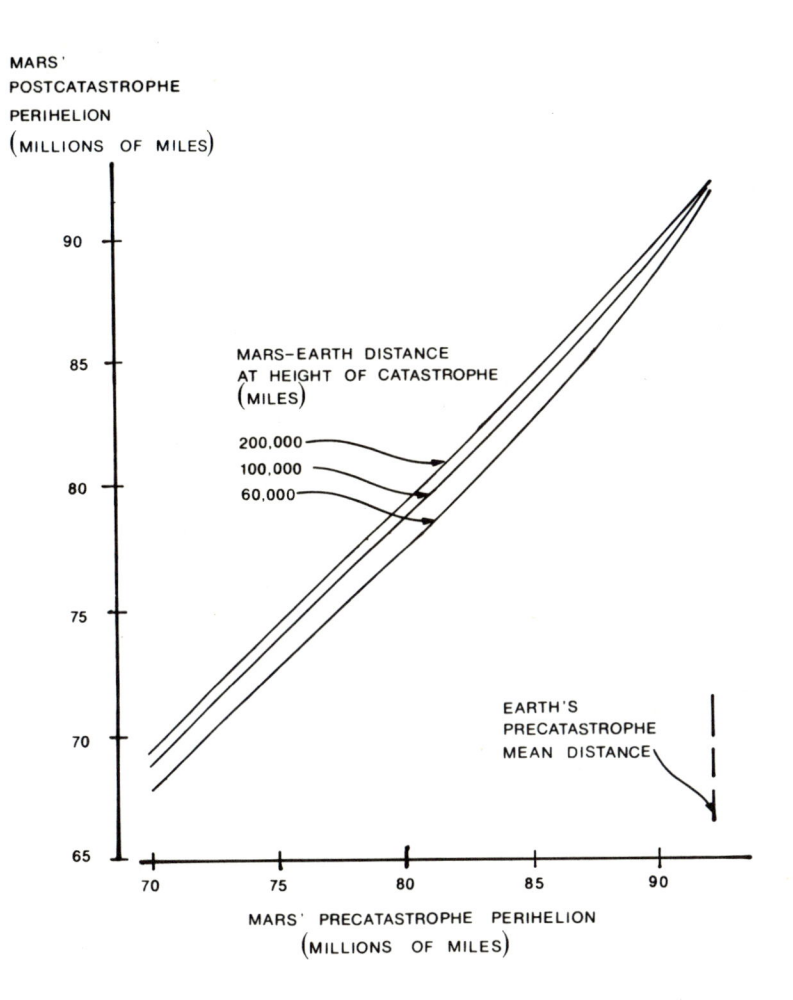

MARS' POSTCATASTROPHE PERIHELION

FIGURE 11
The shift of the perihelion of Mars.

On Difficulties With Model: Post-Resonance Orbital Decay

The most obvious difficulty with the Mars-Earth orbital resonance model seems to be with the transition from the post-Isaiahic orbital scheme to the present order. It is not possible for a single violent Mars-Earth interaction to effect the necessary transition. Mars, after the catastrophe, would still cross Earth's orbit (through not synchronized with Earth's passing as in the resonant condition). In the present order, Mars gets no closer than 35,000,000 miles to Earth's orbit. Thus the question is, "Does there exist a mechanism which could, in a couple thousand years, change Mars' eccentric post-Isaiahic orbit to the present quasi-circular configuration?"

One possible candidate, orbital resonance with Jupiter and/or Earth can probably be discarded since no simple resonance with either would have existed following the breakup of the 2:1 pattern. A second possible candidate is a violent near miss (after 701 B.C.) of Mars with an unknown body which changed the Martian orbit to its present configuration. The authors prefer to discard this suggestion which smacks of an "ad hoc" assumption posed to support the model. Furthermore, there is no known body of sufficient size that could have so altered Mars' orbit in a single pass. A third candidate is that the combined small perturbations of distant Jupiter and Earth effected the changes. This is the preferred suggestion although the difficulty remains; could such a change be brought about in a time scale of only a couple of thousand years?

If this is indeed the explanation, then this means that Mars is still in its decay orbit, at the very end of a transient decay curve. And such a rate at this date, some 2678 years after the encounter, would be expected to be of a magnitude of several feet per century, an amount too low for current astronomical instruments to measure.

The answer to the mystery is not known, and this is indeed a weakness of the model. Nevertheless, there are dozens of categories in which the model correlates well with historical records, geophysical evidences, and scientific principles. Thus in view of the weight of evidence, the authors are comfortable with the present model, in spite of this and other areas that remain mysteries.

The Effect of Martian Fly-Bys on Earth's Geomagnetic Field

Many different theories have been proposed to account for Earth's geomagnetic field. But even the most popular theories are unsubstantiated.[41] When lava solidifies, the polarity of the geomagnetic field is recorded in the molecular structure.[42] Recent studies have shown a history of magnetic field reversals and realignments (see footnote 2 of this chapter). What is perhaps less well known is that these flows are ancient in terms of thousands, not millions of years. We suspect that on *each* of these seven closest fly-bys, 2500 B.C. to 701 B.C., there was a reversal of the Earth's magnetic field, followed by a drift or migration of the magnetic poles. Thus, Earth appears to have had several different magnetic poles as well as several different geographical poles in "recent" times.

The Canals of Mars

It has been less than 20 years now, that astronomy books have finally ceased printing theories and presuppositions (which almost took the dimension of fact) about canals on Mars. *Canali* were first reported by Giovanni V. Schiaparelli in 1887, the year of an exceptionally favorable opposition of Mars. He reported what he thought to be a considerable network of fine lines cov-

---

[41]Dr. Melvin A. Cook suspects that gravity is of electrical and magnetic origin. We quote in part from his Appendix III, *The Science of High Explosives*. Huntington, New York: Krieger Publishing Co., 1971 pp. 422-423, 426. We quote:
$G^{1/2}$ is dimensionally charge/mass and is $2.58 \cdot 10^{-4}$ e.s.u. per gram. That it may actually be electrostatic charge per gram thus offers itself as an explanation of gravity. But this naive interpretation has been avoided because of the formidable problems incurred by the apparently complete nonpolarity of gravity and the absence of a satisfactory mechanism for the accumulation of the required amount of charge on one body, e.g., $1.54 \cdot 10^{24}$ e.s.u. for the earth and $5.16 \cdot 10^{29}$ e.s.u. for the sun. On the other hand there are several reasons to believe that gravity is actually of electrical and magnetic origin. Let us summarize several of these reasons. . . . [*7 are listed*].

[42]The geomagnetic field is frozen at the instant the temperature drops below the Curie point which is actually colder than the temperature of solidification.

ering much of the surface of the planet. The Italian word *canali* meaning channels quickly became "canals" in English and during the next three decades, about half of the astronomers studying Mars reported "seeing" the canals and the other half failed to "see" them.

Lowell, for instance, drew conclusions about the "canals" of Mars. He suggested that "canals" could only be built by intelligent beings, and he speculated their purpose was to bring water from melting ice caps to the equatorial deserts. It is all fairy tale. Any such canal would have had to have been 20 *miles* wide to be seen through telescopes on Earth. But Lowell imagined, if biological evolution had occurred on Earth, it must also have occurred over a similar amount of time alleged for Mars, and the canals were his "proof." How beautiful the logic appeared.

The fact is that Mars is a very hostile planet, with a very low barometric pressure, with probably no free oxygen and almost no free water vapor in its thin atmosphere. However, astronomers and space navigation researchers have been astonished to observe (1) the innumerable craters, ranging from 400 miles across to tiny pitlets, much more numerous than the Moon's, (2) massive rifts (3) massive, recent basalt outflows and (4) river like erosion patterns. Our catastrophic model would predict this, and indeed Immanuel Velikovsky did predict just this kind of evidence in 1950, in *Worlds in Collision*.

Velikovsky theorized, but today we can say with certainty that the surface of Mars is severely marred with astonishingly recent-looking upheavals. In light of our model, is that not what one would expect? Did not Mars and Earth interact heavily at least seven times within the last 5,000 years? And if Mars is about one-ninth as massive as Earth, would not Mars be fractured about nine times as severely as the Earth with lava outflows and rifts? We predict that if and when cores of basaltic outflows on Mars are analyzed and corroborated, (and if Mars has a geomagnetic field, which is not certain), here too we may find evidences of several magnetic polar locations or reversals in the various outflows.

The Tidal Effects Caused by the Fly-By

Tidal Effects on Earth's Crust

The tidal effects of Mars on Earth at 70,000 miles can only be estimated, and our estimate is that there would have been an 85 foot crustal tide, as measured from the Earth's core to the crust. See Table VIII, Chapter VIII. Even in the most conservative of estimates, the Earth's crust must have experienced a tidal swell of 50 feet as measured from Earth's core. This compares to a two- to three-inch crustal tide caused by the Moon. This effect for the Isaiahic Catastrophe we estimate at perhaps 350 times the normal lunar crustal tide.

No one with a seismograph or other measuring instruments was available in the eighth century B.C. However, there are some interesting descriptions of crustal deformation in books such as Habakkuk, Isaiah and others, by men who lived during the event.

> He stood, and measured the earth: he beheld, and drove asunder the nations; AND THE EVERLASTING MOUNTAINS WERE SCATTERED, THE PERPETUAL HILLS DID BOW. . . .
>
> I saw the tents of Cushan [*the eastern horizon*] IN AFFLICTION: and the curtains of the land of Midian [*the southern horizon*] DID TREMBLE.
>
> THE MOUNTAINS SAW THEE, AND THEY TREMBLED: the overflowing water passed by [*tidal waves on the Mediterranean and Red Seas?*]: the deep uttered his voice, and lifted up his hands on high. (Habakkuk 3:6, 7, 10)
>
> . . . for the windows from on high are open, and THE FOUNDATIONS OF THE EARTH DO SHAKE. (Isaiah 24:18)
>
> Thou shalt be visited of the Lord of hosts with thunder, AND WITH EARTHQUAKE, and great noise, with storm and tempest, and the flame of devouring fire. (Isaiah 29:6)
>
> Therefore will not we fear, though the earth be removed, AND THOUGH THE MOUNTAINS BE CARRIED INTO THE MIDST OF THE SEA; though the waters thereof roar

and be troubled, THOUGH THE MOUNTAINS SHAKE WITH THE SWELLING THEREOF. (Psalm 46:2-3, [*probably penned by Isaiah, summer, 701 B.C.*]).

When Israel went out of Egypt [*March 20-23, 1447 B.C., the Exodus Catastrophe*]. . . . The sea saw it, and fled: Jordan was driven back. THE MOUNTAINS SKIPPED LIKE RAMS, AND THE LITTLE HILLS LIKE LAMBS. (Psalm 114:1, 3-4)

The book of Isaiah and the Isaiahic Catastrophe simply cannot be understood until these utterances are taken as eye-witness accounts. Perhaps there is an element of hyperbole, either in the original manuscript or in translation, on occasion. For instance, Isaiah 24:1 suggests, literally, that the Earth was turned upside down. Isaiah 24:19 says it was removed exceedingly, and 24:20 says it reeled to and fro (spin axis wobble) like a drunkard. A polar relocation of 300 miles is clearly not turning the world "upside down," but it could cause Jerusalem's latitude to slip down by 5°.

How many times was it, according to archaeologists, that Troy, or Lachish, or Jericho, or other Middle Eastern sites, were rebuilt out of their own rubble? How many times was it, according to the Earth-Mars resonant orbit model, that our planet suffered a very close fly-by? The answer to the question about Troy rebuilt in its rubble is approximately seven times.

In addition, a 50 to 100 foot crustal tide would renew hundreds of dormant and "extinct" volcanoes like Stromboli, Sinai and Rainier. Such a crustal tide would create a sudden outpouring of volcanic ash, cinders and dust into the atmosphere, darkening the world temporarily in many places, as did Vesuvius in 79 A.D. for the region surrounding Pompeii. Many renewed volcanoes would be submarine volcanoes, causing immense tidal waves in their upheavals.

The Tidal Effect on Mars' Crust

Abundant basaltic outflows, gargantuan rifts, crustal cleavages, as well as immense craters have been photographed on Mars. Mariner IX spotted fifteen collapsed volcanoes (calderas). Geologic faults and vulcanism are apparent on a scale far more dynamic than anything the Moon exhibits, or anything expected by most astronomers of ten years ago. If the fly-by's effect on

THE ISAIAHIC CATASTROPHE AND SCIENCE   113

Earth's crust was 50 to 100 foot crustal tides, that effect would have been nine times greater in the Martian crust, Earth being nine times as massive. For example, Mars has one deep, wide rift valley an astounding 2,800 miles long and ten miles deep.

Tidal Effects on Earth's Oceans, Atmosphere and Ionosphere

Tides of unusual magnitude and tidal waves of devastating scope would be expected during a near fly-by of Mars.

> The mountains saw thee, and they trembled: THE OVERFLOWING OF THE WATER PASSED BY: the deep uttered his voice, and lifted up his hands on high. (Habakkuk 3:10)

> Was the Lord displeased against the rivers? was thine anger against the rivers? was thy wrath AGAINST THE SEA, that thou didst ride upon thine horses and thy chariots of salvation? (Habakkuk 3:8)

Earth's magnetic field is pear-shaped, being distorted by the solar wind. It extends well out beyond the Moon, some 240,000 miles distant. Thus while Mars in its last fly-by did not "hit" the Earth, nevertheless Mars would pass *through* Earth's geomagnetic sheath, creating deep disturbances. It is entirely possible that there were loud and terrible exchanges of static electricity between the planets.

> He stood and measured the earth. . . . (Habakkuk 3:6)

> . . . THE DEEP UTTERED HIS VOICE, and lifted up his hands on high. (Habakkuk 3:10)

A GENERAL THEORY OF SPIN AXIS PRECESSION

The Precession of Earth's Spin Axis

What would be the effect of such a close fly-by upon Earth's spin axis? The Earth is a giant spinning gyroscope, floating not in water but freely through space.

The spin axis of a sphere or a cylinder can be caused to precess, that is, to rotate around two axes simultaneously. One example is a tire or wheel which is rolled down hill. If it is set upright before released, it will roll straight down. If it is set up leaning before released, it will roll downhill on a path describing a curve. This is because it is precessing, or in other words, its spin axis is changing direction.

A precession of Earth's spin axis involves three different phenomena. These are:

1. A change in the location of
the spin axis on the Earth   (a polar migration)

2. A change in the tilt of the
the spin axis   (a realignment to space)

3. A change in the rate of spin   (an increase in spin rate)

Each of these three phenomena is dependent upon the same mechanism for its occurrence.

This mechanism comprises some rather complicated physical principles. As a result, no attempt is made to give quantitative results. The magnitude of the forces involved is a strong function of the closeness of the approach of Mars to the Earth. The magnitude of the forces involved is also a function of the angle of Mars to Earth's ecliptic plane, a 45° angle either north or south providing the maximum torque.

GRAVITY GRADIENT. Involved in the spin change mechanism is the concept of gravity gradient. Gravity gradient is simply another way of expressing Newton's inverse square law. It states that the gravitational force between two masses (in this case the Earth and Mars) is inversely proportional to the square of the distances between them. This means that as the two planets approach, the gravitational interaction increases in geometric proportions as the distance decreases. This law has been applied to Earth satellites to make them point to the Earth at all times, for example, navigation satellites. This concept is illustrated in Figure 12 for a dumbbell-shaped satellite.

Assuming that the mass of the satellite is concentrated at the two ends and assuming an initial orientation of the satellite as shown, then the force on the mass closer to the Earth (labelled f_1) will be stronger than the force on the other mass (labelled f_2). The average of these two forces is f^a and is equal to one-half f_1 plus f_2. This is the force which causes the satellite to travel a curved path around the Earth. (It is equivalent to the string

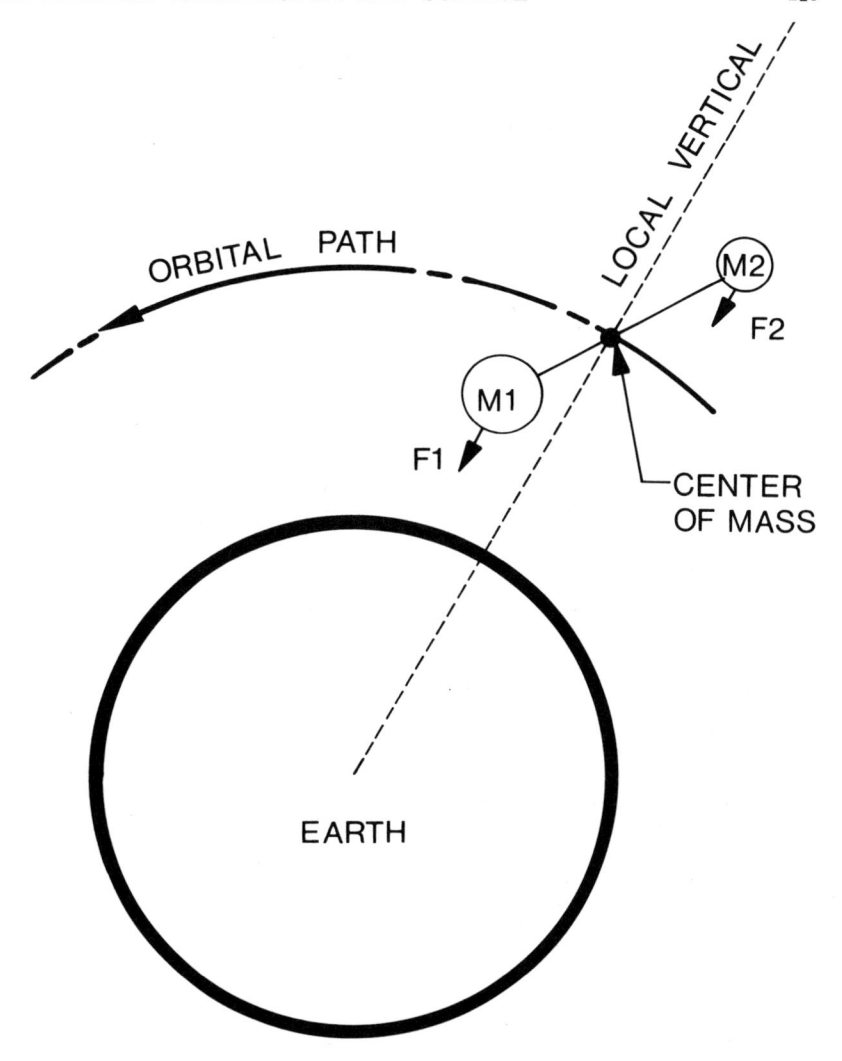

GRAVITATIONAL FORCES ACTING ON A DUMBBELL-SHAPED SATELLITE

FIGURE 12

on which one twirls a mass, constraining the mass to follow a circular path.) Since this average force would cause all parts of the spacecraft to follow the same path (even if the parts were not tied together), it can be subtracted off to see what forces remain on the spacecraft due to the fact that it is tied together.

In Figure 13, it is seen that the remaining force on mass #1 is $(f^1-f^2)/2$ *toward* the Earth, and on mass #2 it is $(f^1-f^2)/2$ *away* from the Earth. But these forces can be separated into two components. The first, $(f_1-f_2)(\cos A)/2$ is that which tries to fragment the satellite (i.e., the pulling apart force). The second, $(f_1-f_2)(\sin A)/2$ is that which tries to rotate the satellite so that angle A decreases. Since this last force is proportional to the sine of A, it is zero when the angle is zero. Thus, it tries to align the satellite to point at the Earth.

The effect of both of these forces is visible in the solar system. The Moon, which is slightly larger in diameter in one direction,[42] has been aligned by this gravity gradient effect always to point the longer diameter to the Earth. This explains why the Moon does not rotate relative to the Earth, why until recently man had never viewed the other side.

The "pulling apart" component of the gravity gradient force is exactly the mechanism which causes the smaller of two planetary bodies to shatter if they approach too closely.[43]

EARTH OBLATENESS. The gravity gradient effects discussed above would have a reduced effect upon the spin of the Earth during the Earth-Mars interaction if the Earth were perfectly spherical in shape (i.e., not a dumbbell shape). However, the Earth's spin rate, about 1,000 miles per hour at the equator, results in a sizeable centrifugal force. This outward force results in a bulging of the equatorial zone, and a flattening in both of the polar regions. As a result of centrifugal force counteracting

---

[42] The Moon's average equatorial diameter is approximately 2,850 feet longer than its polar diameter. Further, since the Moon's equatorial zone is itself oblate or pear-shaped, its equatorial diameter also varies. This variance is approximately 800 feet, with the bulge pointing toward the Earth.

[43] Roche's Limit describes this for stellar bodies and circular orbits, and Steinhauer's redefinition describes this for planetary situations and non-circular orbits.

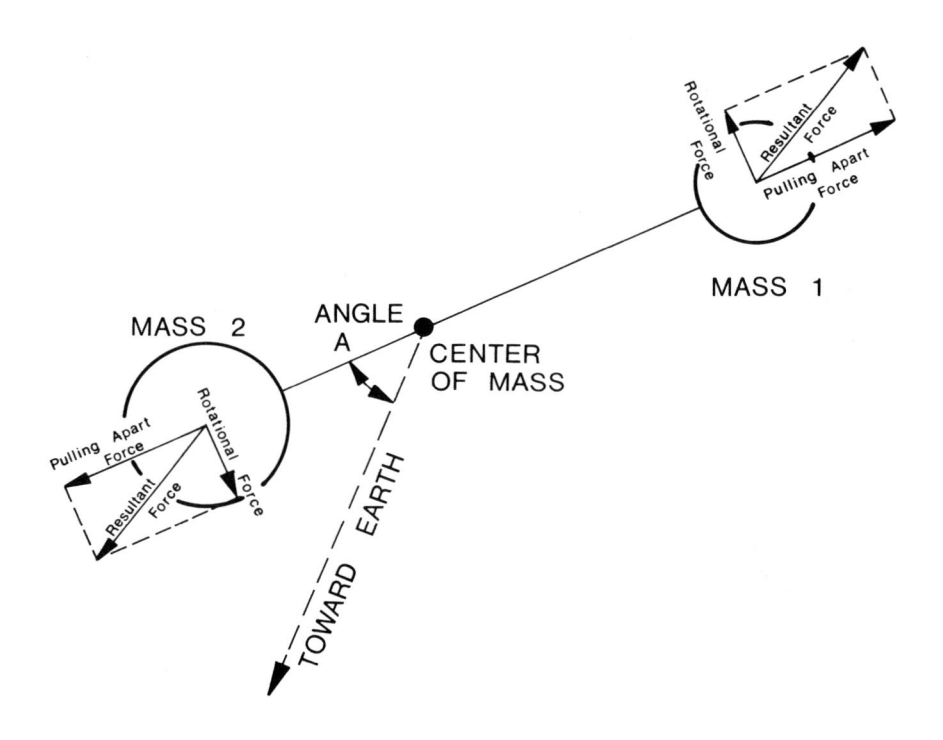

"ROTATION" AND
"PULLING APART" FORCES

FIGURE 13
Alignment functions of a dumbell-shaped satellite.

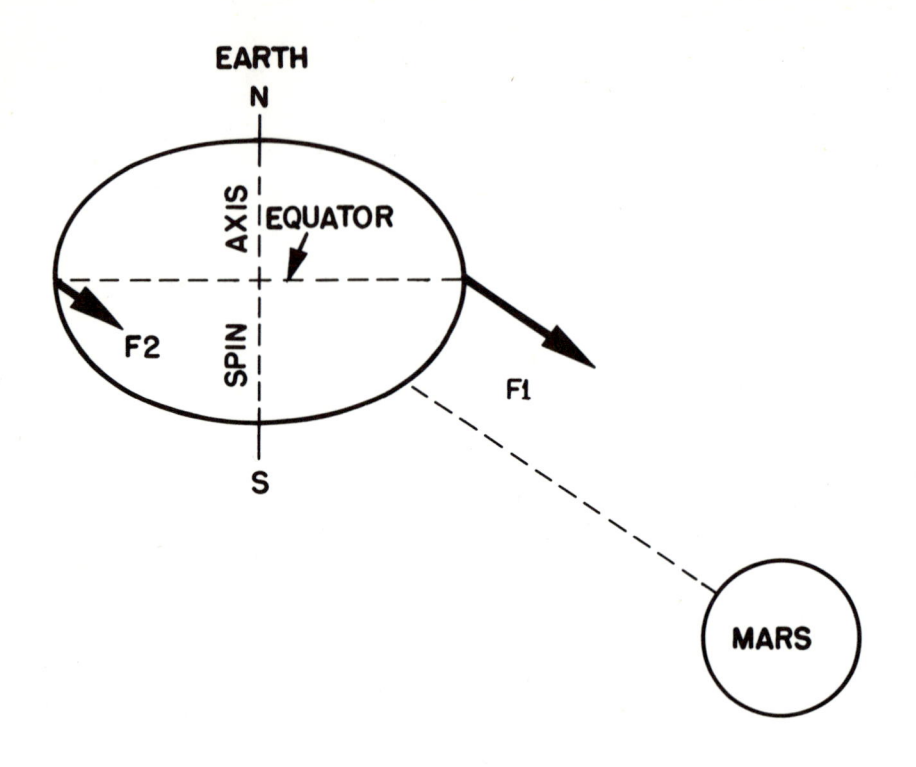

**GRAVITY GRADIENT EFFECT OF MARS ON EARTH
— AN OBLATE SPHEROID**

FORCE F1 IS GREATER THAN FORCE F2

FIGURE 14
Mars gravitational effect on the Earth with an exaggerated bulge zone.

the force of gravity, the equatorial diameter of the Earth is 26.86 miles longer than the polar diameter. This shape is referred to as an *oblate spheroid,* and it functions in space like a gyroscope. This flattening of the poles and bulging of the equatorial zone would result in a significant rotational force, as is shown in Figure 14 if the passing of Mars were very close, and were not along the equatorial plane.

GYROSCOPIC EFFECT. The application of the rotational force (torque) to the Earth does not result in a simple rotational motion that the dumbbell satellite and the Moon undergo. Rather the Earth, because it is spinning, acts like a giant gyroscope and responds to torques just as does a gyroscope.

The effect of a torque on a gyroscope is shown in Figure 15. Gravity, acting on the center of mass, tries to rotate the axis on the gyroscope downward. But because it is spinning, the actual motion that results is in a different direction. This resulting axis rotation is called *precession.* The direction of *precession* is at right angles to both the gravity force and the spin axis. Figure 15 illustrates.

The effect can be easily demonstrated. A spinning bicycle wheel is a gyroscope. When a bicycle wheel is spun rapidly and then held by only one end of the axis rather than by both ends, the wheel will *precess.* If the wheel is spun in the opposite direction, or held by the opposite axis, then the precession is in the opposite direction.

When the bicycle wheel is being held by one axis while spinning, and as it is twisting or "precessing", if it is tossed into the air it will appear to the human eye to be "wobbling". In reality it is temporarily rotating around some axis other than its normal spin axis. This temporary and abnormal axis is a combination of the two spin forces, the normal and the induced.

A CHANGE IN THE SPIN AXIS. The twisting force exerted on the bulge of the Earth would cause the spin axis to begin to precess. We believe the spin axis is an easily displaced, easily relocated function, partly because it is precessing several meters under current conditions for no known, observable reason at all.

Figure 8, page 100, illustrates the Earth-Mars-Sun geometry for the 701 B.C. fly-by. We believe Mars buzzed Earth as close as 70,000 miles, on the inside, and north of the ecliptic plane. Mars

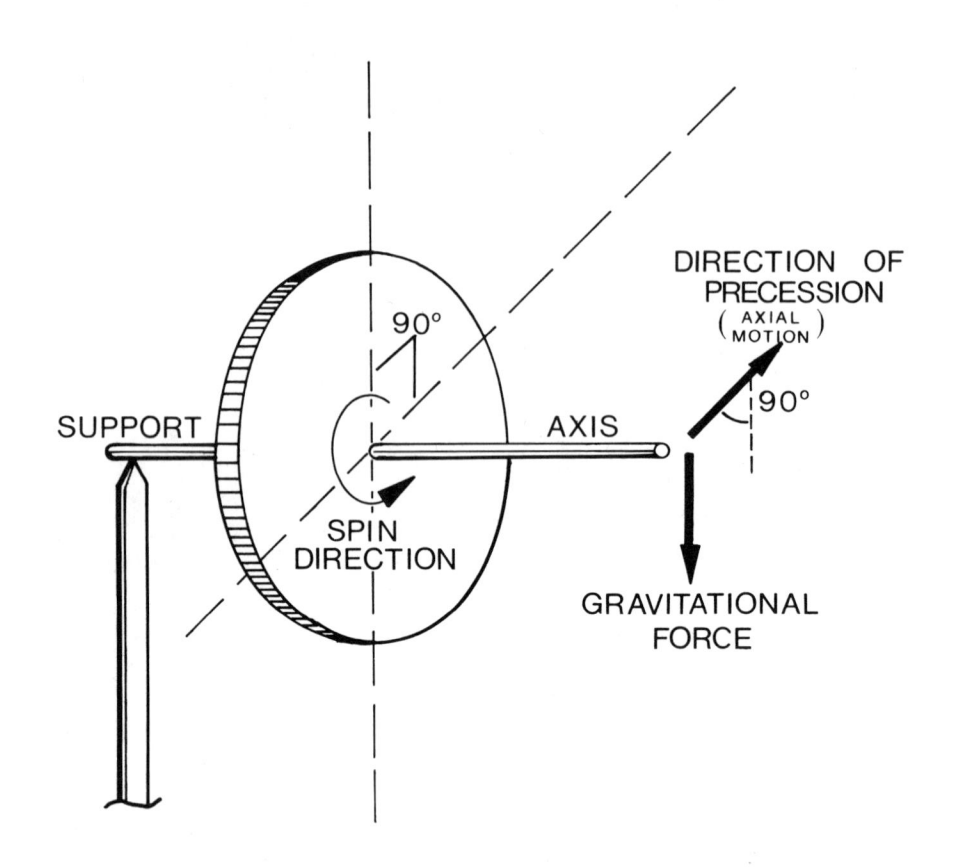

GYROSCOPIC PRECESSION
THREE DIMENSIONAL DIAGRAM

FIGURE 15

THE ISAIAHIC CATASTROPHE AND SCIENCE

[Figure: Diagram showing vector A (Pre Catastrophe Spin Vector) pointing toward Polaris, vector B (Precession Spin Vector During Catastrophe) pointing toward Sun, and vector C (Post Catastrophe Spin Vector) as the resultant.]

VECTOR A — THE EARTH'S SPIN BEFORE PRECESSION

VECTOR B — THE EARTH'S TOTAL PRECESSION DURING THE CATASTROPHE

VECTOR C — THE EARTH'S NEW SPIN AFTER PRECESSION

IN EACH CASE: THE DIRECTION REPRESENTS THE AXIS

THE LENGTH REPRESENTS THE SPIN RATE

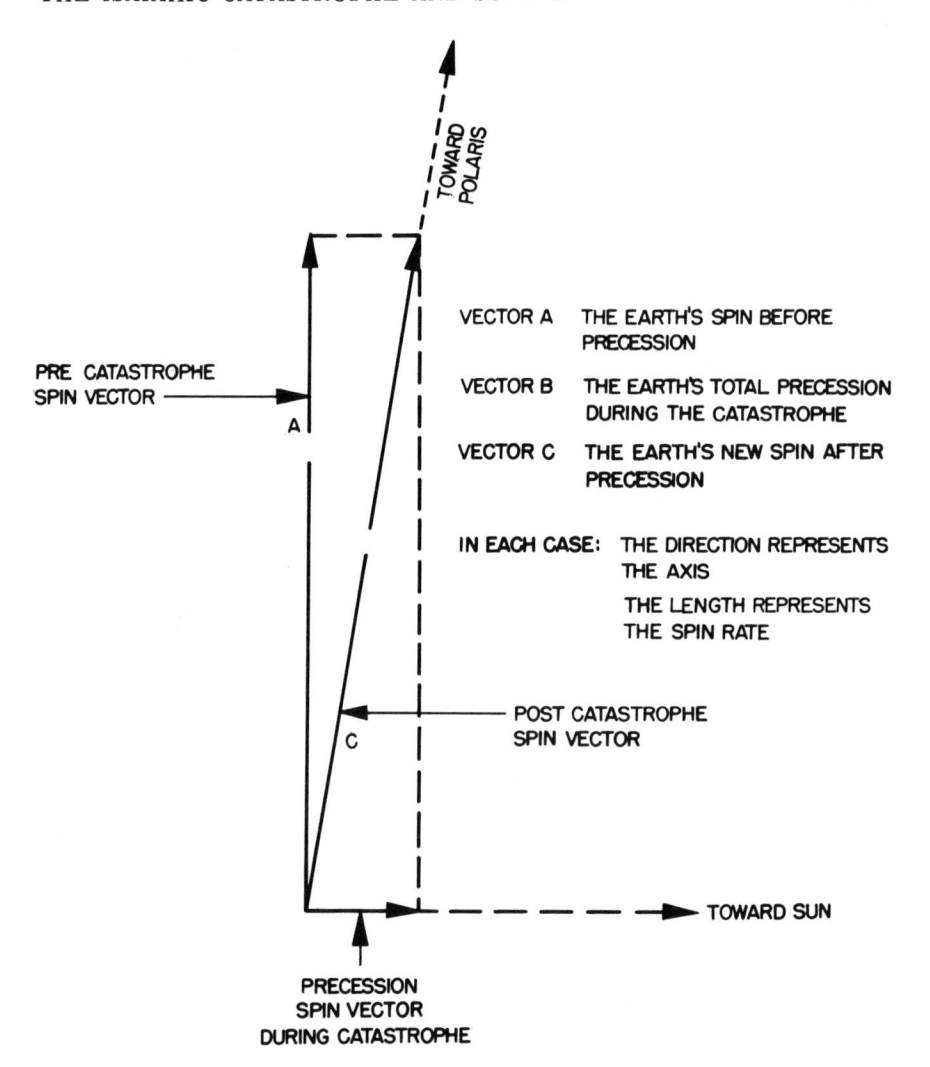

PRE AND POST CATASTROPHE SPIN VECTORS OF THE EARTH

FIGURE 16
Gyroscopic precession as applied to the Earth. The length of vector C compared to vector A illustrates the increase in spin rate. The angle between vector C and vector A illustrate some combination of tilt shift and polar relocation.

was advancing on Earth at a relative speed of about 22,500 miles per hour, with a slight tendency to increase speed on approach, and decrease speed on retreat.

It was during the climax hours of that fateful evening, a "passover" night, that our planetary spin axis temporarily precessed. The bulk of the precessing force was temporary, lasting the better part of a day. As it was removed, the angular velocity of the normal spin axis *combined* with the angular velocity of precession to result in a new spin rate and a new spin axis location. This addition, or combination, resulted in:

1.	A new spin axis location on Earth	Perhaps a 300 mile relocation
2.	Probably a new tilt for the axis relative to the fixed stars.	Perhaps a $1\frac{1}{2}°$ decrease in tilt
3.	A new and increased spin rate	Perhaps an 0.3% increase in rate

This is illustrated in Figure 16. In Figure 16, Vector A represents the Earth's old spin axis. Its length represents the spin rate. Vector B represents the induced spin or the precessing force caused by the Mars fly-by. A combination of these two spins is represented by Vector C. Vector C represents by its *increased length* that the spin rate was now slightly faster (resulting in more days per year). Vector C represents by its *new angle* (a) a relocation of the spin axis on Earth, plus (b) a relocation of the spin axis to space, or shift in tilt, in some combination.

It is not clear how much change in axial tilt, and how much polar relocation was involved but it totaled $6\frac{1}{2}°$ in Sun angle. However, whatever the extent was, from this particular geometry of fly-by, and presuming the height of the passage was during late afternoon for Palestine then the shift in polar relocation would be *toward Alaska* and *away from Europe*. Europe and the Middle East would acquire a significantly lower latitude, being advanced toward the equator, and experience a somewhat warmer climate following this particular kind of spin axis precession.

THE SUN DIAL OF AHAZ. This was an obelisk used for measuring the sun's shadow and especially advantageous was measuring it at the Sun's zenith, or noontime. An analysis of extant Egyptian obelisks has been made, and the average of the largest of them is 86 feet high.[44] We estimate that Ahaz' sun dial in Jerusalem, the capital city, was a smaller replica of Egyptian models, about 60 feet high and 8 to 10 feet wide at the base.

> And Isaiah the prophet cried unto the Lord: and he brought the shadow ten degrees [*steps or feet*] backward, by which it had gone down in the dial of Ahaz. (II Kings 20:11)[45]

Our model proposes that the North Pole was relocated between 300 and 350 miles closer to Alaska. There may have been a spin axis tilt shift from 25° down to the current 23½°. We propose that the combination of change in latitude and change in spin axis tilt was 6½°, of which at least 5° was a change southward in Jerusalem's latitude. Hence, we propose that the former latitude of Jerusalem was 37° N. or even 38° N. compared to the current 32° N. A raising of the angle of the sun at noon of 6½° will result in a shorter shadow. If the obelisk or tower was 60 feet tall, the shadow at noon would be shortened from 47.7 feet to 37.5 feet.[46]

A SPIN AXIS PRECESSION FOR MARS. If Earth's spin axis precessed by a significant amount during this fly-by, one would presume that Mars, affected by a planet nine times as massive as itself, would have an even greater spin axis precession. There has been no work done on this subject, but there is a strange observation which must not escape our attention. Earth

---

[44] The tallest Egyptian obelisks whose heights are known are
1. Heliopolis (Tethmose II)   105' 9")
2. Axum (Ethiopia)   100   )
3. Karnak   97 6"   ) average 86 feet
4. Syene (in quarry)   80   )
5. Heliopolis (Ramtheses II a) 77   )
6. Heliopolis (Ramtheses II b) 75   )
7. Heliopolis Senwosri I   68   )

[45] The amplified version translates "degrees" as "steps." (Isaiah 38:8). Ten steps on the floor of the astronomical edifice is a more likely translation.

[46] Credit is given to physicist C. William DeCeault, Seattle, for recognizing that this observation, recorded in the books of Isaiah, II Kings and II Chronicles is a "scientific" kind of observation.

AHAZ' SUN DIAL

BEFORE
47.7 FEET
60 FEET
38 ½°

LATITUDE 38°
TILT OF AXIS 25°

AFTER
37.5 FEET
60 FEET
32°

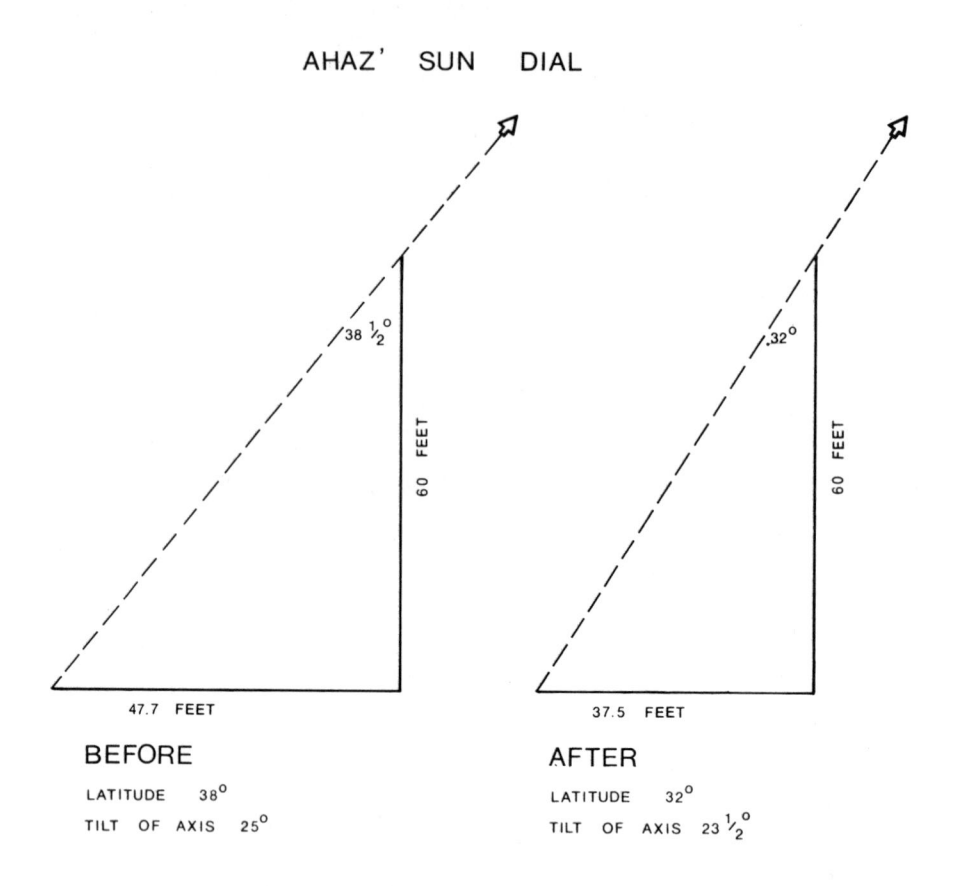

LATITUDE 32°
TILT OF AXIS 23 ½°

THE SHADOW OF AHAZ' SUN DIAL

FIGURE 17
The shift downward, or shortening of the shadow of Ahaz' sun dial illustrates the new path of the sun was higher in the sky. Some combination of change in latitude (downward) and shift in tilt (downward) resulted in about a 6½° increase in the angle of the Sun.

has a spin axis rate of one rotation per 23 hours 56 minutes (sidereal time). Mars has a spin axis rate of one rotation per 24 hours 37 minutes (sidereal time), or about 2.2 percent slower. This could be chance, but there are no other two planets in the solar system with such a harmonious spin rate.

Further, Earth has a spin axis tilt of 23°27′, whereas Mars has a spin axis tilt of 24°50′. This is a tilt of about 1.4 degrees steeper, which again is so remarkably similar to Earth. Since the planets interacted so many times and in a cyclic pattern, the question to be raised concerns whether there is a harmonic principle involved, yet undiscovered.

According to our model, with at least seven heavy planetary interactions, there must have been several spin axis precessions for Mars, perhaps more than seven within the past 5,000 years. Is there any evidence of polar migration on Mars? One of the greatest surprises presented by the Mariner 9 pictures was the discovery of circular geographic features, plate-like regions averaging 200 miles in diameter with outward-sloping edges. The slopes or edges showed evenly spaced light and dark bands. They have been studied by Bruce C. Murray and Michael C. Malin. Murray and Malin theorize that the plate-like features were formed when frost trapped atmospheric dust. The dust was left as a residue after the frost evaporated. In such case, they say, the center of each plate would represent a former spin axis location of the Martian pole.

In the following quotation, the subconscious (rather than conscious) uniformitarian outlook is seen. Murray and Malin suggest a slow "nodding" or nutation, for which no mechanics exist. Our model suggests rapid, recent, catastrophic shifts, or "precessions" due to torque caused by the Earth.

> The time scale of the hypothetical pole wandering is difficult to assess. . . . If each individual lamin of the laminated terrain corresponds to the 50,000 year period in the polar climate of Mars postulated by Leighton and Murray (20), then an estimate can be made of the age of a single plate by noting the number of such laminae visible. This was done by Murray et al. (10) and they estimated that the laminated terrain under observation at the south pole probably represented a few million years of accumulated deposits. In the north as many as 20 or 30 plates can be recognized . . . Thus, we are led by these arguments to sup-

pose that polar wandering of 10° to 20° has occurred over the last 10^8 years or so. . . . [47,48]

On Plutarch

During Hezekiah's, Isaiah's and Numa's time, the calendar needed revision from the former 360 days to the current 365+ days. Whether about 70% or up to 95% of this change is due to orbital expansion, and whether about 5% or up to about 30% of this change is due to an increase in spin rate is a matter for further research. However, it is definite that a change of calendars occurred, and this is reflected in Plutarch as well as in the Bible.

> "Hermes playing at draughts with the moon, won from her the seventieth part of each of her periods of illumination, and from all the winnings he composed five days, and intercalated them as an addition to the 360 days."[49]

Plutarch was forwarding from ancient sources, probably Etruscan sources, a "scientific" kind of observation. This parallels Isaiah's "scientific" kind of observation that the shadow of the Jerusalem obelisk shortened ten steps on this occasion. Notice the significant points that Plutarch touches upon:

1. Ancient literatures and architectures referred to a 360 day year.

---

[47] Bruce C. Murray and Michael C. Malin, "Polar Wandering on Mars?", *Science,* Vol. 179, pp. 997-1,000, March 9, 1973.

[48] Murray and Malin point toward gradual nutation of the Martian spin axis to explain various spin axis locations. Nutation is a phenomena very similar to spin axis precession, only it suggests a slow nodding or shifting whereas we consider it to have been sudden, and considerably more recent than they assumed. Obviously the spin axis shifts are related to the massive volcanism and rifting which are also astonishingly revealed by the Mariner 9 photography. But then such cataclysmic events are expected, and their evidence is not astonishing when one assesses the model we are proposing together with its effects. Spin axis precessions are but one of these effects, crustal deformation but another, fragmentation of Electra into asteroids being yet a third of the effects in this cause-and-effect episode in the recent past of our solar system.
Murray and Malin theorized that the plates are a combination of frost and atmospheric dust. This suggests wind-driven or wind-generated dust. Our model would propose the plates are a combination of frost with volcanic ashes, cinders and dust rather than wind-driven materials primarily.

[49] Immanuel Velikovsky, *op. cit.,* p. 337, citing Plutarch's *Isis and Isiris.*

2. Ancient literatures and architectures allowed for a 30 day month.

3. The length of the year increased by 5 days, approximately $1\frac{1}{2}\%$.

4. The length of the period of the moon decreased somewhat. (A decrease from 30 days to the current $29\frac{1}{2}$ days (synodic period) is a decrease by a similar $1\frac{1}{2}\%$.)

Of course the construction of our model differs from the account of Plutarch, and differs as follows:

1. It was Mars (Ares-Apollo) and not Hermes (Mercury) made the assault.

2. The bonus in winning was more like $5\frac{1}{4}$ days than 5 days.

3. Mars assaulted not just the Moon but the Earth-Moon system, primarily the Earth.

4. The winning planet was neither Mars (which lost energy and angular momentum) nor Mercury-Hermes (an apparent misidentification) but rather was the Earth, which gained days per year, angular momentum and energy.

Nevertheless the information from Plutarch is most interesting, and is in agreement that the Moon lost about $1\frac{1}{2}\%$ of its period, and likewise, Earth gained about a similar amount in its count of days per year (360 to $365\frac{1}{4}$).

Further research in the area of the general theory of spin axis precession is needed; this is the first work to our knowledge on spin axis precession proposing and analyzing an Earth-visiting planet interaction and resultant spin axis shift. Included in the research should be ancient sun dials, pyramid star charts and so forth, for it is reported that one pyramid star chart shows a star in the Big Dipper as the polar star, replacing Polaris. This can only suggest a change in the tilt of Earth's spin axis.[50]

---

[50] Louis Ginzberg, *The Legend of the Jews*, Philadelphia: Jewish Publication Society of America, 1913, Vol. IV, pp. 267 ff. "With this vast army Sennacherib hastened onward, in accordance with the disclosures of the astrologers, who warned him that he would fail in his object of capturing Jerusalem, if he arrived there later than the day set by them . . . In the

Conclusion

An ancient orbit of Mars in 1:2 resonance with the Earth-Moon system has been proposed and modelled. It has been evaluated through analogy with the 2:1 and 3:1 asteroids currently resonating with Jupiter. This model includes a 54-year cycle of conjunctions, a period of the same magnitude as the conjunctive cycle of the 2:1 asteroids, and also of the same magnitude as the conjunctive cycle of the resonating Pluto, in 3:2 resonance with Neptune.

An ancient fragmentation of a small planet, once orbiting between Mars and Jupiter has been proposed, and the planet has been named "Electra" after similar themes in Greek cosmo-mythology. Evidence that Mars was the planet causing the fragmentation was presented.

An interaction of the magnitude we model will include the following:

1. A perturbation of Earth's orbit — and of Mars' orbit

2. A reversal of Earth's geomagnetic field — and of Mars' "geo"magnetic field, if such exists

3. A severe, temporary tide in Earth's lithosphere — and in Mars' crust

4. A severe tide in Earth's oceans and atmosphere — and in Mars' tiny atmosphere

5. A wobble of Earth's spin axis, a "precession" — and of the Martian spin axis

---

following night, WHICH WAS THE PASSOVER NIGHT, when Hezekiah and the people BEGAN TO SING THE HALLEL PSALMS, the giant host was annihilated. The archangel Gabriel, sent by God to ripen the fruits of the field, was charged to address himself to the task of making away with the Assyrians. . . . The death of the Assyrians happened when the angel permitted them to hear THE SONG OF THE CELESTIALS. Their souls were burnt, though their garments remained intact." [*We presume that the singing of the Hallel Psalms commenced shortly after sundown, or about 8:00 P.M. on the fateful night of Friday the 13th of Nisan, our March 20, 701 B. C.. There was a time lag of perhaps two hours between the Martian perigee during the fly-by and the timing of the Jerusalem Bolide. The "song of the celestials" and the report that "their souls were burnt" we compare with the flash-burn effect of the Tunguska Bolide, radiating in shock waves from the subpoint of that cometary holocaust.*

However, a thorough understanding of the Isaiahic Catastrophe remains incomplete, until we have assimilated the actions and reactions of the people observing, awaiting this fearful holocaust, the dreaded encounter between Earth and Mars. Would some have one last fling—eat, drink and be merry—even up to the day of the holocaust? Would some carefully watch and note or even record the astronomical scenery? Would some contemplate pillaging or vandalism in the wreckage of cities levelled by earthquakes? Would some turn to God and prayer and wonder about the end of the world? Would some offer even more Venus-cakes to Aphrodite (Ashtoreth), or offer an increasing number of cherished babies in human sacrifice to the pot-bellied furnace, the idol Baal-Mars? Might such a horrendous offering placate the wrath of this idol or its celestial consort? Perhaps enough Venus-cakes would encourage Aphrodite to apply her influence with the wild one and lead him away where he could not do harm to the Earth. These questions are too important to neglect, even if this study is one primarily devoted to Earth's cosmological history. Therefore, the preceding chapter was devoted to the reactions of eight persons living under the dreaded threat of imminent astronomical holocaust in 701 B.C.

Once the model of the Isaiahic Catastrophe is comprehended and mentally digested, then variations of it will serve to explain the other more ancient holocausts for which correspondingly less data are available. The cyclic pattern did repeat itself. Based on our model, the variations could include closer or farther fly-bys, inside or outside fly-bys, holocausts with or without spin axis shifts, and holocausts with little or much fire and brimstone (bolides and meteorites), and with severe or moderate earthquakes and volcanic activity.

Chapters V through X will be devoted to gathering and assessing of more details about each of the other six major catastrophes which have occurred since the Deluge.

> The ignorant refuse to have respect for authority; they rush recklessly into a fight, relying on their numbers and the protection of tradition, which is impervious to the weapons of truth. But after the edge of the ax has been struck against iron, it does not cut wood any longer either. Let this be understood by anyone who is interested.—Johannes Kepler

chapter **V**

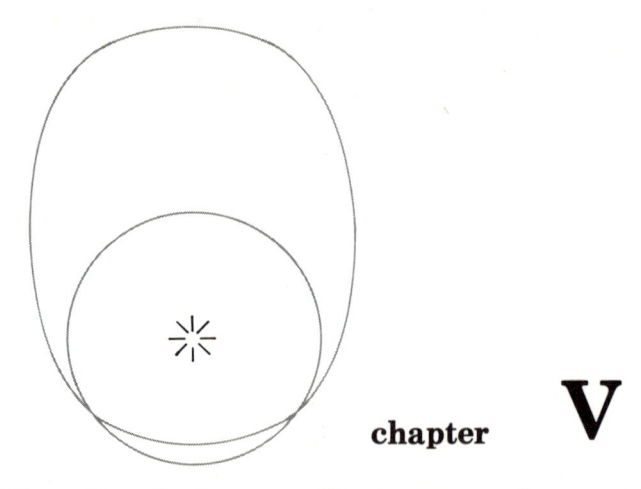

The Joel-Amos Catastrophe

circa October, 25, 756 B.C.

This chapter discusses the literary descriptions and expectations of the catastrophe which occurred just 54 years 4½ months earlier than the Isaiahic Catastrophe of 701 B.C. The descriptions come from four Hebrew "fire and brimstone" prophets, namely Amos, Joel, Jonah and Nahum.

The catastrophe, severe as it was, was but a prelude to the one which followed 54½ years later. Similarly, it will be seen in a later chapter that the Tower of Babel Catastrophe (October 25, 1930 B.C.) was but a prelude to the Sodom-Gomorrah Catastrophe (March 20, 1877 B.C.), just 52½ years later. To understand one pair of catastrophes is to understand the other pair, identical in the time of the month dating, almost identical in intensity, and separated by about 1174 years.

Naming The Catastrophe

WHEN LEWIS AND CLARK, early American explorers, first came upon the three forks at the headwaters of the Missouri River, they of necessity had to select names. The names chosen were in honor of important contemporary statesmen, Gallatin, Jefferson and Madison, a president and two members of his cabinet.

THE JOEL-AMOS CATASTROPHE   131

We are the first to identify and differentiate the series of catastrophes and their cyclic nature. Each requires a name. For example, the catastrophe of 701 B.C. has been named "The Isaiahic Catastrophe" since Isaiah was the dominant figure of the time in Hebrew history.

Concerning the catastrophe of October 25, 756 B.C., there was no single dominant figure in Judah, either militarily, politically or theologically. (The king, Uzziah, had desecrated his own image in the eyes of the prophets and priests.)[1] Four prophets, each of whom wrote briefly of this catastrophic era, are in the canon of scripture. They are Amos, Joel, Jonah and Nahum. Of the four prophets, the two more significant men are Joel and Amos, hence the "Joel-Amos Catastrophe."

Dating The Catastrophe

Dating the Isaiahic Catastrophe was easy, for there is no doubt of the exact day. This is not so with the Joel-Amos Catastrophe, for the literatures of these prophets are not precisely-dated. We have five ways of arriving at a date and not all five harmonize. These five methods are as follows:

1. By Model
2. By the book of Amos
3. By the book of Jonah
4. By Josephus *(Antiquities of the Jews)*
5. By the *Talmud*

1. BY THE MODEL. The model presented in Chapter IV indicates that 54 years was *the average* for the cycle of conjunctions from one catastrophic intersection location to the other. The average is not the rule. Therefore the model, if valid, suggests any one of the three following dates:

    a.   October 25   754 B.C.

    b.   October 25   756 B.C.   (date preferred by the authors)

---

[1] Flavius Josephus, translated by William Whiston, *Antiquities of the Jews*, Bridgeport, Connecticut: M. Sherman, 1828, Vol. II, Book IX, Chapter X, section 4, p. 236.

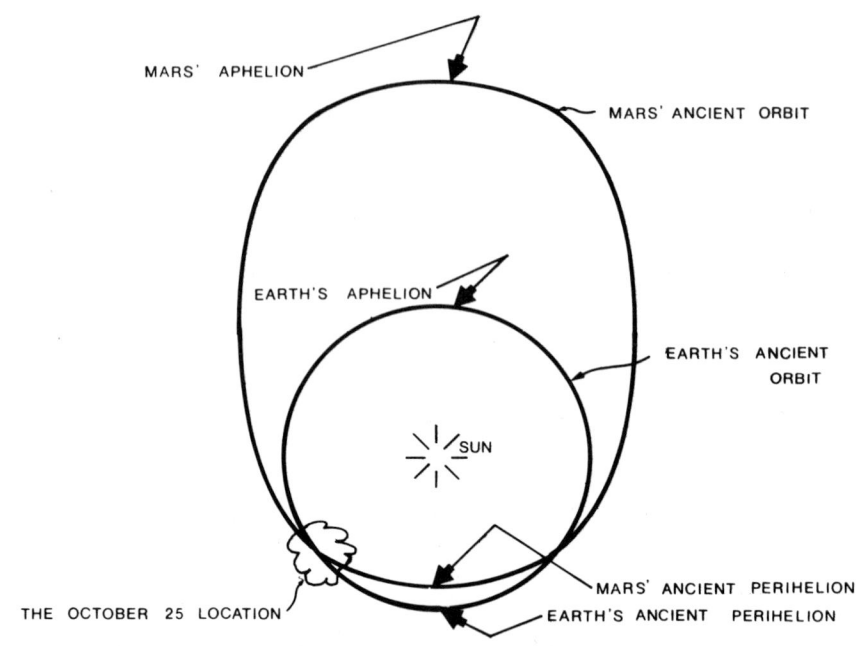

THE GEOMETRY OF THE JOEL-AMOS CATASTROPHE

ORBITS AS SEEN FROM POLARIS

FIGURE 18

The geometry of this catastrophe will be repeated in Figures 23, 24 and 34. It is believed that all four of these catastrophes occurred during the last week of October, in the years 756 B.C., 972 B.C., 1404 B.C. and 1930 B.C.

THE JOEL-AMOS CATASTROPHE

c. October 25   758 B.C.

2. BY AMOS. Amos described the catastrophe (as a *raash*, or "earth-shaking"), and dated it, but in an incomplete way by modern standards.

> The words of Amos, who was among the herdmen of Tekoa, which he saw concerning Israel in the days of Uzziah, king of Judah, and in the days of Jeroboam the son of Joash, king of Israel, TWO YEARS BEFORE THE EARTHQUAKE. (Amos 1:1)

The "earthquake" was not a localized earth tremor as we think of today, but a planetary catastrophe, a "day of commotion," better translated as an "earth-shaking." This particular day (which we believe was October 25, 756 B.C.) was sufficiently memorable and vivid in contemporary times, that 200 years later the prophet Zechariah described it quite strikingly:

> And ye shall flee to the valley of the mountains . . . yea, ye shall flee, like as ye fled from before the EARTHQUAKE in the days of Uzziah king of Judah. . . . (Zechariah 14:5)

Zechariah was talking about coming catastrophism as modelled after the historical catastrophic scenes, in this case, the Joel-Amos holocaust. Localized earthquakes today are hardly a subject for casual point-making in contemporary literature; however, contemporary earthquakes are no comparison to the condition being described. The same word, "earthquake," describes two rather different phenomena.

In Amos' introductory verse, he indicates he began to prophesy two years before the celestial holocaust. (Since Mars was in a two-year resonance orbit with Earth, Amos saw Mars pass over roughly a million miles away during the autumn of 758 B.C.)[2] This close fly-by may have had something to do with his prognostication of the next fly-by, and of his call to the prophetic office. He plainly predicted that the next scheduled fly-by

---

[2]From an extrapolation from Table V, page 103.

would be replete with celestial wrath which no nation in the Middle East (his world) could escape;³ it would be fierce. The two year warning period in the book of Amos must have been based on his cosmic observation and insight that the next pass would indeed be severe, so severe that it would rival the historic holocausts of The Long Day of Joshua, Sodom-Gomorrah and the Exodus Catastrophe.

Amos dates his message as being during the reigns of Jeroboam II, King of Israel, and Uzziah, King of Judah. A knowledge of the precise dates of their reigns will enable us to further define or limit the time period for Amos' catastrophic pronouncement. The dates of their reigns are as follows:

Jeroboam II	co-regency with Jehoash	798-781 B.C.
	sole regency	781-753 B.C.
Uzziah or Azariah	co-regency with Amaziah	791-767 B.C.
	sole regency	767-750 B.C.
	co-regency with Jotham	750-739 B.C.⁴

The overlapping dates of the sole regencies of Jeroboam II and Uzziah (also known as Azariah) are 767 B.C. to 753 B.C.

In Chapter 7 of the book of Amos, Amos had a confrontation with the religious establishment of Northern Israel, specifically the council leader of the priests of Bethel (the king's chapel). Amos considered these priests, involved deeply in Baalism, to be representatives of the apostasy, not of bona fide faith. Because of his insight into the corrupt character of the nation and coming political instability, Amos prophesied the approaching demise

---

[3] In chapters 1 and 2 of the book of Amos, he predicts a blizzard of bolides and meteors (fire) will fall on seven Middle Eastern Nations, all of them contiguous with Northern Israel or Southern Judah.

[4] Edwin R. Thiele, *The Mysterious Numbers of the Hebrew Kings*, Grand Rapids: Wm. B. Eerdmans Pub. Co., 1965, p. 205. Our list is a simplification of Thiele's where he allows for the inexact correspondence between the Hebrew civil calendar beginning in September, the Hebrew Religious calendar beginning in March, and our Julian calendar, an adaptation of the revised Roman calendar.

(by assassination) of Jeroboam's dynasty.[5] Tradition indicates that Amos was eventually put to death[6] for his opposition to establishment apostasy (which also happened to Isaiah).

Amos' dire prophecy of the end of the dynasty was certainly pronounced in the latter years of the reign of Jeroboam II, after 760 B.C. Amos' prophetic career began at least two years before Jotham's co-regency in 750 B.C. This picture of Amos' persecution, inspired by apostate clergymen, suggests a date of about 758 B.C. The celestial holocaust enveloped the Middle East two years after Amos' call as the first of the writing prophets.

3. BY JONAH. Jonah was another fire and brimstone prophet who is best-known because he was swallowed by the big fish. More important was Jonah's call, a mission directed by God to go to the huge, growing militaristic Nineveh[7] (capital of Assyria) and preach. His message was not a message of brotherhood or disarmament, neither was it a popular message. It was to be about the coming judgment from the Lord—fire and brimstone.

> And Jonah began to enter into the city a day's journey, and he cried, and said, Yet forty days, and Nineveh shall be overthrown. (Jonah 3:4)

Observe the specificity of timing. Forty days before the Joel-Amos holocaust, September 15, 756 B.C., Mars was visible and visibly approaching 20,000,000 miles distant. The leadership of Northern Israel had little time for Amos. In contrast the leader-

---

[5] For this unpleasant pronouncement Amos was banished from Israel, and then was persecuted even in exile. Subsequently Jeroboam II died in 753 B.C., apparently of natural causes. He was succeeded by his son Zechariah who was assassinated in 752 B.C., and the dynasty was ended. Other assassinations of regents in Northern Israel occurred in 752 B.C. (Shallum, Zechariah's slayer and successor), 740 B.C. (Pekahiah) and 731 B.C. (Pekah).

[6] Louis Ginzberg, *The Legends of the Jews,* Philadelphia: Jewish Publication Society of America, 1913, Vol IV, p. 262. "However, the fearlessness of Amos finally caused his death. King Uzziah inflicted a mortal blow upon his forehead with a red-hot iron."

[7] Nineveh was a city of over 1,000,000 persons at this time, and the world's leading metropolis. It was what Moscow is to Russia, nerve-center and capital of a cruel, expanding state.

ship of Assyria, and of its capital, Nineveh, received Jonah's message with sobriety, not scorn.

> So the people of Nineveh believed God, and proclaimed a fast, and put on sackcloth, FROM THE GREATEST OF THEM even to the least of them. For word came unto the king of Nineveh, and he arose from his throne, and he laid his robe from him, and covered him with sackcloth, and sat in ashes.
>
> Who can tell if God will turn and repent, and turn away from his fierce anger, that we perish not? (Jonah 3:5-6,9)

The Scriptures indicate that the city was not destroyed in 756 B.C. but neither was it left fully intact according to a Talmudic account:

> But at the end of forty days they departed from the path of piety, and they became more sinful than ever. Then the punishment threatened by Jonah overtook them, and they were swallowed up by the earth.[8]

The schedule of the catastrophe, or even the fact of the catastrophe is necessary background missed to date by all Christian and Jewish Biblical commentators. Assuming Jonah had some cosmic knowledge, some calendaric knowledge and some historical perspective, and since Mars was 20,000,000 miles away and approaching, logically the leadership of Assyria would listen to Jonah. They did listen, however briefly.

Jonah is mentioned in *Antiquities of the Jews* by Josephus. His "sojourn" to Nineveh is discussed (Book IX, Chapter X, section 2), and the death of Jeroboam II is discussed next, in the first line of section 3. The implication is that Jonah's series of sermons and prognostications in Nineveh were given toward the end of the reign of Jeroboam II. The king's death occurred in 753 B.C. Thus either the date 756 B.C. or 754 B.C. would satisfy the general context for the occurrence of the catastrophe. Our preference is 756 B.C.

4. BY JOSEPHUS (*Antiquities of the Jews*). Josephus de-

---

[8]Louis Ginzberg, *op. cit.*, Vol. IV, p. 252-253.

THE JOEL-AMOS CATASTROPHE

scribes some of the crustal shift, and the urban geography in and around Jerusalem (Book X, Chapter IX, section 4). A part of a mountain broke off, and formed a landslide, which rolled as far as the king's garden. The landslide is recorded as having rolled four furlongs, or about half a mile. Such an earth deformation (together with the associated astronomical commotion) was remembered for generations. This landslide of splitting off of part of a mountain formed the basis of prophetic notes such as have already been quoted from Zechariah.

Josephus recorded this geophysical event on "that remarkable day" when Uzziah went into the temple, not just to worship, but to offer incense sacrilegiously upon the golden altar, a function reserved only for the temple priesthood. (Uzziah apparently had been seized with some degree of dread, fear and panic. We suspect the source of his fear was the immediate and close Martian approach of 756 B.C., by that eventful day, well within the Earth-Moon system.) One development that day was Uzziah's sacrilege, a second was the landslide, and yet a third was a severe breaching or bowing of joists and rafters in the temple.

> And when they cried out, that he must go out of the temple, and not transgress against God, he was wroth at them, and threatened to kill them, unless they would hold their peace: in the meantime, A GREAT EARTHQUAKE shook the ground, and a rent was made in the temple, AND THE BRIGHT RAYS OF THE SUN SHONE THROUGH IT . . . And before the city, at a place called Eroge, half the mountain broke off from the rest on the west, and rolled itself four furlongs, and stood still at the east mountain, till the roads, as well as the king's gardens, were spoiled by the obstruction.[9,10]

---

[9] Josephus, *op cit.*, Vol. II, Book IX, Chapter X, section 4, pp. 236-237.

[10] The "bright rays of the sun" which Josephus discusses indicates that severe structural damage was done to the temple. Josephus and rabbinic commentary in the *Talmud* suggest that these unusual rays, shining on Uzziah while he was in the sanctuary in his sacrilegious act, were the cause for his subsequent "leprosy." That it was a nervous disorder is not doubted, but whether it was a nervous breakdown or an infection of *Mycobacterium leprae* is an open question.

Ginzberg's *Legends of the Jews* (Vol. VI, p. 358), a compilation of rabbinic commentary, says the following: The statement of Josephus that a ray of sunlight caused Uzziah's leprosy is evidently based on haggadic interpretation of [Hebrew word] meaning "shone" in regard to the sun. See, however, also Vol. III, p. 303, also note 197 on p. 90 in connection with

5. BY THE TALMUD. Another method of dating the Joel-Amos Catastrophe is to determine when Uzziah first discovered "leprosy." Jotham assumed his co-regency at about this time. The *Talmud* indicates that Jotham's co-regency began in 756 B.C. if he died in 731 B.C. with which Thiele concurs.

> Afflicted with leprosy, Uzziah was unfit to reign as king, and Jotham administered the affairs of Judah for twenty-five years before the death of his father.[11]

Thus we conclude that Jotham's reign extended over 25 years as the *Talmud* indicates, and ended in 731 B.C. Uzziah's nervous disorder was a progressive condition, beginning in 756 B.C. and forcing his retirement from public life. This establishes more firmly our preferred date of 756 B.C. for the Joel-Amos holocaust.

A Historical Frame Of Reference For Cosmic Catastrophism

Isaiah foresaw and pictured the coming holocaust of 701 B.C. in terms of earlier ones such as the Sodom-Gomorrah, the Exodus and the Long Day of Joshua. Amos thought as Isaiah thought. Amos also used history and past catastrophic holocausts as models or patterns for the imminent cosmic crisis. This is to say that a good cosmologist in that era[12] had to be a good historian, and a good historian had to have a catastrophic frame of reference.

> *AMOS USING THE EXODUS CATASTROPHE AS A MODEL.* Shall not the land tremble for this, and every one mourn that dwelleth therein? and it shall rise up wholly as a flood; and it shall be cast out and drowned,

> death by CELESTIAL FIRE as a punishment for the laity usurping the priesthood. . . . As to the earthquake taking place on the day on which Uzziah attempted his sacrifice, see references cited . . . in Jerome on Amos 1:3.

[11] Louis Ginzberg, *op. cit.*, Vol. IV, p. 264.

[12] The same is true today.

AS BY THE FLOOD OF EGYPT. (Amos 8:8, see also Amos 9:5)[13]

AMOS USING THE SODOM-GOMORRAH CATASTROPHE AS A MODEL. I have overthrown some of you, as God overthrew Sodom and Gomorrah, and ye were as a firebrand plucked out of the burning. . . . (Amos 4:11)

AMOS USING THE ANTITHESIS OF THE LONG DAY OF JOSHUA (A SHORTENED DAY) AS A MODEL. And it shall come to pass in that day, saith the Lord God, that I will cause the sun to go down at noon, and I will darken the earth in the clear day. (Amos 8:9)

In these three references, we believe Amos compares the coming holocaust to the ancient holocausts, to the Long Day of Joshua, to the Exodus Catastrophe and to the even more ancient Sodom-Gomorrah holocaust. There were differences. The Long Day of Joshua Catastrophe occurred primarily in the morning, whereas Amos was predicting a similar *kind* of polar migration, only in the afternoon, Palestine time, and polar migration in another direction (the day would shorten rather than lengthen). Amos advised his contemporaries that they could understand what was coming by understanding the earlier holocausts. We shall indicate also that when these more ancient catastrophes are better understood (as they are discussed in Chapters VII, VIII, and IX), a more complete understanding of this Joel-Amos Catastrophe will be achieved.

The Joel-Amos Catastrophe
As Forecast And Described By Amos

THE SCHEDULE   Woe unto you that desire the DAY OF THE LORD! to what end is it for you? the DAY OF

---

[13]Greek cosmo-mythology tells of two floods. One ended the era of the Titans and the other ended the era of the Minoans, or the dynasty of Minos of Crete. Amos differentiates between the two floods, the first of which we believe was global and the second was but regional. The era of the Titans was the age of Noah; the time of Minos was the time of Moses.

THE LORD is darkness, and not light. (Amos 5:18)[14]

Shall not the DAY OF THE LORD be darkness, and not light? even very dark, and no brightness in it? (Amos 5:20)

THE EARTHQUAKES   And I will smite the winter house with the summer house; and the houses of ivory shall perish, and the great houses shall have an end, saith the Lord. (Amos 3:15)[15]

For, behold, the Lord commandeth, and he will smite the great house with breaches, and the little house with clefts. (Amos 6:11)

THE VULCANISM   . . . and I will darken the earth in the clear day. (Amos 8:9)

THE BOLIDES AND METEORS   But I will send a fire upon Judah. . . . (Amos 2:5) (See also Amos 1:4, 1:7, 1:10, 1:12, 1:14 and 2:2.)

I have sent among you the PESTILENCE after the manner of Egypt. . . . (Amos 4:10)

I have smitten you with blasting and mildew. . . . (Amos 4:9)

---

[14] When the volcano Krakatoa blew up in August, 1883, the sky was dark at noon at towns in Java which were hundreds of miles distant, and at various elevations including at Bandung, 2600 feet above sea level. This was due to the air pollution caused by volcanic dust, ash and cinders. A symphony of volcanic eruptions due to a close Mars fly-by is believed to be the "day of the Lord," a day of darkness and gloominess. It is an explanation for why the sun would become red in the sky, as it is in the localities near forest fires.

[15] There would be extreme crustal distortion caused by tides of magma, and many collapsed buildings. The *Talmud* states that Jotham, who assumed co-regency about 756 B.C., went to great endeavors to repair the breaches in Jerusalem's walls, and refurbish other damaged architectures including the temple.

THE JOEL-AMOS CATASTROPHE

"Blasting" is from the Hebrew word *shdephah* meaning paleness, scorch, to blast.

"Mildew" is from the Hebrew word *yeraqown* meaning paleness, as perhaps in persons from fright. This word appears five times in the Old Testament, each time accompanied by "blasting" and twice in a triad with "pestilence."

PRAIRIE FIRES

Seek the Lord, and ye shall live; lest he break out like fire in the house of Joseph, and devour it, and there be none to quench it in Bethel. (Amos 5:6)

ON ASTROLOGY[16]

But ye have borne the tabernacle of your Moloch and Chiun your images, the star of your god, which ye made to yourselves. Therefore will I cause you to go into captivity.... (Amos 5:26-27)

ORBITAL MOVEMENTS

It is he that buildeth his STORIES in the heaven, and hath founded his TROOP in the earth; ... (Amos 9:6)

"Stories" might suggest buildings to us. This is the Hebrew word *ma'alah* which has meanings such as elevation, ascending in the heavens, moving in the celestial scene, spheres in stellar movement, climactic progression, degrees of progression. (It may be related to the word *ma'or* or *me'orah,* meaning a luminary, which we suspect is the ancient Hebrew word for Mars.)

---

[16] Amos, like Elijah and Isaiah, chastised his people severely for their belief in astrology rather than faith in God the Creator. Astrology was associated with worship of Baal-Mars and Ashtoreth-Venus, idolatry, sexual orgies, infant sacrifice, witchcraft and Satanism, forming an unholy religious system.

> "Troop" is the Hebrew word *aguddah* which has meanings including to bind, a band, bundle, an arch, like an arch in the heavens.[17]

Amos was not, by modern standards, a well-travelled man. Probably he did not travel beyond the confines of Palestine, but he did travel in both Northern Israel and Southern Judah. Yet in Amos' book, chapters 1 and 2, Amos reveals himself as a regional, if not global, prophet. In the year 758 B.C., just as Mars had completed its final orbital lap before the holocaust, he prophesied that fire and brimstone would fall on eight different lands or nations in the Middle East. The lands doomed to fire and brimstone destruction two years hence included Ammon, Edom, Judah, Moab, Northern Israel, Philistia, Phoenicia (Tyre), Southern Judah and Syria. These are all nations contiguous to Judah or Israel. Even though he was not a "world" traveller, his prognostication included the idea that astronomical judgment was in the offing for all lands, not just Jerusalem or Samaria, Judah or Israel.

The Joel-Amos Catastrophe
As Described And Forecast By Joel

Joel, the prophet, in his written text, did not refer to historical holocausts for the pattern of coming astronomical crisis; however, he may have been a well-read and astute historian of cosmic crisis like Amos and Isaiah, for certainly he was a prophet of cosmic crisis.

THE SCHEDULE	Alas for THE DAY! for the DAY OF THE LORD is at hand, and as a destruction from the Almighty shall it come. (Joel 1:15)
THE EARTHQUAKES	. . . let all the inhabitants of the

---

[17] We believe Amos was describing first the path of Mars in the heavens and second the Earth's rotation or spin nature. Translators have missed both the word translation and the surrounding context.

land TREMBLE: for the day of the Lord cometh, for it is nigh at hand. (Joel 2:1)

The earth shall QUAKE before them; the heavens shall TREMBLE: the sun and the moon shall be dark, and the stars shall withdraw their shining. (Joel 2:10)

THE VULCANISM

And I will shew wonders in the heavens and in the earth, blood and fire, and PILLARS OF SMOKE. The sun shall be turned into darkness, [*as perhaps with an occluded volcanically-polluted atmosphere*], and the moon into blood, before the great and terrible day of the Lord come. (Joel 2:30-31)

THE BOLIDES AND METEORS

A fire devoureth BEFORE THEM; and BEHIND THEM A FLAME BURNETH. . . . (Joel 2:3)

Like the noise of chariots on the tops of the mountains shall THEY leap, like the NOISE OF A FLAME OF FIRE that devoureth the stubble, as a strong people set in battle array. (Joel 2:5)

The Joel-Amos Catastrophe As Described And Forecast By Nahum

Traditional Bible commentaries place the message of Nahum about the time of the fall of Nineveh to Babylonian armies, about 612 B.C. Dake, in *Dake's Annotated Reference Bible,* dates Nahum between 786-757 B.C., a dating in which we concur. His description of cosmic holocaust points toward his living during the era of catastrophism, and this ended in 701 B.C. We conclude that he, Jonah, Amos and Joel form a quartet of fire and brimstone prophets of circa 760-750 B.C. Two (Amos and Joel) addressed their messages to the Hebrews and two (Jonah and Nahum) addressed their messages to Nineveh and the militaristic Assyrian Empire.

THE SCHEDULE	The Lord is slow to anger, and great in power, and will not at all acquit the wicked: the Lord hath his way IN THE WHIRLWIND AND IN THE STORM. . . . (Nahum 1:3)
THE EARTHQUAKES	The MOUNTAINS QUAKE at him, and the hills melt, and the earth is burned at his presence, yea the world, and all that dwell therein. (Nahum 1:5)
THE VULCANISM	The mountains quake at him AND THE HILLS MELT. . . . (Nahum 1:5)
THE BOLIDES AND METEORS	Who can stand before his indignation? and who can abide in the fierceness of his anger? his FURY IS POURED OUT LIKE FIRE, and THE ROCKS ARE THROWN DOWN BY HIM. (Nahum 1:6)
	. . . the CHARIOTS [*bolides*] shall be with flaming torches in the day of his preparation, and the fir trees shall be terribly shaken . . . they shall seem LIKE TORCHES, they shall run LIKE THE LIGHTNINGS. (Nahum 2:3-4)

Here are four prophets of the eighth century B.C., Amos, Joel, Jonah and Nahum. Two record a similar outline of a wayward, drifting Israel suffering from poor religious leadership and inadequate political leadership. Of the three cities (Samaria, Jerusalem and Nineveh) addressed by these men, the most pagan was Nineveh. It was, surprisingly, the king and leadership of this metropolis who listened and repented, however briefly. They at least honored Jonah and Nahum and their words. Jerusalem, on the other hand, was tired of the prophets, and Samaria would not tolerate the hard-hitting words of Amos.[18]

The Geometries Of The Catastrophes

CASE ONE. If Mars is approaching the Earth from within Earth's orbit (i.e. Mars has recently passed its own perihelion), then an inside pass of Mars (inside Earth's orbit) leads to Mars *passing ahead of Earth,* hence losing energy. This is required for Earth's orbit (year) to be lengthened and Mars' orbit to be shortened. This case occurred during the Isaiahic Catastrophe.[19]

CASE TWO. If Mars is approaching Earth from outside Earth's orbit (i.e. from its remote aphelion), then an inside pass of Mars is also going to occur, that is, *Mars passes behind Earth.* In this case Mars will gain energy and Earth will lose energy and will lose angular momentum, just the opposite of Case One.

During the 1800 years (2500 B.C. to 701 B.C.) when Mars

---

[18]Samaria was the capital city of Northern Israel. Here Ashtoreth and Baal (Venus and Mars) were the supreme deities, not Jehovah. Those faithful to Jehovah were few and with modest influence. The priesthood was apostate, and the morality of the nation was in poor condition, immorality being a part of the Baalish system. The feeling against Biblical doctrine was somewhat vicious, although rejection was not yet total. The postscript to this situation is that Samaria's days were numbered. Assassinations in a series took four of her kings within 25 years, and her political and economic stability deteriorated rapidly. Many emigrated. By 720 B.C. the idolatrous city was destroyed by Assyria and the survivors removed as slaves; the nation disappeared forever. Samaria would have done well to heed Amos, and had it done so it would have survived. This is because faith and spirit are the heart and soul of a nation, and when a nation loses its faith it loses a great deal. Amos compared Samaria and Bethel to Sodom and Gomorrah, two earlier cities whose days had been numbered. Five steps of moral and spiritual deterioration of the nation are foreseen and outlined by Moses in Leviticus 26. The fifth stage results in national destruction and captivity; Amos foresaw that Israel was well along on this path into the fifth cycle of discipline, as outlined by Moses, and he warned the nation to return to the Lord.
For further information on these five cycles of discipline and five increasingly decadent generations, see Kenneth L. Jensen, *Wisdom The Principal Thing,* Seattle: Pacific Meridian Publishing Co., 1971, pp. 101 ff.

[19]The resonance model requires Mars to pass inside of Earth in both cases. The one exception to this was the Exodus Catastrophe when Mars passed outside Earth, and apparently almost went out of resonance, because the next catastrophe occurred in 42 years instead of the normal 54-year cycle.

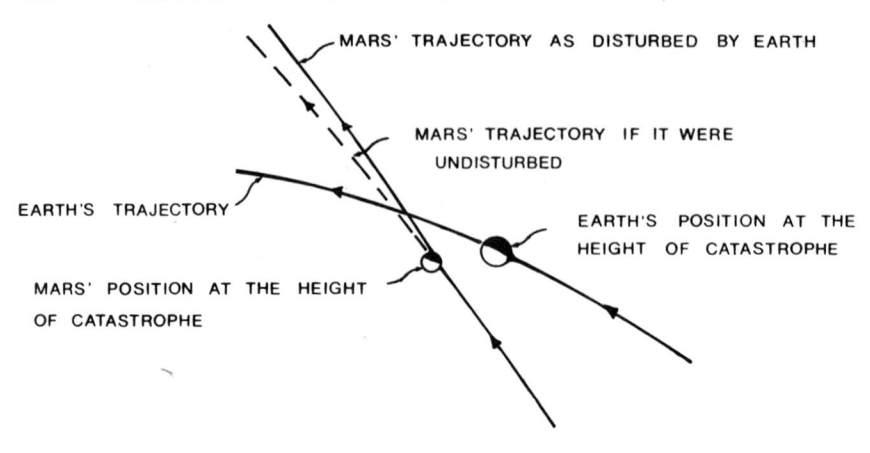

146 THE LONG DAY OF JOSHUA AND SIX OTHER CATASTROPHES

CASE 1 TRAJECTORIES
MARCH 20–21 OCCASIONS

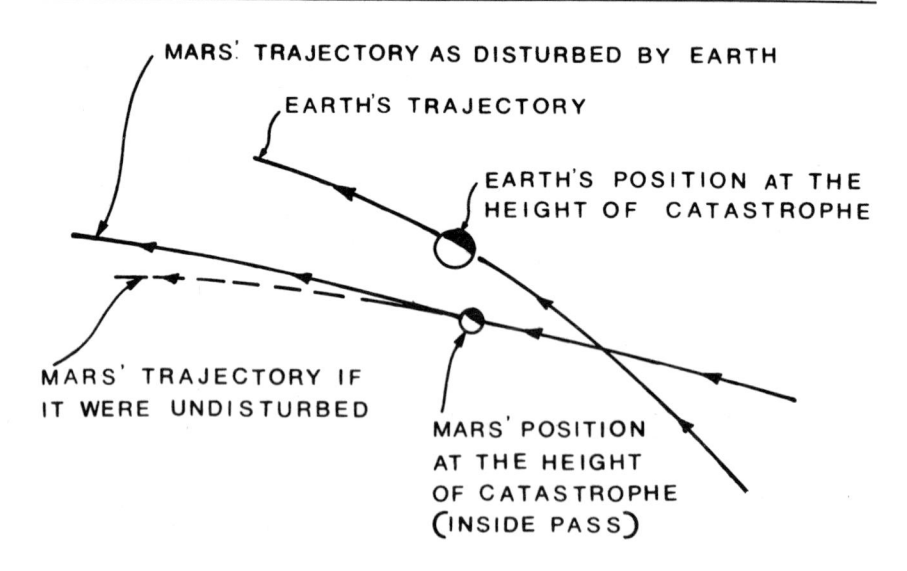

CASE 2 TRAJECTORIES
LATE OCTOBER OCCASIONS

FIGURE 19

Case 1 trajectories apply to all March catastrophes. The normal condition is an inside pass or fly-by by the Martian planet. Case 2 trajectories apply to all October situations. The normal condition, as with the Case 1 trajectories, is an inside fly-by for Mars.

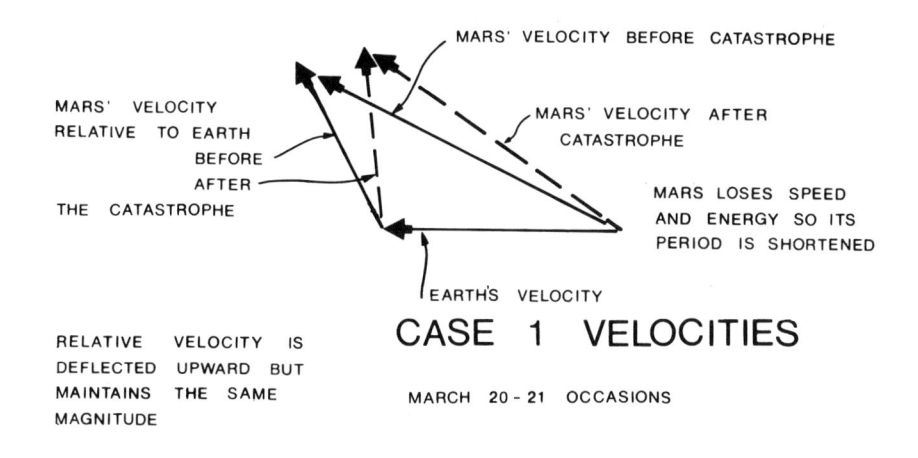

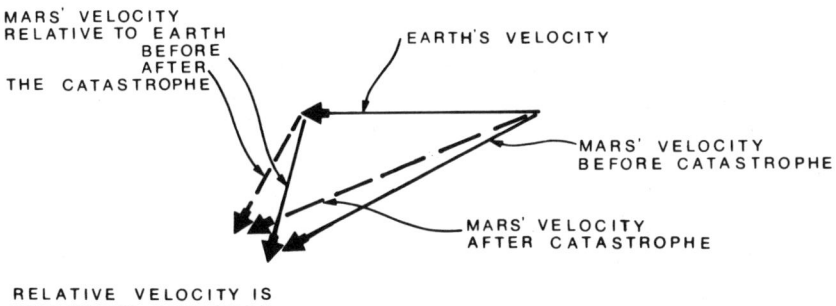

THE JOEL-AMOS CATASTROPHE

MARS' VELOCITY BEFORE CATASTROPHE

MARS' VELOCITY RELATIVE TO EARTH BEFORE AFTER THE CATASTROPHE

MARS' VELOCITY AFTER CATASTROPHE

MARS LOSES SPEED AND ENERGY SO ITS PERIOD IS SHORTENED

EARTH'S VELOCITY

RELATIVE VELOCITY IS DEFLECTED UPWARD BUT MAINTAINS THE SAME MAGNITUDE

CASE 1 VELOCITIES

MARCH 20 - 21 OCCASIONS

MARS' VELOCITY RELATIVE TO EARTH BEFORE AFTER THE CATASTROPHE

EARTH'S VELOCITY

MARS' VELOCITY BEFORE CATASTROPHE

MARS' VELOCITY AFTER CATASTROPHE

RELATIVE VELOCITY IS DEFLECTED DOWNWARD BUT MAINTAINS THE SAME MAGNITUDE

MARS GAINS SPEED AND ENERGY SO ITS' PERIOD IS LENGTHENED

CASE 2 VELOCITIES

LATE OCTOBER OCCASIONS

FIGURE 20
Case 1 velocities apply to all March catastrophes. The normal condition is with an inside fly-by by Mars. An outside fly-by would reverse the velocity change. Case 2 velocities apply to all October situations. An outside fly-by will reverse the effect illustrated by an inside fly-by.

FIGURE 21
The Great Rift Valley of Mars. A panoramic view of the equatorial region of Mars, covering an area of about 4½ million square miles, about 8% of the planet's surface. The center section of the mosaic contains an enormous canyon, 2500 miles long, 75 miles wide and nearly 20,000 feet deep. Courtesy of Office of Public Information, Jet Propulsion Laboratory, NASA, Pasadena, Calif.

FIGURE 22
The South Polar Region of Mars featuring light and dark contour representing layered deposits of volcanic ash and dust particles and ices of water and carbon dioxide. Various plates suggest different polar locations for Mars in the past. The area covered is about 1070 square miles, 2% of Mars' surface area. Courtesy of Office of Public Information, Jet Propulsion Laboratory, Pasadena, California.

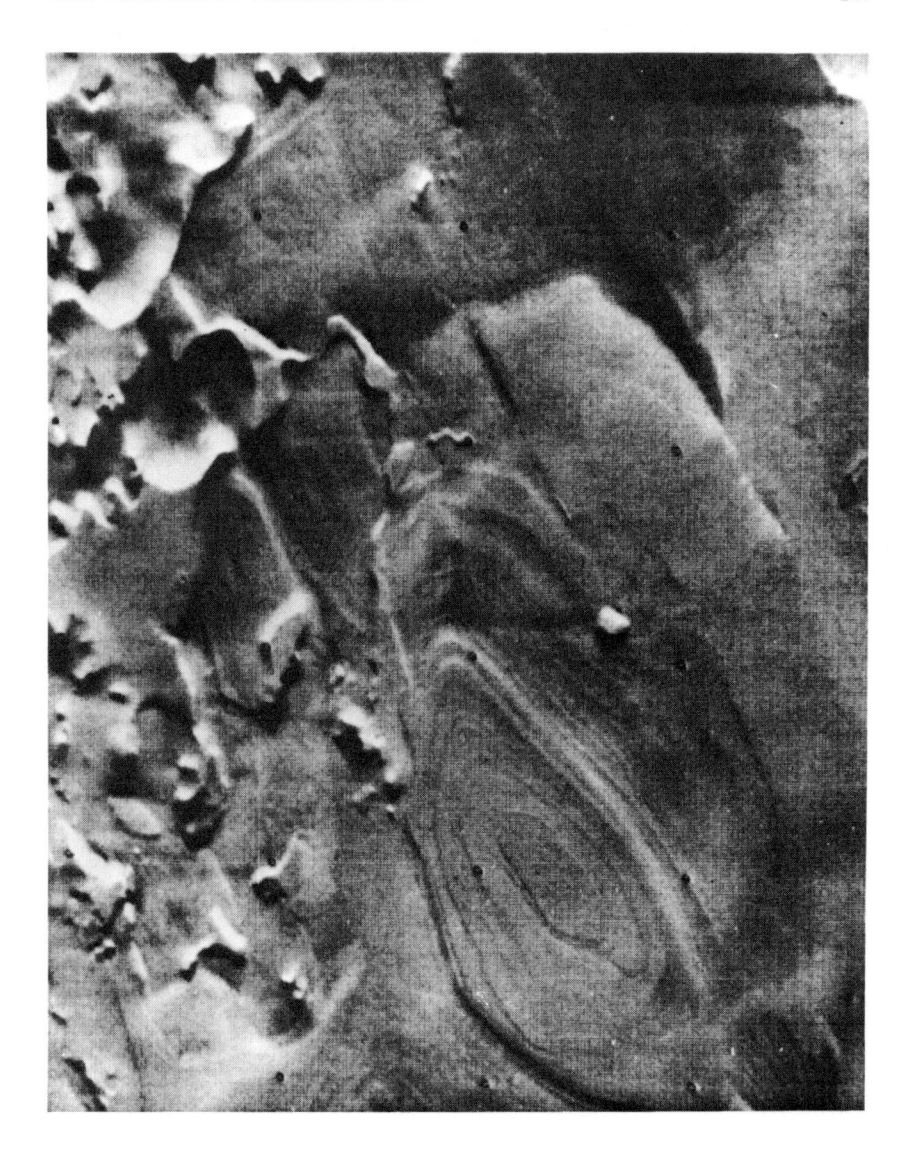

was in the resonant orbit, and having its conjunctions oscillating back and forth once every 108 years on the average, there were about 33 half-cycles. It is something like a ping-pong game in which each opponent hits the ball back across the net for 16 consecutive times, the net corresponding to the perihelions of both Earth and Mars in early January. Then on the 17th cycle, like a ping-pong ball which overshoots the end of the table, Mars finally went out of resonance and into an entirely new orbit.

In the approaches which are all Case One, Mars will appear to rise in the early part of the morning and will set about 12 hours later, or about 8 P.M. At the height of the catastrophe, Mars will appear close to the Sun (and an eclipse of Earth is possible). As it approaches conjunction, the Sun is shining on the opposite side of it, and it will diminish in its image to a bright slit of reflected light.

In the approaches which are Case Two, the October catastrophes (such as this one), Mars will rise about 2 P.M. and set about 2 A.M. It will appear as a three-quarter crescent in the eastern sky, which crescent narrows as Mars approaches the Earth, and looms larger in size. Normally in the Case Two events, Earth passed the intersection location of the two orbits ahead of Mars, and Mars then lapped Earth on the inside, as its three-quarter crescent diminished to a shiny but thin slit. Again in this geometry an eclipse of Earth was possible. This is what the Celtics of Britain saw, when they developed the lore of a celestial witch on a broomstick, screeching and traversing across the heavens, the cosmic broom being her trailing symbol, portrayed as celestial locomotion.

TABLE VI
CASE ONE AND CASE TWO GEOMETRIES

	CASE ONE	**CASE TWO**
Date	3rd week of March	4th week of October
Geometry	Leaving perihelion	Approaching perihelion
Geometry	Inside fly-by normal	Inside fly-by normal
Distance of Mars	60,000 to 200,000 miles	60,000 to 200,000 miles
Time of Day in Palestine	Varies	Varies

We have already discussed a "Case One" catastrophe, the Isaiahic event. We have just completed discussion of a "Case Two" catastrophe, the Joel-Amos event. This catastrophe was typical in its timing, the 54 and 108 year cycles. It was also typical in its geometry. But it was somewhat atypical in its severity. Of the 30 or 35 close Martian fly-bys since 2500 B.C., only a half dozen equalled it in severity; only two or three exceeded it.

Summary

Isaiahic   Date   March 20, 701 B.C.
Catastrophe   Distance   Mars estimated at 70,000 miles perigee
  Geometry   Mars north of Earth's ecliptic plane
  Pass   Mars passed inside of Earth's orbit
  Rotational Scheme   Palestine at mid-day during perigee
  Case   Case One

Joel-Amos   Date   October 25, 756 B.C.
Catastrophe   Distance   Mars estimated at 100,000 miles perigee
  Geometry   Mars north of Earth's ecliptic plane
  Pass   Mars lapped inside of Earth's orbit
  Rotational Scheme   Palestine at mid-morning during perigee
  Case   Case Two

The brighter the light that a new theory sheds on its proper field, the darker and more distorting the shadows in which it submerges the experience which lies around the borders of its true scope.—M. Polyani

chapter VI

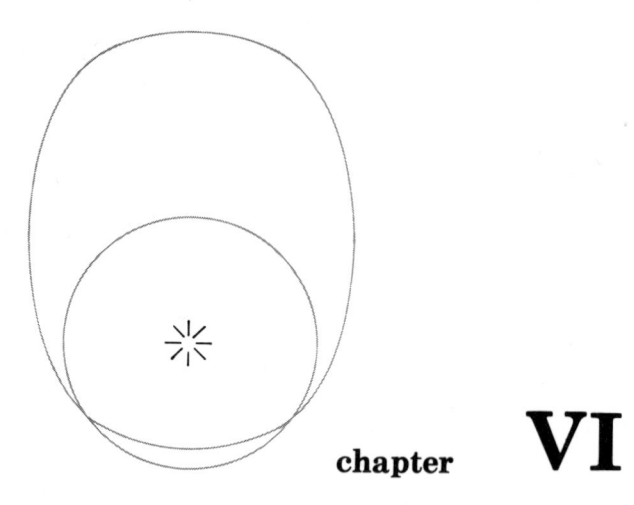

Catastrophes of the Davidic Era

864 B.C., 972 B.C., 1080 B.C. and 1188 B.C.

This chapter shall be concerned with reports of catastrophism during the era of 864 B.C. to 1188 B.C. as detected in Greek and Hebrew literature. There are five catastrophes which come under observation. Of these several catastrophes, only one is considered major (being about as severe as the Joel-Amos Catastrophe). The rest are considered minor, with some bolidic and meteoritic activity, but no spin axis shifts.

THE RESONANT ORBIT MODEL suggests that we should look for ancient catastrophes or threatening conditions every 54 years or every 108 years. Interestingly, they did occur, apparently exactly on the 108-year schedule. The five holocausts, cyclic catastrophes, each successively 108 years earlier, are as follows with our suggested dating:

The Joel-Amos Catastrophe	October 25, 756 B.C.	(Case 2)
The Elijahic Catastrophe	October 25, 864 B.C.	(Case 2)

The Greater Davidic Catastrophe	October 25, 972 B.C.	(Case 2)
The Samuelic Catastrophe	October 25, 1080 B.C.	(Case 2)
The Deborah Debacle	October 25, 1188 B.C.	(Case 2)

The two Davidic Catastrophes of 1025 B.C. and 972 B.C. are contemporary with Homer, author of the *Iliad,* a poetic saga describing events surrounding the Trojan War. It is concerned with military conquest, but also it is mixed with concern about cosmic warfare. A study of the relationship between Greek history and Hebrew history of this era would be beneficial. (Such will be presented in a future publication by geographer and historian Charles McDowell.)

The Elijahic Catastrophe
864 B. C.

This minor catastrophe is minor indeed, yet not without significance. Some meteoritic activity occurred. Little earthquake activity occurred by ancient standards. (It would be great by contemporary standards.) Mars passed over the Earth-Moon system, perhaps as distant as 200,000 miles. How much fire and brimstone fell is difficult to judge from the abbreviated Biblical record. However, that some did fall is significant, and what day of the month and the year is equally significant. Its dating bears on the faithfulness or reliability of the 108 year cycle of conjunctions we have analyzed and described.

The first description is by the cosmologist Isaiah, who recalled two of the most recent astronomical threats in order to project the great one coming in 701 B.C.

> Nevertheless the dimness shall not be such as was in her VEXATION, when AT THE FIRST HE LIGHTLY AFFLICTED the land of Zebulun[1] and the land of Naphthali, [*the Elijahic Catastrophe of 864 B.C.*], and afterward did more grievously afflict her by the way of the sea, [*the*

---

[1]Elijah's confrontation with the 450 astrologer-sorcerers, priests of Baal, occurred on Mt. Carmel overlooking the Mediterranean Sea, near the province of Zebulun, a province named after one of the twelve tribes of Israel.

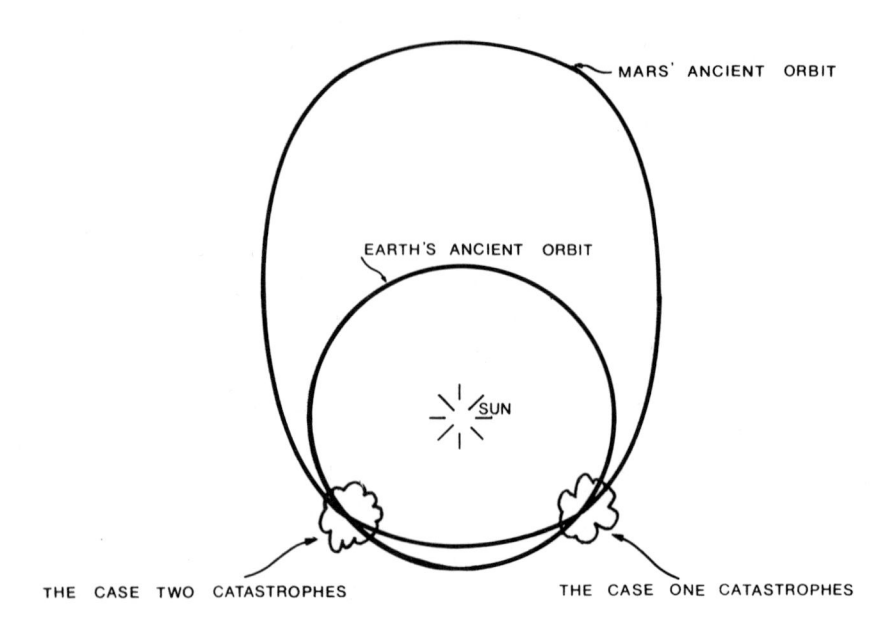

[Diagram showing Mars' ancient orbit as a large oval enclosing Earth's ancient orbit (smaller circle) around the Sun, with two intersection regions labeled "THE CASE TWO CATASTROPHES" (left) and "THE CASE ONE CATASTROPHES" (right).]

THE ELIJAHIC CATASTROPHE	864 B.C.	THE LESSER DAVIDIC
THE GREATER DAVIDIC CATASTROPHE	972 B.C.	CATASTROPHE 1025 B.C.
THE SAMUELIC CATASTROPHE	1080 B.C.	

THE GEOMETRY OF THE CATASTROPHE LOCATIONS OF THE DAVIDIC ERA

FIGURE 23

Catastrophes occurred probably in late October in the years 864 B.C., 972 B.C., 1080 B.C. and possibly 1188 B.C. (the suspected Deborah debacle). These are 108 year increments beginning with the Long Day of Joshua, 1404 B.C., a possible unreported event in 1296 B.C., a suspected event in 1188 B.C., 1080 B.C., 972 B.C., 864 B.C. and finally the last Case 2 catastrophe, 756 B.C.

Joel-Amos Catastrophe of 756 B.C.], beyond Jordan, in Galilee of the nations. (Isaiah 9:1)[2]

THE SETTING. Rather often in ancient history, two battling nations would tacitly arrange to have their military encounter on a day of expected cosmic visitation, concluding that the side which would be decimated was the one which the cosmic deities disfavored. This is seen in the literatures of several ancient nations. The confrontation in Palestine in 864 B.C., on the date of expected cosmic intervention, was not a military, but rather a theological confrontation. The political background of the time includes the reign of King Ahab and Queen Jezebel, a Phoenician princess and ardent idolater.[3] The worship of Jehovah was being severely persecuted as Baal had become the favored deity of the establishment.

Under these conditions, the prophet Elijah suddenly appeared in Ahab's court and predicted a three-year drought.[4] He predicted three years of drought as a judgment upon the land for their apostasies.[5] Because of this unfavorable pronouncement, he was forced to flee the palace, in fact flee the land, and hide for his life.

The drought Elijah announced lasted from spring 867 B.C.

---

[2]Isaiah apparently is pointing out, as a historian, that the catastrophe of 756 B.C. was more severe than the one of 864 B.C., and also that its disastrous effects were greater east of the Jordan River than west of it.

[3]Jezebel, daughter of a Phoenician king, was not merely an adopted queen, but was also co-regent, a position of authority not delegated to women in the Hebrew commonwealth. Israel was in the process of becoming virtually a Phoenician state.

[4]This was in accord with the constitutional prophecy for Israel in Leviticus 26:18-20.

[5]This period coincides well with the 11-year cycle of sunspot activity which has been recognized since 1800. This more recently has been correlated with the migration of the *center of mass* of the Sun and its nine known planets which migrates as far as two radii outside the Sun's surface. We suspect a tide-causing line-up of Jupiter and Saturn occurred during this time, causing an unusual period of sunspot activity and period of magnetic storms on the Sun, which in turn affected the pattern of jet streams and weather patterns on Earth.

to fall 864 B.C. At the end of this period, by appointment, a contest was scheduled between Elijah, the lone prophet of the Lord, and the apostate clergy of the land. These were 450 prophets and priests of Baal, sorcerers, who practiced incantations and sacrifices to their chief deity, Baal-Mars. The only one solitary spokesman for the faith in Jehovah was the bold, the hunted, the feared, and the dramatic Elijah.

Late October is the beginning of the rainy season for mid-latitude climates bordering on the western edge of oceans in the Northern Hemisphere. This is the so-called "Mediterranean" type of climate. This type of climate occurs in Southern Italy and Greece but is somewhat modified; it occurs in Morocco and California, and also in Western Australia, Central Chile and Southern Africa during the winter of the Southern Hemisphere. Autumn was the scheduled date for the onset of the rainy season in the land if there was to be rain. There had been little or none in the years 867 B.C., 866 B.C. or 865 B.C., and the land was suffering famine conditions.

This confrontation occurred on the date of the expected passover of Mars. The prophets of Baal "cried aloud, and cut themselves after their manner with knives and lancets, till the blood gushed out upon them."[6] They were persistent and incanted from midday until eventide, but nothing happened. Then Elijah took center stage. Without a word spoken, he gathered 12 stones, each symbolizing one of the 12 tribes of Israel.[7] He prayed a recorded prayer of 63 words as it occurs in the King James translation (I Kings 18:36-37). Once again the scene was replete with drama:

---

[6] I Kings 18:28.

[7] When Elijah called for 12 stones, it was a symbol of the 12 tribes of Israel which were formerly in one united country, but for the last 100 years had been under a divided condition with one capital in Jerusalem and one in Samaria. Northern Israel, with its capital at Samaria, had become virtually a vassal of Phoenicia economically, and culturally, that is it had become predominantly a pagan state. With this single symbol, and without a spoken word, Elijah was demonstrating that the paganized Samaria was functioning outside of the Divine will. It would be comparable to Lincoln as President referring to all the states as part of the union during the Civil War when such was a hope more than a reality.

> Then the fire of the Lord fell, and consumed the burnt sacrifice, and the wood, and the stones, and the dust, and licked up the water that was in the trench. And when all the people saw it, they fell on their faces. . . . (I Kings 18: 38-39)

This is the second description of the Elijahic Catastrophe, complementing Isaiah 9:1. It was no common fire caused by embers of burning cedar or olive wood. Dake observes:

> After a 63-word prayer [*by Elijah*] the fire of God fell from heaven and consumed the sacrifice, the wood, the stones, the dust, and the water in the trench. The blazes must have been intense to burn up the very stones and dust. It was no common fire, but one which nothing could resist; and it burned from the top down instead of the bottom up. It was altogether miraculous; and the people fell on their faces at once declaring that Jehovah was God.[8]

Interestingly, when Palestine was experiencing eventide, Palestine was also turning its face from inner space toward outer space, where it would face the oncoming, onrushing planet and its blizzard of swarming meteors, asteroid-like debris.[9]

This was a confrontation between two religious systems on a catastrophic date. Fire falling from heaven up to eventide on Mt. Carmel, apparently would symbolize that Baal-Mars and Ashtoreth-Venus were the controllers of the solar realm, and were in fact worshipped for such alleged powers. The Hebrews, rather, believed God to be the controller of all the luminaries in the solar system. The Hebrews, in fact, had a history of deliverance on these catastrophic days (the Long Day of Joshua and military battle, the Exodus Catastrophe and Egyptian servitude, Sodom-

---

[8] Finis Jennings Dake, *Dake's Annotated Reference Bible*, Atlanta: Dake Bible Sales, 1963, p. 383, commentary column.

[9] Talmudic tradition relates that Elijah prayed somewhat like Joshua's prayer, and for the same purpose, a sign from heaven and national deliverance. This, we believe, was 540 years (or five 108-year cycles) after the Long Day of Joshua. See Louis Ginzberg, *The Legends of the Jews*, Philadelphia: Jewish Publication Society of America, 1913, Vol. IV, p. 199.

Talmudic and Biblical literature alike indicate Elijah expected God to speak through either the wind, earthquake or fire falling from heaven. Note that at least one occurred, the fire, and if Earth tremors occurred simultaneously, it would not be surprising in the slightest.

Gomorrah and institutional debauchery, Tower of Babel and internationalism, even the Flood Catastrophe and the survival of the Noachian family).

Interestingly, Elijah (ever bold and dramatic) after God had answered with fire from heaven, fire falling from above, fire hot enough to vaporize the water and melt the rocks, announced that the end of the drought was at hand. "Hurry home, people, or your dusty chariots and wagons will get stuck in the mud" is our paraphrase of Elijah's advice (I Kings 18:44) as a tiny cloud began to form on the western horizon, the harbinger of a driving rain.

THE DATING. Dating this catastrophe requires two dates, the day and month, and the year. Since mid-autumn is the only logical time in this climatic zone that droughts are ended (whether it be the normal half-year drought or an abnormal three-and-a-half year drought), a date of around late October is logical.

The second category of dating is the year of the event, one which combined the end of the drought with a close fly-by of the marauding planet. Biblical literature does not date this event. However, the context places it at around the middle of the reign of King Ahab. Ahab's reign extended from 874/873 B.C. to 853 B.C.[10] The midpoint of this reign was circa 864 B.C. or 863 B.C. We date it at 864 B.C. by the resonant orbit model, with the 108-year average for time spans.

THE FIRE. The fire was not lighted by Elijah or any of his Mars-worshipping adversaries. The fire fell from the astronomical heavens. It was sufficiently hot to consume the sacrifice (a steer), the wood under the sacrifice, the water in a trench surrounding the wood, and reportedly even the stones, which must have melted. These were extremely hot meteoritic-type temperatures, not charcoal-type temperatures. It would be interesting to undertake an archaelogical search on the sides of Mt. Carmel, for that meteorite may well exist today under the debris and soil of this lovely hill overlooking the Mediterranean Sea.[11]

---

[10] Edwin R. Thiele, *The Mysterious Numbers of the Hebrew Kings*, Grand Rapids, Michigan: Wm. B. Eerdmans Publishing Co., 1965, p. 205.

[11] Mt. Carmel early became sacred to both the worship of Jehovah and Baal. It is about 1800 feet high, and has been a favorite site for monasteries, especially for the Order of the Carmelites, founded in 1156 A.D.

This catastrophe, a minor one, includes three of five conditions our model anticipates for a cosmic event:

1. It should occur 108 years earlier or later than another similar holocaust.

2. It should involve the dumping of bolidic or meteoritic materials—Mars-asteroids.

3. It should occur in mid-autumn.

Earthquakes and recorded celestial movements in the heavens are also a part of the rabbinic tradition concerning Elijah.[12]

The Greater Davidic Catastrophe
972 B. C.

So the Lord sent PESTILENCE[13] upon Israel: and there fell of Israel seventy thousand men. And God sent an ANGEL[14] unto Jerusalem to destroy it: and as he was destroying, the Lord beheld, and he repented him of the evil, and said to THE ANGEL THAT DESTROYED, It is enough, stay now thine hand. . . . (I Chronicles 21:14-15)

And David lifted up his eyes, AND SAW the angel of the Lord stand between the earth and the heaven, having a drawn sword[15] in his hand STRETCHED OUT OVER JERUSALEM. . . . (I Chronicles 21:16)

So the Lord sent A PESTILENCE upon Israel from the

---

[12] See Louis Ginzberg, *op. cit.*, Vol. IV, pp. 219-220.

[13] "Pestilence" is from the Hebrew word *deber*, from the root *dabar*, and is elsewhere translated murrain, pestilence or plague. It is meteoritic, and more specific, it describes Mars-asteroids dumped on Earth "even to the time appointed." (See II Samuel 24:15.)

[14] "Angel" is from the Hebrew word *mal'ak* meaning a deputy, or a messenger.

[15] "Sword" is from the Hebrew word *chereb* meaning a cutting instrument or a plunging instrument. The word usually describes an axe, dagger, knife, mattock or rapier. However, this is a celestial plunger, a sword of the Lord, being quite different than the sword of Ahab or Tiglath-Pileser, for example. It is probably a description of visible phenomena such as plunging meteorites associated with the catastrophe.

morning EVEN TO THE TIME APPOINTED: and there died of the people from Dan even to Beersheba seventy thousand men. And when the angel stretched out his hand upon Jerusalem to destroy it . . . . (II Samuel 24:15-16)

THE DATING. This event occurred shortly after the last political event of David's illustrious career, and shortly before his death. Since David's death was in 971 B.C.,[16] it is reasonable to assume this catastrophe to have been toward the end of the year 972 B.C. The year of this catastrophe was 972 B.C., just 108 years earlier than the Elijahic episode, and just 216 years earlier than the Joel-Amos holocaust.

The dating for the year (972 B.C.) is thus relatively easily established. The dating for the day and the month can only be ascertained from indirect evidence, as it was in the Elijahic Catastrophe. At the risk of being repetitious, we shall quote Dr. Charles McDowell's work as it will appear in a future publication:

> In the closing days of David's reign, a tense international situation developed. Baal/Mars was again expected to closely approach the earth. According to the Patten-Hatch model of orbital movement, Mars approached the earth every two years, coming successively closer each time. At 1000 B.C. the planets may have been within 8,000,000 miles of each other. By 972 B.C. the distance was probably reduced to 150,000 miles.
>
> Under these circumstances, no government could exercise real authority. Destruction from the close encounter of the planets could destroy cities, and armies, navies, perhaps even decimate whole coastlines. Who would escape the destruction? Nations began to arm themselves for the looting and pillaging that they knew must certainly come from marauding bands of warriors on the land and on the sea. Civil authority would break down in many places. In this context the Philistines began a revolt (I Chronicles 21).[17]

---

[16] Edwin R. Thiele, *loc cit*. Rehoboam assumed the throne upon the death of Solomon, who reigned 40 years. Thus Solomon's ascendancy was in 971 B.C., the year of David's death.

[17] Charles McDowell, "A History of Middle East Catastrophes, 1500-972 B.C.", Unpublished Manuscript. Dr. McDowell is chairman of the department of geography and history, Cuyahoga Community College, Parma, Ohio.

David chose to undertake a census of the people before the expected cataclysm. A census would logically be completed in the months just preceding the expected calamity. Beyond this, we can only conclude that the ancients by tradition and by observation over the centuries knew that if a holocaust were coming, it would be on a 108-year or 54-year schedule. The text in I Samuel declares the pestilence occurred "even to the time appointed." It was indeed on schedule.

By as early as 980 B.C., David felt impelled to build a temple to the glory of God, a monumental edifice. He was advised by the prophet Nathan that he should not, primarily because he was a man of war and had been involved in too many battles and too much blood shed. In addition to this primary reason for the delay in the construction of the temple, we note that the construction of such an edifice could take as much as ten to fifteen years. The delay in construction of this great edifice was not only proper due to David's background, but fortuitous with respect to the coming holocaust. A half-built temple would have been ruined by the 972 B.C. holocaust. Of comparable significance is a verse of scripture in I Kings describing the celestial serenity of Solomon's reign:

> But now Yahweh my God has given me rest on every side: not one enemy, NO CALAMITIES. I therefore plan to build a temple for the name of Yahweh my God. . . . (I Kings 5:5 New Jerusalem Bible).

The import of this verse is lost in the King James translation. Ground for the temple was broken in 967 B.C., five years after the Davidic Catastrophe, four years after Solomon assumed the throne.

DEPOPULATION. During the Isaiahic Catastrophe, an estimated 5 to 10% of the population of Palestine that night was destroyed. The Joel-Amos Catastrophe destroyed an estimated 3 to 5%. The Greater Davidic Catastrophe is recorded as killing 70,000 men *(not including women and children)* in the united Israel, which may have had a population of nearly 4,000,000. The seventy thousand deaths are recorded as including the area "from Dan to Beersheba," their counterpart for "from Maine to California," the national boundaries. If Israel had a population of 1,400,000 men, the true casualty rate may have been close to

200,000 or 5% of the populace. There was a census to account for the living and the dead. (A comparable depopulation for the United States in 1973 would be 10,000,000 person in one day.) Depopulation occurred through four modes:

1. Through bolidic explosions destroying large areas, and meteors destroying smaller spots.
2. Through prairie fires, set by meteoritic debris.
3. Through earthquakes, causing the collapse of buildings and city walls.
4. Through fright and heart attacks among an apprehensive populace.

If this catastrophe claimed the lives of 5% of the populace, it can hardly be classified as a minor holocaust.

In the Elijahic Catastrophe, three of five major keys were observed indicating the nature and the timing of the catastrophe as one among the long, cyclic series. The literature (I Kings and I Chronicles) includes the following keys highlighting the astronomical nature of this Davidic catastrophe:

1. It occurred 108 years before the Elijahic event, 216 years before the Joel-Amos event.
2. It occurred at the expected time, "the time appointed" which we conclude was on the 108-year schedule and in late October.
3. It involved bolidic and meteoritic outpourings, Mars-meteors from on high.
4. It included descriptive cosmological movements:
   a. The angel of the Lord passing over.
   b. The sword of the Lord, threatening Jerusalem from on high.

Our fifth category, severe earthquakes, is not mentioned specifically. However, since 70,000 men lost their lives in this one small section of our planet, unrecorded earthquake activity with associated collapsing structures is suspected.

Under such cosmic conditions, it is little wonder that the Hebrews were reluctant to start the temple until after "the appointed time" of cosmic disturbance. When they did build, huge quarried stones were carefully hewn and secured together with mortar, hopefully to make the structure earthquake-proof. (Fitting the stones together was a trade requiring the best of ancient skills.) Apparently the temple did last until the 756 B.C. episode. At that time, cracks allowing sunlight to come in developed during severe earthquake activity. That is, the temple stood without need of refurbishing for 211 years, from 967 B.C. to 756 B.C.

HOMER'S *ILIAD*. The Greater Davidic Catastrophe of 972 B.C. was the background for the staging time for launching a Greek attack on Troy. The catastrophic day in the year 972 B.C. must have been the issue behind Book I of the *Iliad*. Here, Calchus,[18] the son of Thestor, was the augur or seer "wisest of the augurs, who knew things past present and to come. . . ."[19]

> "Son of Atreus," said he, "I deem that we should now turn roving home if we would escape destruction, for we are being cut down by war and pestilence at once. Let us ask some priest or prophet, or some reader of dreams (for dreams, too, are of Zeus) who can tell us why Phoebus Apollo is so angry. . . ."[20]

The personal behavior of Agamemnon, one of the Greek rulers and generals, was also considered serious enough, potentially, to anger Apollo and his orbital movements. Thus the Greeks, seers and generals alike, felt they were facing difficult questions:

> ". . . Surely Zeus, who thunders from Olympus, might have made that little glorious. It is not so. Agamemnon, son of Atreus, has done me dishonor, and has robbed me of my prize by force. . . ." "On this the rest of the Achaeans with one voice were for respecting the priest and taking the ransom that he offered; but not so Agamemnon, who spoke fiercely to him and sent him roughly away. So he went back in anger, and Apollo, who loved him dearly, heard his prayer. Then the god sent a deadly dart upon the Argives [*one of the Greek tribes*], and the people died thick

---

[18] Calchus' Hebrew counterpart was the prophet Gad, concerned about David's census and the timing of the construction of the national temple.

[19] Homer, *Iliad*, Book I, p. 9.

[20] Homer, *Iliad*, Book I, pp. 8-9. Apollo is merely the Hellenized form of Baal or Bel. Intercultural flows of goods and ideas between Greece and Phoenicia were abundant during this era.

on one another, for the arrows went every-whither among the wide host of the Achaeans. At last a seer in the fullness of his knowledge declared to us the oracles of Apollo. . . ."[21]

The balance of the account of conflict in the *Iliad* is in reality a double conflict, both quite casualty-ridden. One conflict is between the Earth-Moon system and Mars (Hera and Apollo/Ares, the bane of mortals, the marauding celestial, hardly controllable by father Zeus or by sister Venus-Aphrodite). The second conflict, going on simultaneously, was the marine assault across the Aegean Sea on the stronghold of Troy. Both conflicts caused many casualties.

This is the Troy which Heinrich Schliemann discovered in 1868, based on his insight that the geography of the *Iliad* had a solid core of truth.[22] Up to and during Schliemann's time, the *Iliad,* along with the book of Joshua and others, had been classified as myths, as fairy tales, as folklore, by cynics, "superior" scholars, reacting out of the frame of reference of the nebular hypothesis. We doubt seriously that the *Iliad* can be really well-understood unless one realizes that there is also a solid core of truth in the *cosmology* of the *Iliad* as well as the *geography* contained therein.[23]

---

[21]Homer, *Iliad*, Book I, pp. 15-16.

[22]Reference is made to C. W. Ceram, *Gods Graves and Scholars,* New York: Alfred A. Knopf, Chapters IV and V, pp. 29 ff. and to the section on Schliemann on p. 169 of this volume.

[23]For an example of the celestial cosmology in the *Iliad*, we quote the following:

Thus did the gods spur on both hosts to fight, and rouse fierce contention among themselves. The sire of gods and men thundered from heaven above, while from beneath Poseidon shook the vast earth, and bade the high hills tremble. The spurs and crests of many-fountained Ida quaked, as also the city of the Trojans and the ships of the Achaeans. . . . Such was the uproar as the gods came together into battle. Apollo with his arrows took his stand to face King Poseidon, while Athene took hers against the god of war; the archer-goddess Artemis with her golden arrows, sister of far-darting Apollo, stood to face Hera; Hermes, the lusty bringer of good luck, faced Leto. . . . The gods, then, were thus ranged against one another.

The *Iliad, op. cit.,* p. 310. Note and compare the description of Homer that the oceans were in tidal wave upheaval while the high hills trembled, the spurs and crests of Crete quaked. Moses, in Psalm 114 (describing an earlier but similar catastrophe) wrote that "the mountains skipped like rams, and the little hills like lambs." He continues to also discuss oceanic

The picture of cosmology in the background of events is:

1. Ares-Apollo in its biennial pass near (and on occasion through) the Earth-Moon system.
2. Ares-Apollo and its deep biennial appointment with "father" Jupiter (Zeus-pater) in the cosmological deep, a resonance appointment for Apollo-Mars.
3. Ares-Apollo and its biennial lap or line-up with Aphrodite-Venus, where, as it would appear, Aphrodite might influence its "brother" away from Hera.

The Lesser Davidic Catastrophe
Estimated 1025 B.C.

This catastrophe is considered more of a threatening condition than a genuine holocaust, more of a minor catastrophe. It is dated by the model, and evidence from Biblical sources is extremely limited.

David was born about 1041 B.C., and died at the age of 70 in 971 B.C. He was 18 years old when he met the giant, Goliath, on the field of battle and emerged, surprisingly, victorious. He was 15 or 16 years old during the close conjunction of 1024/25 B.C. David's cosmic description of what we *think* is this event occurs both in II Samuel 22:8-19 and Psalm 18:7-18.

> Then the earth shook and trembled; the foundations of heaven moved and shook, because he was wroth. There went up a smoke out of his nostrils, and fire out of his mouth devoured: coals were kindled by it. He bowed the heavens also, and came down; and darkness was under his feet.
>
> And he rode upon a cherub, and did fly: and he was seen upon the wings of the wind. And he made darkness pavil-

upheaval, "What ailed thee, O thou sea, that thou fleddest? thou Jordan (Lake Menzelah) that thou wast driven back?"

Moses was observing near the Mediterranean Sea on the Suez Isthmus in 1447 B.C. whereas Homer was reporting from somewhere in the Aegean, perhaps from Crete, in 972 B.C., both being preoccupied with celestial events and physiographical effects on Earth. David observed the threatening condition in 1025 B.C. from an interior location (near Bethlehem) where no sea or ocean in upheaval was apparent, but where celestial and crustal disturbances were a concern, and his observations are quoted in the next section.

ions round about him, dark waters, and thick clouds of the skies. Through the brightness before him were coals of fire kindled. The Lord thundered from heaven, and the most High uttered his voice.

And he sent out arrows, and scattered them; lightning, and discomfited them. And the channels of the sea appeared, the foundations of the world were discovered, at the rebuking of the Lord, at the blast of the breath of his nostrils. He sent from above . . . . (II Samuel 22:8-17)

This text contains (in abundance) three of the five categories of evidence for which we look concerning an astronomical catastrophe. They are:

1. Meteoritic and bolidic blizzards from on high.
2. Severe earthquakes and probably associated vulcanism.
3. Descriptive cosmic scenery.

The dating is but an educated estimate based on the resonant orbit model.

The Samuelic Catastrophe
Estimated 1080 B.C.

And as Samuel was offering up the burnt offering, the Philistines drew near to battle against Israel: but THE LORD THUNDERED WITH A GREAT THUNDER ON THAT DAY upon the Philistines, and discomfited them. . . . (I Samuel 7:10)

This text, extremely brief in the Bible, is expanded in *The Antiquities of the Jews* by Josephus. His source material was much more abundant than ours; among his sources were Egyptian, Babylonian, and Phoenician literatures in addition to much more Hebrew source material.

But things so fell out, that they would hardly have been credited, though they had been foretold by anybody; for in the first place, God disturbed their enemies WITH AN EARTHQUAKE, and moved the ground under them to such a degree, that he caused it to tremble, and made them to shake, insomuch that by its trembling he made some unable to keep their feet, and make them fall down, and by opening its chasms, he caused that others should be hurried down into them: after which he caused such a noise of

> thunder to come among them, and made FIERY LIGHTNING SHINE SO TERRIBLY ROUND ABOUT THEM. . . . [24]

Philistine armies like later Assyrian armies, were given over to the idea of confronting their enemy (Israel) on the date of expected cosmic intervention; "let the deities be involved in the decision of battle." In 701 B.C. the Jews were facing the Assyrians; in 972 B.C. the Greeks were facing the Trojans; in 1080 B.C. the Hebrews were facing the Philistines; and in 1404 B.C. the Hebrews were facing the Canaanites in the decisive battle for the control of central Palestine.

Some destruction enveloped the Philistine forces; even more so, fear and panic caught them. The Jewish armies were quick to seize the advantage. According to our calculations, this holocaust was 324 years later (to the day) than the Long Day of Joshua in 1404 B.C. Thus the Samuelic Catastrophe was 324 years after the Long Day of Joshua, even as the Joel-Amos Catastrophe was just 324 years in the future.

> . . . and there he [Samuel] set up a stone as a boundary of their victory, and their enemy's flight, and called it the "Stone of Power," as a signal of that power God had given them against their enemies.[25]

The "stone of power" was a large, impressive meteorite, and it was selected, appropriately enough, for an historical monument.

That kind of monument occurs elsewhere on the Arabian peninsula. During one or another of these many cyclic catastrophes a meteorite fell in or near Mecca, for the black stone of Kaaba in Mecca is also a meteorite. In ancient times, it, too, fell from the sky, and became a holy thing to surrounding tribes. Later it was brought into the Islamic faith, an adoption from local cosmic lore. One ancient Arabian legend relates that it was brought down by the Archangel Gabriel, an archangel or celestial being sometimes considered a governor of the luminaries.

---

[24] Flavius Josephus, *The Antiquities of the Jews*, translated by William Whiston, Bridgeport: M. Sherman, 1828, Book VI, Chapter II, section 2, p. 8.

[25] Flavius Josephus, *loc. cit.*

While Muslim pilgrims may travel thousands of miles to kiss the holy stone, it is also true, earlier, that the holy stone tumbled millions of miles orbiting through space before it finally arrived at Mecca. This is to say that the meteorite was a celestial pilgrim, in all likelihood a Mars-asteroid, once a part of the fragmented planet, Electra. It has found its current resting place in Mecca, probably two millenia before Mohammed was born.

THE DATING. There is no specific dating in extant literature for this catastrophe. It occurred while Samuel was still a young priest. The likely dates of Samuel's life are circa 1115 B.C. to 1015 B.C. Samuel was a young priest in the year 1080 B.C., our projected year of cosmic intervention. Any other particulars on dating have eluded these researchers.

Many comparisons could be drawn between Hebrew catastrophic literature of the Davidic era and Greek cosmic descriptions of the Homeric era. Two Homeric descriptions follow. The reader may want to compare them to previously-cited Hebrew texts:

> All had then been lost and no help for it, for they would have been penned up in Ilium like sheep, had not the sire of gods and men been quick to mark, AND HURLED A FIERY FLAMING THUNDERBOLT which fell just in front of Diomed's horses with a flare of burning brimstone.[26]

> Thus did the gods spur on both hosts to fight, and rouse fierce contention also among themselves. The sire of gods and men THUNDERED FROM HEAVEN ABOVE, WHILE FROM BENEATH POSEIDON [*lord of seas and tidal waves therein*] SHOOK THE VAST EARTH, and MADE THE HIGH HILLS TREMBLE. The spurs and crests of many-fountained Ida quaked, as also the city of the Trojans. . . . Such was the uproar as the gods came together in battle.[27]

---

[26] Homer, *Iliad*, Book VIII, p. 116.

[27] Homer, *Iliad*, Book XX, p. 310. When Schliemann undertook his startling mission to discover Troy, the Turkish natives pointed him toward Hisslarik, the traditional site for the ancient city. Schliemann, being too familiar with the *Iliad*, did not find the spring of Ida at Hisslarik and looked a few miles elsewhere. Schliemann's geographical insight was the difference between success and failure, and his attention to literary detail provided his basic geographical insight.

On Schliemann's Archaeology

Schliemann, the great German pioneer of archaeology of 100 years ago, was sufficiently sure that Homer's *Iliad* was good history, and good geography, to undertake extensive archaeological diggings at his own personal expense. He had no foundation funds backing his expedition. He discovered the ancient site of Troy, and smuggled out gold and silver coins, masks, implements of war and so forth, which made even his most dubious critics respectful, if not envious. When he followed this coup by duplicating the feat at Mycenae (discovering in the process Agamemnon's mask) the critics folded their tents and joined, even led the enthusiasm for Schliemann's work.

Homer's cosmology was just as good, and just as important as was his geography, but today's scholars, laboring under the evolutionary-uniformitarian delusion, have been entirely unaware. The following observation well-describes Schliemann's unusual motivation for his history-moving (if not earth-shaking) theory and venture:

> Every plane of advance is first laid by retroduction alone, that is to say, by the spontaneous conjectures of instinctive reason.—Charles Sanders Peirce

The Deborah Debacle

Estimated 1188 B.C.

They fought from heaven, the stars[28] in their courses[29] fought against Sisera. (Judges 5:20)

According to a literal interpretation of the chronicles of Judges (which we favor), the theocracy under Barak and Deborah lasted 40 years (Judges 5:31), 1228 B.C. to 1188 B.C. The above cited brief reference indicates that celestial concerns were not dormant during the 12th century B.C.

---

[28]"Stars" is from the Hebrew word *kowkab*, a blazing or rolling star, a shining star, a luminary, and we propose, a rotating planet such as Mars.

[29]"Courses" is from the Hebrew word *mecillah*, which Strong's Concordance translates as a viaduct, a staircase, a causeway, a course, a highway, a path, a terrace, and our belief is it could also be accurately translated "an orbit", or "orbits", paths of the luminaries.

SUMMARY

Isaiahic Catastrophe Case One
- Date: March 20, 701 B.C.
- Distance: Mars estimated at 70,000 miles
- Geometry: Mars passed north of ecliptic plane
- Pass: Mars fly-by on Earth's sunward-side
- Rotational Scheme: Palestine at mid-evening (perigee)

Joel-Amos Catastrophe Case Two
- Date: October 25, 756 B.C.
- Distance: Mars estimated at 100,000 miles
- Geometry: Mars passed north of ecliptic plane
- Pass: Mars fly-by on Earth's sunward-side
- Rotational Scheme: Palestine at mid-afternoon (perigee)

Elijahic Catastrophe Case Two
- Date: October 25, 864 B.C.
- Distance: Mars at 200,000 miles
- Geometry: Mars passed north of ecliptic plane
- Pass: Mars fly-by on Earth's sunward-side
- Rotational Scheme: Palestine at mid-evening (perigee)

Greater Davidic Catastrophe Case Two
- Date: October 25, 972 B.C.
- Distance: Mars at 120,000 miles
- Geometry: Mars passed north of ecliptic plane
- Pass: Mars fly-by on Earth's sunward-side
- Rotational Scheme: Palestine at early afternoon (perigee)

Lesser Davidic Catastrophe Case One
- Date: March 20/21, 1025 B.C.
- Distance: Mars at 200,000 miles
- Geometry: Mars passed north of ecliptic plane
- Pass: Mars fly-by on Earth's sunward-side
- Rotational Scheme: Unknown, possibly in Palestine night

Samuelic Catastrophe Case Two
- Date: October 25, 1080 B.C.
- Distance: Mars at 150,000 miles
- Geometry: Mars passed north of ecliptic plane
- Pass: Mars fly-by on Earth's sunward-side
- Rotational Scheme: Palestine at mid-day

Deborah	Date	October 25, 1188 B.C.
Debacle	Distance	Mars at 150,000 miles
Case Two	Geometry	Mars passed north of ecliptic plane
	Pass	Mars fly-by on Earth's sunward side
	Rotational Scheme	Fly-by during Palistine daytime

Perhaps Hamlet is right that there are more things in heaven and earth than are dreamed of in our philosophy; but on the other hand it may be said that there are a good many things in our natural philosophy books, of which neither in heaven nor on earth may any trace be found. — G. C. Lichtenstein

One can spend years of searching in the dark for a truth that one feels but cannot express.—Albert Einstein

chapter **VII**

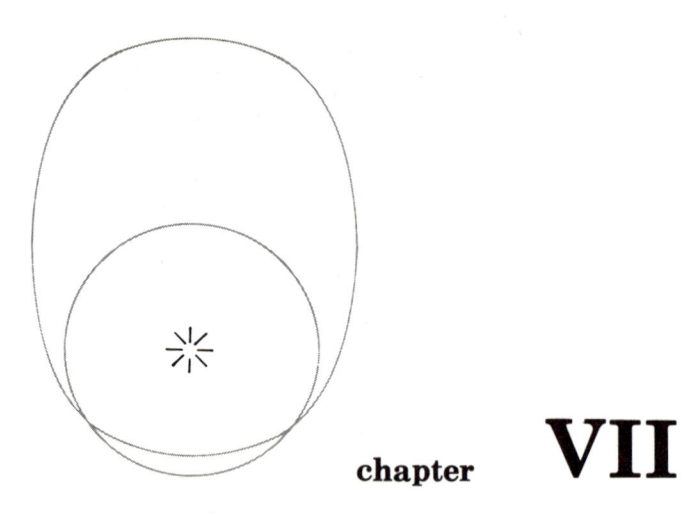

The Long Day of Joshua

circa October 25, 1404 B.C.

This chapter concerns the famous if never understood "Long Day," which was indeed longer, but not as long as tradition states. There were other days, both before and after, when Earth's spin axis relocated or shifted, but the shift on each of the other crisis days was not quite like the shift or relocation of this day. We will offer a reason why.

This chapter will consider astronomical, geographical and historical aspects of this renowned day. There were two spin axis precessions within 50 years of each other in this catastrophic century, the fifteenth century B.C., and there was little guarantee (to the ancients) that there would not be more. If so, sightings of the marauding planet would be ever more necessary, and the locations of due east, due north, the rising and setting of the Sun in the several seasons and of the solstices, and other astronomical data would be essential to gather and to understand.

We believe this was the reason for the construction of many ancient sun or planet temples, obelisks and gnomons, sun caves and astronomical charts. We suspect that the astronomical temple of Stonehenge in England was constructed before, not after this crisis day, and in response to the Tower of Babel event rather than to this particular

THE LONG DAY OF JOSHUA

catastrophe. However, the two crises were quite similar. Both were "Case Two" crises. Both occurred in late October, one in 1404 B.C. and the other in 1930 B.C.

Dating The Catastrophe

THE DATING OF THE LONG DAY OF JOSHUA will be considered in four ways. One is by the resonant model for the ancient Martian orbit. A second is based upon the chronicles of Scripture. A third is based on the records of Josephus, and Talmudic information. (Josephus is somewhat sketchy, but both are helpful.) Our fourth perspective in dating is not concerned with the year date, or the day of the month, but rather with the observation that heavy holocausts tended to bunch in pairs every five to six centuries.

Dating By The Resonant Orbit Model

Figure 24 illustrates again the resonant orbit model as it applies to the fifteenth century B.C. and the Long Day of Joshua. This is the century of the Long Day of Joshua and its immediate predecessor, the Exodus Catastrophe. According to our model, catastrophes or threatening catastrophes should be expected once every 54 years, or once every 108 years on the average. We observe the following:

The Joel-Amos Catastrophe	Oct. 25, 756 B.C.	add 108 years
The Elijahic Catastrophe	Oct. 25, 864 B.C.	add 108 years
The Greater Davidic Catastrophe	Oct. 25, 972 B.C.	add 108 years
The Samuelic Catastrophe	Oct. 25, 1080 B.C.	add 108 years
The Deborah Debacle	Oct. 25, 1188 B.C.	add 216 years
The Long Day of Joshua	Oct. 25, 1404 B.C.	

Figure: orbital diagram showing Mars' Aphelion, Mars' Ancient Orbit, Earth's Old Orbit, Sun, Mars' Perihelion, The October 25 Location, The Case Two Location

THE LONG DAY OF JOSHUA CATASTROPHE REGION

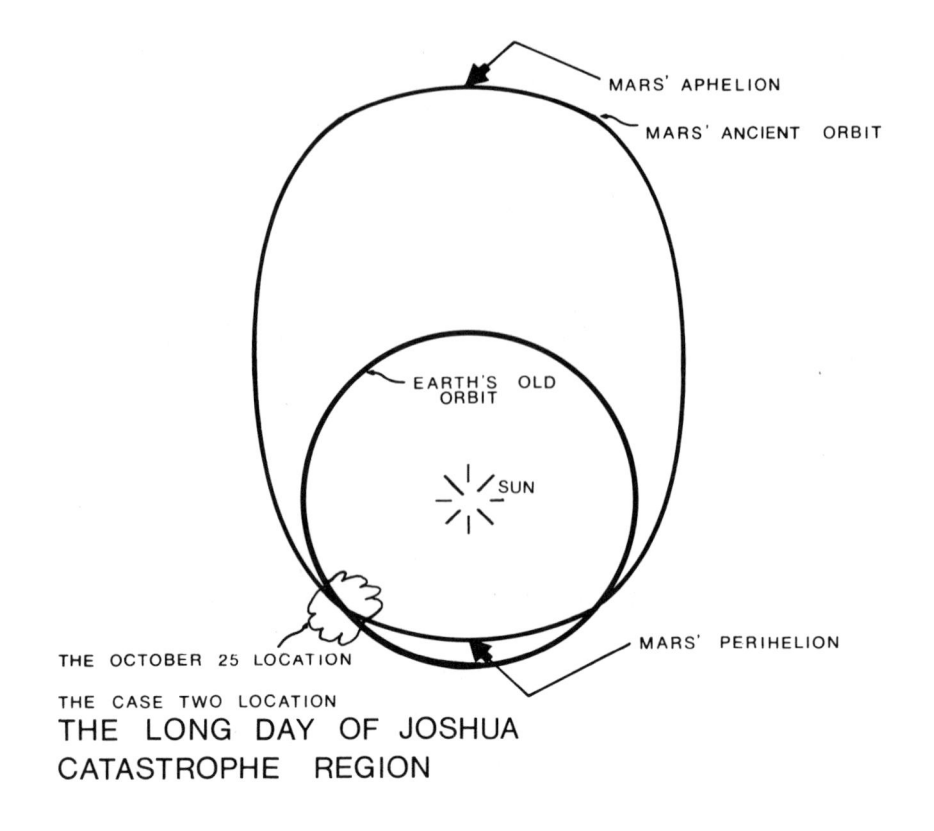

THE GEOMETRY OF THE LONG DAY OF JOSHUA CATASTROPHE

ORBITS AS SEEN FROM POLARIS

FIGURE 24

This geometry is a repeat of the Tower of Babel event some 526 years earlier, and the Joel-Amos event 648 years later. This event may be the basis for the Phaethon story (see Figures 40 and 41), or it may possibly be a return performance of the Phaethon story, thus a reinforcement of the frightful story in Greek cosmological lore.

Note that 216 years, the suspected interlude between the Deborah Debacle and The Long Day, is a multiple of 108. This list suggests that there were six full cycles of inferior conjunctions, six pendulums of 108 years, between the Joel-Amos event and the Joshuaic event, or 648 years. This makes an impressive list if one can allow that minor holocausts may have threatened or even occurred in 1080 B.C., 1188 B.C. and 1296 B.C., and for which there are few extant records.

This may not be a complete analysis. We have not searched the records of the *Vedas* of India nor the spectrum of other ancient literatures including Greek, Persian, Chinese and others. We understand that catastrophic themes are easily recognizable, but to date them is difficult and elusive. Hebrew history, on the other hand, is generally well-dated.[1]

Dating By Scriptural Chronologies

First of all, Scripture indicates that the Exodus events occurred during the year 1447 B.C. as we now calibrate time. This was just 480 years earlier than the laying of the foundation, and the building of Solomon's temple. This is recorded in I Kings 6:1. If David died in 971 B.C., which is established, and if Solomon had no co-regency with David, then Solomon's temple was started in 967 B.C. The four year interval between 971 B.C. and 967 B.C. was the period when Solomon consolidated power and finished the architectural plans.

> And it came to pass in the four hundred and eightieth year after the children of Israel were come out of the land of Egypt, in the fourth year of Solomon's reign over Israel, in the month Zif, which is the second month, that he began to build the house of the Lord. (I Kings 6:1)

Following the Exodus events of 1447 B.C., such as the flight from Egypt, the astronomical passover, the sea-swelling and the giving of the Decalogue on Mt. Sinai, there ensued 40 years of wandering in the wilderness. This continued through 1407 B.C. Following this were the conquests of Bashan and Gilead east of

---

[1]The most poorly-dated era of Hebrew history is the era of the Judges, 1400 B.C. to 1000 B.C., the era of our attention. Later events and earlier events are much more carefully dated as well as being more widely discussed.

the Jordan, and the crossing at Jericho which we believe was captured in the spring of 1404 B.C. Its walls shuddered and collapsed about the time of the vernal equinox.[2] Following the capture of Jericho was the assault on the Central Highlands, especially on Ai and Gibeon. By the time the Canaanite armies federated, gathered and challenged the Hebrew invasion, it was autumn of 1404 B.C., and the day of celestial crisis was approaching.

Dating By The Works Of Josephus

If we assume from Scriptural chronologies that 1447 B.C. was the year of the Exodus, then Josephus records that by 1402 B.C., two years after the Long Day of Joshua, Hebrew forces had conquered Eastern Palestine, Central Palestine, and Southern Palestine, as well as a good portion of Northern Palestine.

> The fifth year was now past, and there was not one of the Canaanites remained any longer, excepting some that had retired to places of great strength.[3]

Thus we conclude that the campaign of Joshua in Central Palestine, and the battle at Bethhoron (on the Long Day) was in 1404 B.C., or less likely, in 1406 B.C.

The *Talmud* also indicates Canaan was subdued within 47 years of the Exodus Catastrophe, or by 1400 B.C.

> At the end of seven years of warfare, Joshua could at last venture to parcel out the conquered land among the tribes.[4]

Centuries Of Double Catastrophes

The phenomenon of heavy twin catastrophes across the cen-

---

[2] The vernal equinox time (March 20-21), the first day of spring, continues to be a time of magnetic storm activity, and especially when the Moon is in perigee, a time of earthquake activity. The majority of the severe earthquakes in the twentieth century A.D. have occurred in the months of March and April, when the moon was in perigee.

[3] Flavius Josephus, *The Antiquities of the Jews*, translated by William Whiston, Bridgeport: M. Sherman, 1828, Book V, Chapter I, section 19, pp. 292-293.

[4] Louis Ginzberg, *The Legends of the Jews,* Philadelphia: Jewish Publication Society of America, 1913, Vol. IV, p. 15.

turies should be observed. If a century had one very severe holocaust, very likely it also had another. See figure 34, Page 253.

The Eighth Century B.C.	Case 1	The Isaiahic Castastrophe, March, 701 B.C.
	Case 2	The Joel-Amos Catastrophe, October, 756 B.C.
The Fifteenth Century B.C.	Case 1	The Exodus Catastrophe, March, 1447 B.C.
	Case 2	The Long Day of Joshua, October, 1404 B.C.
The Twentieth Century B.C.	Case 1	The Sodom-Gomorrah Catastrophe, March, 1877 B.C.
	Case 2	The Tower of Babel Catastrophe, October, 1930 B.C.

Thus, double catastrophes occurred in the eighth century, the fifteenth century, the twentieth century and perhaps the twenty-fifth century B.C. This phenomenon could be explained by the theory that approximately every five centuries, literary figures with cosmic styles just happened to blossom. This would be the "chance" theory. However, this phenomenon of twin catastrophes every five or six centuries may be a result of a grander cycle. A discussion of the grand cycle of catastrophism, involving cycles of 500 to 600 years, is reserved for Chapter X. It concerns the influences of both Jupiter and Saturn on the orbit of Mars.

We have discussed the two-year cycle of the period of the former Martian orbit. We have also discussed the 108-year average cycle of inferior conjunctions of Earth and Mars. Now we note the possibility of yet another, greater cycle operating, one yielding particularly severe crises (in pairs) every five to six centuries. This grander cycle may well be the basis for ancient writers who discuss world ages coming to abrupt closes, followed by successive world ages. Ovid is one example of this (in his discussion of the four ages) and Josephus is another example.

> Now when Noah had lived three hundred and fifty years after the flood . . . and because their food was then fitter for the prolongation of life, might well live so great a

number of years: and besides, God afforded them a longer time of life on account of their virtue, and the good use they made of it in ASTRONOMICAL AND GEOMETRICAL DISCOVERIES, which would not have afforded the time for foretelling [the periods of the stars], unless they had lived six hundred years, for THE GREAT YEAR IS COMPLETED IN THAT INTERVAL.[5]

Characteristics Of The Long Day Of Joshua

There are five characteristics which we look for in the later Mars catastrophes, discussed in Chapters III through VII. They are:
1. Threatening conditions should occur every 54 years or every 108 years.
2. Major holocausts should occur on or about March 20/21 or October 25th.
3. Such should involve the dumping of meteoritic and bolidic materials on Earth.
4. Such should involve earthquakes and perhaps spin axis wobbles.
5. Such should include descriptive cosmic developments or scenery.

Dating By Day And Month

If our dating of this holocaust is correct, it occurred just exactly 216 years, 324 years, 432 years, 540 years and 648 years earlier, respectively, than the later catastrophic days just discussed.

There is only one way, other than circumstantial evidence, of deducing that the Long Day of Joshua was in the autumn; however the model dictates this. There is a strange passage in the *Talmud* accompanying the general discussion of the parcelling out of the land of Canaan among the Israelites. (The Hebrew month of Marchesvan may have been named after *ma'or* or Mars and began about October 7.) This strange statement teaches that persons living in that era could freely travel about from the close of the harvest season (roughly July) until the seventeenth day of Marchesvan, after which travel was dan-

---

[5] Flavius Josephus, *op. cit.*, Book I, Chapter III, section 7, p. 87.

gerous and not recommended. Any who died in travel during this period after Marchesvan 17 were to be buried "on the spot" and not given burial ceremonies.[6] Marchesvan 18 in the Hebrew calendar (October 25) is the day we presume for the Long Day of Joshua in 1404 B.C.

Meteoritic And Bolidic Materials

This is one of the two great features of the Long Day of Joshua. On this day of celestial warfare, perhaps a third of a million men met on the field of battle at Bethhoron, the Canaanite general militia and the Jewish invading hordes.

> And it came to pass, as they fled from before Israel, and were in the going down to Bethhoron, that the Lord cast down GREAT STONES[7] from heaven upon them unto Azekah, and they died: they were more which died with HAILSTONES[8] than they whom the children of Israel slew with the sword. (Joshua 10:11)

In the Greater Davidic Catastrophe, 972 B.C., 70,000 men (perhaps 5% of the populace) were destroyed. In the Isaiahic Catastrophe, 701 B.C., an even greater number of casualties occurred. If the Canaanite armies numbered 200,000 men (not an unreasonable possibility) and half perished, then the number of casualties approximated the toll of the Greater Davidic Catastrophe. Some we believe were slain by meteoritic hits, some by sweeping prairie fires, but most by exploding bolides. Bolides, like the Tunguska Bolide, can explode with forces rivalling nuclear bombs.

Earthquakes And Earth-Shakings

Earthquakes are defined as crustal tremblings, fractures and faulting of the crust. Earth-shakings we define as spin-axis

---

[6]Louis Ginzberg, *op. cit.*, Vol. IV, p. 16.

[7]"Stones" is from the Hebrew word *'eben* suggesting stones or weights. These were not ordinary stones shot from catapults, but "great" *(gadol,* high, loud, mighty, exceedingly) stones, and they came DOWN from the astronomical skies, not across open countryside.

[8]"Hailstones" is from the Hebrew word *barad* and indicates bolides and/or meteorites.

shifts or precessions. There are no records of earthquakes in the Bible, nor in Josephus nor in *The Book of Jasher,* during the Long Day of Joshua, but there is record in the *Talmud:*

> The earth quaked and trembled from the noise of Thy thunder against them. . . . [9]

Concerning "earth-shakings," spin axis shifts, the one of the Long Day of Joshua is the one which has received the most publicity, although we doubt that it was the worst in terms of distance for polar migration or for change in tilt.

> Then spake Joshua to the Lord . . . and he said in the sight of Israel, SUN, STAND THOU STILL upon Gibeon [*to the east*]; AND THOU, MOON, in the Valley of Ajalon [*to the northwest*]. And the sun stood still, and the moon stayed. . . . So the Sun stood still in the midst of heaven, and hasted not to go down about a whole day. (Joshua 10:12-13)

The following account describes a similar event, coming from the neighboring Greece, the famous Phaethon story of Greek cosmo-mythology:

> Phaethon, in Greek mythology, was the son of Helios, the sun-god, and the nymph Clymene. He persuaded his father to let him drive the chariot of the sun across the sky, but he lost control of the horses and, driving too near the earth, scorched it. To save the world from utter destruction Zeus killed Phaethon with a thunderbolt. . . . [10,11]

---

[9] Louis Ginzberg, *op. cit.,* Vol. IV, p. 12. This describes the Long Day of Joshua occasion.

[10] *Encyclopaedia Britanica,* Chicago: Wm. Benton, publisher, 1958, Vol. 17, p. 687. "The story is most fully told in the *Metamorphoses* of Ovid (i, 750, ii, 366, and Nonnus, *Dionysiaca,* xxxviii)."

[11] See also Ingri and Edgar Parin D'Aulaire, *Book of Greek Myths,* New York, Doubleday and Co. Inc., 1962, pp 82-84. Helios was the sun-god; Phaethon was his son.
   "One morning as Helios was about to set off on his daily journey across the sky, Phaethon came to him and begged him to grant his dearest wish. . . . He tried in vain to make his son change his mind, for what Phaethon wanted was to drive the sun chariot for one day, and Helios knew that no one but he himself could handle the spirited steeds.
   Phaethon was determined to have his wish, and Helios had to give in.

Among many other nations, including the Maori or Polynesian story of Maui (discussed in Chapter II), there are similar traditions. Early morning in Palestine (the Long Day of Joshua was a morning phenomenon), was late afternoon or evening in Maori-land. Perhaps the Maori rendition of a spin axis precession comes from the Long Day of Joshua. It could also have originated during the Exodus Catastrophe of 1447 B.C., when the height of the catastrophe was at the midnight hour, Palestine time, and was early afternoon in Polynesia. We are not sure.

Traditionally, in the "intellectual circles" of Western society, the Phaethon story has been classified as fanciful myth along with the Long Day of Joshua. This is partly because there has been no place for catastrophism in the popular if feeble evolutionary nebulous hypothesis. This is also partly because "ration-

> Sadly, he put his golden rays on his son's head and rubbed divine ointment on his skin so he could withstand the searing heat of the chariot. He barely had time to warn him to stay well in the middle of the heavenly path when the gates of the palace were thrown open, and the rearing horses were brought forth. Phaethon leaped into the chariot, grasped the reins, and the horses rushed out.
> At first, all went well and Phaethon stood proudly in the glowing chariot. But the fiery steeds soon felt that unskilled hands were holding the reins. They veered off the heavenly path and brushed by the dangerous constellations that lurked on both sides of it. The animals of the zodiac were enraged: the bull charged, the lion growled, the scorpion lashed out with its poisonous tail. The horses shied and Phaethon was thrown half-way out of the chariot. Without a firm hand to guide them, the horses bolted. . . .
> Zeus stood on Olympus and shook his head. He had to stop the careening chariot to save the earth from destruction, and he threw a thunderbolt at it. In a shower of sparks, the chariot flew apart and Phaethon plunged into the river Po. . . .
> Hephaestus had to work the whole night through to mend the broken chariot so Helios could drive it again the next day. Helios grieved over his lost son, and he never again allowed anyone to drive his chariot except for Apollo, the god of light."

We cannot guarantee that either the Phaethon story from Greece, or for that matter the Maui story from New Zealand describes the Long Day. The latter may well describe the more ancient Sodom-Gomorrah catastrophe of 1877 B.C. And it may possibly be a double description of both days. There is a hint that this was a case 2 catastrophe in October from the citation of the activity of Scorpio. Scorpio's period in the zodiac was October 7 to November 6 whereas the Sodom-Gomorrah event was in March. Therefore we favor the conclusion that the Phaethon story is just the Hellenized version of the Long Day of Joshua, but our confidence is of the range of 80% as to the particular, specific catastrophe which the Phaethon story describes. See Figures 40 and 41, pp. 284-285.

With 100% confidence, however, we can affirm that modern cynics, radicals and rationalists, who ascribe this story to mere fancy, are entangled in a mistaken set of assumptions.

alists" have had a major influence on Western education and have been hostile to the good history of the Scriptures.

The Phaethon story is *not* an ancient Greek yarn; it *does* contain a significant core of truth: a crazily wandering sun in the sky and scorching bolts falling on Earth. Ancients, of course, lacked telescopes, lacked celestial mechanics and gravitational theory, lacked most forms of calculus and mass publication. However, since they lived during the era of the fearful Martian holocausts, this kind of "Phaethon" explanation helped satisfy the Greek mind. The human mind indeed has a need for explanation. (That such stories have *amused* some of today's "experts" is insignificant because the theories of some contemporary "experts" may indeed amuse future experts of another century.)

Gyroscopic theory informs us that a sphere, or for that matter a cylinder, can, while rotating, be caused to precess and/or to spin about a second axis. Examples are numerous. A bicycle wheel that is spinning and held by one hand on one end of the axis will precess. If it is tossed in the air while precessing then the gravitational force causing the precession is removed, and the wheel will spin around a new axis. This appears to the eye as a wobble. In the Earth the analogy is a geographical relocation of the spin axis on the Earth, which defines a new north pole. The Earth is a giant gyroscope with an 8000 mile diameter traveling freely in space while rotating. Under the proper conditions, Earth too can wobble, or precess. The question surrounding the Long Day of Joshua is not "Was there a spin axis precession on that day?," but rather, "What kind of spin axis precession occurred?"

There are several different possible geometries for the Martian fly-by. Hence there can be many directions of polar migration plus two directions for a shift in tilt. Also there can be several different distances possible for the fly-by causing different intensities of interaction. Therefore a variety of distances of polar migration are possible as well as many different directions possible.

If Mars was on a fly-by pattern about 70,000 miles distant and passed almost directly over the North Pole, the spin axis would precess first in one direction and then another. This is a unique type of spin axis precession, first forward and then backward; first one way and then the other. This, we propose, is why "there was no day like that before it or after it." (Joshua 10:14)

The Lengthening Of The Day

The Book of Jasher has an interesting account of this unique day. This has come from ancient Hebrew sources and its authority has been questioned; however, we feel it is of historical value. Its account is as follows:

> And the Lord hearkened to the voice of Joshua, and the sun stood still in the midst of the heavens, and it stood still SIX AND THIRTY MOMENTS,* and the moon also stood still and hastened not to go down a whole day. (Chapter 88:64)[12]

> *עתים, literally *times*; what portion of time, I cannot understand by this term, never used in scripture to express any division of time, so I have translated it *"moments."*[12]

The word for "day" in Joshua 10:13 is *yowm* in Hebrew. It is used to describe several divisions of time, not just 24 hours as it is used today. It often connotes "a time" such as a time of day or a time of year or a time of a season.

The exact amount of lengthening of the day may have been due in part to a change in latitude, and in part to a retilting of the spin axis. This resulted in a lengthening of the afternoon and evening. The lengthening may have been of the order of two to four hours. The change in the spin rate would have been negligible. The precession phenomenon could have made this autumn day like a midsummer day in length.

Scriptures hint that the spin axis shift was a matter of two to four hours in the following verse:

> And the sun stood still, and the moon stayed, UNTIL the people had avenged themselves upon their enemies. Is not this written in the book of Jasher? . . . (Joshua 10:13)

Up to this point a two-to-four hour extension of the day with shifting polar locations is within the text. But, not the following:

> . . . So the sun stood still in the midst of heaven, and hasted not to go down ABOUT A WHOLE DAY. (Joshua 10:13)

---

[12]*The Book of Jasher*, New York: M. M. Noah and A. S. Gould, 1840, p. 260.

Our conclusion is that in the original text some kind of time increment was indicated, but that the word used was misunderstood by later rabbinical translators and translated into something they could grasp. This is probably because the later rabbis could not conceive of the nature of the planet nor the nature of the spin axis shift. They had to write in terms which they could understand.

This problem of translation is related to the problem of the rabbis who criticized Hezekiah for adding a whole month onto the calendar between Nisan and Ziv, the first and the second months. (This would be like inserting a special month between January and February to users of the Julian calendar.) The rabbis felt it would be more logical to add one month at the *end* of the year. However, they asked the wrong question. "Why did Hezekiah add a month *after Nisan?*" should have been rephrased "Why did Hezekiah have to add a month *at all* to the ancient calendar?" This is one example of translators and copyists asking the wrong questions and coming up with dubious answers. Many have thus made calendaric errors. Similarly, we suspect that an addition to, or a corruption of, this original text occurred. The translator of *The Book of Jasher* is probably closer to the original meaning than are the modern Bible translations in this case. The time increment was two to four hours rather than "about a whole day."

Descriptive Cosmic Movements

This is the fifth of five categories for which we look in the ancient astronomical holocausts and their literatures. We believe that the Phaethon story of Greece applies to this particular catastrophe. If so, this is an example of descriptive cosmic movements, for it is a word picture of the Sun moving in an abnormal path across the sky, amid falling thunderbolts on Earth. We believe there is nothing in the Biblical record and almost nothing in the *Talmud* describing the actual passover of Mars. However, there is an interesting description in the book of Judges which may possibly be a *double description,* applying first to the Long Day of Joshua, and secondly to the Deborah Debacle some 216 years later.

> They fought from heaven; the stars [*planets*] in their courses fought against Sisera. (Judges 5:20)

Thus the four of the five types of phenomena we expect for holocausts have all been detected concerning the Long Day of Joshua. The spin axis precession indicates that Mars passed over particularly closely, and perhaps uniquely over the North Pole sector.

The Geographical Scene Of This Catastrophe

> Then spake Joshua . . . and he said in the sight of Israel, Sun, stand thou still UPON GIBEON [*in the eastern or morning sky*] . . . . (Joshua 10:12)

The Scriptural account suggests the major spin axis shift started in the very early morning, whereas the bolidic and meteoritic dumps arrived some two to three hours later, arriving at relative speeds of about 30,000 miles per hour.[13] It was a long afternoon, especially for the Canaanite forces which were decimated, if not annihilated. Gibeon was at the crest of the Central Highlands, the mountainous spine of Palestine running north and south. It was to the east of the battle scene around Mount Perizim and Bethhoron. This suggests the Martian fly-by was an early morning fly-by. The timing of the Phaethon story is similar; the Sun began to wander crazily across the *morning* sky. The bucking steeds drawing the solar chariot began bucking in the *morning*.

> . . . and thou, Moon, IN THE VALLEY OF AJALON. And the sun stood still, and the moon stayed. . . . (Joshua 10:12-13)

The Valley of Ajalon, on the other hand, is northwest of the battlefield scene, and at a lower elevation. It is a wadi[14] running into the Mediterranean Sea. The Moon (in the western sky) was out of the way of the onrushing Mars. It did not be-

---

[13]The arrival of the bolides and meteors in the mid-morning and during a spin axis precession in the morning indicates Mars was 70,000 to 80,000 miles distant, the meteoric showers falling toward Earth at speeds of more than 30,000 miles per hour.

[14]A water-course that is dry except during the rainy season, an arroyo, a dry creek bed.

come cratered or tidally disfigured on this fly-by. Figure 25 illustrates the geography of the battle site.

At this juncture in the development of the Long Day of Joshua, another issue must come to the forefront, and then we shall return to the ancient accounts of this particular holocaust. Thus we shall take a small excursion into the effects of the Long Day of Joshua on modern thought. Modern Western Civilization emerged out of the Medieval Era, about the time of Columbus, Copernicus and Luther, circa 1450 A.D. to 1550 A.D.

On Cosmology In Western Civilization

In ancient times, there is ample evidence that a heliocentric viewpoint of the solar system predominated, both in the Mediterranean area and in the Near East. It fell into disfavor gradually as interest in cosmologies, such as the Olympic deities, waned. Largely through the influence of Claudius Ptolemy, a Greek astronomer and geographer in Alexandria, Egypt, in the second century A.D., a "geocentric" view of the solar system was undisputed in academic circles. Most people *assumed* Ptolemy knew his material, and Ptolemy *assumed* that the Sun, like the Moon and the few planets, went around the Earth. For 13 centuries throughout Christendom, Islam and Judaism alike, Ptolemy's view went unchallenged.

By the fifteenth century A.D., in the zone of Christian civilization in Europe, some profound questions were beginning to be asked both in astronomy and in geography by such men as Copernicus and Columbus. One of these venturesome thinkers, Copernicus, lived near the banks of the Vistula river in Kulm, in what is now Poland. Nicolas Copernicus, or Koppernik, was more of a German than a Pole in his methodology and language of thought. Copernicus was a clergyman, an astronomer, a skilled medic, and a bishop of some authority. He wrote his great work, *De Revolutionibus Orbium Coelestium,* beginning about 1505 A.D., although its final publication occurred in 1543. This work described the theory that the planets revolve around the Sun, and that the turning of the Earth on its axis accounts for the apparent rising and setting of the stars. It became the basis for modern astronomy. (Incidentally, the first copy arrived from the printer's shop on the day Copernicus died.)

Martin Luther, by this time a very important figure in the

THE LONG DAY OF JOSHUA

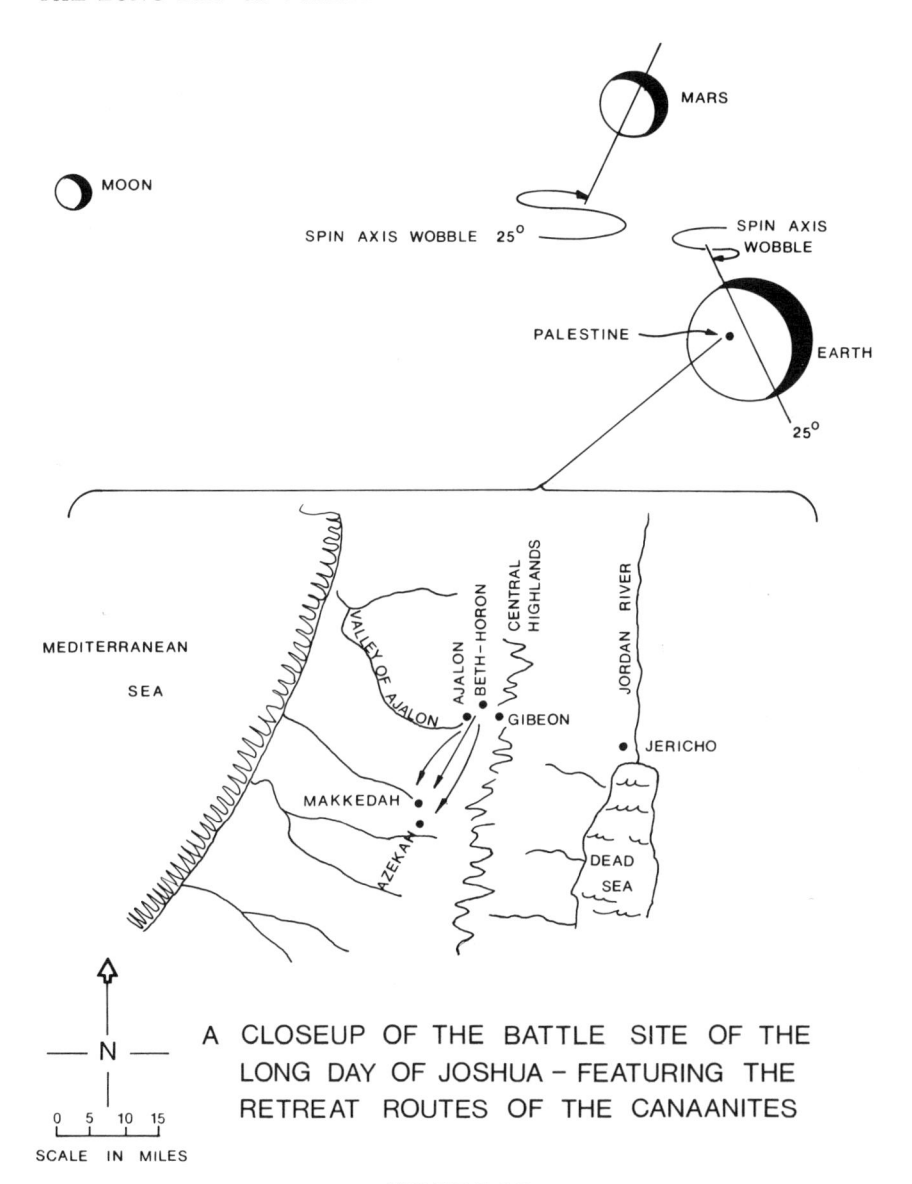

A CLOSEUP OF THE BATTLE SITE OF THE LONG DAY OF JOSHUA – FEATURING THE RETREAT ROUTES OF THE CANAANITES

FIGURE 25
Earth's spin axis and the Martian spin axis are almost equal in angle but opposite in direction of tilt, an indication of interaction causing mutual precessions. Were the spin axis angles equal but parallel, it would be a contradiction to the rationale and celestial mechanics of catastrophism. This is another evidence favoring the catastrophic model.

German theological scene, was severely disturbed by the theories of the clergyman Copernicus.

> But even before the publication of his book, Copernicus had been severely criticized by Luther, who, in conversation, used to denounce "the new astronomer who wants to prove that the Earth goes round, and not the heavens, the Sun, and the Moon; just as if someone sitting in a moving wagon or ship were to suppose that he was at rest, and that the Earth and the trees were moving past him. . . . The fool will turn the whole science of Astronomy upside down. But, as Holy Writ declares, it was the Sun and not the Earth which Joshua commanded to stand still."
>
> Luther's colleague, Philip Melanchton, also argued against the Copernican theory in a little book on physics which he published some six years after the astronomer's death. Like Luther, he laid especial stress on texts in the Bible which seemed to suggest that the Earth was at rest.[15]

In all fairness, it is to be observed that another Lutheran clergyman, Rheticus, did champion the Copernican system. In fact, *De Revolutionibus Orbium Coelestium* would never have been published but for the insistence of Rheticus. Some clergymen also took the lead in the defense of Copernicus, even as others took the lead in the discreditation campaign.

Two facets in the Copernicus question need to be examined more closely than is usually the case. One concerns Luther's evaluation and the other concerns contemporary evaluation of revolutionary theory.

Luther was a theologian who was not able to synthesize new scientific data with the ancient Biblical record because of a narrow frame of reference. His concern was that this new theory might disprove the Bible. Due to his lack of astronomical understanding,[16] his only alternative was to claim that the Copernican

---

[15] Angus Armitage, *Sun, Stand Thou Still*, New York: Henry Schuman, 1947, p. 116.

[16] Luther thought from a world view that was being shaken, and especially for men over 35, it is easier to close their minds and criticize than to think afresh; and many younger students under 35 get their minds closed for them at some universities.

THE LONG DAY OF JOSHUA

theory was totally wrong. He considered theology to be the queen of the sciences.

Conversely, today, we have a heritage in Western Civilization in which much of the academic establishment harbors an anti-Biblical prejudice, often based on misinformation and erroneous assumptions. This prejudice exists in almost every field from cosmology to geology to biology. Simultaneously, the fundamentalist theologians, insisting on the historicity of the Scriptures but unable to explain the details, claim that every time there is an upheaval difficult to understand, such as the Long Day of Joshua, God waved His hand, and everything fell into place. This is a "theomagical" approach.[17]

We must assert that *neither* the "theomagical" nor the "nebulous"[18] approach (as postulated by Darwin and Kant) is valid. This is important to recognize, because it is into one or the other of these two wide ruts which almost all of today's thinking in cosmology has been channeled. Neither channel is satisfactory.

It is widely asserted that there is some kind of conflict between the Bible and science. In this conflict, the Bible is said to be unscientific because it does not agree with the "scientific" theories currently in vogue. We propose that there is indeed a conflict, but that this conflict exists because the *history*[19] *in the Bible is accurate,* and popular evolutionary theory is in error.

One conflict, for example, is between the evolutionary cosmology and the catastrophic evidences present and observable in our solar system, in Earth's crust, in Mars' crust, and in the lunar crust. Historical holocausts are not "bunny-out-of-the-hat" propositions. These ancient astronomical crises did occur, they were astronomical, they were mechanical, and they were divinely guided and providential, in our view.

Concerning the anti-Biblical prejudice, we note that several

---

[17]"Theomagical"—like a magician who pulls a bunny out of the hat at will. See R. E. D. Clark, "Creator God or Cosmic Magician?" *Symposium on Creation IV*, Grand Rapids: Baker Book House, 1972, pp. 108-122.

[18]The proper term is 'nebular' but we believe the word 'nebulous' aptly describes the theory of cosmology by Kant.

[19]This includes its scientific kinds of observations.

of the earliest proponents of the Copernican system *were* clergymen, both of Catholic and Protestant persuasion, even as was Copernicus himself a man of the cloth. Why, then, has so much *unfavorable* recognition been given to Luther, and so little *favorable* recognition been given to Rheticus? Why is it not well known that Copernicus, apart from his astronomical work, was an esteemed clergyman, known for his piety? Might the answer to this seeming perversion of reformation era history be due to the fact that humanists generally have an emotional block against the church and the Scriptures? Could it be that *discredit* to the church satisfies their inner harmony, and *credit* given to a God-centered view frustrates their inner harmony?

The same issue recurred in the Galileo controversy, almost 100 years later. The scene changed and the religion changed, but human nature was the same. Galileo wished to offer evidence for the legitimacy of Copernicus' basic insight, which would incidentally undermine Aristotelian physics and Ptolemaic astronomy. This Greek view of science had became establishment view (i.e. "scriptural"). Important churchmen including Cardinal Bellarmine and, temporarily, Pope Urban, encouraged Galileo's quest for knowledge, part of his appreciation of God in nature.

But others reacted with alarm, anxiety, bewilderment, confusion and doubt. In time his opponents (through an ecclesiastical commission) succeeded in suppressing his doctrine and making him suspect of heresy. This is reaction in the history of the church.

But establishment scientists opposed Newton, Pasteur, Semmelweiss, Einstein, Jenner, Joule, Lister, and inflicted much punishment on them in the name of science. And the list of examples is of mistreatment in the history of science is rather long actually. Mendel is another passing example, whose theories were spurned during his lifetime by scientists. So this reactionary tendency should not be attributed to one religion, or all religions, but rather to a fossilized, self-centered human nature, of which we all participate in considerable degree.

Finally, we must observe that with all of its failures, still, Christendom has led to the productive climate of human grace, of which Copernicus himself is as good an example as any. And this attitude of grace has been the cradle of science, as well as the bedrock of Western Civilization. On this note, we return to the ancient accounts.

The Historical Scene Of The Long Day Of Joshua

Ancients fought and won or lost a thousand battles, very few of which had much real significance on the flow of history. This was one of those few battles which completely changed the course of history.

THE SECOND GENERATION OF ISRAEL. The first generation of Israel died in the wilderness, by and large an unfaithful generation in the eyes of the prophets. In contrast, this second generation was hardy, buoyant, valorous and faithful to Divine precepts. They met and conquered many enemy armies. (Some are mentioned in the Biblical account and others are not mentioned.) On some occasions, with divine guidance, they annihilated enemy armies which were larger. This aggressive generation firmly rejected idolatries, astrologies and other decadent depravities. They were a staunch, hardened, cooperating people, and as such, they broke the back of Amorite power which had dominated the Middle East for perhaps as much as 600 years, almost back to the era of Nimrod of Chaldea. This was an empire-breaking campaign which Joshua led. The critical battle of the Palestine campaign occurred on or about October 25 (Marchesvan 17 or 18) of 1404 B.C. This particular conflict was not just a battle, but was the "Gettysburg", the "Stalingrad", the "Waterloo" of the entire campaign.

There were four phases of the Israelite invasion of the promised land, of which the critical stage was the second. These four stages were:

1	The Eastern Theatre	Bashan, Gilead, Jericho, the Jordan Valley
2	The Central Theatre	Central Highlands, Gibeon, Plain of Sharon
3	The Southern Theatre	Hebron, Debir, Azekah, Makkedah, The Negev
4	The Northern Theatre	Galilee, Valley of Megiddo, Palestinic League.

The 40 years in the wilderness transformed the people from paganism and slavery into monotheism and martial spirit. The society in one generation changed from one of slaves, complaining and touchy, into freedom fighters valuing liberty and property (the promised homeland) very highly. Faith, hardship and cooperation transformed the national character in just one generation.

In stage 1 of the campaign, the Israelites conquered Bashan and Gilead, and parried with the Moabites and Edomites. They defeated the Ammonites, a division of the Amorites, and a strong incursion of Midianites from the upper Mesopotamian Valley. Israelite victories east of the Jordan were no great threat to the powers west of the river Jordan. However, when Jericho and Gilgal fell in the Jordan Valley, the league of Amorite princes was duly alarmed, and the word for battle went up and down Amorite provinces ranging from the border of Egypt to the border of Chaldea.

Upon the fall of Jericho, whose walls fell about March of 1404 B.C., the Israelites assaulted the heart of the promised land. Onward, upward and westward their forces moved, sometimes with defeat but usually with victory. Ai is an example of an exceptional but small defeat; Gibeon is an example of a diplomatic victory, since the city surrendered without a shot fired (or an arrow shot). Now the Israelites occupied high ground. Beyond was the productive, well-watered plain of Sharon, and beyond that the shimmering Mediterranean Sea. The Hebrew armies encamped in twelve divisions just west of Gibeon. The Amorite League, composed of about twelve tribes of Canaanites, made their bivouac just across the wadi (or valley) at Bethhoron.[20] Both armies probably planned to join the battle on the same day as the expected cosmic crisis.[21]

In mid-morning, before the maneuvering armies entered into a full engagement, the spin axis precession was effecting an abnormal path of the Sun in the eastern sky. Soon, the expected astronomical holocaust began, involving bolides and meteorites, which exploded, decimating the Canaanite forces. Perhaps exploding bolides consumed most of their northern flank, an experience similar to that of Sennacherib some 700 years later.

---

[20] Bethhoron is about ten miles northwest of the site of Jerusalem, on lower ground than the holy city.

[21] "Besides, he [*Joshua*] noticed that the heathen were using sorcery [*astrology*] to make the heavenly hosts intercede for them in the fight against the Israelites." Louis Ginzburg, *op. cit.*, Vol. IV, pp. 10-11.

> ... the Lord cast down great stones from heaven upon them unto Azekah, AND THEY DIED: THEY WERE MORE WHICH DIED WITH HAILSTONES THAN THEY WHOM THE CHILDREN OF ISRAEL SLEW WITH THE SWORD. (Joshua 10:11)

> And the Lord discomfited them before Israel, and slew them with a great slaughter at Gibeon, and chased them along the way that goeth up to Bethhoron, and smote them to Azekah, and unto Makkedah. (Joshua 10:10)

The riddled, ravaged, decimated armies of the Canaanite League withdrew, mostly to the southwest about 20 miles, to two or three walled cities. It was a long, long day for the vanquished. In fact, it was a "long day" for the victors as well.

After the Israelite soldiers broke Canaanite resistance in the Central Highlands and on the Plain of Sharon, stage three of the campaign began immediately, winter rains and winds notwithstanding. The assault on the holed-up Amorite forces in Southern Palestine became simply a "mopping up" operation. After the "mopping up," the full attention of Joshua could be (and was) directed to Northern Palestine, Galilee and the Valley of Esdraelon (or Megiddo). Here again, Joshua and his divisions were successful, although their success was not total as it had been in the first three stages of the campaign. The assault on Central Palestine, stage two, was the critical phase of the entire campaign, a highly offensive campaign (which might compare with the assaults of Attila or Genghis Khan). The critical battle at Bethhoron was decided more by cosmic forces from on high than by Hebrew forces positioned on the ground.

There are significant comparisons, but also significant contrasts between this military encounter and the encounter in 701 B.C. The Joshuaic campaign was an offensive one, whereas the effort of Hezekiah was a defensive one, to hold Jerusalem. Catastrophism occurred in the mid-morning in the Long Day of Joshua, whereas it occurred in the evening in the Hezekiah- Sennacherib encounter. The 1404 B.C. event pitted Israel against the Canaanite-Amorite League, one that had been generally in power for 600 years and had treated Israel badly over the centuries. (Amorite kings introduced anti-Semitism and slavery into Egypt, for instance.) The 701 B.C. event pitted Israel against Assyria, Jerusalem against Nineveh. Assyria was a young nation, Nineveh was a young city. In 1404 B.C. the Canaanite armies were chewed up piecemeal by bolides, whereas in 701 B.C. the destruction of the bulk of the Assyrian army was caused by a single, large bolide.

Cosmic Intervention In History

The broadest view of catastrophism concerns its effect on national thinking, not just its effect on the society's architectures, agriculture, army or navy. Of prime consideration is the Deluge, or Flood Catastrophe, the greatest of them all. In that catastrophe the human race was nearly obliterated, leaving Noah, his three sons and three daughters-in-law to repopulate several continents. It also left them free to develop an entirely new society, based on principles of a theocracy, a government of God. The former society, reportedly, was hopelessly involved in corruption, sorcery, tyrrany and violence. Catastrophism in that case resulted in (1) a new start for the human race, and (2) a residue of trillions of fossils. This is not just Hebrew tradition; originally, it was the heritage of all peoples,[22] but the Hebrews preserved the records more carefully than did other peoples.

The Tower of Babel Catastrophe was a twentieth century B.C. holocaust. Nimrod, tyrant of Chaldea, astrologer magnus mediocrita, had completed the Tower of Babel and was completing the outlying buildings and streets when disaster from the planetary regions overtook him and his efforts. What was to be the United Nations building of the twentieth century B.C. was destroyed, partly through fire falling from heaven, partly through earthquakes. Both the astrological system and the Chaldean tyrrany suffered a setback of major proportion. (This was "good.")

The Sodom-Gomorrah holocaust overtook two, perhaps as many as five, cities in a once fertile region, and left them in shambles, amid cinders, ash and lava. Sodom was known for its extremes in moral depravity; Gomorrah was known far and wide for its cruelties. These corrupt societies ceased to exist and plague their neighbors. (This was "good.")

The Exodus Catastrophe involved the flight of Israelites

---

[22] Arthur C. Custance, "Flood Traditions of the World," *Symposium on Creation IV*, Grand Rapids: Baker Book House, 1972, pp. 9-44.

from Egyptian slavery into the freedom of Sinai. (This was "good.") It involved the water destruction of Pharaoh's army, bent on recapturing the fleeing fugitives. (This was "good.") Amid thunderings, earthquakes and some lava outflow from the volcanic Sinai they received the decalogue, the Ten Commandments. This became the constitution of what developed into the greatest commonwealth in human history. (This was "very good.")

The four preceding providential events were very much in the minds of the Hebrew people. Now, a fifth astronomical holocaust, cosmic intervention on an appointment day, resulted in the conquering of Canaan, in fulfillment of an old covenant from the Lord dating back reportedly to the era of Noah, Ham, Shem and Japheth.[23] After this fifth illustration of providential intervention and/or protection for Israel from on high, it was concluded that there was a Divine plan or a Divine Protector for Israel.

Later, minor catastrophes such as the Elijahic and Samuelic were considered providential, but the heavier Greater Davidic and Joel-Amos events were interpreted by the prophets as judgments on the unfaithful nation.

Thus Israel had approximately six providential experiences with catastrophism. In these experiences, Amorite armies, Assyrian armies, Egyptian armies and Philistine armies all suffered severely on catastrophic occasions. Therefore, high councils of prophets and priests came to the conclusion that God would *always* deliver Jerusalem from foreign armies, normally by an intervention from the heavens. Reasoning in this way, the clergy, in alliance with heretical commercial groups, counselled the king in 590 B.C. to resist Babylonian vassalage, even as Hezekiah had resisted Sennacherib in 702 B.C.

However, Jeremiah sensed coming national discipline and total divine disfavor on the city given to idolatries and harlotries.

---

[23] In *The Book of Jubilees,* it is said that Noah, Ham, Shem and Japheth agreed on a division of the then-known world among their three families. Japheth was to have the north and west (Turkey, Europe, Siberia). Shem was to have the Middle East (Mesopatamia, Persia, Arabia including Palestine and Syria). Ham was to have the south, which is Africa. Ham reportedly broke the ancient covenant and his descendants seized Palestine Phoenicia and most of Syria. The Palestinic Covenant in Genesis should be considered in this light. Perhaps the Israelites considered they were claiming an ancient heritage of which they had been deprived for 800 years. This may have been part of their invasion rationale.

The cosmic good fortune which the council of high clergymen relied on for assistance in 587 B.C. did not come. The surrounded city starved and capitulated in 586 B.C., and was obliterated. As Jeremiah had predicted, there was no deliverance this time.

The same pattern occurred in New Testament times. Most of the populace, including the leaders, required some kind of "sign from heaven" before they would consider the Nazarene to be the Messiah.[24] As it had been in the time of Isaiah, and again in Jeremiah's time, high councils chose to rebel once more. This time the rebellion was against Rome. Once again, no sign from heaven appeared, and no cosmic deliverance occurred as Roman legionnaires systematically surrounded and destroyed the holy city, a rebellious city.

Times had changed as the solar system became reorganized. Planets had become sorted out, each into its own non-catastrophic orbit.[25, 26] The general climate or environment for mankind changed after 701 B.C., and this discussion reflects how catastrophism was helpful to Israel on certain occasions. (Isaiah in 701 B.C. is the supreme example, as is Moses in 1447 B.C.) An unrealistic reliance on catastrophic deliverance (a sign or intervention from heaven) was part of the disaster of 586 B.C., and the disaster in 70 A.D.

Thus when all is considered, even though the Biblical account of the Long Day of Joshua is not as precise as one would wish, its date can be carefully reconstructed by various methods. Not

---

[24] The curing of a few blind, lame and lepers was impressive, even amazing. But such did not qualify as divine credits in the minds of the doctorate of Jerusalem. This was because these achievements, marvellous in themselves, were not bolides, celestial fly-bys, meteors, or spin axis wobbles, "signs from heaven" such as had accompanied the leaderships of Isaiah, Joshua and Moses.

[25] Under a catastrophic frame of reference, the Bethlehem star (if it were a planet-sized body with a comet-like orbit and a period of thousands of years) would have indeed aroused ample interest. The Magi who visited Palestine in about 2 B.C. to 1 A.D. were Zoroastrian scholars. Zoroaster reportedly was a student of Daniel, one of the leading Jewish prophets in Babylon. Thus the Zoroastrians were quite sympathetic to the Jewish commonwealth. A Persian Zoroastrian, Cyrus, a king, had ordered the rebuilding of Jerusalem in the late fifth century B.C.

[26] Pluto's orbit crosses that of Neptune, but since they are in 3:2 resonance around Pluto's aphelion, this is no illustration of latent cosmic catastrophism.

THE LONG DAY OF JOSHUA   197

only was Joshua correct in his observations; it would seem that
Deborah, one of the judges, was quite accurate in her post-dated
description of a similar fly-by 216 years later.

> They fought from heaven, the stars [*planets*] in their
> courses fought against Sisera. (Judges 5:20)

> And there was no day like that before it or after it. . . .
> (Joshua 10:14)

Conclusion

Thus, when all is considered, the Biblical account of the Long Day of Joshua is neither as detailed as one would wish, nor even as precise. Nevertheless it is of superior literary quality to either the Maui story or the Phaethon story in both its datability and in the eye-witness preservation of the account. Joshua was correct in his historical observations.

The question for centuries has been, "How many spin axes did the Earth have during this remarkable, unique day?" Luther's retort was none since he believed the Earth didn't rotate. Bellarmine and other Biblicists also concluded none since somehow a brake temporarily had occurred on the normal spin axis. Galileo affirmed that no braking effect could be applied to such a dynamic planet and have it survive; therefore Earth rotated around but one unchanging spin axis. Galileo's assumptions have been similar to the assumptions of modern rationalists and cynics who usually are hostile to the Scriptures. Galileo had no hostility to the Scriptures but he required horizontal and vertical consistency between history and science, and he had no understanding of gyroscopes or the nature of gyroscopic precession.

Our analysis is that neither the traditional Biblicists (advocating an unexplained braking effect) nor the rationalists (advocating a uniformitarian rationale) have properly understood the nature of that catastrophic day. Earth, like any gyroscope, can rotate around two spin axes simultaneously under the proper conditions. And the proper conditions existed on that particular day, which was October 24th or more likely October 25th of

1404 B.C. Thus not zero, not one, but TWO spin axes is the solution for that particular, renowned unique day.

SUMMARY

The Isaiahic Catastrophe 701 B.C.	Mars fly-by at 70,000 miles Case One
The Joel-Amos Catastrophe 756 B.C.	Mars fly-by at 120,000 miles Case Two
The Elijahic Catastrophe 864 B.C.	Mars fly-by at 150,000 miles Case Two
The Greater Davidic Catastrophe 972 B.C.	Mars fly-by at 120,000 miles Case Two
The Lesser Davidic Catastrophe 1025 B.C.	Mars fly-by at 200,000 miles Case One
The Samuelic Catastrophe 1080 B.C.	Mars fly-by at 150,000 miles Case Two
The Deborah Debacle 1188 B.C.	Mars fly-by at 150,000 miles Case Two
The Long Day of Joshua 1404 B.C.	Mars fly-by at 70,000 miles Case Two, modified*

*The Long Day of Joshua *may* have occurred with a Mars fly-by above the North Pole.

Let us first sweep away some cobwebs. One of these is the contention that whereas science encourages the critical attitude, religion is based solely on uncritical acceptance of authority.—Robert E. D. Clark

It is easy to speculate that science might have been able to develop in the absence of Christianity, but in fact it never did. Why?—Robert E. D. Clark

chapter **VIII**

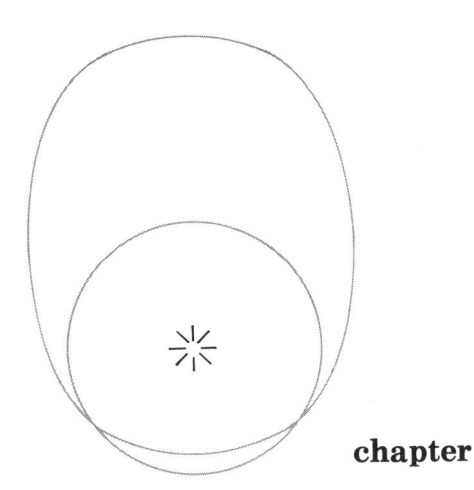

The Exodus Catastrophe

March 20/21, 1447 B.C.

The Exodus Catastrophe occurred during the midnight hour (Palestine time) of March 20/21, 1447 B.C. This catastrophe was roughly at the midpoint of the "resonant orbit era," circa 2500 B.C. to 701 B.C. This was also the worst catastrophe of the entire fire and brimstone series, (but much less in intensity, and of a different nature than the Deluge of circa 2500 B.C.).

The March 20/21 dating of the Exodus Catastrophe is similar to the March 20/21 dating of the Isaiahic Catastrophe, and as will be seen, of the Sodom-Gomorrah Catastrophe. All three of these were Case One catastrophes, where Mars was north of the ecliptic plane, and the timing was at the vernal equinox. However, there is one major difference. This catastrophe was an outside pass, a modification of the Case One geometry, and this modification produced significant results. Thus the modified Case One geometry, and the nearness of the Martian fly-by are unique to this particular catastrophe.

This is the last catastrophe for which there is considerable extant literature. Our primary sources describing this catastrophe are (1) the book of Exodus in the Bible, (2) the Exodus Psalms also in the Bible, (3) the Talmud, (4) the works of Josephus and, surprisingly, (5) Plato, in his Critias and Timaeus. These contain the story of Atlantis as we know it. These works describe somewhat the Exodus Catastrophe as it affected the Aegean, even as the Mosaic account describes this holocaust as it affected Egypt and the Sinai Peninsula.

The Job Catastrophe
Estimated 1663 B.C.

SINCE THIS BOOK reverses the normal flow of history (early to late), attention to historical settings may seem like "jumps" backward. This is indeed a problem in our analysis and description of the Exodus holocaust. Some of the historical background will occur in Chapters IX and X on the Sodom-Gomorrah Catastrophe and the Tower of Babel Catastrophe, respectively. However, some background will be included at this juncture.

Understanding the Isaiahic Catastrophe of March 20/21, 701 B.C., helps immeasurably in understanding both the generalities and the specifics of the Exodus Catastrophe. The geometries were similar.[1] So also was the fly-by similar to the Sodom-Gomorrah event, for this Exodus Catastrophe occurred on the four hundred and thirtieth *anniversary* of the Sodom-Gomorrah debacle, one which Abraham and Lot both witnessed with their own eyes.

> And it came to pass at the end of the four hundred and thirty years, EVEN THE SELFSAME DAY IT CAME TO PASS, that all the hosts of the Lord went out from the land of Egypt. It is a night to be much observed unto the Lord for bringing them out from the land of Egypt. . . . (Exodus 12:41-42)

This historic passover is the basis for the passover celebration in Judaism. This is the night of the tenth and worst of the plagues which left Egypt in shambles. That it was a memorable night is indicated in the above text. That is was the four hundred and thirtieth anniversary of the earlier historic catastrophe day is a

---
[1]The Isaiahic Catastrophe was a Case One fly-by while the Exodus Catastrophe, with Mars passing on the *outside*, was a variation of the Case One geometry.

THE EXODUS CATASTROPHE

point which has been missed by most, if indeed not all, Biblical commentators.[2]

There were minor catastrophes and catastrophes which threatened between 1447 B.C. and 1877 B.C., the Sodom-Gomorrah event. Such shall be as relevant to Chapter IX as to the subject at hand. Two examples in literature are described as follows:

> And when Jacob ceased praying to the Lord the earth shook from its place, and the sun darkened, and all these kings were terrified and a great consternation seized them.[3]

Another significant catastrophe, a major disaster to Job, is somewhat described in the opening chapter of this work of high drama the book of Job:

> While he was yet speaking, there came also another, and said, THE FIRE OF GOD IS FALLEN FROM HEAVEN, and hath burned up the sheep, and the servants, AND CONSUMED them.... (Job 1:16)
>
> And behold, there came A GREAT WIND[4] from the wilderness, and smote the four corners of the house, and it fell

---

[2] Galatians 3:17 also refers to the 430 year period. Genesis 15:13 refers to the period until the Exodus as about 400 years. Biblical commentators have varied widely in attempting to locate the event in Abraham's life which began the 430 year period. One common guess has been the year Abraham migrated into Canaan. But the capitalized words in the above quotation, coupled with Talmudic information that the Sodom-Gomorrah Holocaust was also on the vernal equinox, supplies what we consider to be a pivotal issue to this historic question.

[3] *The Book of Jasher*, New York: M. M. Noah & A. S. Gould, 1840, 37:17. According to our model, threatening close fly-bys of Mars should have occurred in 1502 B.C., 1555 B.C., 1610 B.C., 1663 B.C., 1718 B.C., 1771 B.C., 1826 B.C. and 1877 B.C. Our guess is that this event, about the middle of Jacob's life, coincided with the threat in 1718 B.C., which would have been a Case Two kind of event like the Elijahic event or the Greater Davidic event.

[4] "A great wind" in the above text suggests in English a sudden gust on a stormy, windy day. This suggestion is quite mistaken. The Hebrew word for "wind" is *ruwach* which sometimes does mean wind in other texts, but was seen in Isaiah 37 and II Kings 20 as the "blast" or the exploding bolide which destroyed almost 200,000 Assyrian troops. Among its meanings as found in *Strong's Exhaustive Concordance* are "air, anger, blast,

upon the young men, and they [*Job's sons*] are dead; and I only am escaped alone to tell thee. (Job 1:19)

Thus, minor catastrophes are detected between the cycles of major catastrophes in this era, even as such were in the era just preceding the heavy events of the eighth century B.C.

The children of Israel went into Egypt to seek food and security. The date was about 1662 B.C. as gleaned from Dake's commentary, 215 years after the Sodom-Gomorrah event and 215 years before the Exodus event.[5] This two hundred fifteenth year between the two catastrophes was also apparently:

(1) One year after a Case One catastrophe in 1663 B.C., the Job Catastrophe.

(2) At the beginning, the first or the second year of a period of famine.[6] Thus there are indications of intermediate catastrophism between the Sodom-Gomorrah and the Exodus events, but of what intensity is unknown.

The family of Jacob, numbering 70 in all, went into Egypt to seek *food and security* in 1662 B.C. At that time, Joseph, the son of Jacob, was also the premier of Egypt, second only to the Pharaoh. Under Joseph's leadership, food supplies in abundance had been reserved for the expected dearth; indeed, Egypt temporarily became the granary of the Levant-Suez region. Egypt

---

breath, tempest, whirlwind." Since this occurred along with falling fire, it must suggest the effects of a bolide which are so comparable to the effects of a nuclear explosion. This cosmic holocaust, in the prelude to the book of Job, so disastrous to the patriarch of Uz, occurred in the year 1663 B.C., in which case it would have been a Case One catastrophe like the Isaiahic or the Sodom-Gomorrah episode.

[5]Finis Jennings Dake, *Dake's Annotated Reference Bible,* Atlanta: Dake Bible Sales, 1961, p. 13.

[6]This period of dearth was foreseen by Joseph. "The seven years of dearth began to come, according as Joseph had said [*in 1662 B.C.*], and the dearth was in all lands; but in all the land of Egypt there was bread." (Genesis 41:54). Could it be that Joseph, then governor of Egypt, foresaw the seven years of plenty followed by the seven years of famine in a cosmic, catastrophic context? Could it be that this catastrophe of 1663 B.C. deranged much of the productive facilities throughout the Middle East?

flourished culturally. This was the era of the authorship of the book of Job, the oldest book in the Scriptures. It was the era of pyramid-building at its best. It was an era of much commerce and trade and of arts and sciences. Defenses were organized along Egypt's northeastern border by Joseph against Amalekite and Amorite incursions. Eventually, however, Joseph died after 80 years of premiership, about 1590 B.C.

The succeeding Pharaoh was weak. His dynasty disappeared as Amorite invaders from Palestine conquered, and established their own dynasty, the "shepherd kings," or the Hyksos.[7] The Amorites and Hebrews were mutually antagonistic. Gradually increasing degrees of servitude were induced upon the Hebrews until they became extremely distressed, longing for release and freedom, but utterly unable to achieve these hopes. This condition lasted for about 100 years, during which Moses was born, and became an adopted son of Bathia,[8] an Amorite Pharaoh's daughter. He grew up, was educated, and became a successful general of the armies. However, in time he renounced the adopted culture of the Amorites for his natural birthright, the Hebrew. He sensed a calling in the role of emancipator of his people. (His rejection as would-be emancipator occurred in 1517 B.C., resulting in Moses' 40-year exile from Egypt.)

The Book of Job—A Cosmological Reference For The Hebrews[9]

The book of Job is a great drama, a literary work, but one with a deep spiritual message for the Hebrews in Egypt. Their bondage was in a harmony with Job's suffering. Beyond the

---

[7] Charles McDowell, "A History of Middle East Catastrophes," Unpublished Manuscript.

[8] Bathia is the name of Pharaoh's daughter in the *Talmud;* Josephus gives her name as Thermuthis.

[9] Cosmology—a theory or perspective of the *development* of the solar system. Cosmogony—a theory or perspective of the *origin* of the solar system. In the evolutionary world view, (the nebular hypothesis in which it is stated that planets condensed out of a gaseous filament), cosmology and cosmogony are one and the same. In a catastrophic world view, cosmology considers the arrival of the planets at their current orbits, the asteroids

pathos and the theology of the book of Job, we call attention to its cosmology. This book[10] reflects the cosmological thought of both Hebrews and Egyptians of the seventeenth century B.C., to the fifteenth century B.C.

ON EARTHQUAKES	[*God*] Which removeth the mountains, and they know not: which overturneth them in his anger. (Job 9:5)
ON COSMOGONY	[*God*] Which alone spreadeth out the heavens. . . . Which maketh Arcturus,[11] Orion, and Pleiades, and the chambers of the south. (Job 9:8-9)
ON ORBITAL CHANGE	[*God*] Which shaketh the earth out of her place, and the pillars thereof tremble. (Job 9:6)
ON SPIN AXIS SHIFT	[*God*] Which commandeth the sun, and it riseth not; and sealeth up the stars. (Job 9:7)

and Mars being of special interest in this work. The *origin* of the planets, their cosmogony, is quite another matter than their arrivals at their present orbits, their cosmology.

[0]It is our belief that the "publisher" of the book of Job was Joseph, not Moses. Eliphaz, one of the leading characters, one of the quartet of unhelpful friends, was a son of Esau, and therefore a first cousin of Joseph. Elihu and Bildad were also distant cousins of Joseph. Egypt, having papyrus and population, was a center of arts, of writing and drama; and the Hebrews under Joseph were very interested in theological drama, as Joseph's life history itself reveals. The trial of Job, tried by Satan, was a foreshadow of the trial of the Hebrews under the Hyksos (Amorite) dynasty. The Amorite culture included the Baal-Ashtoreth system.

For further information regarding the interrelationships of Eliphaz the Temanite, Bildad the Shuaite, and Elihu the Buzite, see Christine L., Benagh, *Meditations on the Book of Job;* Houston, St. Thomas Press, 1964, pp. 33-50, "The Mysterious Generation". Eliphaz, Bildad, Elihu and Joseph were all descendants of Abraham or Abraham's brother; all were relatives. And their gathering around Job's sick bed included the dimensions clan-type gathering for a seminar on the nature of suffering.

[1]Arcturus, Orion and Pleiades are discussed also in Job 38:31-32, along with a fourth planet, Mazzaroth. Traditional commentaries suppose these three are constellations, whereas actually they were visible planets moving across the constellation areas. Our supposition is that Arcturus was Mars, Orion was Jupiter, Pleiades was Venus, and the "chambers of south" in Job 9:9 was the Milky Way.

THE EXODUS CATASTROPHE

ON SPIN AXIS SHIFT	The pillars of heaven tremble and are astonished at his reproof. (Job 26:11)
ON EARTH'S ROTATIONAL SCHEME[12]	He stretcheth out the north over the empty place and hangeth the earth[13] upon nothing. (Job 26:7)
ON TIDAL WAVES AND TIDES	He divideth the sea with his power. . . . (Job 26:12)
ON A "WILD" PLANET	By his spirit he hath garnished the heavens; his hand hath formed THE CROOKED SERPENT. (Job 26:13)
ON A "WILD" PLANET	Canst thou bind the sweet influences of Pleiades, or loose the bands of Orion? Canst THOU BRING FORTH MAZZAROTH IN HIS SEASON? or canst thou guide Arcturus with his sons? (Job 38:31-32)
ON THE COMPOSITION OF A "WILD" PLANET	His heart is as firm as a stone; yea, as hard as a piece of the nether millstone [*iron and nickel*]. (Job 41:24)
ON OBSERVATIONS OF A "WILD" PLANET	By his neesings a light doth shine and his eyes are like the eyelids of the morning. Out of his mouth GO BURNING LAMPS, and SPARKS OF FIRE leap out. Out of his nostrils goeth smoke, as out of a seething pot or caldron. HIS BREATH KINDLETH

---

[12]This suggests the Hebrews realized the Earth was a free planet in space, not supported by elephants or giant turtles at the pillars of Hercules, Gibraltar. Also they were aware that the Earth's path of movement (ecliptic plane) was on an east and west basis. It indicates that Egyptian science was aware of Earth's rotational scheme.

[13]"Earth" is *'erets* in Hebrew, meaning the earth, country, land, wilderness, world.

	COALS, AND A FLAME GOETH OUT OF HIS MOUTH. (Job 41:18-21)
ON METEOR STREAMS	Canst thou send lightnings, that they may go, and say unto thee, Here we are? ... or who hath given understanding to the HEART?[14] (Job 38:35-36)
ON COSMOLOGY	Who can number the clouds in wisdom? or who can STAY the BOTTLES[15] of heaven. (Job 38:37)
ON COSMOLOGY	Knowest thou the ordinances of heaven? canst thou set the dominion thereof in the earth? (Job 38:33)

In Job, Chapters 40 and 41, there are two mysterious figures which were large, ferocious figures of ancient times. Persons without a catastrophic cosmology have suggested that they were great, fearsome animals of ancient times, perhaps "hippopotamus" and "crocodile." Their names in Job are Leviathan and Behemoth. Behemoth, or "hippopotamus" is an interesting "hippo."

> "His strength is in his loins, and his force is in the navel of his belly.
> The sinews of his stones are wrapped together.
> His bones are as strong pieces of brass; his bones are like BARS OF IRON.
> He drinketh up a river.
> He can draw up Jordan into his mouth.
> He taketh it with his eyes; his nose pierceth through snares. (Portions of Job 40)

---

[14]"Heart" is from the Hebrew *sekvee* and is translated in the Amplified Version as "the meteor." The idea seems to concern also the directing of the meteor.

[15]"Bottles" in Hebrew is *nebel* which includes the idea of a pitcher, a bottle, a vessel, a container. "Luminaries" or "planets" may be a better translation.

This is a remarkable hippopotamus indeed. And the crocodile is even more remarkable. Concerning the "crocodile," Leviathan:

> His scales are . . . shut up together as with a close seal:
> By his neesings a light doth shine.
> Out of his mouth go burning lamps, and sparks of fire.
> His breath kindleth coals, and a flame goeth out of his mouth.
> His heart is a firm as a stone, yea, as hard as a piece of the nether millstone.
> He esteemeth iron as straw, and brass as rotten wood.
> The arrow cannot make him flee.
> He maketh the deep to boil like a pot.
> Upon the earth there is not his like. . . .
> He beholdeth all high things. (Portions of Job 41)

These are not descriptions of crocodiles and hippopotami. Neither is this fairy tale mythology. Leviathan and Behemoth represent two planets, probably Mars and Mercury, whose "bones" are made of iron. Mars seems to be represented as Leviathan, and Mercury as Behemoth,[16] two great, ancient, fearsome beings, but not conventional dragons or even dinosaurs.

William Ward, without understanding catastrophic cosmology, has yet somehow captured the essence of Leviathan and Behemoth. He discusses them with remarkable skill:

> Then God resumes his questionnaire, revealing His power and glory in the natural world. But in chapters 40 and 41 we find this done in a different way; we have long descriptions of two creatures called Behemoth and Leviathan. Behemoth is translated hippopotamus, and Leviathan crocodile. The detailed descriptions of these two animals, occupying most of two chapters, seem exaggerated and out of place here, and some scholars have suggested they were not a part of the original poem. This is to miss the point completely.
> The descriptions here are not of ordinary animals, as in God's first speech, but are two symbolic creatures which played a most significant role in ancient mythology. The great sea monster was a symbol of the primeval chaos God had to conquer to bring His creation under control. One of

---

[16] Mercury, not Mars, is the planet we believe interacted with Earth during the Flood-Ice Catastrophe, the Deluge, circa 2500 B.C.

the earliest stories of creation was of God's destroying the monster of the deep, Tiamat or Rahab or Leviathan, representing the primeval chaos, to make the universe an orderly one under His control. This story is often referred to in ancient apocalyptic literature, and occasionally in the Old Testament.[17]

We have merely touched upon, and hardly developed the cosmology contained in the book of Job and must resist the temptation to exhaustively analyze the cosmology therein, even as others have analyzed the drama or the theology. Our point is that catastrophic cosmology was unquestioned in that drama. The cosmology of Job 9, for instance, must be considered as closely reflecting their literal experiences. One of these experiences, circa 1930 B.C. or perhaps as early as 2146 B.C. was the creation of the Rift Valley, stretching from Syria into the South Indian Ocean, across the Red Sea and the African Highlands, a cleavage in the Earth's crust 5000 miles long. "Which removeth the mountains, and they know not: which overturneth them in his anger," was tragically literal as were other phrases of the cosmology of Job 9. We must try to think as the Hebrews (and Egyptians or others of that era) thought in order to understand their times, their literatures, their migrations, their architectures and so forth. This has been an excursion into the era of 1663 B.C., of Job, and of its suspected catastrophe.

The Ten Plagues in Egypt
March 1447 B.C.

Note that the flight of the Israelites from Egypt came during the "passover" night, and amidst the Lord's ten plagues upon the land of Egypt. These plagues are listed in the Bible as follows:

1.	The waters turned to blood	Exodus 7:17-25
2.	Frogs	Exodus 8:2-15
3.	Lice	Exodus 8:16-18
4.	Flies	Exodus 8:21-32
5.	Murrain (Pestilence)	Exodus 9:2-7

---

[17]William Ward, *Out of the Whirlwind,* Richmond: John Knox Press, 1958, p. 103.

6.	Ashes of the furnace	Exodus 9:9-12
7.	Hail mixed with fire	Exodus 9:15-35
8.	Locusts	Exodus 10:4-20
9.	Oppressive darkness	Exodus 10:21-29
10.	Death throughout the land	Exodus 11, 12:1-42

How many of these ten plagues were a direct result of catastrophism? How many were results of indirect effects? We are not sure, but the following guidelines may be helpful.

1. WATERS TURNED TO BLOOD — This may have been iron dust (from orbiting around the red planet) which turned to a brilliant crimson when entering Earth's atmosphere, rich in oxygen. Raphael's painting of the waters of the parting sea as "red" waters was perceptive. The waters of the Nile also were red and badly polluted as the red dust became intermixed and coagulated in such bodies as the "Red" Sea.[18]

2. FROGS IN THE LAND — We shall offer two thoughts concerning this rather unusual plague. One view is that, with the invasion of volcanic dust and pumice, and meteoritic dust, water conditions rapidly deteriorated; plants were covered. Faced with a sudden change in their natural environment, frogs came up out of the waters in marshes, canals and rivers to die on the shores, in the streets and almost everywhere.

Normally in Egypt frogs multiply in July and August after the Nile River floods. We cannot place this event within the normal climatic regime.

---

[18] See Immanuel Velikovsky, *Worlds In Collision*, pp. 48-51.

A second view is that the original Hebrew word, *tsephardea* ("frogs"), was animated by later Hebrew scholars who had no experience with catastrophism. *Tsephardea* ("frogs") is derived from either tsaphar, meaning "to skip about" or from *tsephar* meaning "a bird." In this view, the original *tsephardea* corresponded to volcanic pumice and ash which descended thickly throughout the land in marshes, in canals, in rivers, on the shores, in the streets and almost everywhere.

3. LICE THROUGHOUT THE LAND

The Hebrew word *ken* includes the sense of fastening like a gnat, or stinging. When Krakatoa exploded on August 26, 1883, in the afternoon, the sky began to yellow and darken as fine volcanic particles descended amid drops of rain.

This plague may describe voracious mites, suddenly denied their normal habitat due to the volcanic fallout, turning in vast numbers upon man and beast alike. Or it may possibly be an animated description adopted by later scholars to describe volcanic fallout they failed to fathom.

4. GRIEVOUS SWARMS OF FLIES

The Hebrew word *arob* can mean diverse sorts of flies such as stinging dragon flies, mosquitoes and other insects. This plague may, like the third, be a result of insects suddenly denied their normal habitat, turning upon man and beast.

Or again, it may be an animated translation of a scene which originally involved a fallout of volcanic cinders, ash and fine powder amid wind and rain. When Krakatoa exploded, the volcanic fallout rose as high as 80,000 feet before descending. And during the Exodus holocaust, with such a close Martian fly-by, there must have been hundreds of dormant volcanoes suddenly become active on a scale dwarfing Krakatoa.

5. A GRIEVOUS MURRAIN

"Murrain" is from the (by now familiar) Hebrew word *deber*, elsewhere translated as "pestilence" and "plague." It describes meteoritic fallout as contrasted to volcanic fallout. It describes fire and brimstone.

6. ASHES AS IN A FURNACE

"Ashes" in the Hebrew is *piyach* and describes ashes, dust or powder. It may be very similar to the aforementioned "lice," or perhaps volcanic dust. They caused boils on animals and man alike.

7. HAIL MIXED WITH FIRE

"Hail" in the Hebrew is *barad* indicating fiery meteors. This is seen also in Psalm 78:47-48 and 105:32. It is also the word describing meteors in Joshua 10:11 where it is translated "hailstones." This was the worst blizzard of meteorites of all of the seven major catastrophes. It was "very grievous, such as there was none like it in all the land of Egypt since it became a nation," (implying that meteors had fallen during other catastrophes, but not in this intensity). That it was accompanied by thunderings, and that "fire ran along the ground" indicates it included both bolides and meteorites. Many prairie fires must have been ignited by them.

8. WIND-BORNE LOCUSTS

The Hebrew word *'arbeh* means a locust, or a grasshopper, a large, flying insect. This word is derived from *rabah* meaning to enlarge, to increase in whatever respect, to heap up, to overtake.

As in our discussion of frogs, lice and flies, we offered two lines of thought. One was that insects such as grasshoppers suddenly finding the fields denuded, began to migrate and invade human dwellings in great numbers. A second line of thought is that this could be a word, later animated, which described a fallout of volcanic powder, dust and cinders.

When Krakatoa blew up August 26-27, 1883, so much volcanic material was released into the atmosphere that, 14 weeks later the bark Ta Lee passed through a bank of pumice extending about 25 miles, some pieces as large as two feet square.

9. OPPRESSIVE DARKNESS

The explosion of Krakatoa in 1883 resulted in Batavia (100 miles distant) being darkened, even at noon, for about a day. The Exodus darkness in 1447 B.C. was worse, darkness caused by volcanic smoke, ashes, cinders and dust so thick that sunlight could not penetrate for three days. This was a darkness which could be "felt," indicating the maximum volcanic pollution of Egypt's atmosphere.

10. DEATH THROUGHOUT THE LAND

Scriptures indicate death on the night of the cosmic fly-by was so widespread that in Egypt, the "first-born" of every family died (that is every family which did not have the blood

THE EXODUS CATASTROPHE

of the lamb on the door).[19] Under these conditions, destruction was so widespread that no count could possibly be made. Some entire communities perished with falling bolides. Earthquakes levelled most structures.

The word "firstborn" in Hebrew is *bekowr* meaning elder, chief or firstborn, and comes from the prime verb *bakar,* to burst from the womb. We suspect the death toll throughout Egypt that cataclysmic night was 15% to 25% and that, on the average, "one born"[20] of most families perished. This principle also extended to animals as earthquakes, bolides, meteors, prairie fires, respiratory reactions and shortly, tidal waves, took an unimaginable toll.

Thus we propose that plagues 2, 3, 4, 6, 8 and 9 were directly related to the massive vulcanism in nearby areas. Plagues 1, 5, and 7 were related to astronomical red dust (from the red planet), and from bolides and meteors (fire and brimstone). Plague 10 is tidal. Mars was causing an immense tide in Earth's crust, especially at the midnight hour, the hour of the height of the fly-by. This extreme earthquake was extreme in both duration and intensity. See Table VIII, Page 224.

It may be interesting to note that there is a parallel to the ten plagues of Egypt in the plagues in Greek myth of Cephalus.

---

[19]Goshen, where the Hebrews lived, was a county or province at the very northeasterly edge of the Nile delta, adjacent to the Suez Isthmus. It was a frontier province, and would be the *first* to suffer from any invasion from Arabia or Palestine. Scriptures repeatedly observe that this province was largely bypassed by both the meteoritic outpouring and the volcanic envelopment.

[20]Immanuel Velikovsky first suggested this interpretation. See *Worlds in Collision,* p. 63. "In *Ages in Chaos* (my reconstruction of ancient history), I shall show that 'first-born' *(bkhor)* in the text of the plague is a corruption of 'chosen' *(bchor)*." [*The* "smiting of the houses," *part of this massive tenth plague, also indicates extreme seismic disturbance.*]

Greece, even more so than Egypt, is located in a region of crustal weakness, including submarine volcanoes. This suggests that the plagues as recounted in the Exodus were not just a localized event, but in one form or another, in one intensity or another, were global in scope. The plagues of Egypt occurred, it is believed, over a period of about seven days, possibly less.

The Timing Difficulty of the Ten Plagues

A significant difficulty arises in trying to place this Exodus catastrophe into a calendaric scheme with the ten plagues. The time scale for global events (crustal tides, spin axis precession and polar relocation, electrical discharges, etc.) directly associated with a Mars fly-by is a day or two. Local after effects (earthquakes, tidal waves, vulcanism etc.) might continue for some time. By comparison, the time scale for the ten plagues in the book of Exodus seem to have spanned many weeks or even months.

Such a lengthy period is conceivable if the Mars passover occurred first, causing a global upheaval for a day or two, and perpetuating a lengthy series of local violent after-effects extending over several weeks or even months. According to the Biblical record, the most violent events seem to be the 5th plague of grievous murrain (an intense blizzard of fire and brimstone). the 7th plague of hail mixed with fire (also fire and brimstone, bolides and meteors), the 10th plague (intense earthquake activity) and the "postscript," the tidal wave. We might call the "postscript" the 11th plague, the tidal bore sweeping across the coasts of the eastern Mediterranean Sea. These plagues, the 5th, the 7th, the 10th and the postscript are far from the earliest events *(assuming* the Biblical record is in *chronological* order). Neither did they occur within a day or two of each other. Furthermore, dating the 10th plague, the "passover" or fly-by at March 20/21, 1447 B.C. places the nine other plagues *after* the scheduled passover rather than preceding.

The Bible dates the Mediterranean Sea flooding with tidal waves after the Mars passover, since this could have been caused by continuing vulcanism and earthquakes. But it doesn't seem possible to locate the whole series of plagues *after* the tenth which is the climax and capstone of the whole series, and which is known to have been on the night of March 20/21.

We cannot even venture an answer to this problem at the

present time. A study of the Greek account of plagues (the Cephalus myth) and the Egyptian account (by Ipuwer) may help resolve the mystery. Further studies of Near and Far Eastern literature and mythology (with an open mind toward the catastrophic world view) may furnish significant information.

Comparisons Between the Exodus Catastrophe and the Isaiahic Catastrophe

A lengthy discussion has already been presented concerning the Isaiahic Catastrophe, its celestial mechanics, historical background and eye-witness description. To understand the Isaiahic Catastrophe is to largely understand the somewhat more intense, and somewhat more ancient Exodus Catastrophe.

We can detect three major differences between these two similar catastrophes. First, Mars was closer to the Earth on the Exodus fly-by, possibly closer than 60,000 miles. Second, the display of meteoritic and bolidic activity was more intense, indeed it had no equal among all the other post-flood cosmic holocausts. It was truly

> ... a night to be much observed unto the Lord for bringing them out from the land of Egypt: this is that night of the Lord to be observed of all the children of Israel in their generations. (Exodus 12:42)

> So there was hail, and fire mingled with the hail, very grievous, such as there was none like it in all the land of Egypt since it became a nation. And the hail smote throughout all the land of Egypt. . . . (Exodus 9:24-25)

Thirdly, Mars made an outside fly-by rather than an inside fly-by. This suggests why the Long Day of Joshua was only $43\frac{1}{2}$ years later rather than $53\frac{1}{2}$ years which was normal for the resonant orbit model.[21] That is, Mars gained angular momentum with an outside fly-by whereas it lost angular momentum with an inside fly-by. Probably the two orbits very nearly went out of resonance on this occasion, whereas on the fly-by of 701 B.C. they *did* finally break out of resonance, and Mars into an entirely new or-

---

[21]Immanuel Velikovsky favored a 52 year period between the Exodus holocaust and the Long Day of Joshua. See *Worlds in Collision*, pp. 153 ff.

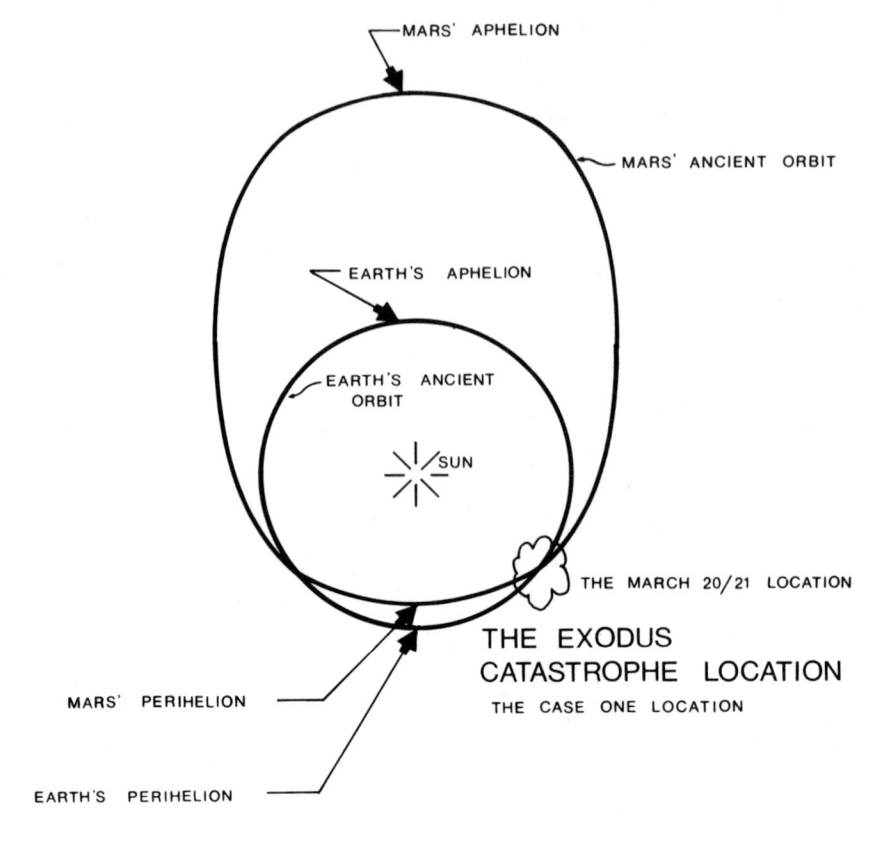

THE GEOMETRY OF THE EXODUS CATASTROPHE

AS SEEN FROM POLARIS

FIGURE 26
The Geometry of the Exodus Catastrophe (1). This March 20/21 catastrophe was simiar to the Isaiahic event (701 B.C.) and the Sodom-Gomorrah holocaust (1877 B.C.) in date. But it was dissimilar in that it is believed to have been an outside fly-by.

THE EXODUS CATASTROPHE

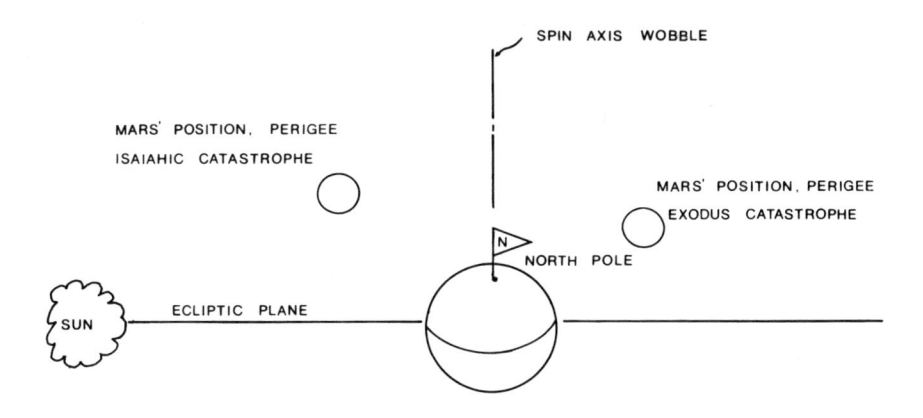

THE GEOMETRY OF THE EXODUS CATASTROPHE AS SEEN FROM WINTER SOLSTICE (EARTH'S NORTH POLE IS LEANING BACKWARD 25° TO ITS PATH)

MARS ON AN OUTSIDE PASSOVER — EXODUS CATASTROPHE (UNIQUE)
MARS ON AN INSIDE PASSOVER — ISAIAHIC CATASTROPHE (NORMAL)

FIGURE 27
The Geometry of the Exodus Catastrophe (2). Geometry illustrating an outside fly-by, north of the ecliptic plane. A comparison is made with the geometry of the Isaiahic event.

bital scheme. Figure 26 illustrates the geometry of the Exodus Catastrophe as the orbits are seen from the celestial north. Figure 27 illustrates the geometry of the Exodus Catastrophe as seen from the Earth's celestial location on January 1 of 1447 B.C.

TABLE VII

COMPARISON OF THE EXODUS AND THE ISAIAHIC CATASTROPHES

Category	Exodus Catastrophe	Isaiahic Catastrophe
The Date	1447 B.C.	701 B.C.
The Day	March 20/21	March 20/21
The Time of Day	Midnight	Evening
Geometry of Mars	North of Ecliptic Plane	North of Ecliptic Plane
Geometry of Mars	Outside Passover	Inside Passover
Estimated Distance	60,000 Miles	70,000 Miles
Bolides, Meteors	Intense	Spotty
Earthquakes	Very severe	Severe
Vulcanism	Extreme	Substantial
Polar Migration	8° to 10° Latitude	5° to 6½° Latitude
Tilt Shift	More than 1½°	0 to 1½°
Calendaric Reform	Calendar Reorganized	Five Days Added
Depopulation of the Land	15% to 25%	5% to 10%
Celestial Visitor in Scripture	Angel of the Lord	Angel of the Lord
God's Prophet	Moses	Isaiah
The Prophet's Advice	To Flee Egypt	To Stay in Jerusalem
The Victims	Egyptian Cavalry	Assyrian Troops
The Hebrews' Celestial Help	Mediterranean Tidal Wave	Astronomical Bolide

Dating the Exodus Catastrophe

The dating of the Exodus Catastrophe is established from the Scriptural record already discussed in I Kings 6:1. The temple, founded in 967 B.C., was 480 years after the Exodus. The Exodus was in 1447 B.C. This closely correlates with carbon-14 dating of contemporary artifacts, as will be demonstrated by Charles McDowell in a future publication and is already available in publications by J. V. Luce and James Mavor, Jr.

In terms of the resonant orbit model, the Exodus Catastrophe would be expected $53\frac{1}{2}$ years earlier than the Long Day of Joshua, which was in November, 1404 B.C. Thus, a resonant orbit model, assuming normal conditions, would propose a date of March, 1457 B.C. However, because Mars made an *outside* fly-by in the Exodus event, it *gained* angular momentum rather than lost it. Therefore the Long Day of Joshua, the next cosmic crisis, came ten years earlier than the model would dictate. This is due mainly to the outside pass, and perhaps partially to the unusually close fly-by of this occasion. The expected calendaric date, March 20/21 was the correct day as Mars still intersected Earth's orbit at this location.

Ramifications of the Exodus Catastrophe

The many facets of this catastrophe are listed as follows, and are subsequently discussed, one by one in this chapter.

1. On Depopulation—The Plague of Death
2. On Crustal Tides and Earth Shocks—The Plague of Death
3. On Renewed Vulcanism—The Plague of Darkness
4. On Iron Dust—The Plague of Blood, or Red Snow
5. On Meteors and Bolides—The Plague of Hail Mingled with Fire
6. On Orbital Shift—Resulting in Calendaric Reorganization
7. On Spin Axis Shift—Resulting in a Change in Latitude
8. On Cosmic Scenery

9. On Cosmic Imagery—The Golden Calf

10. On Astrology

11. On Ancient Catastrophes in the Aegean—The Atlantis Story by Plato

12. Vestiges of Ancient Cosmic Catastrophic Lore in Current Life

Depopulation of Egypt—The Plague of Death

It was estimated that up to 3% to 5% of the population of Palestine was destroyed during both the Greater David Catastrophe and the Joel-Amos holocaust. Perhaps as much as 5% to 10% of the population was destroyed during the Long Day of Joshua and the Isaiahic Catastrophe, (including 185,000 from one single bolide). All of the texts and the context of the Exodus Catastrophe deal with its widespread severity. Some of these Scriptural accounts are found in Exodus; other corroborating accounts are found in the Exodus Psalms.

> So there was hail, and fire mingled with the hail, very grievous, such as there was NONE LIKE IT IN ALL THE LAND OF EGYPT SINCE IT BECAME A NATION. And the hail smote THROUGHOUT ALL the land of Egypt. . . . (Exodus 9:24-25)

The height of the catastrophe for Egypt was the midnight hour, as Palestine on the globe swept past evening, facing Mars on its outside fly-by, or passover. The depopulation of Egypt was considerable.

> And it came to pass, that at midnight the Lord smote all the firstborn in the land of Egypt, from the firstborn of Pharaoh that sat on his throne unto the firstborn of the captive that was in the dungeon; and all the firstborn of cattle. And Pharaoh rose up in the night, he, and all his servants, and all the Egyptians; and there was a great cry in Egypt; FOR THERE WAS NOT A HOUSE WHERE THERE WAS NOT ONE DEAD. (Exodus 12:29-30)

In some parts of Egypt, where bolides chanced to fall, we propose that entire communities were demolished, (as in the case of the collapsed building where Job's children were having a birth-

THE EXODUS CATASTROPHE 221

day party exactly 216 years earlier). In addition, as we shall soon show, tidal waves perhaps 100 feet high swept the Mediterranean coast of Egypt. (When the tidal wave emanated from Krakatoa in 1883, it was a maximum of 100 feet high on the nearby coasts of Java and Sumatra and 36,000 people were drowned.) A tidal bore sweeping up the Nile Delta would also create ample havoc for that, the richest part of Egypt.

On Crustal Tides and Earth Shocks—The Plague of Death

The following description of crustal upheaval sounds to the modern mind (unaccustomed to planetary catastrophes) like fancy, myth or poetic imagination. Let the reader realize that it is authentic description under near fly-by conditions. Observe the magnitude in this, the worst of the series we are discussing:

> The sea saw it, and fled: Jordan[22] [*Lake Menzilah, at that time a swampy lagoon of the Mediterranean Sea*] was driven back. The MOUNTAINS SKIPPED LIKE RAMS, and the LITTLE HILLS LIKE LAMBS. . . . Tremble, thou earth, at the presence of the Lord. . . . (Psalm 114:3, 4, 7)

SOLID EARTH DISTORTION BY MARS. Mars would have a greater effect on Earth's crust at 60,000 miles than at 120,000 miles, but greater by how much? Gravitational interaction follows the principle of Newton's inverse square law, that is, if the distance between the Earth and the Moon were halved, the gravitational attraction would be increased *fourfold* rather than twofold. This applies to freely moving fluids, but for SPHERICAL DISTORTION OR TIDAL DISTORTION, gravitational interaction follows the *inverse of the cube.*[23]

---

[22] In the Hebrew, the word is *yarden*, indicating the principal river. It is derived from the root *yarad*, to descend, to go downwards, and conventionally used to describe a lower region, as a shore, a boundary. The shore in this case was the shore of the Reed Sea (Lake Menzilah) in the Suez Isthmus, a lagoon which has subsequently been silted up. (This is not today's Red Sea.)

[23] Sydney Chapman, *The Earth's Magnetism*, London: Methuen & Co., 1951, p. 76. "This conclusion is supported by the fact that L appears to increase from apogee (when the moon is furthest from the earth) to perigee (when it is nearest) in approximately the same ratio as the moon's tide-producing force, that is, inversely as the cube of the moon's distance." ["L" *refers to deformation.*]

FIGURE 28

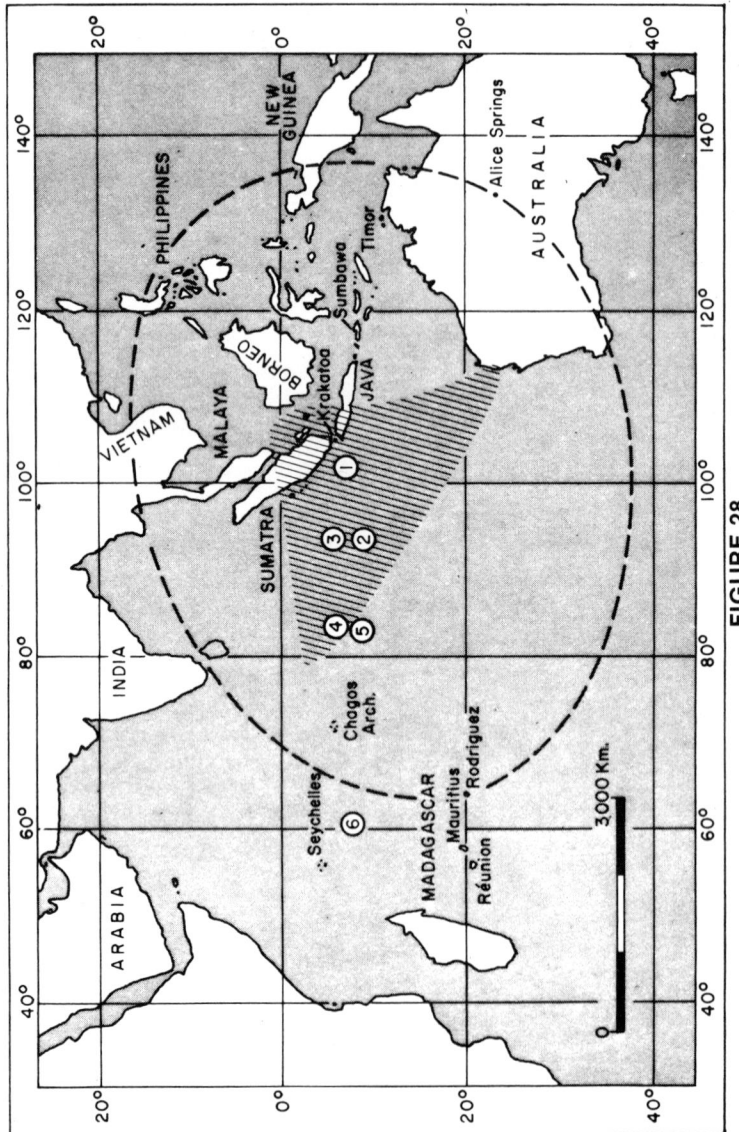

The effects of the Krakatoa eruption in 1883. The shaded area indicates localities at which ash is reported to have fallen after the eruption (suggesting northeasterly winds prevailing at the time). The dotted line indicates the area over which the explosions were heard. (Alice Springs is 2300 miles from Krakatoa; Rodriguez is 3000 miles distant.) The numbers refer to sightings of floating pumice. From Lost Atlantis, page 79, courtesy of McGraw-Hill Book Co.

THE EXODUS CATASTROPHE

The current crustal tide caused by the Moon is two to three inches. The Moon's average distance from the Earth is 240,000 miles, and its mass is .0123 of Earth. Mars, we believe, was at perigee with Earth on this particular fly-by, we estimate, at 60,000 miles. The mass of Mars is .107 of Earth. Table VIII is an endeavor to sketch the tide-raising ability of Mars on a close fly-by with respect to Earth's crust. The two to three inch tide which the moon currently causes is sometimes reinforced by the influence of the Sun, and is sometimes opposed by that same influence depending on their geometries at any particular time.

Velikovsky discovered the Papyrus Ipuwer[24] in the Leyden Library. It purports to be an ancient Egyptian account, an eyewitness account of this same event, only penned by an Egyptian rather than by a Hebrew.

> Ipuwer witnessed and survived this earthquake. "The towns are destroyed. Upper Egypt has become waste. . . . All is ruin." "The residence is overturned in a minute." [*Papyrus Ipuwer 2:11, 3:13*]. Only an earthquake could have overturned the residence in a minute. The Egyptian word for "to overturn" is used in the sense of "to overthrow a wall."[25]

> Also, Hieronymus (St. Jerome) wrote in an epistle that "in the night in which Exodus took place, all the temples of Egypt were destroyed either by an earthshock or by the thunderbolt." . . . An inscription which dates from the beginning of the New Kingdom refers to a temple of the Middle Kingdom that was "swallowed by the ground" at the close of the Middle Kingdom.[26]

Under these conditions, many tents would collapse, resulting in little injury to the tent-dwelling Israelite slaves, living in Goshen, (adjoining the Suez Isthmus). Conversely, many obelisks, city walls, temple structures and other heavy architectures would topple in ruins, decimating the more urbane populace, in this case mostly Egyptians. During the midnight hour of this fateful catas-

---

[24] Another discussion of the Papyrus Ipuwer is found in Donovan A. Courville's *The Exodus Problem and its Ramifications*, Vol. 1, Loma Linda, Calif.: Challenge Books, 1971, pp. 129-132.

[25] Immanuel Velikovsky, *Worlds in Collision*, pp. 62-63.

[26] Velikovsky, *op. cit.*, p. 64.

TABLE VIII
SOLID EARTH DISTORTION BY MARS

Distance of Mars	Crustal Distortion*
240,000 Miles	25 Inches
120,000 Miles	200 Inches
60,000 Miles	1,600 Inches (about 130 feet)

* This distance is measured from the core of the Earth.

trophe, destruction was so intense that, as we have indicated, as much as 20 per cent of the populace died. Some died perhaps due to bolidic explosions, other due to respiratory and heart conditions, others soon to die in the imminent tidal wave, and perhaps most of all due to the earth-shocks and their terrible effect on structures.

Renewed Vulcanism—The Darkness Plague

A crustal distortion such as we have suggested in Table VIII (or even a fraction of the magnitude thereof) would renew thousands of dormant or "extinct" volcanoes, both volcanoes on land, and submarine volcanoes. This discussion is limited to volcanoes on land, terrestrial volcanoes.

> He looketh on the earth, and it trembleth: he toucheth the hills, AND THEY SMOKE. (Psalm 104:32)

How many volcanoes on the Sinai Peninsula were reactivated at this time we have no idea, but there was at least one. Mount Sinai, the mount of lawgiving (the decalogue), is located about 200 miles from the delta of the Nile. It, for one, became a renewed volcano. Depending on the prevailing wind systems of that week, ashes, dust and cinders from this volcano (and presumably others) were the source of the plague of darkness. Volcanic action may also have been related to the plague of frogs, the plague of locusts, and the plague of ashes from the furnace. This one particular mountain, Mount Sinai, was still quaking and in volcanic activity 50 days after the Mars fly-by, the day of lawgiving.

> And Mount Sinai was altogether in a smoke, because the Lord descended upon it in a fire: and the smoke thereof ascended as the smoke of a furnace, and the whole mount quaked greatly. (Exodus 19:18)

When Krakatoa in the East Indies blew up in 1883, it was reported that darkness even at noonday was great in Batavia (100 miles distant) and in Bandung (150 miles distant). Bandung is 2000 feet above sea level.[27] The delta of Egypt was 200 miles from volcanic activity in Sinai, but possibly an entire symphony of belching volcanoes east of the Gulf of Suez added to the effect. While darkness in Indonesia lasted for about a day, the Biblical account suggests a more intense regional volcanic activity:

> ... and there was a thick darkness in all the land of Egypt three days. (Exodus 10:22)

This darkness was so intense that it was "even darkness which may be felt." (Exodus 10:21)

Volcanic action took place not only in Egypt but also elsewhere in the Mediterranean, (note Etna, Stromboli, Vesuvius). The subject of marine vulcanism is reserved for later in this chapter.

On Iron Dust—A Red Snow

We have proposed that Mars at 200,000,000 miles in orbit once fragmented a smaller planet (Electra) sometime between 2400 B.C. and 2100 B.C. Orbiting around Mars were tens of thousands of larger asteroidal fragments from Electra, but also

---

[27] James W. Mavor, Jr., *Voyage to Atlantis*, New York: G. P. Putnam's Sons, 1969, pp. 71-72. "Observations made at Batavia (now Djakarta), on Java, 100 miles from Krakatoa, give us a clear picture of the sequence of events following the ash eruption as observed from some distance away. At 7 a.m. the sky was clear. It then began to darken and become yellow. There was a fall of fine watery particles followed by a few grains of dust. By 11 a.m., there was a regular heavy dust rain followed by complete darkness. The heavy rain continued until 3 p.m., and in the latter phases the dust fell in small rounded accretions resembling hail and we know that complete darkness for a matter of several hours occurred at distances of more than 150 miles from Krakatoa."

orbiting around Mars (the red planet) were billions of particles or granules and dust also from Electra. Such dust must have orbited in a ring, a reddish ring, around Mars at least as far out as 25,000 miles. (This compares to Saturn's icy ring.) When on this occasion, the red planet came as close as perhaps 60,000 miles, much of the iron dust must have been captured by the Earth, and drifted down into the atmosphere, where it oxidized into a rusty hue, and fell as an impressive if unwelcome blanket. Falling in water it precipitated out as orange-red, like blood. In this particular catastrophe the iron oxide was merely one aspect of other more severe phases of catastrophism, hot thunderbolts and lightnings, earthquakes, vulcanism, tidal waves.

> . . . and all the waters that were in the river [*Nile*] were turned to blood. (Exodus 7:20)[28]

On Meteors and Bolides—The Plague of Hail Mingled With Fire

Deber, translated "murrain," has been also translated "pestilence" 48 times in addition to having been translated about 17 other ways. It is meteoritic activity, meteors and bolides. This is the nature of the murrain, the fifth plague. Apparently there were little particles (dust), middle-sized particles (murrain), and big particles (bolides and meteors).

> He gave up their cattle also to the hail, and their flocks to hot thunderbolts. (Psalm 78:48)[29]

> . . . thine arrows also went abroad. The voice of thy thunder was in the heaven; THE LIGHTNINGS LIGHTENED THE WORLD; the earth trembled and shook. (Psalm 77:17-18)

> So there was HAIL, AND FIRE MINGLED WITH THE HAIL, VERY GRIEVOUS, such as there was none like it in all the land of Egypt since it became a nation. And the

---

[28]"Blood" in Hebrew is *dam* which means blood of man or an animal, or perhaps the juice of a grape. Compare this to '*adam* which means to turn rosy, to be dyed red, to be ruddy. From this word comes the name of our earliest ancestor.

[29]"Thunderbolt" is from the Hebrew word *resheph,* a burning coal, an arrow flashing through the air, hence, a meteor.

hail smote throughout all the land of Egypt. . . . (Exodus 9:24-25)

The Long Day of Joshua, compared to this, was "moderate" in meteoritic activity.

The world view of catastrophism, and the Jewish experience in catastrophism (more often than not, deliverance from invasion or oppression) is seen in Psalm 91.

> Surely he shall deliver thee from the snare of the fowler [*the devil*], and from THE NOISOME PESTILENCE . . . Thou shalt not be afraid FOR THE TERROR BY NIGHT; nor for the ARROW THAT FLIETH BY DAY; nor for the PESTILENCE THAT WALKETH IN DARKNESS; nor for the DESTRUCTION THAT WASTETH AT NOONDAY. (Psalm 91: 3, 5, 6)

"Pestilence that walketh in darkness" could describe the midnight hour of the Exodus Catastrophe. "The terror by night" could describe the eventide hour of the Isaiahic Catastrophe. "The arrow that flieth by day" could describe the dawn hour of the Sodom-Gomorrah holocaust. "The arrow that flieth by day" could also describe the afternoon hour of the Tower of Babel Catastrophe. "The destruction that wasteth at noonday" probably best describes the Long Day of Joshua. Thus the holocausts were known to the ancients to come from one direction (from on high) but at varying times of the day or night, as would be expected in a long series.

On Orbital Shift—Resulting in Calendaric Changes

In Chapter IV, we discussed the geometry of the Isaiahic Catastrophe. It was quite similar to the Exodus Catastrophe except it was less intense, and Mars made an inside fly-by. Hence, we conclude:

(1) The spin axis precession was greater during the Exodus Catastrophe.

(2) The polar migration was in another, but not necessarily opposite direction upon our globe.

(3) The position of Palestine at Mars' perigee was about six hours later (midnight rather than evening).

Assuming the correctness of our model, the spin axis relocation during the Exodus Catastrophe may have been in the range of 400 to 800 miles. "True" east and "true" north once again changed their position somewhat. Possibly some change in axial tilt accompanied the polar relocation.

In the Isaiahic Catastrophe, it was also noted that the year changed from 360 days to 365¼ days. While a minor part of this change may have been due to an increase in spin rate, the major part (as much as 70%) of the change in day count per year was due to an expanded orbit. The result in 701 B.C. was the sudden need among ancient people for a calendaric revision. Some peoples revised by adding five days per year, some revised by adding a month every few years. A calendaric revision is an indication, then, of an orbital shift, either an expansion (which would require more days per year) or a contraction (which would require less), or a spin rate change.

According to the model, the Exodus fly-by was a modified version of the Case One geometry, the modification being an outside pass. The normal geometry, the inside pass would result in an increase of angular momentum for Earth (and a decrease for Mars). In this modification, the outside pass, we would expect the opposite, that is, a *decrease in angular momentum* of the Earth, thus contraction of the orbit to some degree, and fewer days per year.

In Chapter II, we observed that the Teutons, in response to catastrophic cosmology in their early ages, named the days of the week after the planets. The Latins named the first several months of the year after the planets, probably following the Etruscan pattern. Other ancient civilizations followed comparable patterns in their veneration of the planets. The names of some of the Hebrew months may also be of interest, especially the month which was roughly October 7 to November 6, which was the month of all the autumn catastrophes. The name Marchesvan is related to *ma'or (me'orah),* ancient Hebrew for "Mars."[30,31]

---

[30] *Strong's Exhaustive Concordance of the Bible,* "Dictionary of the Hebrew Bible," p. 60. "Other forms are *ma'owr, m'owrah, m'orah,*" defined by Strong as a luminous body, a luminary, a light, a brightness. It compares to *mazzalah* which we suspect means planet in the general sense, and *mazzarah* which appears in Job 38:32.

[31] Personal correspondence between Charles McDowell and Patten.

FIGURE 29

Left: One of "Cleopatra's Needles," set up by Thothmes III at Heliopolis, removed to Alexandria in 23 B.C., and thence to New York where it now stands. It is 67.2 feet high excluding pedestal. This compares with Ahaz' sun dial which we estimated at 60 feet high. (see Fig. 17). Center: the second of "Cleopatra's Needles," 68.4 feet high removed to London. Right: obelisk of Senusret I still standing on its original emplacement near Heliopolis, the earliest obelisk known to us. From Wonders of the Past, Vol. II, p. 530, courtesy of G. P. Putnam's Sons.

ANCIENT HEBREW CALENDAR

MARCHESVAN[32] (Bul)	October 7 — November 6
Chisleu	November 7 — December 6
Tebeth	December 7 — January 6
Sebat	January 7 — February 6
Adar	February 7 — March 6
Nisan	March 7 — April 6
Iyyar (Ziv)	April 7 — May 6
Sivan	May 7 — June 6
Tammuz	June 7 — July 6
Ab	July 7 — August 6
Elul	August 7 — September 6
Tishri	September 7 — October 6

It is entirely possible that names of some of the months are related to the planets. For instance, note the similarity of Iyyar (April) with the Chaldean Ishtar, or Venus, the same month corresponding to the Latin Aprilla, also after Venus. Marchesvan was the ancient month in which the Case Two catastrophes occurred, and a variant name for Marchesvan is "Bul," after Bel or Baal, already identified as Mars in Chaldean and Ugaritic.

The calendaric change instituted by Hezekiah about 696 B.C., while significant, appears modest when compared to the calendaric revision instituted by Moses. Moses did the equivalent of switching January into July. He shifted Tishri, or September, from the first month in the Hebrew calendar to the seventh. Similarly, Nisan (March-April) was shifted from the seventh to the first. Perhaps cumulative discrepancies due to the Sodom-

---

[32] This same month of October 7—November 6 is *Araksamna* in Chaldean, perhaps related to the Greek Ares. The Phoenician calendar called the month October 7-November 6 "Bul," after Baal or Mars. The Araksamna should be noted in conjunction with the Celtic Samhain, already discussed as the end of the year, and the time of the flying witches in the heavens with their sweeping broomsticks, panic, dread and so forth, for "Samhain" may have a Chaldean derivation. In Hindu, the same month of October 7-November 6 is known as "Margasira" which again suggests Mars' month. In Sanskrit, the astronomical solar month begins with one "samkranti" of the Sun. This again suggests a common etymology of the Chaldean *Araksamna* and the Celtic *Samhain*. This may also be the origin for the English word "Sun." This brief comment suggests how much study in etymology especially in astronomical terms needs to be undertaken.

THE EXODUS CATASTROPHE

Gomorrah holocaust and the suspected Job Catastrophe (1663-B.C.) were demanding a revision even before this particular fly-by. At any rate, the older Hebrew calendar prior to the Exodus Catastrophe suddenly became obsolete.

> And the Lord spoke unto Moses and Aaron in the land of Egypt, saying, This month [*the month of the 1447 B.C. fly-by*] shall be unto you THE BEGINNING OF MONTHS: it shall be the first month of the year to you. (Exodus 12:1-2)

This day, the fourteenth of Nisan (and the thirteenth, its eve) became the most memorable day in the Hebrew calendar. The same day, later, was designated by Numa to become Rome's New Year Day.

In the ancient Hebrew calendar, the month of Tishri (including the time of the autumnal equinox, September 21, the first day of autumn) had been the first month, and had included the original New Year Day. Josephus describes this time of calendaric reform. The earlier Tishri calendar had been in use for 1,000 years, back to the era of the Flood Catastrophe.

> This calamity happened in the six hundredth year of Noah's government [*age*] in the second month, called by the Macedonians Dius, but by the Hebrews Marchesven; for so did they order their year in Egypt. But Moses appointed that Nisan, which is the same with Xanthicus, should be the first month for their festivals, because he brought them out of Egypt in that month: so that this month began the year, as to all the solemnities they observed to the honour of God, although he preserved the original order of the months as to selling and buying, and other ordinary affairs.[33]

Marchesvan (Bul) was originally the second month, and this month saw such catastrophes as the Tower of Babel Catastrophe, the Long Day of Joshua, and the Joel-Amos Catastrophe.

Shortly after the Isaiahic Catastrophe in 701 B.C., King Hezekiah not only introduced a calendaric revision, but also closed the east gate of Jerusalem, for it no longer identified or

---

[33] Flavius Josephus, *Antiquities of the Jews,* Book I, Chapter III, section 3, pp. 83-84.

portrayed "true" east. (It very likely had a surveying significance.) In the Isaiahic Catastrophe we believe the geographical poles shifted some 300 miles to 400 miles, and latitude shifted between 5° and 6½°. The Exodus Catastrophe was worse; a 500 mile polar relocation could be a conservative estimate. Egypt and Palestine may well have changed between 5° and 10° of latitude.

With a relocated pole and a shift in axis tilt, up to a month could be either added to, or removed from the calendar (depending on the geometry of the case). Rather than make a minor adjustment to patch up the calendar (as Numa, who added five days per year, or Hezekiah, who added one month every five years), Moses merely rescheduled entire calendar, making the vernal equinox of the Northern Hemisphere the New Year Day. A new direction for true north was also the new order, but surveying concerns were not uppermost in the Hebrews minds as they were leaving Egypt anyway, and becoming a nomadic people for the next 40 or 45 years.

On Spin Axis Shift—A Change in Latitude[34]

Comparisons to the Isaiahic Catastrophe have already been made in terms of calendaric revision, orbital shift and suspected spin axis shifts. The discussion was based on the precedent of the Isaiahic Catastrophe, and general theory of precession derived from Chapter IV.

The Sinai Peninsula is the region to which the children of Israel migrated, and camped for the better part of their 40 year

---

[34]In his work, *Worlds in Collision,* pp. 105 ff., Velikovsky refers to ancient literature, especially Egyptian source material, to conclude that in a former age, the Earth rotated on an east-to-west basis. "In the Papyrus Ipuwer it is similarly stated that 'the land turns round [*over*] as does a potter's wheel' and the 'Earth turned upside down.' " (p. 107). " 'A characteristic feature of the Senmut ceiling is the astronomically objectionable orientation of the southern panel.' The center of this panel is occupied by the Orion-Sirius group, in which Orion appears west of Sirius instead of east. 'The orientation of the southern panel is such that the person in the tomb looking at it has to lift his head and face north, not south.' 'With the reversed orientation of the south panel, Orion, the most conspicuous constellation of the southern sky, appeared to be moving eastward, i.e., in the wrong direction.' " (p. 108).

Velikovsky concluded that the rotation of the Earth, during a former age, was from east to west, opposite of today, although he gives no celes-

THE EXODUS CATASTROPHE

period in the wilderness. Their encampments were especially in the southern part of that peninsula. This peninsula today comprises about 25,000 square miles, latitude 29° to 30° N. It is desolate, arid, hostile, a sandy waste, virtually devoid of flora and population. However, in 1447 B.C. to 1410 B.C., it supported an estimated two million persons plus their livestock.

In today's climatology, there is a zone called the "horse latitudes" throughout the Earth. The zone is located from 15° N. to 35° N. on the westerly sides (but not the easterly sides) of all the continents. In this latitude zone, there are deserts in both the Northern and Southern Hemispheres. Deserts in this "horse latitude" zone include the Atacama of Chile, the Sonoran of Northern Mexico, the Kalahari of Southwest Africa, the Great Australian Desert, the Sahara Desert of North Africa and its extension, the Arabian Desert. (This zone has been given the name "horse latitudes" because in such arid zones, horses became a critically essential part of the nomadic culture.) Today Sinai is in the middle of this zone of aridity.

Today the Sinai Peninsula is so deficient in rainfall that the hardiest of scrub plants often fail to survive. Creeks and rivers are nonexistent. Oases are very few, very small and far between. Yet during the era after the Exodus Catastrophe over two million people encamped there with their cattle — a population density of nearly 100 per square mile. There is no record of perishing from thirst; instead the record indicates an experience of hardy survival and *growth in numbers,* both for people and livestock. This kind of population requires ample water, and the only way the Sinai Peninsula could have been moderately-well watered would be for it to catch the rain-bearing winds, either the rain-bearing westerly wind system of the mid-latitudes, a generally cool wind zone, or else the trade winds astride the

---

tial mechanics, and forces causing such a reversal would probably fragment the Earth. Another method of suggesting something comparable would be to suggest that the spin axis of the Earth flipped 180°, either in steps or on a single occasion.

We subscribe to neither of these conclusions, that is, a reversal of rotation or a 180° spin axis flip. But we do subscribe to the idea that the north pole has shifted significantly on a number of ancient occasions, a cumulative number not less than five. The shift in location should be considered in a magnitude of hundreds of miles, not thousands, for each occasion. This may be a better explanation for some of this intriguing, if puzzling data.

equator in a more equatorial latitude. Here, with another latitude, perhaps the Sinai could catch the easterly trade winds of another era.

In the Isaiahic Catastrophe, we proposed a shift of between 5° and 6½° latitude, a southerly shift. Other shifts occurred during the Exodus Catastrophe, the Long Day of Joshua and perhaps also during the Greater Davidic Catastrophe, to change the climatic zone of the Sinai. This is another, indirect method of concluding that the location of the geographic poles migrated significantly during these ancient catastrophic days, or, to quote the book of Job, "the pillars of the earth trembled."

On Cosmic Scenery

In *The Book of Enoch* and other Jewish apocryphal and Talmudic writings, six archangels are named and their functions are associated with the luminaries.

> . . . I beheld seven stars of heaven bound in it together, like great mountains, and like a blazing fire. . . . These are those of the stars which have transgressed the commandment of the most high God. . . . (*The Book of Enoch* 21:3)

> Then the angel said: This place, until the consummation of heaven and earth, will be the prison of the stars, and the host of heaven. The stars which roll over fire are those which transgressed the commandment of God before their time arrived; for they came not in their proper season. . . . (*The Book of Enoch* 18:15-16)

Various ancient Jewish literary works including Talmudic commentaries are helpful in understanding the term "the angel of the Lord," an archangel, which passed over Egypt on the night of March 20, 1447 B.C., and which passed over Jerusalem on the days of the Davidic Catastrophe and the Isaiahic Catastrophe.

> . . . The Lord will PASS OVER the door, and will not suffer THE DESTROYER to come in unto your houses to smite you. (Exodus 12:23)

> And the angel of God, which went before the camp of Israel, removed and went behind them; and the PILLAR OF THE CLOUD went from before their face, and stood behind them . . . it was a cloud and darkness to them, but it gave light by night to these. . . . (Exodus 14:19-20).

THE EXODUS CATASTROPHE

> And the Lord went before them by day IN A PILLAR OF A CLOUD, to lead them the way; and by night IN A PILLAR OF FIRE, to give them light; to go by day and night: He took not away the pillar of the cloud by day, nor the pillar of fire by night. . . . (Exodus 13:21-22)[35]

> . . . It is the sacrifice of the Lord's PASSOVER, who passed over the houses of the children of Israel in Egypt. . . . (Exodus 12:27)

> It is a night to be much observed unto the Lord for bringing them out from the land of Egypt: this is THAT NIGHT OF THE LORD to be observed of all the children of Israel in their generations. (Exodus 12:42)

As with most peoples, later generations of the children of Israel scarcely remembered, and could little appreciate the earlier events of the nation's dramatic history:

> They kept not the covenant of God, and refused to walk in his law; And forgat his works, and HIS WONDERS that he shewed them. Marvellous things did he in the sight of their fathers, in the land of Egypt. . . . In the daytime also he led them with a cloud, and all the night with a light of fire. (Psalm 78:10-12, 14)

On Cosmic Imagery — The Golden Calf[36]

In Habakkuk 3:4, the Martian passover is described as having "horns." These horns are thought to describe the thin but silvery and fearful crescent of Mars as it assaulted Earth. It came somewhat from an "out of the Sun" in direction. The sacred Egyptian bullock also had two long curved horns. This bullock, Apis, was the god of the ancient cult. It was identified in Egyptian religion with the marauding planet we now know to be Mars. Worship of the sacred bovine was widespread during those days of astrological lore and astronomical catastrophism. (Vestiges of this worship survive in India today where the Brahmans still worship the "sacred" cow. Celestial cows which hurl their fire upon

---

[35] We believe the "cloud by day, and the pillar of fire by night" was Mars. Mars has an albedo (or reflectivity) of 15% compared to the Moon's dull 7% ability to reflect sunlight, and Earth's 39% (including clouds and oceans). At 240,000 miles from Earth, the average lunar distance, Mars-shine would exceed moonlight by a factor of 8.15. At 700,000 miles, Mars and the Moon would have about equal brightness.

[36] In Exodus 32:4, "calf" is from the Hebrew word 'egel meaning a steer or bullock, a male calf nearly grown.

FIGURE 30

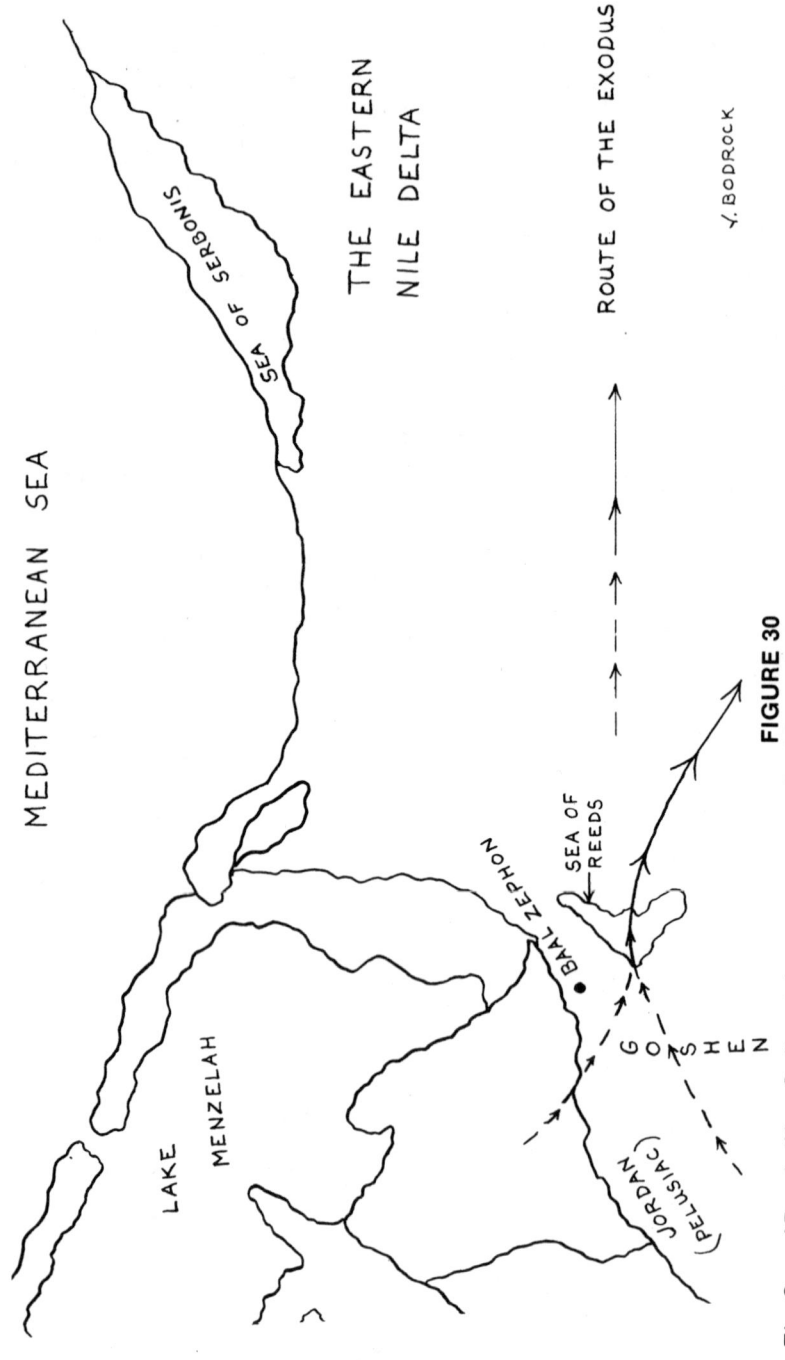

The Sea of Reeds (Yam Suf), not the contemporary Red Sea, is believed to have been the route of the Hebrew exodus. Much of the local geography has changed as lakes have silted up, river courses have shifted and desert sands have moved in. Courtesy of Charles McDowell and V. Bodrock, Cuyahoga Community College, Parma, Ohio.

the Earth are described in passages of the Hindu Ramayana.)

Many of the Hebrews leaving Egypt were still oriented to Egyptian religious themes, idolatrous and polytheistic. Several weeks after their escape through the "Red" Sea, Moses climbed the volcanic Mt. Sinai where he was to receive the decalogue. In his absence, the children of Israel reverted to idolatry. They gathered all the golden jewelry, melted down the gold and cast it into a model of the bullock Apis, a golden image replete with horns. It was a symbol of the astronomical destroyer, the marauding planet in its crescent appearance, which had just caused the massive holocaust.

On Astrology

The Hebrew understanding of cosmology was that the planets were part of God's creation and purpose, whether bringing catastrophes or not, whether regular or irregular in their periods. The pagan rites involved the worship of Baal, or Mars, and of Ashtoreth, or Venus. Baal was the evil god of fire and destruction which needed placating; Ashtoreth was the goddess of restoration and fertility. Child sacrifices were offered to the former, sex orgies to the latter. The Baal cult was influential in Babylonia at least as early as the twenty-second century B.C.[37] Canaanite, Greek, Phoenician, Egyptian and to a lesser extent Roman cultures were influenced by this cult.

Associated with the worship of Ashtoreth and Baal were astrological omens, incantations, licentious rituals, sacrificial murders, orgiastic music, sorceries and witchcraft. During times of national crises, there was a rash of human sacrifice rituals. One such time was the night before Carthage fell, when Roman troops could smell strongly the burning flesh of the Carthaginian children. Other national crises included eves of the planetary holocausts. If planetary catastrophism came anyway, it was rationalized that an insufficient number of sacrifices had been made.

With this general background, we can see that, especially

---

[37] Louis Ginzberg, *Legends of the Jews*, Vol. I, p. 186. Concerning Serug, grandfather of Abraham: "When he grew to manhood, the name was seen to have been chosen fittingly, for he, too, worshipped idols, and when he himself had a son, Nahor by name, he taught him the arts of the Chaldees, how to be a soothsayer and practice magic ACCORDING TO SIGNS IN THE HEAVENS."

in the general region of Palestine, clashing religious views paralleled the clashing orbits and the clashing geomagnetic sheaths of Earth and Mars. The origins of astrology were established early within this era of history, certainly before 2100 B.C. It is the strong Hebrew tradition of monotheism which clashed head-on with the Amorite-Chaldean-Phoenician system of Ashtoreth and Baal.[38] Since Amorite kings assumed power in Egypt about 100 years before the Exodus holocaust, circa 1550 B.C., this background may be helpful in understanding why the Hebrews were singled out for slavery, for pyramid-building, and for gradual genocide, seen as the state policy at the time of the birth of Moses.

On Ancient Catastrophism in the Aegean

One final episode of the Exodus Catastrophe remains to be considered, an episode which is of considerable import. In our model, Mars approached perhaps as close as 60,000 miles, justifiably causing worldwide panic. The Earth's crust experienced a tide of perhaps 130 feet, compared to the normal two to three inches induced by the Moon and Sun. Volcanic activity occurred on land. Mount Sinai was one illustration:

> And Mount Sinai was altogether on a smoke ... the smoke thereof ascended as the smoke of a furnace, and the whole mount quaked greatly. (Exodus 19:18)
>
> ... the earth trembled and shook. (Psalm 77:18)
>
> He looketh on the earth and it trembleth: he toucheth the the hills, and THEY SMOKE. (Psalm 104:32)

Terrestrial vulcanism has been discussed, and among the effects were a thick darkness which accompanied the passover. This darkness was explained as a result of volcanic ashes, cinders and dust which virtually shut out sunlight for three days. This was *terrestrial vulcanism*. There is a second kind of vulcanism equally as significant, namely *marine vulcanism*. This occurs

---

[38]The Baal cult had gathered much influence and fostered much international ambition. Its most famous endeavor was the construction of the Tower of Babel, with an astrological temple or observatory at its apex. This system required slavery (600,000 slaves were conscripted to build the Tower), high level taxation, international power lust, intrigue, tyranny, loose marital bonds, and so forth. It was quite contrary to the Noachian heritage of creation, freedom, marital bonds and the heritages of nationalism.

when volcanic islands, or submerged volcanic cones suddenly become active. Boiling, discolored water, earthquakes and tidal waves are among the results of marine vulcanism.

THERA. Thera is an island 70 miles north of Crete in the Eastern Mediterranean Sea, and about 180 miles southeast of Athens. It is a caldera[39], about eight miles across on one side and ten miles across on the other. The rim of the caldera projects above sea level; the crater is below sea level. A caldera is formed when a marine volcano expels several cubic miles of ash, cinder, dust and lava, and the expulsion results in a hollow center. The hollow center is partly below sea level. The volcanic walls then collapse, leaving merely the rim. Thera is the largest known caldera on Earth. See Figures 31, 32, 33.

In ancient times, before 1500 B.C., Thera was closely associated with Crete, and the ancient empire of Minos (the Minoan Empire). Crete was the political capital of that ancient, far-flung, maritime empire, and the island of Thera was the empire's religious capital. The capital on Crete was the historical Knossos. This famous but remote empire disappeared from the scene of history, as it were, overnight.

The eruption of Thera has been correlated within the last two decades with the cataclysmic events simultaneous with the Exodus Catastrophe. The correlation in timing has been by carbon-14 datings, by buried archaeological pottery, and by historical analysis. Certain timbers remain there, buried in the paroxysm, which yield carbon-14 dates identical to those of the Exodus upheaval.[40,41] The correlations in timing have been well documented by Mavor, Luce, and more recently, in *National Geographic*.

> So, between 1450 and 1400 B.C., the greater part of the island of Thera collapsed into the cavernous abyss left by the eruption of cubic miles of ash and pumice, leaving behind the three remnants we know today. Thera, Therasia and Aspronisi are disposed concentrically about a central

---

[39] A caldera is the rim of a volcano, the sides of which have collapsed back into the sea. It forms a crater with a diameter many times that of the volcanic vent formed by the collapse of the central part of the volcano.

[40] J. V. Luce, *Lost Atlantis*, New York: McGraw-Hill, 1969, pp. 63 ff., p. 200.

[41] James W. Mavor, Jr., *Voyage to Atlantis*, New York: G. P. Putnam's Sons, 1969, p. 267 ff.

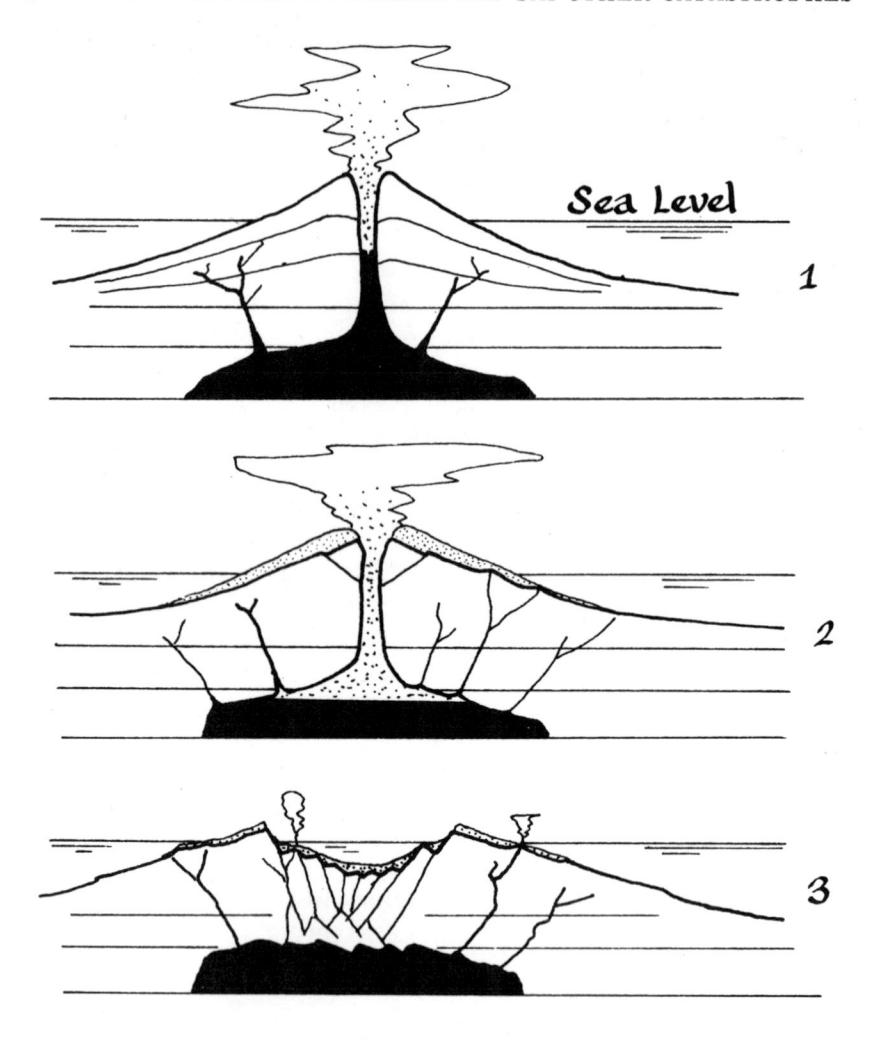

FIGURE 31
Volcanic eruption and collapse, typical behavior of a Theran cone. (1) Eruption. (2) Eruption and partial voiding of the magma chamber below. (3) Collapse of the unsupported cone into the empty magma chamber, creating a great water-filled caldera. From Voyage to Atlantis, *p. 44, by arrangement with G.P. Putnam's Sons.*

FIGURE 32
Possible reconstruction of Thera-Atlantis before the great collapse of the 15th century B.C., and an aerial view of Thera today. From Voyage to Atlantis, p. 78, by arrangement with G. P. Putnam's Sons.

bay some 32 square miles in area, with a maximum depth of 1,300 feet. This enormous hole is the most imposing marine caldera, or collapsed volcano, in the world.[42]

The collapse also created tremendous sea waves, which radiated in all directions as far, certainly, as the coasts of Africa and the Levant....[43]

The morphology of the caldera, however, and the extent of the pumice deposits indicate that it was at least as powerful, and it may well have been more powerful [*than the explosion of Krakatoa*], judging from the greater depth of the *graben*. We do know that fine Thera tephra was scattered over an area of 300,000 sq. km., mainly in a southeasterly direction. THERE IS ALSO SOME INDICATION OF A TIDAL WAVE OVER 200 M. [*meters*] HIGH ON NEARBY ANAPHI....[44]

It is known that this particular volcanic eruption spread nine to ten cubic miles of ash and cinders across at least a 150,000 square mile area of the Eastern Mediterranean, blanketing Crete and reaching almost to Egypt. Compare this single eruption with the eruptions which must have occurred from the volcanic cones on the Sinai Peninsula just 150 to 200 miles southeast of the Nile Delta and the Suez Isthmus.

A massive tidal wave of 200 meters is about 650 feet high, and such a wave is believed to have occurred at this time on the nearby islands.[45] This tidal wave overwhelmed the Cretan coastline and inundated, virtually intact, such cultural centers as Knossos. Assuming that the effect would dissipate with distance, how large would the tidal wave have been on the Levant Coast, or moving up the Nile Delta, or across the Suez Isthmus? A wave

---

[42] Spyridon Marinatos, *National Geographic*, "Thera, Key to the Riddle of Minos," 1972, Vol. 141, No. 5, pp. 702-726.

[43] James W. Mavor, Jr., *op. cit.*, pp. 61-62.

[44] J. V. Luce, *op. cit.*, p. 83.

[45] Among the high points reached on land by the sea as a result of earthquake-caused tsunamis is one in the year 1737 on Cape Lopatka, on Russia's Kamchatka Peninsula, a height of 220 feet. In 1936, following a slump in the Norwegian lake of Loen, a wave 240 feet in height was generated.... Following a large-scale earthquake in the eastern Mediterranean in A.D. 365, a wave carried a ship two miles inland.... (See J. W. Mavor, *op. cit.*, p. 67.)

THE EXODUS CATASTROPHE

of 100 feet in height could be a conservative estimate. The Suez Isthmus is 500 miles from Thera.[46, 47, 48]

The paroxysm of Thera correlates with the Exodus holocaust in Egypt. Three days after the passover, the tidal waves generated by the collapsing walls of the volcanic cone would correlate with the water overwhelming Egyptian charioteers as they pursued the children of Israel across the Suez Isthmus. The site of the inundation of the Egyptian army and deliverance of the fleeing Hebrews is thought to be an arm of Lake Menzilah, an ancient lagoon adjoining the Mediterranean Sea, and was not the Red Sea as we know it today. This should be a good site for archaelogists interested in Egyptian chariots.

The tidal wave of 1447 B.C., affecting Egypt and the Levant, is recounted twice by the historian Amos in his messages warning his people of the coming holocaust in 756 B.C. He uses the "flood of Egypt" as a template of the holocaust he is predicting.

> Shall not the land tremble for this, and every one mourn that dwelleth therein? and it shall rise up wholly as a flood; and it shall be cast out and drowned, AS BY THE FLOOD OF EGYPT. (Amos 8:8; see also Amos 9:5)

It is worth noting that Amos differentiated between the flood of Egypt and the flood of Noah. Ancient Greek texts do the same, differentiating between the floods of Deucalion (Noah) and Ogyges (contemporary with Moses).

---

[46] And the Lord said unto Moses, Stretch out thine hand over the sea, that the waters may come again upon the Egyptians, upon their chariots, and upon their horseman. And Moses stretched forth his hand over the sea, and THE SEA RETURNED to his strength when the morning appeared . . . and the Lord overthrew the Egyptians IN THE MIDST OF THE SEA. And the waters returned, and covered the chariots, and the horsemen, and all the host of Pharaoh that came into the sea. . . . (Exodus 14:26-28)

[47] When Krakatoa, another volcanic island becoming a caldera, exploded in 1883, there were generated three successive waves, 50 and up to 100 feet high on the nearby Java and Sumatra coasts. These waves were 80 miles long. 36,000 lives were lost along these coasts as villages and ports were overwhelmed. The effects of these tidal waves, transmitted through the Indian Ocean, around Cape of Good Hope, and through the South and North Atlantic Oceans, were measured as far distant as England and France, on the English Channel. (See James W. Mavor, op. cit., p. 63, and J. V. Luce, op. cit., p. 83.)

[48] We can estimate conservatively that the sea climbed to heights of 300 feet or more on Crete, coastal Greece and Turkey. Waterborne pumice stone has been found on the Island of Anaphe, near Thera, at an elevation of 750 feet. (Mavor, op. cit., p. 64.)

Following this recounting of the Exodus-Thera tidal wave, the "flood of Egypt," Amos records simultaneously the migration of three peoples. They are the Hebrews out of Egypt, the Philistines (Cretans or Minoans, including Therans) out of Caphtor (or Crete), and the Syrians out of Kir (Amos 9:7). He could have added, with accuracy, the Amalekites out of Northwestern Arabia into the Nile delta, a migration of hungry, plundering nomads which Moses records.

Migrations of unsettled peoples probably followed many times in the wake of the several ancient catastrophes. Many of the Cretans and Therans who survived the Thera disaster settled on the coast of Palestine, where they were known as the "Philistines," and in fact have given their name to "Palestine."

When the walls of Krakatoa were collapsing in August, 1883, and the immense, hundred-foot tidal waves were being generated, it is recorded that sailors on ships passing through the straits noticed virtually nothing at all as their boats gradually were lifted 50 to 100 feet above mean sea level, and were gently let down again. It was with great surpise that they realized they had experienced a tidal wave, even though they had ridden the crest of it. Meanwhile, people by the tens of thousands were drowning on the nearby coasts. This suggests that during the Thera paroxysm, refugees sailing across the open sea were safer than those who had just landed on the shores of Crete, Rhodes, Palestine or other friendly ports. (This also suggests that in the far worse watery catastrophe, the Deluge, a barge or boat in open sea was easily the safest of all places.)

Further describing the Krakatoa explosion, a smaller model of the Thera disaster, is the following:

> A pall of darkness spread rapidly outwards as the great central column of dust and vapour began to descend. By 10:30 a.m. it had become so dark in Lampong Bay that the *Gouverneur-Generaal Loudon* had to anchor. An hour later complete darkness had spred to Batavia 160 km. [*100 miles*] away, and a heavy dust-rain went on till 3 p.m. Eventually the darkness extended to Bandung nearly 240 km. [*150 miles distant and 2400 feet above sea level*] east of Krakatoa.[49]

---

[49] J. V. Luce, *op. cit.*, pp. 78-79.

THE EXODUS CATASTROPHE 245

> The caldera of Thera has a surface area of 32 square miles and is some 1,300 feet deep, with a volume about five times that of the Krakatoa caldera. Based on the volume of collapsed land, a Hungarian scientist, P. Hedervaris, has estimated that the heat energy released during the Thera eruption must have been four and one-half times that of Krakatoa. The total energy unleashed during the Krakatoa eruption has been estimated as 430 times more powerful than the explosion of an Eniwetok H-bomb.[50]

Earlier, we mentioned the pioneer archaeologist Heinrich Schliemann who was convinced that the *Iliad* contained a core of *geographical and historical* truth about Troy. His excavations proved his hypothesis as his finds of relics of ancient Troy amazed the scientific world. What Schliemann failed to also realize was that the cosmology of the *Iliad*, the war between Apollo/Ares and Hera, or Earth (with Aphrodite and Zeus as bystanders), also contained a core of *cosmological and astronomical truth*.

And similarly, Spyridon Marinatos has published on his outstanding hypothesis that the paroxysm of Thera correlates with both the Egyptian plagues and the Atlantis legend. What Marinatos has failed to realize is that a near fly-by of Mars, in the month and year of March 1447 B.C., caused both dormant volcanoes (Sinai and Thera) to mightily erupt. Mars at 60,000 miles would cause a 130 foot crustal tide as measured from Earth's core, ample to renew 1,000 and perhaps 10,000 dormant volcanic cones, both terrestrial and submarine. Thera is at a junction of fault lines crossing the Eastern Mediterranean Sea, and the crust in its area was under particular stress.

ATLANTIS. Marinatos first conceived the idea that the Theran paroxysm and the Atlantis tradition were one and the same. He published on this in 1939, and some 30 years later, this outstanding hypothesis has begun to receive its due credit and become generally accepted. Of course there were serious discussions and unimaginative detractors surrounding him and his startling hypothesis within archaeological circles, especially within Greek archaeological circles. However, the important

---

[50]James W. Mavor, Jr., *op. cit.*, p. 67.

thing is that in time, the evidence became convincing, even overwhelmingly in favor of his view. Not only did he link the Theran paroxysm with the Exodus events; he also linked it with the legend of Atlantis, as is found in Plato's *Timaeus* and *Critias*. Plato described in considerable detail the customs of the empire, the urban geography of this ancient island kingdom of Atlantis, and its associated island which we now know to be Crete. The story originally was cycled through Egyptian sources back to Greece, where Plato copied it several generations later, from Solon's account.

From Plato's account, Atlantis should be located geographically beyond Gibralter due to the number of *stadia* given for its distance. However, Marinatos has proposed that in the translation of the account from Egyptian into Greek, one zero was added into all numbers of 100 or more by a translator's error.

> Dr. Galanopoulos has an explanation for the tenfold discrepancy: in the translation of the Egyptian scripts by Solon, the symbol 100 was unquestionably rendered as 1,000. An example of this same sort of confusion in modern times, is the contrast between the American billion, which is a thousand million, and the English billion, which is a million million.[51]

If this hypothesis is applied, distances, dimensions and populations of the two islands fit Thera and Crete very very well, if not perfectly. This means that Plato's account of Atlantis and other accounts of the sudden demise of an ancient but great civilization describe the fall, virtually overnight, of the great Minoan civilization. This also means that the Atlantis tradition and the ten plagues of Egypt were *contemporary developments*. Egypt suffered terrestrial and astronomical destruction even while Crete and Thera were being inundated and destroyed.

> Moreover, by means of trade and diffusion of religious ritual, in the second millenium B.C., the Cretan connection extended to northern and western Europe as well as to all the Mediterranean lands. And significantly, in all these places—Egypt, Italy, Spain, Sardinia—it ceased about 1500 B.C., just at the time of the Thera eruption.[52]

---

[51] J. W. Mavor, Jr., *op. cit.*, p. 33.

[52] J. W. Mavor, Jr., *op. cit.*, p. 177.

THE EXODUS CATASTROPHE

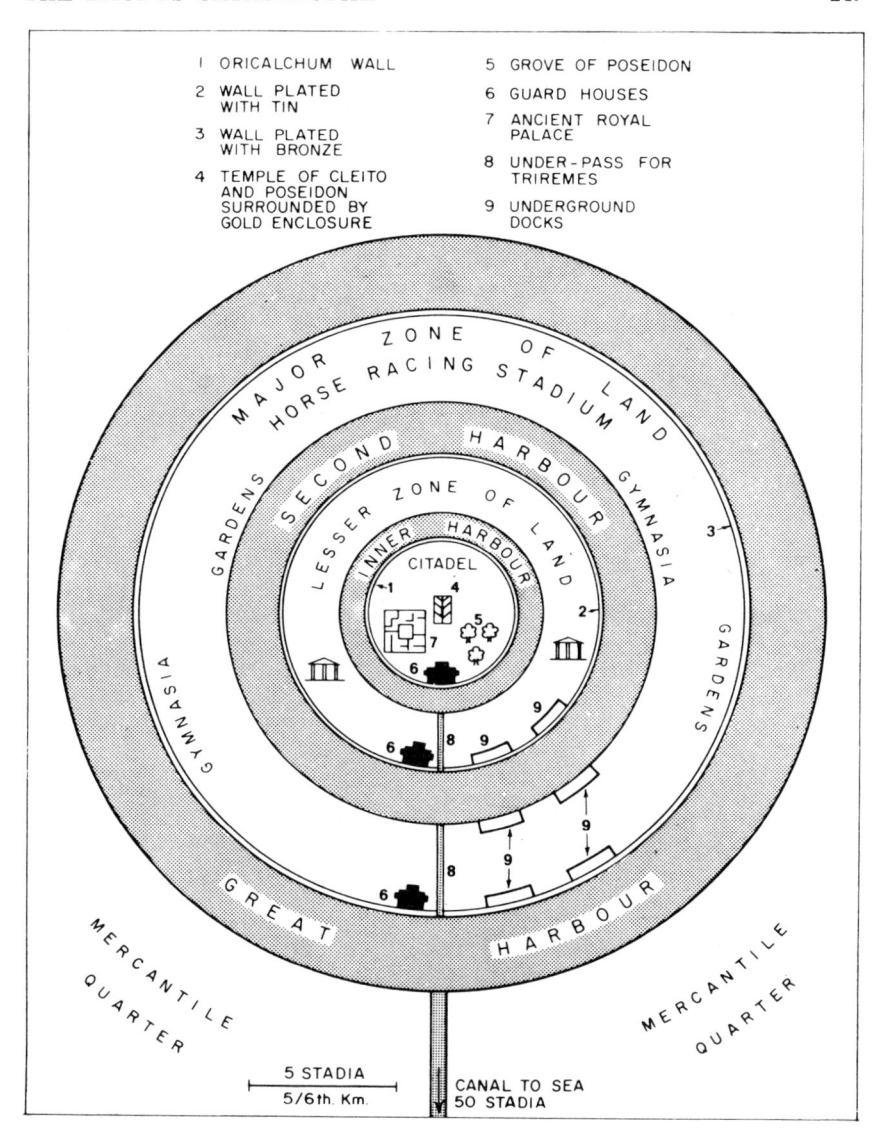

1 ORICALCHUM WALL
2 WALL PLATED WITH TIN
3 WALL PLATED WITH BRONZE
4 TEMPLE OF CLEITO AND POSEIDON SURROUNDED BY GOLD ENCLOSURE
5 GROVE OF POSEIDON
6 GUARD HOUSES
7 ANCIENT ROYAL PALACE
8 UNDER-PASS FOR TRIREMES
9 UNDERGROUND DOCKS

FIGURE 33

The Metropolis of Atlantis according to Plato. From J. V. Luce, Lost Atlantis, *page 39, permission from McGraw-Hill Book Co. (A comparable diagram occurs in* Voyage to Atlantis, *p. 10 by Mavor.)*

For further details on this fascinating excursion into ancient history, ancient geography, ancient literature and archaelogy, we recommend further study of the aforementioned works by Mavor and Luce, as well as the article in *National Geographic*.

The Thera-Atlantis disaster cannot be understood fully without its correlation to ancient cosmology and the fly-by of Mars in March, 1447 B.C., a fly-by which we estimate was perilously close. In the broadest panorama of thought, the Atlantis-Exodus-Thera scene is best understood in terms of the cyclic nature of catastrophes of that millenium, and of the entire era from 2500 B.C. to 701 B.C. The Atlantis-Exodus-Thera event is to be understood in the same cosmic context as is the Long Day of Joshua, or the Isaiahic Catastrophe or the Tower of Babel Catastrophe. Only the dates, the leading actors, and the geographical location of the incidents reported vary. The Exodus Catastrophe was severe in Egypt, where an estimated 15% to 25% of the populace perished during one week; but it was worse on Crete and Thera, twin centers of another, equally-advanced ancient empire and civilization, where mortality may have ranged from 60% to 80%.

Vestiges of Ancient Cosmic Catastrophes in Current Life

Some generalized discussion has already been given for surviving traditions of these ancient catastrophes in traditions, holidays, religions and lores. The Passover Holy Season of Judaism is a direct derivation of the Exodus Catastrophe. The Celtic New Year, which began on November 1, is a recollection of either the Tower of Babel event or the Long Day of Joshua (or perhaps both). October 31 was both the end of summer and a festival for the dead. Astrologies, auguries, divinations and other magical practices were exercised. It was a time when goblins appeared in the ether, and a celestial witch rode across the sky with a cometary, meteoritic broom in her wake, terrifying the populace, inspiring dread, fear and panic. Bonfires were lighted on the hilltops in order to plead with the celestial deities to depart.

This is similar to the beating of conch shells and prayers to Indra whenever there is an eclipse in India, even today. The ancient fly-by of Mars apparently has been equated in India to lunar eclipses, whereas originally when Martian eclipses threatened, all the aforementioned associations also threaten.

In astrology, the first point of Aries, or March 21 is another commemoration of this ancient condition when Earth's and Mars' orbits were in resonance; March 21 was one of the two dates where the orbits intersected. We suggest that the era circa 2500 B.C. to 701 B.C. was a time when augurs, seers, and general sky-gazers really had something worth discussing, in contrast to contemporary astrologers.

Another tradition going back to ancient times is ill luck on Friday the thirteenth. The Isaiahic Catastrophe was the evening preceding the fourteenth of Nisan; as was the Exodus Catastrophe, the Sodom-Gomorrah event, plus such other ancient minor catastrophes as the Job event suggested earlier in this chapter. All of these were Case One catastrophes. The fourteenth of Nisan was always a Saturday in the Hebrew calendar. The evening before the fourteenth of Nisan was obviously Friday the thirteenth, sometimes a day of severe cosmic disturbance. Historically, Friday the thirteenth of Nisan was a night of dread in contrast to other Friday nights of other months. This is to suggest that such a silly superstition as ill luck on Friday the thirteenth has deep historical roots, and that those roots go back to the resonant orbit era. Are these few examples surprising? An analysis of the lore of India and other countries will very likely yield further illustrations of vestiges of the catastrophic era.

> Effectiveness in research is not just proportional to the effort. The airplane, if it does not travel fast enough, does not get airborne.—H. A. Krebbs

SUMMARY*

The Isaiahic Catastrophe 701 B.C.	Mars fly-by at 70,000 miles Case One
The Joel-Amos Catastrophe 756 B.C.	Mars fly-by at 120,000 miles Case Two
The Elijahic Catastrophe 864 B.C.	Mars fly-by at 150,000 miles Case Two
The Greater Davidic Catastrophe—972 B.C.	Mars fly-by at 120,000 miles Case Two
The Lesser Davidic Catastrophe—1025 B.C.	Mars fly-by at 200,000 miles Case One
The Samuelic Catastrophe 1080 B.C.	Mars fly-by at 150,000 miles Case Two
The Deborah Debacle 1188 B.C.	Mars fly-by at 150,000 miles Case Two
The Long Day of Joshua 1404 B.C.	Mars fly-by at 70,000 miles Case Two, modified**
The Exodus Catastrophe 1447 B.C.	Mars fly-by at 60,000 miles Case One, modified***
The Job Catastrophe 1663 B.C.	Mars fly-by at 120,000 miles Case One

*Distances are estimates in all cases and are given to help compare the intensities of the heavier catastrophes with the minor catastrophes.

**The Long Day of Joshua may have occurred with a fly-by *over the North Pole.*

***The Exodus Catastrophe did occur with a fly-by on the outside of the Earth. This angular momentum added to Mars, was subtracted from Earth, and resulted in the unique 42-year period, or fast cycle for the next cosmic event in 1404 B.C.

chapter **IX**

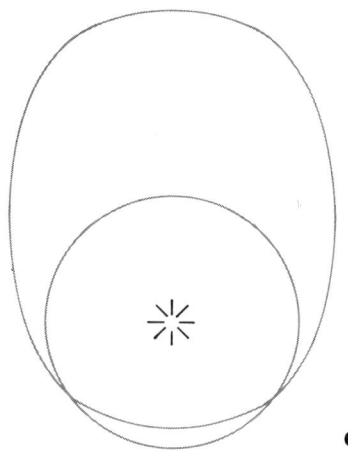

The Sodom-Gomorrah Catastrophe

circa March 23, 1877 B.C.

The Sodom-Gomorrah Catastrophe in geometry, location and date, was much like the Exodus Catastrophe and the Isaiahic Catastrophe. All three were major holocausts, and all three were on or about March 20/21, thus Case One types. All three featured bolides and meteorites, earthquakes and earth-shakings (spin-axis precessions), described cosmic scenery and renewed vulcanism.

The accounts of the Sodom-Gomorrah Catastrophe in Scripture are scant, but are somewhat enlarged in the Talmud and works of Josephus, in addition to other apocryphal Hebrew writings. Much of the cosmic, catastrophic material in the book of Job relates especially to the Sodom-Gomorrah Catastrophe.

THE PATTERN OF HEAVY CATASTROPHES in pairs every four to six centuries has been mentioned. The eighth century B.C. had one pair. The fifteenth century B.C. had another very heavy pair. The twentieth century B.C. also had a heavy pair. In each of these centuries, we have established that one was a Case One catastrophe[1] (on or about March 20/21) and the other a Case Two catastrophe, around the last week of October.

This is not to imply that all was serene between the Sodom-Gomorrah holocaust and the Exodus holocaust. A suspected Job Catastrophe in 1663 B.C. was at the mid-point of the 430 year interval. A suspected Jacob Catastrophe in 1718 B.C. has already been mentioned in Chapter VIII. Description of the former comes from the Bible, and description of the latter from *The Book of Jasher*.[2,3]

Dating The Sodom-Gomorrah Catastrophe

BY ANCIENT LITERATURES. The Bible (in the book of Exodus) suggests both the day and the year of the Sodom-Gomorrah event, for the Exodus holocaust was on its four hundred and thirtieth anniversary:

> And it came to pass at the end of the FOUR HUNDRED AND THIRTY YEARS, EVEN THE SELFSAME DAY it came to pass that all of the hosts of the Lord went out from the land of Egypt. It is a night to be MUCH OBSERVED unto the Lord for bringing them out from the land of Egypt: this is that night of the Lord to be observed of all the children of Israel in their generations. (Exodus 12:41-42)

---

[1]Technically, the Sodom-Gomorrah event occurred in 1877 B.C. and the Tower of Babel Catastrophe just 52 years earlier in 1930 B.C. One is in the last half of the twentieth century B.C. and the other in the first half of the nineteenth century B.C.

[2]*The Book of Jasher,* New York: M. M. Noah & A. S. Gould, 1840, 37:17.

[3]We do not propose that each half cycle was 54 years; some were 52, some were 54 and some were 56 in this era. There are literatures describing catastrophism for the dates with stars. The other dates were probably dates of astronomical threat, although full catastrophes could have occurred, descriptions of which did not survive the ravages of time.

March 20/21	1447 B.C.	October 25,	1500 B.C.
March 20/21	1555 B.C.	October 25,	1608 B.C.
March 20/21	1663 B.C.	October 25,	1716 B.C.
March 20/21	1771 B.C.	October 25,	1824 B.C.
March 20/21	1877 B.C.	October 25,	1930 B.C.

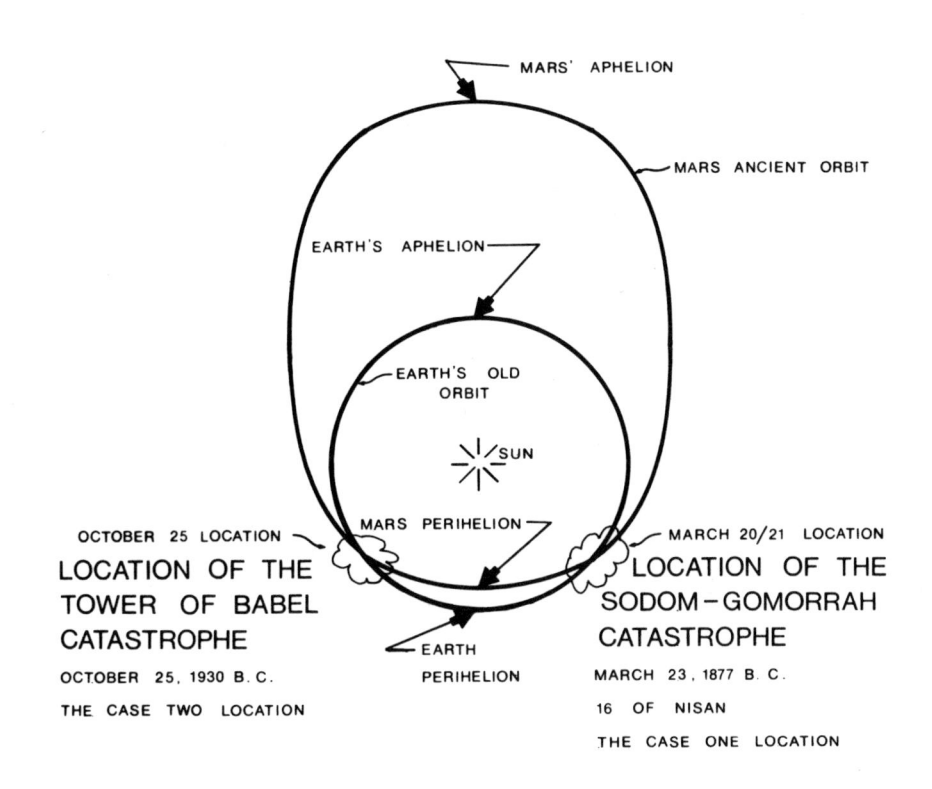

THE SODOM-GOMORRAH CATASTROPHE 253

MARS' APHELION

MARS ANCIENT ORBIT

EARTH'S APHELION

EARTH'S OLD ORBIT

SUN

MARS PERIHELION

OCTOBER 25 LOCATION
LOCATION OF THE TOWER OF BABEL CATASTROPHE
OCTOBER 25, 1930 B.C.
THE CASE TWO LOCATION

EARTH PERIHELION

MARCH 20/21 LOCATION
LOCATION OF THE SODOM–GOMORRAH CATASTROPHE
MARCH 23, 1877 B.C.
16 OF NISAN
THE CASE ONE LOCATION

THE GEOMETRY OF THE 20th CENTURY B.C. CATASTROPHES

FIGURE 34
This geometry is a repeat of the two holocausts in the 8th century B.C. and the two of the 15th century B.C.

This 430 year period is also cited in the book of Galatians (3:17). On both historic occasions, (1447 B.C. and 1877 B.C.) Mars, surrounded by swarms of Mars-asteroids, engaged the Earth in a close fly-by, an expected day of appointment. Thus the first "passover" was not in 1447 B.C., only the most memorable "passover."

The *Talmud* also dates the Sodom-Gomorrah holocaust in terms of day and month.

> The destruction of the cities of the plain took place at dawn of the SIXTEENTH DAY OF NISAN, for the reason that there were moon and sun worshippers among the inhabitants. God said: ". . . and if I destroy them by night, the sun worshippers will say, Were the sun here, he would prove himself our savior. I will therefore let their chastisement overtake them on the SIXTEENTH DAY OF NISAN at an hour at which the moon and the sun are both in the skies."[4,5]
>
> AT THE SAME TIME the rain that was streaming down upon the two cities was changed into brimstone.[6] [*Shades of the Murrain Plague of the Exodus Catastrophe*]

BY MODEL. The model would anticipate March 20/21 (or Nisan 13/14) for the catastrophe, and the literature dating is within two days of the model. The model would anticipate the year 1879 B.C.; the literature dating is within two years of the model. The conjunctive cycle *averaged* 108 years. There was one short cycle just after the Sodom-Gomorrah event, and as we shall see in the next chapter, one short cycle just before the Sodom-Gomorrah event. Each short cycle was short by just two years.

---

[4]Louis Ginzberg, *Legends of the Jews,* Philadelphia: Jewish Publication Society of America, 1909, Vol. I, p. 256.

[5]The *Talmud* suggests the sixteenth rather than the thirteenth or fourteenth of Nisan as the date for this Case One catastrophe. The Exodus and the Isaiahic Catastrophes were on the nights of the 13/14 of Nisan, our March 21, and vernal equinox. In the Sodom-Gomorrah Catastrophe, there is a two day variation from the pattern. This may be attributed to fluctuations of the orbits of the two planets, or perhaps fluctuations of the ancient calendars measuring the orbits. Either way, it was close enough to the day of appointment, the vernal equinox, to support the total pattern.

[6]Louis Ginzberg, *op. cit.,* Vol. I, p. 255.

The Tower of Babel holocaust occurred 52 years earlier than the Sodom-Gomorrah Catastrophe according to the *Talmud:*

> This city [*Zoar in the Rift Valley trench*] had been founded a year later than the other four [*including Sodom and Gomorrah*]; it was only fifty-one years old, and therefore the measure of its sins was not so full as the measure of the sins of the neighboring cities.[7]
>
> For fifty-two years God had warned the godless; He had made mountains to quake and tremble.[8]

Today the crater lake, Lake Bolsena, stands as mute evidence of the Joel-Amos Catastrophe. Rome was founded in its wake. Similarly, the Rift Valley of Palestine stands as further mute evidence of second millenium B.C. catastrophism, a cleavage of the Earth's crust. The five cities of the plain were founded in the wake of this cleavage in 1930 B.C., only to be swallowed up in the very next cycle, in 1877 B.C.

The model predicts that the passover of 1447 B.C. was not the only passover, only the most spectacular. Earlier holocausts on or about March 20/21 occurred in 1659 B.C. and in 1877 B.C. However, unless the ancient rabbis arbitrarily bunched various dates, we have other significant Biblical events occurring on this same day of appointment. For example, Abraham was circumcised on the thirteenth or fifteenth of Nisan, March 19 or 21.[9] Also Abraham[10,11] and his small militia routed the Chaldean

---

[7]Louis Ginzberg, *op. cit.*, Vol. I, p. 256.

[8]Louis Ginzberg, *op. cit.*, Vol. I, p. 253.

[9]Louis Ginzberg, *op. cit.*, Vol. V, p. 233.

[10]Louis Ginzberg, *op. cit.*, Vol. I, p. 231. "The battle fought . . . happened on the FIFTEENTH OF NISAN, the night appointed for miraculous deeds." Abraham with some 300 militia men [*and perhaps with some bolidic artillery*] routed the forces of Chedalaormer, the Chaldean general.

[11]"His victory was possible only because the celestial powers espoused his side. The planet Jupiter made the night bright for him, and an angel, Lailah by name, fought for him. In a true sense, it was a victory of God." Louis Ginzberg, *op. cit.*, Vol. I, p. 232. [*Where did the rabbinical translators get "Jupiter?" Our research suggests Jupiter's son, Mars.*]

force on a midnight raid made on the same night circa 1890 B.C. to 1900 B.C.

Thus by several methods we have shown that the March 20/21 anniversary was meaningful to ancients, and the four hundred thirtieth anniversary of the Sodom-Gomorrah holocaust was the spectacular and destructive Exodus Catastrophe. This was a slight two-year deviation from the model's average.

In our discussion of each of the catastrophes, five categories of data have been selected for analysis. These five categories include (1) the 54 year half-cycle or the 108 year full cycle of conjunctions, (2) the third week of March or the end of October in timing cycle, (3) earthquakes and/or earth-shakings (spin axis precessions), (4) bolides and meteorites (fire and brimstone), and (5) descriptive cosmic scenery. Categories 1 and 2 have just been discussed.

Bolides and Meteorites

> Then the Lord rained upon Sodom and upon Gomorrah BRIMSTONE AND FIRE from the Lord out of heaven; And he overthrew those cities, and all the plain. . . . (Genesis 19:24-25)
>
> God then cast A THUNDERBOLT upon the city, and set it on fire . . . and laid waste the country with the like burning. . . .[12]
>
> And in this month the Lord executed his judgments on Sodom, and Gomorrah, and Zeboim, and all the region of the Jordan, and He burned them with FIRE AND BRIMSTONE, and destroyed them. . . .[13]

That Abraham was concerned with the movements of the planets, the regular and irregular, the close and the distant, is suggested many times in extra-Biblical literature:

---

[12] Flavius Josephus, *Antiquities of the Jews*, Book I, Chapter XI, section 4, p. 101.

[13] R. H. Charles, *The Apocrypha and Pseudepigrapha of the Old Testament*, Vol. II, "The Book of Jubilees," Oxford: Clarendon Press, p. 37.

THE SODOM-GOMORRAH CATASTROPHE

> And in the sixth week, in the fifth year thereof, Abram sat up throughout the night on the new moon of the seventh month to observe the stars from the evening to the morning, in order TO SEE WHAT WOULD BE THE CHARACTER OF THE YEAR....[14]

> This his [Abraham's] opinion was derived from the irregular phenomena that were visible both at land and sea, as well as those that happened to the sun and moon, and all the heavenly bodies thus: "If [said he] these bodies had power of their own, they would certainly take care of their own regular motions; but since they DO NOT PRESERVE SUCH REGULARITY ... For which doctrines, when the Chaldeans, and people of Mesopotamia, raised a tumult against him, he thought fit to leave that country ... he came and lived in the land of Canaan...."[15]

> Berosus mentions our father Abram without naming him, when he says thus: "In the tenth generation after the flood, there was among the Chaldeans a man, righteous, and great. AND SKILFUL IN CELESTIAL SCIENCE."[16]

Thus we see that not only did fire and brimstone occur, but it was astronomical as well as volcanic, that is, meteorites as well as cinders. The coming and going of Mars, or Bel, was watched carefully by many twentieth century B.C. observers, Abraham being one of the leading astronomical observers of the time.

Earthquakes and Earth-Shakings

Earthquakes are crustal tremors; earth-shakings are spin axis precessions, involving especially a shift in the location of the two geographical poles. Both are alluded to in the book of Job. Unless these happened during the Job Catastrophe of 1663 B.C., they must be observations of the catastrophe under scrutiny, that of 1877 B.C.

---

[14] R. H. Charles, op. cit., p. 31.

[15] Flavius Josephus, op. cit., Book I, Chapter VII, section 1, pp. 94-95.

[16] Flavius Josephus, op. cit., Book I, Chapter VII, section 2, p. 95.

[*God*] WHICH REMOVETH THE MOUNTAINS, AND THEY KNOW NOT: which overturneth them in his anger.	(crustal deformation)
Which shaketh the Earth OUT OF HER PLACE	(orbital shift)
AND THE PILLARS THEREOF TREMBLE.	(spin axis shift)
Which commandeth the sun, and it riseth not; and sealeth up the stars.	(spin axis shift)
...Which maketh Arcturus [*possibly Mars*], Orion [*possibly Jupiter*], and Pleiades [*possibly Venus*], and the chambers of the south [*possibly the Milky Way*]. (Job 9:5-9)	(planet identities)

A crustal tide of 50 or 100 feet (as measured from Earth's core) was not a common occurrence, but did occur with the occasional catastrophes of this era. We believe there is something more occurring, and some background must be presented here.

The Great Rift Valley

Today, the Earth has a polar diameter which is 26 or 27 miles shorter than the equatorial diameter, a result of the spin rate of the Earth causing an equatorial bulge.[17] We have postulated in *The Biblical Flood and the Ice Epoch* that during the year of the Deluge, there were two close passes, by Mercury rather than Mars, and at distances as close as 25,000 miles.[18] The two passes resulted in crustal tides of mountain-forming

---

[17] Earth's polar diameter is 7899.5 miles. Its equatorial diameter is 7926.4 miles. The flattening effect on Earth is one part in 293. Some of the larger planets have a larger spin rate and a greater oblateness. Saturn's oblateness is one part in 15, Uranus' is one in 14; Jupiter's is one in 14.5 and Neptune's is one in 52. The Martian oblateness is one in 192.

[18] Donald W. Patten, *The Biblical Flood and the Ice Epoch*, Seattle: Pacific Meridian Publishing Co., 1966, p. 148.

magnitude, and the formation of two major cycles of orogenesis.[19] We have also postulated that the Flood interaction, including both fly-bys, caused a relocation of geographical poles. This relocation, including both fly-bys, may have been as much as 5,000 miles.[20]

If this massive planetary interaction is correct, then it not only caused a massive relocation of the spin axis locations, but ultimately (not immediately) it caused a relocation of the equatorial bulge due to isostasy. (Isostasy is the tendency of the Earth's crust and underlying magma to maintain a general equilibrium by yielding a flow of molten rock material, magma, beneath the surface under gravitative stress and centrifugal stress.)

A new equatorial bulge zone will develop. It may take centuries for the Earth's new bulge zone to form, and for the former bulge zone to subside. Stresses in some zones developed within the Earth's crust after the Deluge, and an occasion such as a close Mars fly-by would and did trigger the pent up forces within the crust. Earth's new equatorial zone needed to stretch, and this took the form of splits in the Earth's crust, perpendicular to the equator. The Great Rift Valley is the leading example on Earth of one of these splits; a mid-Atlantic Rift Valley is another example. (This is discussed in more depth in *The Biblical Flood and the Ice Epoch.*)[21] We believe that the Rift Valley cleavage first developed perhaps on or about 2146 B.C.,[22] was widened during the Tower of Babel holocaust, and was widened

---

[19] Donald W. Patten, *op. cit.*, pp. 75 ff.

[20] Donald W. Patten, *op. cit.*, pp. 76, 78. There is a basis for postulating that the pre-deluge spin axis was located in the regions of Nigeria and Samoa, not the Arctic Sea and Antarctic continent. The two arcs suggest the fly-by pattern on the rotating planet. That they do not overlap suggests a massive polar relocation on *each* of the two fly-bys, a relocation far greater than the 300-mile and 500-mile relocations of the later Mars fly-bys which we are studying. See Figure 43, page 312.

[21] Donald W. Patten, *op. cit.*, pp. 252 ff. Note the diagrams of the Great Rift Valley, pp. 254-255.

[22] . . . the name of one was Peleg; for in his days was the earth divided. . . . (Genesis 10:25). Peleg was the fifth generation from Noah and he was also five generations before Abraham; thus his generation was in the middle of that ancient age between the Tower of Babel Catastrophe and the greatest of all the catastrophes, the Deluge.

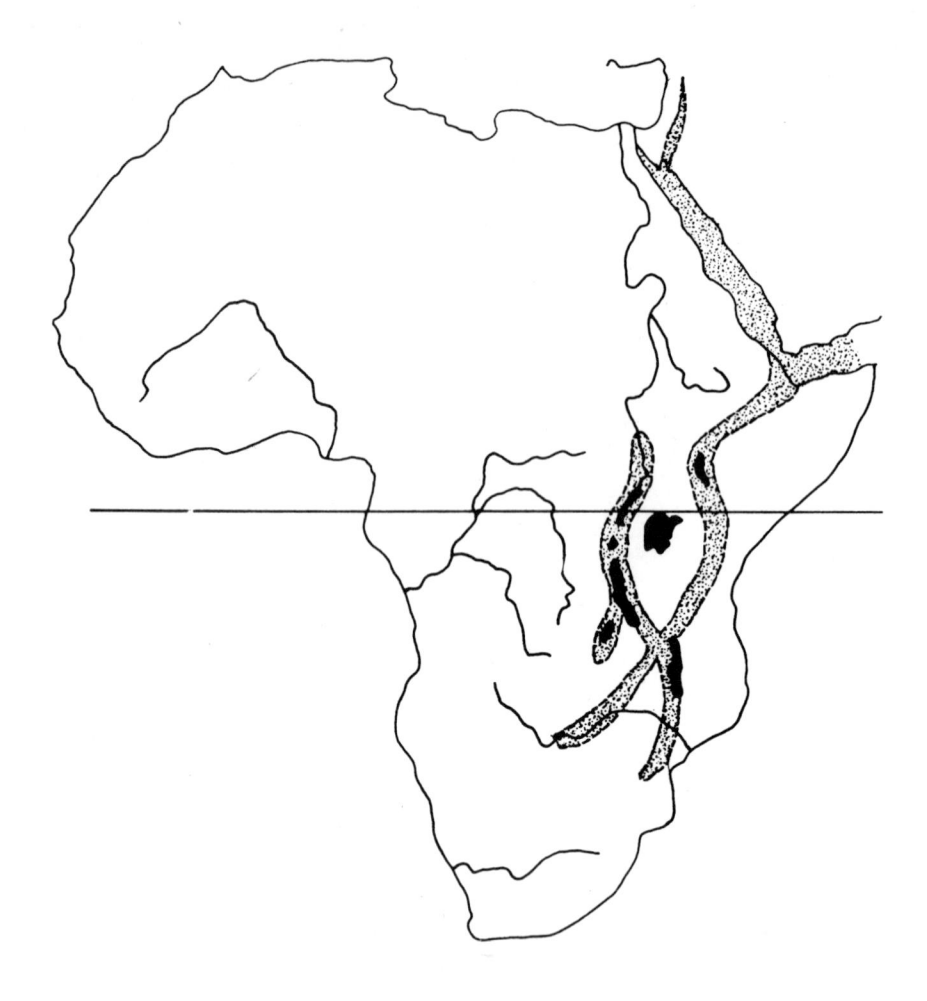

FIGURE 35
The Great Rift Valley of Africa is perpendicular to the equator, and the widest and most complex near the equator. It is a response of our planet's crust to a new bulge zone, a new equatorial zone, required by migrating polar locations. The poles migrated thousands of miles during the Flood catastrophe requiring a new bulge zone. Note also the Great Rift Valley of Mars which is also approximately perpendicular to the current equator of Mars. See Figure 21 page 148.

again by the Mars fly-by in 1877 B.C. Thus the massive vulcanism in this particular location was triggered by a sudden brief stress on an already stress-laden crust.

In Job 9, Job discusses orogeny in past upheavals. He suggests that God "removeth the mountains and they know not; which overturneth them in his anger." His three debating comforters (Eliphaz, Bildad and Zophar) did not dispute this; they too had seen the Job Catastrophe and had heard about the earlier ones. Thus these four men, in discussing the works of God of old, were discussing literal effects of literal catastrophes, which may be phrased in poetic Hebrew or English, but are nonetheless most historical.

> And Abraham gat up early in the morning . . . And he looked toward Sodom and Gomorrah, and toward all the land of the plain, and beheld, and, lo, the smoke of the country went up as the SMOKE OF A FURNACE. (Genesis 19:27-28)

Abraham was an eye witness, standing not far from the edge of the Rift Valley as it cleaved, split, and smoked with volcanic gases, ash, cinders and flowing lava. Needless to say, there is no flood strata at the bottom of the Rift Valley or on its sides, as there is on the surrounding plateaus.

Continental Drift Theory Versus Spin Axis Shift Theory

The continental drift theory of Wegener has become popular in the last two or three decades, probably because uniformitarian geologists have no better ways to explain the data without turning toward catastrophism. Wegener's theory states that over the last several hundreds of millions of years, certain crustal plates or shields drifted across the globe, passing through pre-existing crust. This was allegedly achieved, millimeter by millimeter until Africa and South America finally were at least 3,000 miles distant from the original moorage. This is merely a simplistic jigsaw puzzle exercise, only with continents rather than with puzzle pieces.[23, 24, 25] The long term residual stresses of the relocated bulge zone are even today being measured, minute as they are, some 4,500 years under the original events. Minute separations and movements do occur; the findings are valid. However, this slight residual movement has been misunderstood by evolutionary geologists, and is alleged to "prove" the hypothesis of continental drift. What is actually being measured are the effects of the relocation of the equatorial bulge, some 4,500 years later. The widening of the Great Rift Valley, a cleavage to accommodate the new bulge zone, was part of the isostasy of the twentieth century B.C., even as the current minute deviations are a part of the current isostasy.

Over the last 4500 years, the relocating of the bulge zone and the accompanying adjustments in crustal stress have subsided at *logarithmic* rates, and on a *transient decay curve*. Geologists, thinking with a uniformitarian view point, schedule minute shifts along *arithmetic* rates for hundreds of millions of years. Both the catastrophist and the uniformitarian are thus looking at the same data, current minute shifts in crustal stress, but making vastly different interpretations.

---

[23] In the continental drift rationale, the continental shields should be composed of andestitic rock whereas the oceanic basins should be composed of basaltic rock. In actual observation, the continental shields are andesitic and the Pacific Basin is composed of basaltic rock; however, the Atlantic Basin is composed of andestic rock contrary to continental drift rationale. In addition, the forces of resistance to shield drift exceed by a magnitude of one thousand any drift force which has been postulated.

A better approach to paleography would include "oceanic shift" rather than "continental drift," and one example is the Deluge. During the Flood Catastrophe we postulate that an astronomical ice dump added 7% or more to the Earth's hydrosphere, while simultaneously massively deforming Earth's crust.

[24] Not only *spin axis shift* but its associated *tidal deformation uplift* explains orogeny in a much better manner than does the Wegenerian *continental drift* with its ill-advised assumptions of millions of years of serene Earth experience in the solar system.

[25] Not only have there been spin axis precessions, or relocations. Field reversals and subsequent migrations of the geomagnetic field are suspected. Hence, observing the polarization of the basalt flows from these post-flood lava flows should reflect several locations of the Earth's magnetic poles. We describe seven post-flood catastrophes in this volume, and it may be that there was a field reversal on each occasion.

Descriptive Cosmic Scenery

Footnote 11, page 255, of this chapter portrayed some cosmological scenery which Abraham saw during a time of catastrophism. The rabbis involved in manuscript preservation have judged that Jupiter was the threatening planet, whereas we propose it was Mars. This parallels the current substitution in encyclopedias of Jupiter for Baal, but our research concludes that Mars was the Chaldean Bel and Phoenician Baal.

> God moved, for Abraham's sake, the star Jupiter from the west to the east. . . .[26]

> As a rule, angels proclaim their errand with the swiftness of lightning, but these were angels of mercy, and they hesitated to execute their work of destruction, ever hoping that the evil would be turned aside from Sodom. With nightfall, the fate of Sodom WAS SEALED IRREVOCABLY, and the angels arrived there.[27]

Although the record is scant in the book of Genesis, Josephus, and *The Book of Jubilees,* and is only somewhat enlarged in the *Talmud,* even so, the Sodom-Gomorrah Catastrophe can be quite well understood. One method is to analyze the extensive cosmology of the book of Job.[28] A second method is to study the resonating orbits the planets once had, and to realize that the Isaiahic Catastrophe and the Exodus Catastrophe were similar

---

[26] Louis Ginzberg, *op. cit.,* Vol. V, p. 225.

[27] Louis Ginzberg, *op. cit.,* Vol. I, p. 253.

[28] In the cosmology of the book of Job, the "crooked serpent" in chapter 26:13 is part of the described cosmic scenery. This is parallel to the crooked celestial dragon of Chinese cosmo-mythology, and to the phoenix bird cosmo-myth of ancient Egypt and Phoenicia. When the time came for the phoenix bird to die, it died by setting its nest and the Earth on fire, burning itself alive; but it was an "immortal" bird. It arose from its ashes, which it deposited on Egypt or whatever the locale, to continue its celestial journey near the Sun. From there it returned periodically to the Earth, as the legend tells, to dump more of its celestial plumage. This legend has similar ingredients to the Phaethon story of Greece and other ancient cosmo-mythologies.

to the Sodom-Gomorrah Catastrophe, only on different anniversaries.[29] To understand one catastrophe is, essentially, to understand all three. The differences seem to be the time of day or night in which each occurred, the distance between Mars and Earth during the passover, and an inside versus outside pass in relation to the Earth. The Sodom-Gomorrah event may thus be viewed as a "repeat performance" as we analyze the cyclic nature of the resonant orbit model, and as we analyze the themes of these ancient catastrophes.

Stonehenge, An Ancient Astronomical Temple

Stonehenge is an ancient astronomical temple in Southern England, on the Salisbury plain. The dates generally accepted for its construction are between 1900 B.C. and 1600 B.C.; it was a pre-Druid construction. We conclude that it was built in response to the Tower of Babel and Sodom-Gomorrah catastrophes, due to the spin axis wobbles of these events. Stonehenge was contemporary with pyramid-building in Egypt.

It was not built by neolithic hunters or bumpkins, but rather by some sophisticated "engineers" with some knowledge of astronomy, mathematics and transport.

> At least 82 bluestones, weighing up to 5 tons each, were to be set up in two concentric circles around the center of the enclosure, about 6 feet apart and about 35 feet from the center . . . but the ritual significance of such a structure puzzles the scholars of the past.[30]

What is of equal interest is that these huge stones were quarried in the Prescelly Mountains of Wales, and were each transported over 300 miles across land, water and land again, to their present location near Southampton. Stone 56 weighed about 50 tons. The

---

[29]The Exodus Catastrophe was on the 430 anniversary of the Sodom-Gomorrah debacle; the Isaiahic Catastrophe was on the 1176 anniversary. Perhaps the Sodom-Gomorrah debacle in itself, was an anniversary of an earlier one "in the days of Peleg when the Earth was divided."

[30]Gerald S. Hawkins, *Stonehenge Decoded,* New York: Dell Publishing Co., 1966, p. 48.

THE SODOM-GOMORRAH CATASTROPHE

Photos by S. Sutton

FIGURE 36
Stonehenge, as it is (lower) and a convincing reconstruction of its mighty monoliths (upper). Stonehenge consisted of an outer circle, no less than 100 feet in diameter, formed by thirty great monoliths with large lintel stones. Within this circle and concentric with it was another circle formed of forty small blue stones. Within this was a horseshoe of five huge trilithons formed by ten monoliths with their imposts. Within the horseshoe were nineteen foreign stones and an altar stone. We propose this edifice was used in Mars-Jupiter-Saturn worship rather than Sun worship primarily. From Wonders of the Past, *Vol. III, p. 652, courtesy of G. P. Putnam's Sons.*

central trilithon contained stones one of which was 25 feet long and another 29.7 feet long.[31] Other stones weighed 25 tons as compared to the 45 to 50 tons of the trilithon uprights.

How long did it take to erect Stonehenge, and how many laborers were involved? Hawkins has estimated 1,500,000 man-days at a time when England's population may well have been less than 300,000.[32] He adds that this estimate does not include time for developing the necessary architectural plans. Stonehenge was to be an astronomical gauge and observatory.

Hawkins has concluded that this massive structure was designed to calculate the summer solstice, and perhaps also eclipses of the moon. He assumes the Earth's orbit, the lunar orbit, the Earth's spin axis location and tilt, and the Martian orbit were all the same in 2000 B.C. as they are today. We suggest this ancient astronomical observatory was built to track the journey of Mars, and to calculate it. If these early Celts were concerned with eclipses, it was eclipses of Mars, rather than the Moon. (If Mars was astride the ecliptic plane on the Sodom-Gomorrah Catastrophic Day, then the Earth would have eclipsed Mars during its fly-by.

We have established that there was about a 300 mile to 400 mile polar migration generally toward Alaska and Canada during the Isaiahic Catastrophe. (This resulted in a lowering of latitude for Palestine.) Spin axis shifts occurred during the Long Day of Joshua and the Exodus Catastrophe, and each time a new polar location occurred. Only after each polar location subsequent to the Sodom-Gomorrah Catastrophe is determined will we be able to "decode" Stonehenge. We predict the decoding will involve sighting and logging of the ancient Martian journey across the heavens. Thus, despite some excellent research by Gerald Hawkins, one's conclusions can only be as good as one's assumptions; and his assumptions of a steady state solar system, and of a steady polar location are not valid. Stonehenge has not been decoded. It, and some 500 other temple sites in Great Britain remain wide open for research. Research from a catastrophic world view surely is both more exciting and more productive

---

[31] Gerald S. Hawkins, *op. cit.*, p. 53.

[32] Gerald S. Hawkins, *op. cit.*, pp. 73-74.

than research conducted from a uniformitarian rationale. Uniformitarian geologists bask in the time-worn saying, "the present is the key to the past," a motto of uniformitarianism coined by Charles Hutton in the eighteenth century. What could be more absurd?

One point should be reiterated. Job was an eye witness, as were Eliphaz, Elihu, Bildad and Zophar, to the holocaust in 1663 B.C., however severe it was in a global sense. Abraham, like Lot, was an eye witness to the Sodom-Gomorrah holocaust, and that *eye witness* account, in part, has been preserved in the Scriptures. Other ancient materials are helpful, but by comparison are usually inferior[33]. Eye witness accounts are what the Scriptures give for the Long Day of Joshua, for the Exodus Catastrophe with its spectacular noctural passover, and the Sodom-Gomorrah Catastrophe.

> The vast effort of the present generation in the field of education apparently tends to make people think noncreatively. Education is designed to produce extroversion and social adjustment· but frequently (there are many exceptions) creative people are of the self-sufficient and introverted type.—Liam Hudson

> In almost every scientific problem which I have succeeded in solving . . . the final solution has come to my mind in a fraction of a second by a process which is not consciously one of reasoning. —Irving Langmuir

---

[33] The Phaethon legend of the Greeks is exceptional for its detail in its cosmic description. However in Greek literature it is not dated. And since its description matches the timing of the Long Day of Joshua, we conclude (with about 80% certainty) that it was the Greek version of the Joshuaic scene. It is possible that it describes an earlier scene, such as the Sodom-Gomorrah Catastrophe. This illustrates that both dating and description are essential for historical analysis; one without the other considerably reduces the inherent value of the account.

chapter **X**

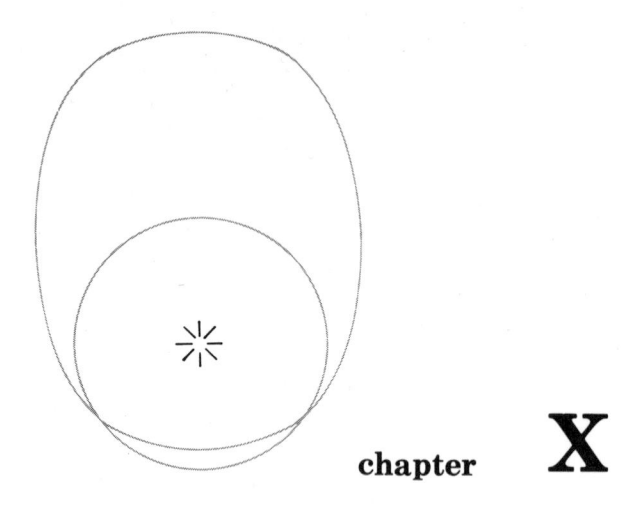

The Tower of Babel Catastrophe

circa October 25, 1930 B.C.

This crisis day is very ancient; it is the first recorded in extant literature after the Deluge, or Flood. It can be best understood by grasping the other, later October 25 catastrophes (the Case Two events), and particularly the Long Day of Joshua and the Joel-Amos holocausts of 1404 B.C. and 756 B.C., respectively.

As THIS STUDY MOVES into increasingly more ancient times, the data becomes increasingly scarce. Ancient libraries and scholarly institutions suffered the ravages of military wars and, up to 701 B.C., celestial wars. To understand the later, better-recorded crisis days helps to understand these more ancient crisis days.

Dating — Short Term

From the literature, there is no way to ascertain the month or the day of this holocaust. However, the resonant orbit model suggests an approximate date of October 25 for the intersection of these ancient orbits. This is considered accurate within 5 days.

However, from the *Talmud* there is a way to ascertain the year of the holocaust.

> For fifty-two years God had warned the godless; He had made mountains to quake and tremble . . . They persisted in their sins, and their well-merited punishment overtook them. . . . they [*the Sodomites and Gomorrahians*] were burnt with fire.[1]

The 52 year period is sufficiently close to the 54 year average of the model to indicate it was another of the cosmic series. It was noted that one of the cycles *after* the Sodom-Gomorrah Catastrophe was also only 52 years. Thus we suggest in the twentieth century B.C. there were two half-cycles in a row containing only 52 years, two years shorter than the normal half-cycle.

Dating — Long Term

There were three kinds of cycles operating simultaneously. One was the two-year cycle, the average period of the orbit of Mars. A second was the 54-year average of the swinging of the conjunctions of Earth and Mars. Sometimes this involved a 52-year cycle, sometimes probably a 56-year cycle, and once just after the Exodus holocaust a particularly short cycle. The third cycle is a grander cycle of catastrophism, a cycle which spanned five to seven centuries. The mechanics of this grander, or grand cycle are now considered.

Josephus seems to have alluded to this grander cycle in his *Antiquities of the Jews* when he wrote as follows:

> *(Speaking of the Noachian era)* . . . and besides, God afforded them a longer time of line on account of their virtue, and the good use they made of it in ASTRONOMICAL and geometrical discoveries, which WOULD NOT HAVE AF-

---

[1]Louis Ginzberg, *Legends of the Jews*, Philadelphia: Jewish Publication Society of America, 1913, Vol. I, p. 253. See also the quotation and footnote 7, Chapter IX, p. 255.

FORDED THE TIME FOR FORETELLING (THE PERIODS OF THE STARS,) unless they had lived six hundred years, FOR THE GREAT YEAR IS COMPLETED IN THAT INTERVAL.

Now I have for witnesses to what I have said all those that have written Antiquities, both among the Greeks and Barbarians; for even Manetho who wrote the Egyptian history, and Berosus, who collected the Chaldean monuments, and Mochus, Hestiaeus, and besides these Hieronymus the Egyptian, and those that composed the Phoenician history, agree to what I here say: Hesiod also, and Hecataeus, and Hellanicus and Acusilaus; and besides these, Ephorus and Nicolaus....[2]

Josephus indicates that the ancients studied the stars in their paths, and more particularly, in their periods.

Ovid (Publius Ovidus Naso, 43 B.C. - 17 A.D.), a later Roman historian, in his *Metamorphoses,* talks about the ancient cycles of catastrophes, or more particularly the intervening years of reconstruction and cultural revitalization, as a series of ancient ages.

The GOLDEN AGE was first, a time that was cherished. . . . The years went by in peace. And Earth, untroubled, unharried by hoe or plowshare, brought forth all that men had need for, and those men were happy, gathering berries from the mountain sides, cherries, or blackcaps, and the edible acorns. Spring was forever. . . . And Earth, unplowed, brought forth rich grain . . . [*This seems to be a discussion of the pre-flood era.*]

After Saturn was driven to the shadowy land of death, and the world was under Jove, the AGE OF SILVER came in, lower than gold, better than bronze. Jove made the springtime shorter, added winter, summer and autumn, the seasons as we know them. That was the first time when . . . icicles hung down in the winter. And men built houses for themselves . . . and the oxen struggled, groaning and laboring under the heavy yoke. [*This seems to be a discussion of the early post-flood era, circa 2500 B.C. to 1930 B.C., ending with the Tower of Babel and the Sodom-Gommorah pair of holocausts.*]

Then came the AGE OF BRONZE. . . . [*Ovid gives no

---

[2]Flavius Josephus, *Antiquities of the Jews,* Book I, Chapter III, p. 9, Bridgeport, Conn., M. Sherman, 1828.

> details of this area. Perhaps it parallels the era 1930 B.C. 1404 B.C., ending with the Long Day of Joshua.]
>
> And last of all the IRON AGE succeeded. . . . Heaven was no safer. Giants attacked the very throne of Heaven, piled Pelion on Ossa, mountain on mountain, up to the very stars. Jove struck them down with thunderbolts . . . Jove was witness from his lofty throne. . . . He summoned them to council. No one dawdled. Easily seen when the night skies are clear . . . Along this road the gods move toward the palace of the Thunder.[3] [*This last of the ages, the iron age, was the era of the founding of Rome, which we already know to be about 750 B.C., between the times of the last two world holocausts of 756 B.C. and 701 B.C.*]

While Ovid indicated a series of ages, Seneca (Marcus Lucius Annaeus Seneca, 54 B.C. - 39 A.D.) has asserted that the ancient Chaleans studied "comets". And he has suggested they studied them in terms of their timing, or periods. What has been termed "comets" undoubtedly includes Mars in its ancient "comet-like" orbit, and the other planets moving across the unmoving constellations.

> It was not till the time of Halley's comet, 1682, that modern astronomy began to consider the question of the possibly periodic character of cometic motions with attention. (For my own part, I reject as altogether improbable the statement of Seneca that THE ANCIENT CHALDEAN ASTRONOMERS COULD CALCULATE THE RETURN OF COMETS. . . .)[4]

We do not claim to have made a perfect analysis of ancient catastrophic history, or ancient cosmology. We suspect a number of catastrophes occurred, and records of them have been blurred or lost across the last 100 or 150 generations of time. However,

---

[3] Ovid, *Metamorphoses*, Bloomington, Indiana, Indiana Univ. Press, 1958, pp. 5-8. Ovid's primary source was Hesiod's *Theogeny*.

[4] Mary Proctor, *The Romance of Comets*, New York: Harper & Brothers, 1926, p. 148. We question Miss Proctor's conclusion about the capacity and performance of the ancient Chaldean mathematicians; we propose that they did understand elemental calculus as well as much geometry. Also, the architects and engineers who supervised the building of the Egyptian pyramids and the Stonehenge Temple in England were certainly not primitive bumpkins or Neanderthals.

the general outline is presented in Figure 37. It is a Master Time Line Scale, and must be classified among the most important figures (or tables) in this opus. It is a grand analysis encompassing 20 centuries. In it three grand cycles of catastrophism are detected, the 20th B.C., the 15th B.C. and the 8th B.C. What might be the celestial cause of this grand cycle? Why did the ancients pay close attention not only to the paths or trajectories, but more importantly to the periods or timing of the planets? Did they somehow consider the timing or periods of the planets to be a key or an indicator of future holocausts as well as an indicator of past holocausts?

In Figure 37, we propose that Ovid's age of gold was the preflood era when a greenhouse type of climate prevailed from pole to pole, and seasons were inconspicuous if existant at all.[5] Ovid's AGE OF SILVER compares to the interlude between the Deluge, circa 2500 B.C., and the 20th century B.C. holocausts. This was "when Saturn was driven to a shadowy land of death, and the world was under Jove." Later, following the 20th century B.C., pair of holocausts studied in Chapters IX and X, came another five century interlude, the AGE OF BRONZE. After the 15th century B.C. catastrophes, cultures were rebuilt, often by migrating peoples, only to be disrupted by the pair of 8th century B.C. holocausts. This was Ovid's AGE OF IRON. Toward the end of this age, "heaven was no safer . . . Jove struck them down with thunderbolts . . .", he summoned the planetary deities (or the planets themselves) to a council, perhaps even some kind of remarkable lineup. After this came the ERA OF ROME, one in which the Olympic dieties, or planetary dieties were increasingly less important, and awarded correspondingly less attention.

A Grand Cycle of Catastrophism Theory

In our total model in this book, there are four legs, three of which were presented in the astronomical discussion and models in Chapter IV. To these three aforementioned legs are now added a fourth and final legs of catastrophe theory.

1. The General Theory of Earth - Mars Resonance   (2:1)

---

[5] See Donald W. Patten, "The Greenhouse Effect", *Symposium on Creation II*, 1970, Grand Rapids, Baker Book House, p. 11.

THE TOWER OF BABEL CATASTROPHE 273

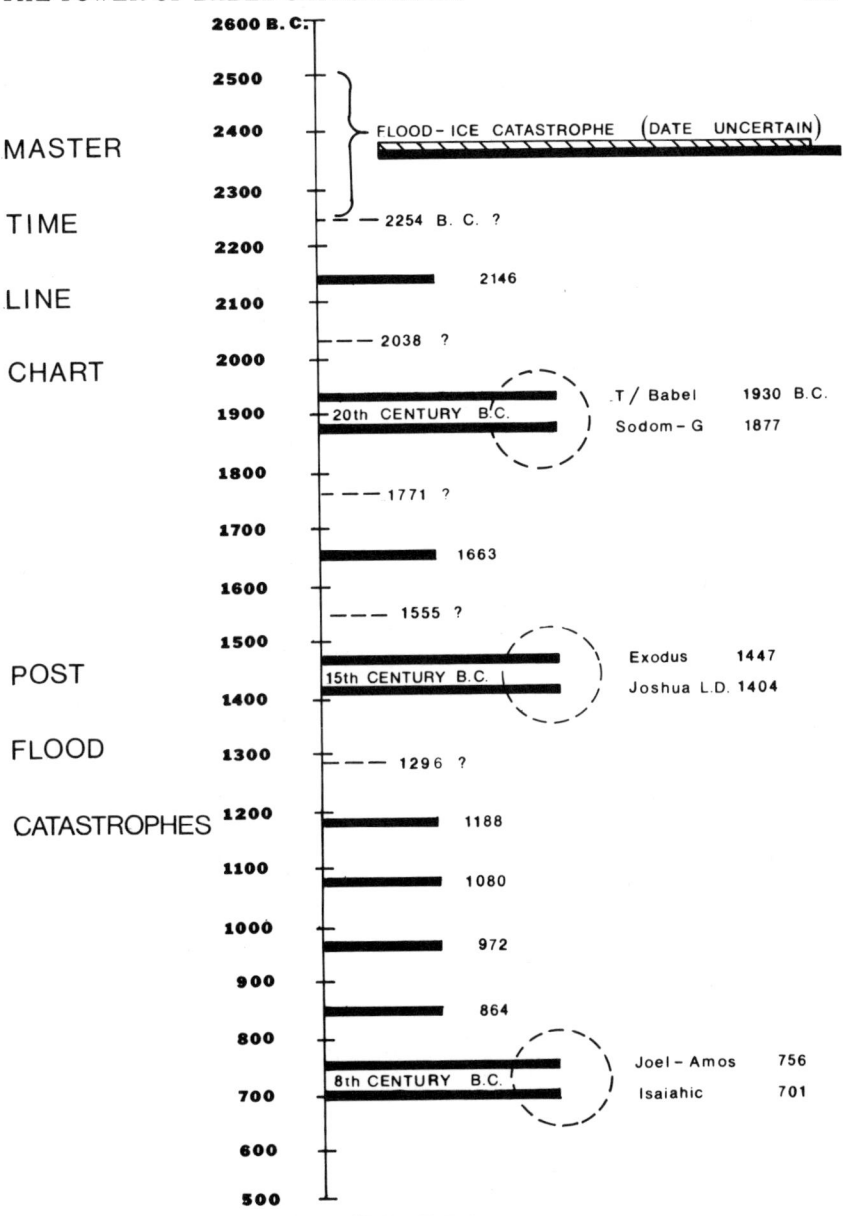

FIGURE 37

The Master Time Line Chart illustrates the cyclic nature of the 1800 years of recorded astronomical catastrophism. This chart indicates gaps which suggest catastrophes that were not reported in the Hebrew chronicles. Almost all catastrophes are undated in the lores and literatures of other ancient nations.

2. The General Theory of Fragmentation

3. The General Theory of Spin Axis Precession

Earth and Mars are subjects of categories 1 and 3 while Electra and Mars are subjects of category 2. We now add category 4 and the subjects are Jupiter and Saturn.

4. The Resonance of Jupiter and Saturn with Earth - Mars

Jupiter In Resonance

Today, Jupiter's orbital period is 11.8653 of Earth's orbital period. However we know as a result of the Isaiahic Catastrophe that Earth lost about 1% of its speed, and gained about 1% in angular momentum. Its former orbit was about .99 of its current orbit, placing it, with Mars, in resonance with Jupiter. Earth was in 12:1 resonance with Jupiter, a relatively distant and weak resonance. Simultaneously Mars was in 6:1 resonance with Jupiter, a closer, stronger and controlling resonance. Figure 38 illustrates this three-body resonance, a 1:6:12 resonance.

The effect of Jupiter on Alinda (which is in 3:1 resonance with Jupiter) is to stabilize its orbit in a teeter-totter geometry. This was seen in Figure 5, page 76. In Figure 5, note that the long axis of Alinda's orbit and the long axis of Jupiter's orbit were perpendicular. The long axis of an elliptical orbit is called the "line of apsides." The particular geometry of this resonance condition results in this perpetual perpendicular relationship of their two orbits.

Note in Figure 38 that the ancient Martian orbit was also perpendicular to Jupiter's orbit, that is, the lines of apsides of the two orbits were perpendicular. Jupiter "stabilized" the Martian orbit. The ancient Martian orbit was stabilized in this sense. Were Earth and Mars acting upon each other alone, without Jupiter, Mars' line of apsides, or its orbit would precess as did its spin axis. Under this condition, Mars would cross Earth's orbit in various months across the centuries as its line of apsides would circulate, or rotate. Jupiter prevented this. Hence Jupiter's influence on Mars was the reason that catastrophes were faithful to the 3rd week of March and the 4th week of October for some 17 or 18 long, catastrophic centuries. Jupiter in a sense "locked Mars in". And this is also why the 54-year cycle of conjunctions was so common. Without Jupiter, and with a circulating line of

THE TOWER OF BABEL CATASTROPHE

A — ORBITAL APHELION

P — ORBITAL PERIHELION

⟵⟶ ORBITAL SEMI-MAJOR AXIS
(LINE OF APSIDES)

S - SUN

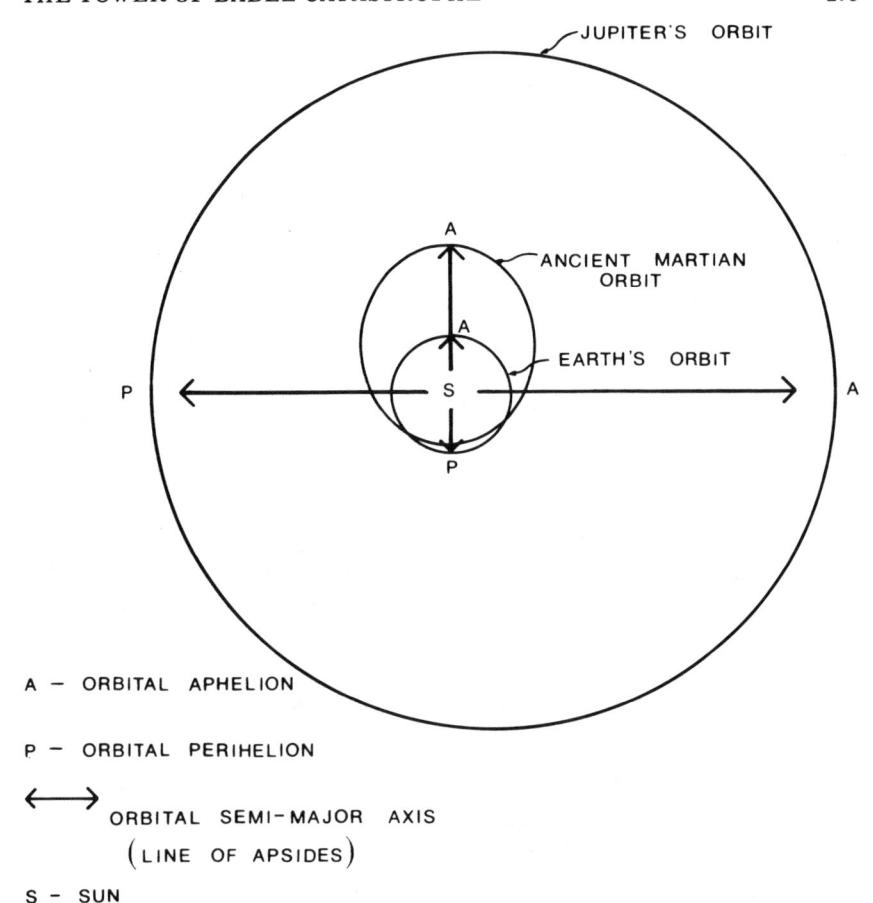

JUPITER – MARS – EARTH GEOMETRY
1 : 6 : 12 RESONANCE SYSTEM

FIGURE 38

Jupiter's current period is 11.8653 of Earth's but our model proposes it was in 1:12 resonance with Earth's orbit and 1:6 resonance with the Martian orbit. Observe that the line of apsides of Earth and the line of apsides of Mars coincides, and both are perpendicular to the line of apsides of Jupiter. Alinda in 3:1 resonance with Jupiter (see Fig. 5) also has its line of apsides perpendicular to Jupiter's, resulting in the "teeter-totter" effect. Jupiter kept Mars in alignment with Earth's orbit. Hence Jupiter kept Mars faithful to its late October and mid-March ancient engagements with the Earth.

apsides for Mars, conjunction cycles would have varied between 50 and 70 or even 80 years.

The principle of resonance has existed in the Creator's framework for a long, long time. Resonance in chemistry is merely an extension of the principle of valence, and has been known for about 100 years. Resonance in sound waves has been studied for about 300 years. Resonance in orbits has just begun to have been recognized within the last 5 years, although it has existed since Creation. We now know for instance that two pairs of Saturn's moons are in 2:1 resonance and another pair is in 4:3 resonance. We know that Neptune and Pluto are in 3:2 resonance. We know that Mercury's spin rate and its orbit are in 3:2 resonance. About 2% of the asteroids are in one kind or another of known resonance.

If Earth's ancient orbit was .9888 in period, or about 1% shorter, its orbit, along with that of Mars, would have been precisely in resonance with Jupiter. (And incidently, Earth at this location would have been very, very close to a 5:8 resonance with Venus; very possibly here was another ancient resonance).

Saturn In Resonance

Saturn has an orbital period of 29.6501 years. Jupiter's is the aforementioned 11.8653 years. These two giant planets are in a 5:2 resonance, a fact just beginning to be recognized in astronomical circles. Saturn is 95 times as massive as Earth; Jupiter is 317 as massive as Earth. This compares to Mars' miniscule .107 mass compared to Earth. This means that there was a Saturn-Jupiter-Mars-Earth resonance system. This resonance was of the order of 2:5:30:60.[6] Figure 39 illustrates the Jupiter-Saturn resonance in the ancient era when it integrated with the Earth-Mars resonance.

We do not want to go too deeply into the details of the Jupiter-Saturn system. But a few observations will be helpful. There are 3 conjunctions, or lineups of the two planets (with the Sun)

---

[6] If it can be further established that Earth was in 5:8 resonance with Venus at this time, it would make a five-planet resonance. The ratios would have been 96 (Venus), 60 (Earth), 30 (Mars), 5 (Jupiter), 2 (Saturn). Earth's ancient orbit we believe was .9888 of the current period. Venus' current orbit is .6152. If Venus has maintained the same orbit, their former ratios were Earth 1 and Venus .6222 and Venus at .625 would have been in a perfect 8:5 resonance with our planet.

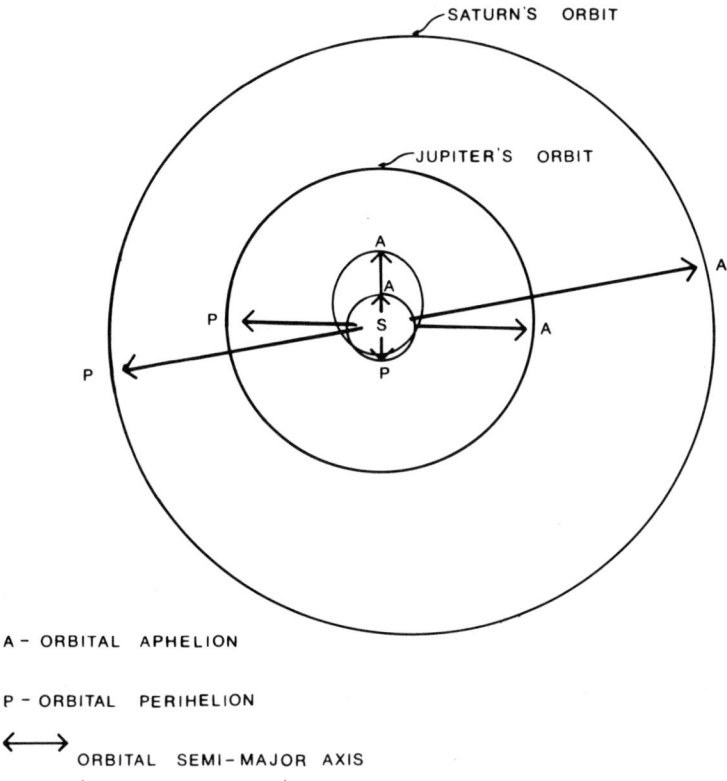

SATURN-JUPITER-MARS-EARTH GEOMETRY

2:5:30:60 RESONANCE SYSTEM

FIGURE 39

Jupiter and Saturn in 5:2 resonance. Jupiter and Saturn shift or perturb each other. The Jupiter-Saturn interaction may be the basis for the ancient grand cycle of holocausts which Ovid reported as ages terminated with celestial interventions.

every 5 Jupiter years. These line-ups are successively at 120° intervals. One is *near perihelion,* where the other two are near aphelion. The near perihelion conjunction is the one of vital concern. The whole system tends to rock. The remote pair of line-ups rocks like a teeter-totter; the near conjunctions like the pendulum we have already observed in the 2:1 asteroid-Jupiter and the 2:1 Earth - Mars conditions. Figure 7, page 85, reminds us that Earth and Mars also had 3 conjunctions, or lineups every Mars-year and there are some parallels between the two situations.

Mars is tiny. Earth is rather small. Saturn is large at 97 x Earth, and Jupiter is massive at 317 x Earth. At their distances, Saturn and Jupiter will disturb each other in a cycle of a larger period. Their perihelion conjunctions cycle like a teeter-totter. What is that period? It has not yet been ascertained.

We do know the Neptune - Pluto system cycles in 40 Pluto years. The Hecuba-Jupiter system cycles in 17 Jupiter years, or 34 asteroid-years. The ancient Earth - Mars system cycled in 27 Mars-years, or 54 Earth-years.

Saturn's period is 29.65 years. It's conjunction cycle with Jupiter (in 2:5 ratio) requires 2 Saturn-years, or about 60 Earth-years. With other cycles of 17, 27 and 40 that are known, could it be that Jupiter and Saturn are disturbing or reversing each other on about a 20 cycle or 22 cycle basis for Saturn? This we suspect. And if this proves to be so, this will strongly indicate that Saturn, shifting or disturbing Jupiter in a 600-year cycle (Earth-years) was the prime influence in the 500-year to 600-year grand cycle which has already been detected in history.

On Models

A good model should contain five characteristics. These characteristics are as follows:

1. HORIZONTAL CONSISTENCY with the understood physical principles of the universe.

2. VERTICAL ALIGNMENT with the known facts of history, be it Earth history recorded in stone, or human history recorded in parchment.

3. FRUITFULNESS OF THOUGHT, catalyzing new research, focusing on new avenues of knowledge.

4. SIMPLICITY OF PREMISE rather than a convoluted premise, overly-flexible to adjust to any kind of incoming data.
5. PREDICTABILITY, or ability to anticipate new discoveries.

Our model should be judged carefully by these criteria. Our prediction is that Jupiter and Saturn will be found to be cycling, in a teeter-totter fashion (like Alinda and Jupiter) on about a 600-year cycle, as measured by Earth years. This data should be forthcoming within the next two or three years.

On Gambling and Dominoes

In an earlier discussion, we cited Plutarch, who described in his own Latin method the changes in celestial realms at the time of the Isaiahic Catastrophe. Plutarch related that Hermes played craps with the Moon, and won heavily. In fact he won from her the seventieth part of each of her periods of illumination, hence the new 29.5 day, the Moon's (Luna's) record of loss. Hermes, possibly confused with Earth, gained one part in seventy, or 5 day per year, hence the new 365 day system. Celestial crap games were significant to Plutarch. Celestial crap games were apparently some pretty exciting and important, even fearful events some 3,000 and 4,000 years ago. We have this on Plutarch's authority, to name one of several.

Another game is dominoes. Some play dominoes by calculations and drawing. Others play dominoes by lining a series up along the edge of a table and tip the lead one over. Knock the lead domino over and the whole series falls over in lock step.

Jupiter, we have already said, more or less locked in, or at least locked in Mars' line of apsides with Earth's orbit. This caused the orbits of the planets Earth and Mars to faithfully cross at the same location, October 25/26 and March 20/21. But Saturn rocked Jupiter. Jupiter rocked Mars. And Mars was then somewhat variable or erratic in its approach geometry to Earth during various cycles. To simplify, let us consider a four-sequence line of dominoes, falling in lock step. The Saturn domino, a heavy one, pushed the Jupiter domino, a very heavy one. The Jupiter domino then pushed the Mars domino, a very light one (1/3000 as heavy). The Mars domino then collided with the Earth domino and bounced off, out of line, even as a domino might be knocked off the table ledge.

We theorize that Mars almost went out of resonance during the Sodom-Gomorrah event. This is based on the general rhythm, but also on the report of the slightly shortened 52-year cycle. Next, after another grand cycle of about 500 years, Mars almost went out of resonance during the Exodus Catastrophe. This too is based on the general rhythm, but also on the observation of the shortened 42-year cycle leading into the famous Long Day of Joshua. The orbit of Mars was alternately under the influence of Jupiter and Earth, but Jupiter shifted back and forth in a grand cycle. The system was under stress, a stress which was theatened during the first grand cycle, which was under even greater stress at the end of the second grand cycle, and which broke up at the end of the third cycle. The era of the third cycle was introduced by the Joel-Amos Holocaust, and was climaxed by the Isaiahic Catastrophe.

This third and last grand cycle broke up during the evening of March 20, 701 B.C. while the youthful Habakkuk watched from the lonely Negev desert, while Hezekiah implored God to deliver his city, while Sennacherib sutured his burns, and while Romulus pondered his "father." This is the era to which Plutarch referred to in his account of the celestial crap game, but it was Isaiah who called the million-to-one shot, the Jerusalem Bolide which delivered his city and his people from scheduled, unmerciful slaughter. And the hand of God, or what Norman Newell refers to (disapprovingly) as "deux ex machina",[7,8] guided these events.

---

[7]Norman Newell, an editor of a geological periodical, holds that geologists in their philosophy 100 years ago threw out the baby with the bath. They threw out catastrophism along with the Bible when they adopted Lyell's uniformitarianism and Darwin's general theory of evolution. He asks and urges geologists to bring back catastrophism (perhaps through the back door,) but never allow it along with "deux ex machina", his term for "the hand of God." Newell is taking a step in the right direction for which we commend him in advocating a renewal of catastrophism in the philosophy of geology.

[8]We advocate understanding catastrophism *with* deux ex machina. In fact we observe design in catastrophism, a pattern which parallels the design which biochemists and geneticists observe in amazing degrees in numberless varieties in the "simple" cells of the many varieties of animals and plants. The magnificence of one of these intricate designs in cell tissue, much less in the numberless varieties, defies all theories of chance and chaos for origin. Design suggests a designer. This magnificence of design in biology demands our attention be turned toward the Creator. We are creationists as well as catastrophists, over-awed with the magnificence of nature. And we are amazed at a parallel, design or pattern which is detected in catastrophism also.

Crap games in general can become catastrophes, much less the kind that Plutarch described, celestial crap games, if one loses. If one lives in an agricultural context, collapse of barns or dams are catastrophes. Perhaps an abandoned barn will stand 50 or 75 years, but eventually, if untended, it will collapse. An untended earthen dam may stand for a century or more before collapsing, depending on construction and local climatic rhythms. The system we describe is not a barn or a dam, but an orbital resonance system. This structure stood for about 1800 years, or three "generations" (i.e. grand cycles) before it too collapsed.

The collapse of barns and dams are unwelcome events in an agricultural context, especially if one lives in a village located immediately downstream of the dam. The collapse of this ancient orbital system, however, was welcomed by the sages of the 4th, 5th, and 6th centuries B.C., sages who somehow understood that planets had shifted and catastrophes threatened no more. This is the basis for shifting attitudes among the sages of this post catastrophe era. Daniel, a sage of ancient Babylon (the second empire) observed that God had changed the times and the seasons (Daniel 2:21). About a century later, Socrates (circa 470 B.C. - 399 B.C.) was awarded a hemlock cocktail because he no longer could recommend the Olympic dieties such as Zeus, Apollo, Chronos and Aphrodite. But Socrates' non-catastrophic world-view was already becoming widespread on the Achaean Peninsula, and elsewhere.

On Saturn

We have already cited Ovid and his attention to Jupiter and Saturn, during the "silver," the "bronze" and the "iron" ages, the catastrophic era. Saturn is extremely dim in the nocturnal heavens. Today probably not one Roman in 50,000 could locate it. It is all but invisible to the naked eye. Yet the Romans built temples to Mars, Jupiter and Saturn within 25 years of the founding of Rome, by 725 B.C. The temple of Mars became the military headquarters on the grassy plain, the Campus Martius. The temple of Jupiter on Capitoline Hill became the political headquarters of the young state. The temple dedicated to Saturn on Palatine Hill became the imperial treasury. Mars, Jupiter and Quirinus were the celestial triad of Rome. Quirinus is not identified by contemporary mythologists, but we are quite sure it is the Latinized form of Chronos, the Greek diety representing Saturn.

Perhaps reasons that transcend our current understanding existed for the ancients. Saturn, though very dim, was considered quite significant to the astronomers and star-gazers of that era, who paid particular attention to its PERIOD. Greek cosmo-mythology suggests, even claims that Chronos, or Saturn, indeed had something to do with the cause of the Deluge. Such an ancient theme is not to be taken too lightly. We have presented a case that Saturn's period (in resonance with Jupiter, and disturbing Mars indirectly) was related to the grand cycle of catastrophism, the extremely severe ones. With his grand cycle theory presented, and some of the correlating mythology presented, we now return to the more mundane matter of details of the Tower of Babel Holocaust, which may be described as a 20th century event, B.C.

Earthquakes and/or Earth-Shakings

For fifty-two years God had warned the godless; He had made the mountains to QUAKE AND TREMBLE. . . .[9]

And as to the tower which the sons of men built, the EARTH OPENED ITS MOUTH and swallowed up one third part thereof, and a fire also descended from heaven and burned another third, and the other third is left to this day. . . .[10]

As for the unfinished tower, A PART SANK INTO THE EARTH, and another part was consumed by fire. . ..[11]

As for the earth, out of it cometh BREAD[12] and under it is turned up as it were fire. (Job 28:5)

From these representative quotations, it is clear that the

---

[9]Louis Ginzberg, *op. cit.*, Vol. I, p. 253.

[10]*The Book of Jasher*, New York: M. M. Noah & A. S. Gould, 1840, 9:38.

[11]Louis Ginzberg, *op, cit.*, Vol. I, p. 180.

[12]In this case the Hebrew word lechem, usually translated as "dough" or "bread," is thought to describe a flowing, plastic-like mass, such as lava. Lava flows and volcanic upheavals were normal for catastrophic days with Mars fly-bys. In the same context is "He putteth forth his hand upon the rock; he overturneth the mountains by the roots", also a literal process which also would necessarily involve fresh lava flows. (See Job 28:9.)

destruction of the famed tower was a two-fold event. Part of the crisis came from the Earth's crust, and part from the celestial zones.

Bolides and Meteorites

> And the Lord sent A MIGHTY WIND against the tower and overthrew it upon the earth, and behold it was between Asshur and Babylon in the land of Shinar, and they called its name 'Overthrow.'[13]

> The Sibyl also makes mention of this tower, and of the confusion of the language, when she says thus: "When all men were of one language, some of them built a high tower, as if they would thereby ascend up to heaven, but the gods SENT STORMS OF WIND and overthrew the tower. . . ."[14]

In Chapter VIII it was seen that the "mighty wind" which blew down the home of Job's oldest son during a birthday party, was not a wind at all, but *ruwach,* a blast. This was the same word used to describe the blast that hit Sennacherib's bivouac in 701 B.C., destroying an entire army in seconds. We believe the mighty wind which hit the tower was shock waves from an exploding bolide, including a flash burn radiation effect or wave, not just a heavy gust of wind or rain storm.

This idea is reinforced by the report that the tower was destroyed one-third by fire descending from heaven which would indicate the falling of meteorites and bolides. It is a typical Case Two catastrophe like the Joel-Amos event or the Long Day of Joshua.

How severe was the catastrophe? It was sufficiently severe to be the leading reported event in two hundred years of time. It was sufficiently severe to cause mass migrations of peoples to the four directions. To underestimate its intensity would be easy, but instead, we are inclined to equate it on a par with the Long Day of Joshua, a Mars fly-by at about 75,000 miles. If this estimate is correct, then this is one of the three worst Case

---

[13]R. H. Charles, *The Apocrypha and Pseudepigrapha of the Old Testament,* Vol. II, "The Book of Jubilees," Oxford: Clarendon Press, p. 29.

[14]Flavius Josephus, *op. cit.,* Book I, Chapter IV, section 3, p. 89.

FIGURE 40
Helios, the original sun deity in Greece, in his regular traverse across the heavens. Helios' regularity brought springtime, seasons and warmth, making livestock, maidens and city folk all happy. From D'Aulaires' Book of Greek Myths, p. 83, courtesy of Doubleday & Co.

THE TOWER OF BABEL CATASTROPHE 285

FIGURE 41
Phaethon in temporary, havoc-filled relief of his father in celestial duties. The solar steeds bucked and the sun wandered crazily across the heavens, i.e., the Earth's spin axis precessed as poles migrated and tilt angle shifted. There is a 50% probability that this cosmic legend originated among Proto-Greeks trying to describe the Tower of Babel holocaust in their region. The Phaethon event may describe BOTH the Tower of Babel and the Long Day of Joshua events, one event reinforcing the other in Greek cosmo-mythology. Observe the prominence of Scorpio, venerated in October in the zodiac. From D'Aulaires' Book of Greek Myths, p. 85, courtesy of Doubleday & Co.

Two catastrophes of ancient times, (along with the Joshuaic holocaust and the Joel-Amos event).

This event, with its bolides and meteors, indicates that Mars fragmented Electra sometime before 1930 B.C. We believe it was some time after the Deluge, circa 2500 B.C. The fire and brimstone, of course, are the Mars-asteroids, part of Electra's heritage to the solar system along with the Sun-asteroids.

Descriptive Cosmic Scenery

> And the Lord said, Behold the people is one, and they have all one language; and this they begin to do: and now nothing will be restrained from them, which they have imagined to do. Go to, LET US GO DOWN, and there confound their language. . . . So the Lord scattered them abroad from thence. . . . (Genesis 11:6-8)

This abbreviated reference to the Tower of Babel Catastrophe indicates the edifice was not sacked and burned by mercenary armies, nor was it looted by Chaldean rioters. It was accomplished from on high ("let us GO DOWN"), by cosmic forces from the heavens. The Tower was intended to be the capitol building of the ruling city for the human race, the idolatrous political and religious capitol of the world. It was something like a United Nations building of the twentieth century B.C. (That the mammoth project failed was considered a benefit to all freedom-loving peoples, according to the ancient Jewish historians.)

The Structure and Purpose of the Tower of Babel

The purposes of the Tower were multiple. One was to make this edifice the masterpiece of world architecture. Another was to make this edifice the political and religious capitol of the world, a center of world control. A third was to worship the planets with astrology, magic and witchcraft. The religious structure at the apex of this six-storied tower was to be the observatory, planetarium and temple. Yet another purpose was to provide the elite of Chaldea a place of refuge "if God should choose again to flood" their world, their "world" being the flat Mesopatamian Plain within their regional context.

Gerald Hawkins, a researcher on Stonehenge, estimated 1:5 million man-days went into construction labor for that megalithic site. And it was just one, although a large one, of some 500 megalithic astronomical temple sites in England and Scotland. The Tower of Babel was clearly an even more impressive effort than Stonehenge in terms of construction labor input (with records indicating a drafted labor force of 600,000 slaves involved in its construction). The Tower of Babel was also more impressive than Stonehenge in terms of its ornamental hardware of gold and other precious metals, and its blue-clay exterior. It could have involved one billion man-days for its planning, its construction and decorating.

> The iniquity and godlessness of Nimrod reached their climax in the building of the Tower of Babel. His counsellors had proposed the plan of erecting such a tower, Nimrod had agreed to it, and it was executed in Shinar by a mob of six hundred thousand men.[15]

Robert Koldewey was an archaeologist who understood that ancient records contained cores of facts and were not myths. He set out to find and excavate the site of the Tower of Babel in 1898 A.D. His find was astonishing. He located the *second* Tower of Babel build by Nebuchadnezzar, and under that he found the foundation of the original Tower of Babel.

> Every large Babylonian city had its ziggurat, but none compared with the Tower of Babel. Fifty-eight million bricks went into the Tower's construction, and the whole landscape was dominated by its terraced mass. The Tower of Babel was built by slaves.[16]

> The original Tower rose up in a series of enormous terraces. Herodotus describes a series of eight superimposed stages, each one somewhat smaller than the one below it. The uppermost terrace formed the base of a temple that looked out far over the land.[17]

The base of the Tower was 288 feet on a side, the total

---

[15] Louis Ginzberg, *op. cit.*, Vol. I, p. 179.

[16] C. W. Ceram, *Gods, Graves, and Scholars*, as translated from the German by E. B. Garside, New York: Alfred A. Knopf, 1951, p. 290.

[17] C. W. Ceram, *op. cit.*, p. 289.

height of Tower and temple also 288 feet. The first stage was 105.6 feet in height; the second, 57.6 feet; the third, fourth, fifth and sixth, 19.2 feet each; and the Temple of Marduk 48 feet in height. The temple housed the most important god in the Babylonian pantheon. The walls of the temple were plated with gold, and decorated with enameled brickwork of a bluish hue, which glittered in the sun, greeting the traveler's eye from afar.[18]

If Herodotus can be credited with accuracy, the gold in the statue and accoutrements amounted to 800 talents of pure gold, worth $24,000,000 at 1951 values. Its weight was 23,700 kilograms or 26.07 tons of pure gold. The gigantic steps leading up to the first terrace rose 105.6 feet in elevation.

The *Talmud* states that the Tower was 42 years in building and was completed, although the surrounding gateways and streets were incomplete when the catastrophe struck.

This is the record of the building planned to house **Bel-Merodech**, or **Bel Marduk**, or **Baal-Mars**. Its construction was undertaken in the tenth generation after the Deluge, in a decadent generation involved in unrestrained, "snowballing" tyranny. Tyranny had replaced freedom; government enterprise with taxation and conscripted labor had superseded private enterprise; astrology and idolatry had superseded monotheism.[19] (By way of analogy, our nation today, in the tenth generation from Plymouth Rock, is becoming decadent in the public sector by statism to the disadvantages of the private entrepreneur. We too are becoming engrossed in one-worldism, in empty churchism and in our era of a *settled* solar system, even in astrology.)

---

[18]C. W. Ceram, *op. cit.*, p. 290. The dimensions of the Tower of Babel, according to the account of Heroditus, included a 5:2 ratio for the 7th story compared to the 6th, at the climax (48 ft. vs. 19.2 ft.). This tower was intended as a celestial temple beyond question. The ancients were concerned about the periods of the planets beyond question. Jupiter was in a 5:2 orbital ratio with Saturn. This ratio happens to coincide with the construction ratio of the two top stories. Is this coincidence, or is there more to it than that?

[19]America is moving toward unrestrained corruption ten generations after the Mayflower Compact. Chaldean civilization moved into unrestrained corruption ten generations after the Noachian event, another "Mayflower-type" event.

> For this reason Reu called his son Serug, because all mankind had turned aside unto sin and transgression. When he grew to manhood, the name was seen to have been chosen fittingly, for he, too, worshipped idols, and when he himself had a son, Nahor by name, he taught him the arts of the Chaldees, how to be a soothsayer and practice magic according to signs in the heavens.[20]

When the Tower of Babel rocked, shivvered and began to collapse, the masonry, artwork and wealth of four decades began to collapse in a series of avalanches of brick, mortar, gold and other accoutrements.

> But as to the plain of Shinar, in the country of Babylonia, Hestiaeus mentions it, when he says thus: "Such of the priests as were saved, took the sacred vessels of Jupiter Enyalius, and came to Shinar of Babylonia.[21]

(This was just after the Tower had fallen, and some of the sacred hardwares were salvaged and kept in adoration at other sites.) Mars-Baal did not perform well. No doubt as Baal-Mars approached closer and closer during that fateful month of 1930 B.C., the frenzied priests and priestesses of Baal-Mars implored Mars to turn aside, but Baal-Mars failed to hear their tortured petitions. Abraham, at this time was about 48 years of age.

Later, when Abraham left Chaldea and migrated into Egypt, he was considered to be an authority on science.

> He communicated to them [*the Egyptians*] arithmetic, AND DELIVERED TO THEM THE SCIENCE OF ASTRONOMY; for before Abram came into Egypt they were unacquainted with those parts of learning, for that science came from the Chaldeans into Egypt, and from thence to the Greeks also.[22]

In the twentieth century A.D., we have telescopes, radio astronomy, spectroscopy, photometry, space modules, booster engines, computers and radar. None of these sophistications existed in the twentieth century B.C. Nevertheless, a large proportion of the citizens of Babylon and other Sumerian cities could locate in the nocturnal skies not only Venus and the wan-

---

[20]Louis Ginzberg, *op. cit.*, Vol. I, p. 186.

[21]Flavius Josephus, *op. cit.*, Book I, Chapter IV, section 3, p. 89.

[22]Flavius Josephus, *op. cit.*, Book I, Chapter VIII, section 2, p. 96.

290 THE LONG DAY OF JOSHUA AND SIX OTHER CATASTROPHES

dering Mars, but also Jupiter, Saturn and numerous constellations, one of which was the first point of Aries (the first sector of the zodiac). Today, hardly one person in 10,000 can locate the dim Jupiter, and few persons know more than a half dozen constellations.

The ancients, too, were interested in the astronomical scene. They were concerned about such matters as paths across the zodiac, lunar eclipses, Mars eclipses, conjunctions, comets, irregular orbits, regular orbits, obelisks, gnomons, sun caves, calendaric systems and reformed systems, catastrophic appointment days and so forth. Today, perhaps ¼% to ½% of our gross national product is involved in space exploration, the lunar missions, the Mariner missions and until cancelled, the "grand tour" in two stages, with space craft containing extremely complicated components. Since 600,000 slaves were employed in the building of the Tower of Babel (only one ziggurat), and since some 26 tons of inlaid gold were used, and since those slaves required tax support, it is quite possible that about 15% or perhaps more of the gross national product of Babylonia went into astrology/astronomy. The same is true for England with its Stonehenge project, and Egypt with its pyramids, its planet temples, and other astronomical-related architectures. Yes, the ancients were interested, very interested, in cosmology and celestial scenery, especially in the years of appointment, every 52 or 54 years in that era.

The Peleg Catastrophe — Estimated 2146 B.C.

Was the Tower of Babel the first of the post-flood catastrophes? Our answer is, in all probability, no. Scriptures contain a vague but significant remark about a special time some two centuries earlier.

> And unto Eber was born two sons: the name of one was Peleg; FOR IN HIS DAYS WAS THE EARTH DIVIDED.... (Genesis 10:25)

Peleg's life span included 239 years in that era of longer life, and the dates of his life are approximately 2168 B.C. to 1929 B.C.

If we pursue dating by the model, earlier crisis years would have been the following:

Case One 1877 B.C.   **Case Two** 1930 B.C. (Tower of Babel)
1985 B.C. 2038 B.C.
2093 B.C. 2146 B.C. (Peleg)
2201 B.C. 2254 B.C.
2309 B.C. 2362 B.C.

The division of the Earth during the days of Peleg was not linguistic. The cleavage was due to a new equatorial zone of oblateness, the forces already welling up within Earth's crust.[23] Our estimated date for the Peleg Catastrophe is 2146 B.C., two cycles before the Tower of Babel holocaust. This estimate compares with our dating of the Job catastrophe two cycles or 216 years before the Exodus event. This dating methodology is patterned after the cyclic pattern of the Greater Davidic Catastrophe, just 216 years (two full cycles) before the Joel-Amos holocaust.

The object of science is not only to apply the different substances in nature to the advantage, benefit, and comfort of man, but likewise to set forth that wonderful and magnificent history of wisdom and intelligence which is written in legible characters both in the heavens and on the earth.
—Sir Humphry Davy

Mine hand also hath laid the foundation of the earth, and my right hand hath spanned the heavens: when I call unto them, they stand up together.—The Bible (Book of Isaiah)

---

[23] We believe there was a radical change of the polar locations during the Flood Catastrophe, or Deluge. Perhaps the poles migrated 3,000 to 5,000 miles. Granting this, there would of necessity have to be a new equatorial bulge generated, a bulge adding about 26 miles in Earth diameter to the new equatorial zone. The Earth's thin crust was thus under great stress in the early post-diluvian era to slowly form its new girdle or bulge. Thus that era would be one of particularly numerous earthquakes.

The Moon also has an equatorial bulge, approximately 5,000 feet in diameter greater than its polar diameter. Since the Moon does not rotate, it has a secondary bulge in alignment with the Earth, a pear-shaped bulge of approximately 2,000 feet. This is called a "dumbbell bulge."

chapter **XI**

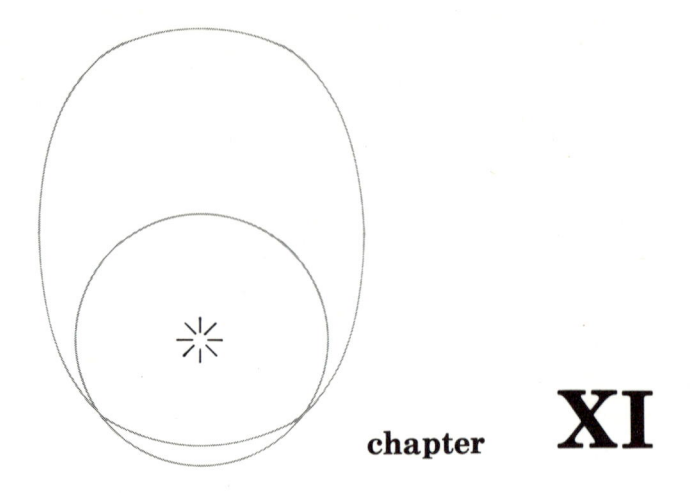

The Two Mysterious Moons of Mars — Deimos and Phobos

Deimos and Phobos, the companions of Ares-Mars, have variously been discussed or described by Homer in the Iliad, circa 970 B.C., by Jonathan Swift in Gulliver's Travels, published in 1726 in London, and by Asaph Hall. Hall was a 19th century astronomer with the U.S. Naval Observatory, Washington, D.C., in 1877. The chapter will endeavor to shed light on how and when Deimos and Phobos were first sighted.

According to the dictionary, a mystery is something which occurs, or has occurred, but cannot (or has not) been explained. There is just such a mystery surrounding the two trabants of Mars. Part I of the mystery is the existence of Deimos and Phobos, tiny asteroid-like fragments, revolving around the red planet. "Why should such a tiny planet have any satellites at all?" Part II of the mystery concerns how Jonathan Swift was able to describe or "guess" their existence, their orbital diameters and their orbital periods so accurately. Part III of the mystery concerns WHEN, and HOW they were first sighted. In our chapter introduction, Greeks, Englishmen and Americans all have some claim on the discovery of these tiny trabants.

Part I — The Existence of Deimos and Phobos

The traditionally-accepted "discovery" of the minscule moons of Mars occurred as recently as 1877 by the American astronomer, Asaph Hall. His discovery was a big surprise since Mars had been studied through telescopes for more than 250 years. As early as 1610, Galileo reported four of the moons of Jupiter along with Saturn's rings. Uranus was discovered by Sir William Herschel in 1781 through a systematic search of the heavens. Then in 1787 he discovered two moons of Uranus, Titania and Oberon, and in 1789 he found two more Moons of Saturn, Mimas and Enceladus. In 1846 Laverrier found the much sought after Neptune and its larger satellite, Triton, nearly 3 billion miles distant. Thus when Asaph Hall announced he had located two hitherto unreported moons on the near-by Mars in 1877, it created a genuine shock in astronomical circles.

The current orbit of Mars varies from 128,000,000 miles to 151,000,000 miles from the Sun. Earth's orbit varies from 91,400,000 to 94,400,000 miles. About every fifteen years, the two planets can come as close together as about 35,000,000 miles.[1]

In 1877, Asaph Hall undertook a search for a satellite of Mars, partly because he had tired of reading in the text books that "Mars has no moons." As recently as the year 1862 a diligent search had been undertaken for just such a satellite, but without success. But in 1877, Hall (on the staff of the United States Naval Observatory) had a better telescope than had existed 15 years earlier. He felt it was worth another try. One thing was certain. It was unlikely such a discovery of a satellite would be achieved without searching for it.

The discovery of Phobos was not easy. This was partly due to its size (about eight miles in diameter), partly because of its irregular, fragment-like shape, changing magnitudes, and partly because of its dark color.[2] A high magnification telescope such as Hall used will allow an observer to scan a section of the sky

---

[1] Earth laps Mars once every 25 months. Of these periodic laps, one in every seven finds the two plants especially close, and provides an excellent opportunity for viewing Mars. 1877 was such a year of close "opposition" for the two planets. The two planets were only 36,000,000 miles distant.

[2] Recent Mariner fly-bys of Mars have shown Phobos to be the darkest body in the solar system, with a reflectivity (or albedo) of 5%.

one-hundredth the apparent width of the Moon. Such an improved magnification would be necessary because the satellite, if existing, would have had to be very tiny or it would have been discovered earlier. A suspicious looking object might easily turn out to be a star of low stellar magnitude. Or it might well turn out to be just another asteroid, which would have a motion similar to that of a Martian satellite.[3, 4]

According to one version, Hall was so discouraged on the night of August 10, 1877, that he would have given up if his wife had not urged him to return to the observatory that night for one more look. This time, Hall spotted a small, star-like object, amazingly close to the planet itself. Then the fog came in from the Potomac River. Clouds prevented further observation until the night of August 15. And by August 21, Hall had convinced himself that there was but one inner moon. The moon completed a revolution around Mars in less than one-third the time of the rotation of the primary planet, about 7 hours, 39 minutes.[5]

A second moon, a little farther out, also was discovered by Hall. The privilege of naming discoveries is granted to the discoverers. Many names were suggested, but appropriately enough, Hall chose the names of those two tiny mythical companions of Mars in Greek cosmology, "panic" and "fear" being their meanings in Greek, Deimos and Phobos.

Ten years later, in 1887, an Italian astronomer, Schiaparelli, also had excellent viewing conditions of Mars, and he also had a fine telescope with an 8-inch refractor. He reported a consid-

---

[3] While searching for a satellite of Jupiter with a 100-inch reflector in 1938, Nicholson picked up 32 asteroids in his photographs. Each had to be eliminated as a possible Jovian trabant, before he found Jupiter X and Jupiter XI.

[4] Jupiter X and XI are also asteroid-like fragments. From our castastrophic framework, assuming Mars fragmented Electra into asteroids, we then have three kinds of asteroids, those revolving around Jupiter subsequent to capture, those revolving around Mars (Deimos and Phobos) and those revolving around the Sun which include about 99.5% of the total of those for which orbits have been plotted.

[5] Thus, to a science fiction "Martian", or a future astronaut, Phobos would appear to rise in the west rather than in the east, unlike any other satellite in the solar system. No similar case was known at that time, and no similar case has been discovered since.

erable network of "fine lines" and thought that his glimpse of a network of lines were channels, or to use the Italian word, *canali*. It was translated as canals in English, not channels. And immediately there was abundant speculation as to "proof" that intelligent life existed on Mars, "proof" (or spoof) of evolution. Schiaparelli's mirage, misinterpreted into canals, was carried over into sober scientific texts for the next 50 or 60 years, until the 1950's. About half of the astronomers observing Mars, incidently, failed to "see" Schiaparelli's *canali,* while the other half thought they "saw" the canals.

Subsequent observations have shown that these two satellites revolve in nearly circular orbits, which lie very close to the Martian equator. Because of the bulge of a planet around the equatorial zone, minute perturbations, cumulative in nature, cause all satellites to revolve around the equatorial zones of the various planets.

While Phobos appears to rise in the west on Mars, Deimos (at a distance of 14,600 miles above the Martian crust) would appear to a science fiction character to virtually hang motionless overhead. This is because its orbital period (30 hours, 18 minutes) is so similar to the rotational period of Mars (24 hours, 37 minutes). Deimos is the closest thing in our solar system to a natural or "stationary" satellite. It rises ever so slowly on the planet's eastern horizon.

Could Deimos and Phobos be remains of a fragmented planet, Electra, fragmented by Mars itself? This is what we have proposed in Chapter III in the part about the general theory of fragmentation. In contrast, observe the *assumptions* (often subconscious) by a traditional, average, contemporary astronomer. This is Richardson's commentary on the two trabants of Mars.

> Phobos and Deimos are the same size as many of the asteroids. On the face of it such a hypothesis [*an evolutionary capture by chance of the two trabants*], sounds quite possible, but upon closer examination it does not stand up so well. A planet only one-tenth as massive as Earth could not easily effect a capture. Suppose that eight small satellites of Jupiter are captured asteroids. Then Mars, with a mass only 1/2950 that of Jupiter, has done extraordinarily well to have been able to latch onto two such bodies. The asteroids revolve in orbits that have no particular relationship to the orbit of Mars.

Suppose one of the satellites is a captured asteroid, captured in such a way that it revolves in a circular orbit in the plane of the planet's equator. . . . But it does seem incredible that Mars could have effected two such very special captures. FURTHER SPECULATION ALONG THIS LINE IS USELESS. This is a problem for a high-speed computor.[6,7]

Richardson suggests that "further speculation along this line is useless". This is true within his limited uniformitarian frame of reference, his limited world view which fails to assess planetary catastrophism. But on the other hand, a catastrophic theory of fragmentation of the former planet Electra by Mars, would *require* the capture of a small percent of the fragments by Mars. Thus Richardson's conclusion about "further speculation being useless" is a very poor conclusion, which is based on a set of poor ASSUMPTIONS. One of his assumptions is the uniformitarian motto, "the present is the key to the past", a patent absurdity. This illustration reveals that *making good assumptions* is more important than making good conclusions.

Part I of the mystery, the PRESENCE of the two Mars-asteroids, is thus adequately explained in the catastrophic world view. There would be many more asteroids and smaller debris than this had Mars not made so many fly-bys near the Earth.

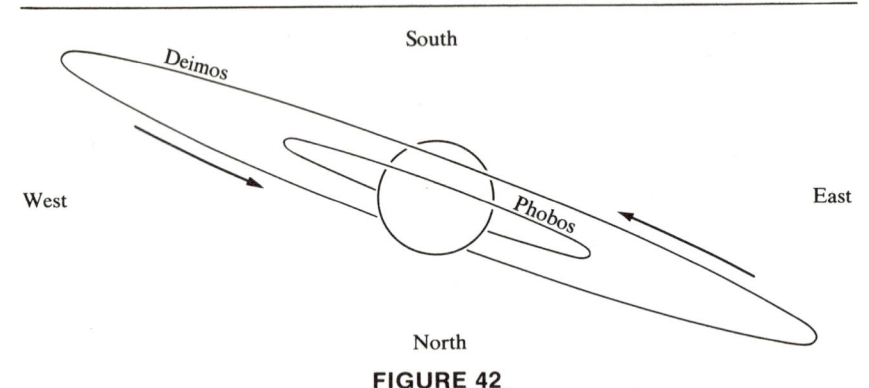

FIGURE 42
The orbits of Phobos and Deimos as they appeared on Dec. 30, 1960. From Mars, p. 91, courtesy of Harcourt, Brace & Co.

---

[6] Robert S. Richardson, *Mars*, New York: Harcourt, Brace and World Inc., 1964, p. 93.

[7] Richardson assumes a capture can occur only during a fly-by. We propose a capture of a fragment can occur during the fragmentation process where the velocities and directions of the suddenly-formed fragments vary widely.

Part II — Swift and the Laputan Astronomers

Part II of the mystery concerns how Jonathan Swift was able to describe or "guess" their existence, plus their orbital diameters and their orbital periods with such amazing accuracy. This appears in his work, *Gullivers' Travels,* published in 1726, some 151 years before Hall "discovered" them. According to Swift, the two Martian moons were well-known to the Laputan astronomers of his time. The Laputans were contemporaries with his miniature Lilliputians and his gigantic Brobdingnags.

Gulliver's Travels, on the surface, is an amusing and pleasant account of Captain Lemuel Gulliver's adventures among strange peoples and around strange places that Englishmen were still in the process of discovering. The "astronomers" on the pleasant isle of Laputa possessed superior telescopes to anything known in Europe during the 1720's. The Laputan astronomers quite assuredly knew about Mars' two tiny satellites, satellites of which the Europeans with their "inferior" telescopes, knew nothing. This is the account of those studious, wise scholars of Laputa:

> . . . they have likewise discovered two lesser Stars or Satellites, which revolve about Mars, whereof the innermost is distant from the Centre of the Primary Planet exactly three of his Diameters, and the outermost five; the former revolves in the Space of ten hours, and the latter in Twenty-one and a Half; so that the Squares of their periodical Times are very near in the same Proportion with the Cubes of their Distance from the Center of Mars, which evidently shews them to be governed by the same Law of Gravitation, that influences the other heavenly Bodies.[8]

When Asaph Hall discovered them, he gave them names quite promptly. Interestingly and in contrast, the Laputans had discovered them, described their orbits, timed them, but had NOT taken the trouble to name them. This is a "strangostrosity." Another strange feature is that Captain Gulliver reported their orbital diameters but not in miles, not in leagues, not in stadii, but in "Mars-diameters." This is very untypical for an Irishman.

[8]Jonathan Swift, *Gulliver's Travels,* New York; Random House, 1958, p. 134.

Why did Captain Gulliver not give their orbital diameters in English miles?

At that time, in 1726, the diameter of Mars was not yet known. At that time astronomers did know that Mars was 1.52 astronomical units from the Sun.[9] But they did not even have an accurate value for the length of the astronomical unit. However, to describe or discuss the distances of the satellites from the primary planet in terms of Mars-diameters implies sighting, implies measurement and implies calculation. Who did this calculation, and where and when? Swift was a clergyman, an Irishman from Dublin, and a wit. But he was not a mathematician, much less an astronomer.

On the other hand, perhaps Gulliver, or the Laputan astronomers, or Swift was "just guessing" about the undiscovered satellites. If the Laputans had superior telescopes, why hadn't they discovered Uranus?[10] Why didn't they discover such satellites as Saturn's Mimas (400 miles in diameter), or Enceladus (500 miles in diameter), or even Jupiter V (100 miles in diameter)? Were they indeed such "superior" astronomers?

TABLE IX

THE LAPUTAN MEASUREMENTS VERSUS RECENT MEASUREMENTS[11]

Satellite	By Swift	By Modern Instruments
Phobos	3 Mars-diameters 12,420 miles	7,879 miles
Phobos	10 hours	7 hours 39 minutes
Deimos	5 Mars-diameters 20,700 miles	16,670 miles
Deimos	21½ hours	30 hours 18 minutes

[9] An astronomical unit, or "A. U." is the average radius of Earth's orbit, about 92,900,000 miles.

[10] Uranus was discovered by Sir William Herschel in 1781.

[11] Swift could have hardly described Deimos or Phobos in any random period. If he were to do so, he could conflict with the Harmonic Law of Planetary Motion discovered by Kepler. Then he would also disagree with such astronomer-friends as Sir Edmund Halley (1656-1742) of comet fame, Sir Isaac Newton (1642-1727) who conceived the idea of universal gravitation, and William Whiston (1667-1752), Newton's laboratory assistant and successor at Cambridge. Whiston, a Greek, Latin and Hebrew scholar and mathematician, translated Josephus' works into English.

Another facet of the mystery merits consideration. Swift goes on to explain:

... the Squares of their periodical Times are very near the same Proportion with the Cubes of their Distances ... .[12]

There is no escape from the conclusion that Swift MUST have had to calculate the period of the outer moon from the equation

$$(\text{Period outer moon})^2 = \frac{5^3}{3^3} \times 10^2 = \frac{12{,}500}{27} = 462.97,$$

which gives: period outer moon = $\sqrt{462.97}$ = 21.5 hours, very closely. Since Swift was a well-educated man, such elementary arithmetic should have been easy for him, although his principal training had been in literature and history.

All this has been known and commented upon for nearly a century now. What seems to have been overlooked is that we can learn still more about Mars from the information Swift gave us about his moons. For when he specified the periods and distances of the moons he necessarily specified something about Mars, too. He specified its MASS.[13]

Part II of our mystery concerns how Jonathan Swift was able to describe or calculate, much less "guess" their existence. Swift (1667-1745), a Londoner, was a contemporary with the famous threesome, Halley, Newton and Whiston. Of these three, Newton and Whiston were particularly interested in Christian theology as well as natural science. London at that time had a population of about 200,000, like Tacoma, Washington, Des Moines, Iowa or Charlotte, North Carolina today. We believe each of these three were all Swift's friends. Perhaps his confidant and calculator was William Whiston, who like Swift had a remarkable but turbulent literary career.

Richardson, after examination of the tales of Captain Gulliver in some depth, proceeds to "throw up his hands".

---

[12] Jonathan Swift, *Gulliver's Travels*, New York; Random House, 1958, p. 134.

[13] Richardson, *op cit.*, p. 97.

> Thus if we accept the values for the distance and period of the satellites found by the Laputian astronomers we get a mass of Mars about 6 times too big. It is disappointing to find it so far off. Swift made a lucky guess about the satellites, but that is the most you can say for it—JUST A LUCKY GUESS.[14]

Similarly astounded is the modern, and prolific science fiction writer, Isaac Asimov:

> This is an amazing coincidence. Of course, Swift might have reasoned as follows: It was known that Earth had 1 moon, Jupiter 4 and Saturn 7 at the time he was writing his book. It was reasonable to suppose that Saturn might have an 8th moon hidden somewhere and, in that case, if Mars had 2 moons, there would be a nice list of numbers.
>
> As one moved outward from the sun, beginning at Earth, the number of moons of each planet would be 1, 2, 4, 8. Then, too, the moons of Mars would have to be small and close to the planet, or even Europeans with their "poor" telescopes would have discovered them.
>
> So far, Swift's thinking can be followed. However, his guess that Phobos would rise in the west and set in the east because of its speed of revolution is uncanny. IT IS UNDOUBTEDLY THE LUCKIEST GUESS IN LITERATURE.[15, 16, 17]

If Swift, or Whiston[18] were "guessing", they did well. If they had source material such as an ancient star chart on which to

---

[14] Richardson, op. cit., p. 99.

[15] Isaac Asimov, *The Kingdom of the Sun,* London: Abelard-Schuman, 1960, p. 128-129.

[16] For Asimov, a writer of fiction to accuse Swift of guessing is like the pot accusing the kettle of blackness. Actually Asimov errs in his facts. Of Saturn's moons, four were discovered by Cassini (Iapetus in 1671, Rhea in 1672, Dione in 1684 and Tethys in 1684). One, Titan in 1655 was discovered by Huygens. Only these five were known during Swift's time. Mimas and Enceladus (Herschel in 1789) complete Asimov's nice group of seven for Saturn, but only five of the seven were known until over 50 years after the publishing of Captain Lemuel Gulliver's travels.

[17] Asmov is doing the guessing while he attributes "guessing" to Swift concerning a mystery he cannot fathom.

[18] Whiston was an astronomer, a historian, and a catastrophist. Among his works are *A New Theory on Earth History* (1696) and *Astronomical Principals of Religion* (1717).

base their cryptic presentation, it makes more sense. Perhaps they were unsure but suspicious concerning some ancient star charts. Whiston knew Greek cosmo-mythology very well. Could it be that they decided to present their hunch in the form of a satire. And if they were correct, someone would sooner or later figure it out, and perhaps give them the proper credit due. And if they were incorrect, no one would be the wiser. Bear in mind that Swift was a Londoner by residence but was an Irishman at heart. He liked a good joke as well as an artistic satire. And he did not hesitate to satirize England, Parliament, the church, mankind, or in this case, science.[19]

Concerning the mystery of the two moons of Mars as "known" by the Laputan astronomers, we propose five possible solutions, and let the reader (by inductive reasoning and instinct) eliminate those least probable.

SOLUTION I Modern astronomers are participating in a giant hoax. Neither Deimos nor Phobos exist, and these normally serious, sober scientists are just having a little collective joke on society.

SOLUTION II Halley, Flamsteed, Newton and Whiston somehow secretly built a superior telescope. They saw, measured and timed Deimos and Phobos. Then they passed their information on to Swift to print in satire, in preference to the Royal Society for learned consideration. Then they destroyed the scope so that no outsider would realize their discovery and publicize their cryptic pun.

SOLUTION III Sometime between 1500 B.C. and 710 B.C., the Greeks built superior telescopes. They recorded their telescopic findings of the distant Mars, some 35,000,000 miles distance, and its satellites. Whiston or Swift stumbled onto their charts and/or literatures, realized the correct interpretation,

---

[19]This is the same Jonathan Swift whom we mentioned in the opening chapter of this work. Swift believed that a civilization needs its widely-held assumptions challenged every two to three centuries, or else society is apt to go to seed.

but doubted if England would listen to such a story, soberly-told.

SOLUTION IV   Mars, with Deimos and Phobos, was in a far different orbit, and made a fly-by near or through the Earth-Moon system about twice a century for some 17 centuries. Greeks, Egyptians, Phoenicians, Goths, Dravidians, Chinese, Japanese and other ancient scholars saw Deimos and Phobos when Mars was within a million miles. Somebody measured the orbits of Deimos and Phobos and timed their periods when they were that close, with the naked eye, possibly assisted by some crude lenses. Somebody left a few ancient star charts somewhere.

SOLUTION V   Asimov and Richardson were correct. Swift made the luckiest guess in all scientific literature.

If Solution IV is chosen among these five, then Deimos and Phobos were known (if not sighted) to the blind Homer, to David, to Isaiah, to Hesoid, to Romulus and to many ancients.

> These were inspired of Ares, but the others by Athene—and with them came Panic [*Phobos*], Rout [*Deimos*], and Strife, whose fury never tires· sister and friend of murderous Ares, who, from being at first low in stature, grows till she uprears her head to heaven. . . . She it was that went about among them and slung down discord to the waxing of sorrow with even hand between them. When they were got together in one place shield clashed with shield and spear with spear in the rage of battle.[20]

> As a dark cloud in the sky when it comes on to blow after heat, even so did Diomed, son of Tydeus, see Ares ascend into the broad heavens. . . . But Hera . . . and Athene . . . now that they had put a stop to the murderous doings of Ares, went back again to the house of Zeus.[21]

---

[20] Homer, *Iliad*, p. 64.

[21] Homer, *Iliad*, pp. 86, 87.

POEM TO ARES. Ares. . . . sceptred King of manliness, who whirls your fiery sphere among the planets in their sevenfold courses through the aether wherein your blazing steeds Deimos and Phobos ever bear you above the third firmament of heaven . . .[22]

Part III—How and When Deimos and Phobos Were First Sighted

HOW. These two tiny trabants were first sighted by the naked eye, and were known to millions of ancients. Asaph Hall was the first to sight them since the 7th century B.C. This is when the two planets went out of orbital resonance.

WHEN. Our material previously presented requires that Mars fragmented Electra at a location some 200,000,000 miles from the Sun, and before 1950 B.C. We suspect the fragmentation occurred later than 2500 B.C.

WHERE. Did Swift, or Whiston (or another colleague) gather ancient star charts and literature tipping them off? Was the source ancient Greece? Medieval Arabie? 17th Century India . . . or China . . . or Japan? The East India Company of Great Britain had just opened up the Orient to trade a few decades earlier. Alert missionary scholars were active in that era. Is 'Laputa' a specific location, some specific island, city or province? Is Swift's 'Laputa' itself cryptic, consistent with Swift's general satire and enjoyment of wit? These questions will be addressed by Charles McDowell in a forthcoming publication expected within the next three years, and we prefer not to reveal his research prematurely, or "steal his thunder" on this occasion. But we will venture an opinion that his material, when presented, will be most interesting.

Conclusions

The modus operandi of science is experimentation. These ancient fly-bys cannot be reprogrammed physically. There are no

---

[22]Hesiod, *The Homeric Hymns*, New York: G. P. Putnam's Sons, 1926, p. 433.

current conditions in our solar system whereby a planet is under a known schedule for catastrophism. Beyond experimentation, observation is also the modus operandi of science. Similar conditions are not being observed today. Therefore, when analyzing these ancient events, we are not dealing with science. We are dealing with HISTORY (albeit measured frequently with scientific tools). Scientists must understand this difference.

Many modern astronomers presume to announce or publish conclusions on ancient conditions because they assume the present is the key to the past, the uniformitarian creed. But since they are not versed in history, they are out of their field (although they may not realize this). These ancient events comprise HISTORY, not science. Even the black plague of medieval Europe is history (whereas it was science when it was being observed).

Richardson's aformentioned conclusion (i.e. "it does seem incredible that Mars could have effected two such very special captures", etc.) illustrates the prevailing philosophy of the astronomical profession. The entire profession lacks a catastrophic framework of thought, just like the geological profession. Astronomers who are not historians would do well to stay with astronomy, and not wander into cosmology. Astronomers seldom are historians; most are fully occupied with mastering one single branch of learning, or a subdivision thereof. This is most proper. But only an astronomer who has a catastrophic world view and an adequate historical background is acceptable as a cosmologist. Perhaps the historian who has educated himself in astronomy and celestial mechanics may also qualify. Cosmology is not astronomy, even as science is not history.

Asimov's aformentioned conclusions (i.e. ". . . his guess that Phobos would rise in the west and set in the east . . . . is undoubtedly the luckiest guess in literature" etc.) illustrates another point. This is the all but universal, and careless acceptance of evolutionary-uniformitarian rationale. This rationale is handed to tens of thousands of students every year without being adequately checked or questioned by either teacher or student. Asimov substituted his own fantasy (of the moons of the solar system being 1, 2, 4 and 8, a "nice list of numbers") as a reasonable thing whereas we found even his basic data was defective. This illustrates that evolutionary-uniformitarians, be they science fiction writers or authors of sober scientific literature should question the facts, allegations and interpretations of history rigorously.[23]

A third conclusion applies to us all. We too must watch and examine our ASSUMPTIONS carefully, long before we make serious conclusions. Assumptions come in two varieties, the conscious and the subconscious. Both require equal scrutiny, although the subconscious variety is usually the more elusive.

A characteristic feature of any new theory, which does not try to fit new facts to any already established representaation, . . . is its irrationality from the point of view of previous ideas.—J. Frenkel

The specialist lives so close to his subject that he often fails to see the wood for the trees. As a result, the great discoveries are often made by those who invade fields of knowledge other than their own.—H. C. Lehman

---

[23] We get our philosophy from history, whereas we get our technology from science.

chapter **XII**

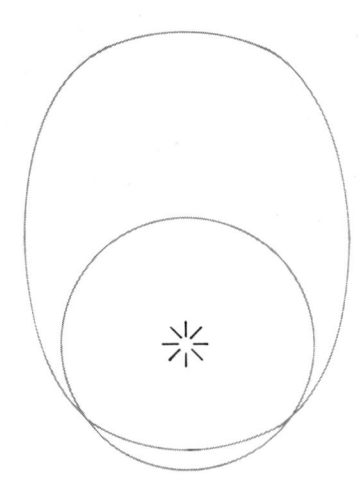

The Flood Catastrophe

Circa 2400 B.C. to 2500 B.C.

The Flood Catastrophe has been the worst by far of all the catastrophes since the creation of man. Its intensity was not merely degrees, but MAGNITUDES more intense than the next worst, the Exodus Catastrophe.

In this chapter (like the previous ones on other catastrophes), we shall follow the general established outline. This outline includes (1) the date, the calendaric month and day, (2) the date, by Julian calendar, (3) bolidic or meteoritic intrusions, (4) earthquakes and spin axis shifts, and (5) descriptive cosmic movements.

This chapter is a supplement to an earlier book on the cosmology of the Flood Catastrophe. It cannot be treated as a synopsis of the earlier work.[1]

In the six hundredth year of Noah's life, in the SECOND MONTH, the SEVENTEENTH DAY OF THE MONTH, the SAME DAY were all the fountains of the great deep broken up, and the windows of heaven were opened. (Genesis 7:11)

---

[1] Donald W. Patten, *The Biblical Flood and the Ice Epoch*, Seattle: Pacific Meridian Publishing Co., 1966.

Thick clouds are a covering to him, that he seeth not; AND HE WALKETH IN THE CIRCUIT OF HEAVEN. (Job 22:14)

For enquire, I pray thee, of the former age [*the pre-flood era*], and prepare thyself to the search of their fathers. (Job 8:8)

Dating By Calendaric Day and Month

THE BIBLICAL FLOOD should be considered more as a catastrophic pair than as a single catastrophe. This is because we conclude the following events occurred astronomically and geophysically in a single 150 day period:

1. A close fly-by of Mercury, between 25,000 and 30,000 miles, an outside pass. This occurred about November 7 of the year of the Deluge.

2. A fragmentation of an icy satellite, drenching the Earth with a 200 to 250 inch rain (average per square inch) across Earth's 197,000,000 square mile surface.

3. At least 50% of the ice particles came in as a sudden rain; the balance formed rings around the Earth (like Saturn's rings). The icy particles therein were deflected along geomagnetic field force lines, assumed elliptic orbits, and descended roughly over the geomagnetic polar areas[2] in a vast, deep subzero icy mist. This occurred also over the next 35 or 40 days, and was completed about December 17.

4. Residual astronomical rain from the ice dump was pretty well over by December 15 or 17, the 40 days and nights being completed as per the Scriptural log.

5. During the first cycle of interaction, the geographical poles shifted or migrated between 2500 and 3000 miles.

---

[2]Technically, the ice particles descended in the two vortices of the radiation belts, which most assume to be over the magnetic poles but in fact are not. The vortex of the radiation belts in the Northern Hemisphere is currently over Northern Greenland, and this coincides with the center of the ice dump in the Northern Hemisphere.

6. The first cycle, about November 7, caused the uplift of the entire Circum-Pacific cycle of mountains.[3]

7. A second fly-by of Mercury occurred about March 20 or 30, this time slightly closer than the first fly-by. This second fly-by was not accompanied by an icy fragmentation nor a sudden astronomical rain. It was an inside fly-by.

8. The second cycle, sometime between March 20 and March 30, caused the uplift of the entire Alpine-Himalayan cycle of mountains, including the Armenian Knot where Mount Ararat was uplifted by crustal tides. The floating ark was in this region when the crust under it was uplifted.

9. During the second cycle, the geographical poles were relocated another 3000 to 3500 miles, the vernal equinox was reset, and the geomagnetic field was again reversed.[4]

In Chapter VIII, discussion occurred regarding the ancient calendar. In the ancient Hebrew calendar, the autumnal equinox (September 21) was the New Year Day. Forty-seven days following the autumnal equinox we are told the flood-tides and the sudden intense rain simultaneously enveloped the locale of the ark and the entire globe. We believe that the apprehensive animals which boarded the ark entered about November 7.[5, 6]

---

[3] In a few hours of fly-by time, as much "work" was accomplished deforming and reforming Earth's crust as evolutionists allow for 200,000,000 years. Both fly-bys include "mesozoic" and "cenozoic" time in Lyell's geological time column which he "created" a priori. With Mercury at 30,000 miles, crustal tides of about 2,000 feet would have been generated. Mercury may have passed as close as 25,000 miles, or even 20,000 miles.

[4] Noah remained in the ark another 210 days before disembarking. It is possible he feared a third cycle and his fears subsided only after a full year had lapsed from the first cycle.

[5] R. H. Charles, *The Apocrypha and Pseudepigrapha of the Old Testament*, Vol. II, "The Book of Jubilees," Oxford: Clarendon Press, p. 21. "And he entered in the sixth (year) thereof, in the second month, on the new moon of the second month, till the sixteenth; and he entered, and all that he brought to him, into the ark, and the Lord closed it from without on the seventeenth evening." [*The sixth year is of the twenty-seventh jubilee of years, the "jubilee of years" being a dating system in ancient Hebrew literature unique to this work.*]

[6] Josephus, *Antiquities of the Jews*, Book I, Chapter III, section 3, pp. 83-84. "This calamity happened in the six hundredth year of Noah's government, [*age*] in the second month, called by the Macedonians Dius, but by the Hebrews Marhesven (sic). . . ."

The works of Josephus, the *Talmud*, *The Book of Jasher* and *The Book of Jubilees* all agree that Noah entered the ark on the forty-seventh day of the old year. We know it began on the autumnal equinox. *The Book of Jubilees* more specifically relates that Noah entered the ark on the evening of that day.

Dating the Year According to the Julian Calendar[7]

BY SCRIPTURE (Masoretic Text). We have established that the Sodom-Gomorrah Catastrophe was in 1877 B.C. This was in Abraham's ninety-ninth or one hundredth year. A literal calculation of the chronologies of Genesis 11[7,8] places the ending of the Flood Catastrophe in the year 2268 B.C., and its onset in 2269 B.C.

BY JOSEPHUS. Data from Josephus supports these calculations.

> . . . his son was Terah, who was the father of ABRAHAM, WHO accordingly was the tenth from Noah, and was born in the two hundred and ninety-second year after the Deluge; for Terah begat Abraham in his seventieth year.[9]

BY THE BOOK OF JASHER. The date of the cessation of the Flood Catastrophe is also 2268 B.C. according to this work.

---

[7]The Julian Calendar supposedly dates from the year of the birth of Christ, but was miscalculated by 4 years so that technically, Christ was born in 4 "B.C." The Julian Calendar is in contrast to the historic Jewish dating of "A.M.," anno mundi, with the traditional, estimated year of creation being year 1 in that system.

[8]Calculations from the Flood: Arphaxad's birth 2 years after the Flood; Salah's birth 35 years later; Eber's 30; Peleg's 34; Reu's 30; Serug's 32; Nahor's 30; Terah's 29; Abraham's 70. Abraham's age at the Sodom-Gomorrah event, 99 years. The date of the end of the Flood Catastrophe is 2268 B.C., that is, 1877 plus 99 plus 292.

[9]Flavius Josephus, *op. cit.*, Book I, Chapter VI, section 5, p. 93. Josephus' accounts, however, are self-contradictory. He seems to draw from the Masoretic texts on some occasions and the Septuagint on others.

... and Arpachshad the son of Shem the son of Noah died in those days, in the forty eighth year of the life of Isaac, and all the days that Arpachshad lived were four hundred and thirty eight years, and he died.[10]

And it came to pass in those days, in the hundred and tenth year of the life of Isaac [*1766 B.C.*], that is in the fiftieth year of the life of Jacob, in that year died Shem the son of Noah; Shem was six hundred years old at his death.[11]

BY MODEL. We believe that Mercury, not Mars, interacted with Earth during the Deluge. However, since they both interacted in October or November in various years, they may once have had similar orbits. Indeed, it is a question as to whether Mars and Mercury in the pre-flood era were actually a binary system (like the Earth-Moon system) only on a cometary-type orbit.

The Flood Catastrophe cannot be dated by the Mars model of 108 year cycles. However, earlier Mars upheavals before Babel, if valid, would favor the following dates:

    2254 B.C.   (three cycles)

    2362 B.C.   (four cycles)

    2470 B.C.   (five cycles)

    2578 B.C.   (six cycles)

In *The Biblical Flood and the Ice Epoch,* a relatively general dating of 2800 B.C., plus or minus 400 years, was suggested. This

---

[10] *The Book of Jasher,* New York: Mordecai M. Noah & Alexander S. Gould, 1840, 25:28, p. 74. (2266 B.C. minus 438 is 1828 B.C. 1828 B.C. plus 48 [*Isaac's 48th Year*] is 1876 B.C. Isaac was born in the year after the Sodom-Gomorrah event of 1877 B.C. Arphaxad was born in the second year after the Deluge, thus placing the Deluge at 2268 B.C.)

[11] *The Book of Jasher,* 28:24, p. 80. Shem was 98 years old the year of the Deluge. *The Book of Jasher* is clear that Abraham was schooled in the home of Noah and Shem, and later, Isaac was schooled at least briefly in the home of Eber. Many of the post-flood generations overlapped and many began to die out in the nineteenth, twentieth and twenty-first centuries B.C. This suggests an explosion of population and civilization. Other references citing similar dating occur but are not given here for the sake of brevity.

would allow for a date between 2400 B.C. and 3200 B.C. Although the dating was general, it did establish the relative recentness of the Deluge. Some have dated it at 5000 B.C., 10,000 B.C. and even more ancient. Such earlier datings assume the chronicles of Genesis 11 either to be mythologies, or to contain large gaps. We reject both of these explanations as accommodations to evolutionary thought. We believe the Deluge occurred SOMETIME IN THE ERA 2268 B.C. TO 2500 B.C. This conclusion of relatively recent dating is in harmony with ancient cyclic astronomical catastrophism. It has been observed that catastrophes occurred in cycles every five or six centuries. The eighth century B.C. experienced two, as did the fifteenth and the twentieth centuries B.C. Within this general pattern, the twenty-fourth or twenty-fifth Century B.C. for the Deluge is possible.

BY TRANSIENT DECAY CURVE. If one plots the life spans and dates of the post-flood patriarchs on a graph, the resulting curve illustrates a typical transient decay curve. We believe that changes in the mixes of ozone and carbon dioxide in the atmosphere, plus a change in the structure of the planetary wind systems (fluxing ozone downward) is at the basis of change in ancient life spans.[12] This curve favors a date in the 24th or 25th century B.C.

Earthquakes and Earth-Shakings

EARTHQUAKES. In *The Biblical Flood and the Ice Epoch,* we suggested Mercury (not Mars) buzzed Earth, and twice in one year. Mercury came within 25,000 miles, perhaps even within 20,000 miles of Earth's *core* (not Earth's crust, which is 4,000 miles closer still). At such a close distance, Mercury would generate crustal tides of 2,000 feet at 30,000 miles, and 5,000 feet at 25,000 miles. Oceanic tides washing around the planet, rinsing the crust, would be superimposed on such a crustal distortion.

We believe gravitational interaction this intense did occur, and we have evidence to verify it. Figure 43 illustrates the great

---

[12]For further discussion see Chapter IX, pp. 194 ff. in *The Biblical Flood and The Ice Epoch,* and "The Greenhouse Effect" in *Symposium on Creation II.*

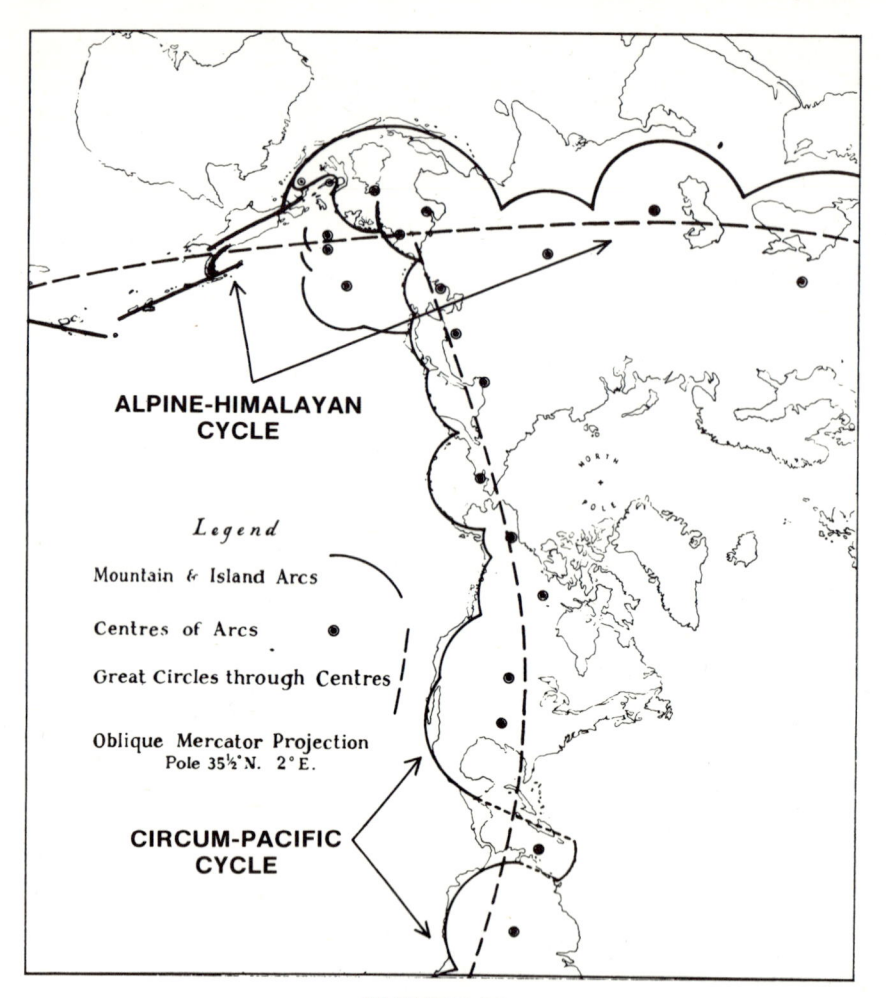

FIGURE 43

Two great circles of mountain uplifts. The vertical cycle, the Circum-Pacific primary arc, is believed to have occurred during the initial week of the Flood Catastrophe. The horizontal cycle, the Alpine-Himalayan primary arc, is thought to have been uplifted during the fifth month of the Flood Catastrophe, toward the end of the 150 days. The two great circles suggest the fly-by patterns of the passing planet, probably Mercury. This pattern suggests that two-thirds of the orogentic (Mountain uplift) activity in the geologic time column occurred within one year rather than within 200,000,000 years as is alleged in the uniformitarian mythology. From The Earth as a Planet *p. 153 courtesy of University of Chicago Press.*

circle patterns of these two recent zones of mountain-uplifting, or crustal deformation. The Circum-Pacific cycle was the first,[13] in November of the year of the Flood; the Alpine-Himalayan Cycle reflects the equator of the Earth facing the second fly-by.[14] "Earthquake" is no word to describe Earth deformation of this magnitude, as entire mountain ranges soared skyward in minutes.

EARTH-SHAKINGS (SPIN AXIS SHIFTS). An examination of Figure 43 will reveal that the second cycle of mountain uplifts straddles Earth's current equator. This "great circle" rises to about 35° N. latitude in the Himalaya-Ararat sector, and descends to about 20° S. latitude in the Pacific Ocean sector, in the region of the Fiji and Samoa island groups. In a very general way, the Alpine-Himalayan cycle reflects a mid-Flood equator. Similarly, in a very general way, the Circum-Pacific cycle reflects the pre-Flood equator. The geographical poles in the pre-Flood era could easily have been in the middle of the African continent and the Pacific Ocean.

On each of the two fly-bys during the Flood Catastrophe, we estimate a polar relocation occurred of no less than 2500 miles and probably more. Thus there was a pre-Flood polar (and equator) location, a mid-Flood polar (and equator) relocation, and a post-Flood third polar (and equator) relocation. Each relocation was due to one of the fly-bys. The March 20/21 post-Flood vernal equinox was established by the last fly-by of the Deluge on or about this date, since that fly-by twisted or reset Earth's spin axis. The Alpine-Himalayan cycle of mountain uplifts reflects the fly-by pattern, a great circle on the rotating Earth opposite to the fly-by path.

The impact of this catastrophic cosmology is that the philosophy of uniformitarianism, accepted in almost all geology departments, is in extreme error. Hundreds of textbooks on

---

[13] The first cycle includes the Andes, the Sierras, the Cascades, the Rockies, the Aleutians, the Brooks Range, the Japanese arc, the Ryukyu arc, the Marianas trench, and so forth.

[14] The second cycle includes the Owen-Stanley range of New Guinea, the Himalayas, the Tien Shans, the Kun Luns (all in India and Tibet), the Elburz Mountains (including the Armenian Knot and Mount Ararat), the Caucasus, the Alps, the Atlas Mountains and so forth. Trenches of course parallel ranges, both above and below sea level. See Chapter V of *The Biblical Flood and The Ice Epoch* for further details.

orogeny (to say nothing of glaciology or stratigraphy) need rewriting. Most students of geological science, being Darwinists, Lyellians and Huttonians, have been looking downward for 150 years; it is time they, too, recognize the ancient wars in the heavens, and their significance. Then the deformed (and reformed) crust of the Earth, or Mars, or even the Moon, will take on an exciting, understandable reality.[15]

Meteors and Bolides

In the post-Flood fire and brimstone catastrophes, blizzards of iron dust, meteors and bolides were repeatedly Earth's experience. During the Flood Catastrophe, there were no iron, nickel or silica (rock) meteors, but there was a fragmentation of an icy satellite. This fragmentation provided, simultaneously, the water for the sudden astronomical rain and frozen deep sub-zero icy mists forming the glacial age. The astronomical rain was the water-ice which made *direct* entry into Earth's atmosphere (as in the Apollo missions when the module's face becomes so warm on re-entry). One of the authors has estimated the icy body was at least 430 miles in diameter and has estimated that at least half of the ice entered Earth's atmosphere as rain and the balance as ice.[16]

The balance of the icy particles interacted with the radiation belts, the solar radiation, and received charges of electricity while in orbit around the Earth. In about a six week period these particles settled down upon Earth, through the vortices of the radiation belts, amid massive volcanic action on Earth. One interesting reflection is that the ice pack in Antarctica today is in places 10,500 feet deep, half below sea level. In drilling and assaying the ice, it has been found that the deeper the core is taken, the greater the admixture of volcanic ash below sea level. This is what the catastrophic theory would predict!

[15]Each of these cycles spans about 75% of a complete great circle. Thus the uniformitarian view that all mountain ranges are local in scope is erroneous. The uniformitarian view that uplifts arise from forces within the Earth's interior is 180° off in finding the direction of the *cause*.

[16]Loren Steinhauer, "Out of Whose Womb Came the Ice?" *Symposium on Creation IV*, Grand Rapids: Baker Book House, 1972. (Patten's original estimate of 10% is thus modified to approximately 50%.

Descriptive Cosmic Scenery

There are no described planetary movements in the Genesis account of the Flood, although an intense, sudden rain is discussed together with a heaving of the oceans ("the fountains of the deep"). The rain, we have already determined, was of astronomical origin, coming from the fragmentation of an icy body between 400 and 500 miles in diameter.

There is a brief cosmological description in *The Book of Jasher:*

> And on that day, the Lord caused the whole earth to shake, and the sun darkened, and the foundations of the world raged, and the whole earth was moved violently, and the lightning flashed, and the thunder roared, and all the fountains in the earth were broken up, such as was not known to the inhabitants before....[17]

Milman, in his work *The History of the Jews,* indicates planet worship dates to the earliest post-Flood times in Chaldea, and also indicates at least one irregular orbit was a matter of much contemplation:

> To this country the first rudiments of astronomy are generally ascribed, and here the earliest form of idolatry, the worship of the host of heaven, planet worship, began to spread.[18]

There is some shadowy flood cosmology in the *Talmud:*

> The flood was produced by a union of the male waters, which are above the firmament, [*the astronomical rain into the pre-Flood canopy*] and the female waters issuing from the earth [*the oceanic tides*]. The upper waters

---

[17]*The Book of Jasher,* 6:11, p. 13.

[18]Henry Hart Milman, *The History of the Jews,* New York: A. C. Armstrong & Son, 1883, p. 51. (Millman identifies the orbiting wanderer, wonder of the ancients, as Venus, whereas we propose it must have been the planet Mars.)

rushed through the space left when God removed TWO STARS out of the constellation Pleiades. Afterward, to put a stop to the flood, God had to transfer TWO STARS from the constellation of the Bear to the constellation of the Pleiades. That is why the Bear runs after the Pleiades. She wants her two children back, but they will be restored to her only in the future world. There were other changes among the celestial spheres during the year of the flood.[19]

There is no cosmological description associated with the flood account in Josephus, but there is an immediate post-flood record of Noah's concern about the possibility of another deluge[20] and several quotations recognizing the post-Flood interest in astronomy and astrology.

Other More Ancient Catastrophes

In Chapter X (the discussion of the Tower of Babel Castastrophe) our discussion was incomplete without a brief mention of an earlier catastrophe "the earth was divided in the days of Peleg." It was suggested that a Peleg catastrophe antedated the Babel event by 108 or 216 years, and may have been the first big post-Flood cataclysm.

Was the Noachian Flood the first catastrophe, even as it was the worst? Both the Scriptures and the works of Josephus are unclear on this issue, leading some to suppose it was the first of

---

[19]Louis Ginzberg, op cit., Vol. I, p. 162. What, if anything, could this discussion of two stars transferred in the heavens at the time of the Flood mean? Is it a hazy, shadowy recollection? If founded on observation, it could indicate that both Mars and Mercury threatened Earth during the Flood catastrophe. This then could lead one to wonder whether Mars and Mercury could have been a binary system like the Earth-Moon system, only in a comet-type of orbit.

Secondly, it could lead one to wonder whether this two luminary transfer could be a hazy recollection of the two planetary fly-bys during this massively catastrophic year. Of further interest is the calendaric dating of the flood catastrophe. Its first cycle began the first week of November, not unlike the later Mars catastrophes which occured the last week of October. The second cycle of the Flood catastrophe occurred during the third or fourth week of March, again not unlike the later March catastrophes. Much continuing research on this great catastrophe is badly needed.

[20]Flavius Josephus, op. cit., Book I, Chapter III, section 7, p. 86.

THE FLOOD CATASTROPHE

the ancient catastrophes. However, *The Book of Jasher* and the *Talmud* are not silent on this matter.

> And the Lord caused the waters of the river Gihon [presumably an ocean or sea in the pre-Flood era as the word for river and sea is the same] to overwhelm them, and he destroyed and consumed them, and he destroyed the third part of the earth. . . .[21]

> The generation of Enosh were thus the first idol worshippers, and the punishment for their folly was not delayed long. God caused the sea to transgress its bounds, and a portion of the earth was flooded. This was the time also when the mountains became rocks. . . .[22]

This shadowy suggestion of a catastrophe is one involving tidal waves only, but not an associated astronomical rain as we saw in the Deluge. In association with this, we quote the apocryphal *Book of Enoch:*

> All the luminaries are agitated with great fear; and all the earth is spared, while it trembles, and suffers anxiety.[23]

There are several reasons to conclude that there was a catastrophic era before the creation of Adam. Crustal scars (mountain cycles of crustal deformation)[24] not attributable to the Deluge are one reason. Strata not attributable to the Deluge are a second reason.[25] There are hints in the book of Genesis (Chapter 1), the book of Proverbs (Chapter 8) and the book of Job (Chapter 38) that ancients viewed catastrophic conditions as preceding the creation of man.

Thus we conclude there was at least one catastrophe of significant proportions after Adam, but before Noah, and at least

---

[21] *The Book of Jasher*, 2:6, p. 4. This is recorded as being in the days of Enosh, midway between the time of Adam and the time of Noah.

[22] Louis Ginzberg, *op cit.*, Vol. I, p. 123.

[23] *The Book of Enoch*, 102:3.

[24] The Herzian-Calendonian cycle, for instance.

[25] Paleozoic strata particularly, as mesozoic and cenozoic strata appear to be Deluge strata.

one catastrophe (perhaps more) preceding the creation of man.

CONCLUSION

Uniformitarianism is the doctrine that "the present is the key to the past." It was assumed by Kant, codified by Hutton, popularized by Lyell and Darwin. This doctrine has become the underlying doctrine of history for communism, humanism and socialism.

The Long Day of Joshua, a gyroscopic spin axis precession amid incoming bolides and meteorites, is an event which illustrates the issue. Kant, the blooming humanist, said the "Long Day" was "impossible" because of his narrow frame of reference, involving a lack of catastrophic probability. We say this event was a historic fact a global upset and a fearful reality. And more important, it was just one of six or seven similar upheavals. Furthermore, such could recur were another intruding planet of appropriate size and nearness to buzz the Earth-Moon system, or Venus, or the Mars-Deimos-Phobos system.

Catastrophism is the doctrine that the Earth has experienced sudden, overwhelming physical events in the past. Catastrophism is the doctrine of ancient historians. It is the Biblical doctrine, and it is the scientific doctrine.

> The existence of an intelligent Creator,
> a personal God, can, in my mind, almost
> be proved from chemistry. —Thomas A. Edison.
>
> Observe creation mercifully hidden
> either in an imaginary Eden,
> or buried in some absent-minded spasm
> of a self-generated protoplasm.
> — Humbert Wolfe.

Selected Bibliography

Abell, George, *Exploration of the Universe,* New York: Holt, Rinehart & Winston, 1964.

Adler, Irving, *Seeing the Earth From Space,* New York: Signet Books, 1961.

Albritton, Claude C. Jr., et al, *Uniformity and Simplicity,* Boulder, Colo.: The Geological Society of America, 1967.

Allan, R. R. "Evolution of Mimas-Tethys Commensurability," *Astronomical Journal,* Vol. 74, April 1969, pp. 497-500.

Alpers, Anthony, *Maori Myths and Tribal Legends,* London: John Murray, 1964.

Armitage, Angus, *Sun, Stand Thou Still* (The Life and Work of Copernicus), New York: Henry Schuman Inc., 1947.

Asimov, Isaac, *The Kingdom of the Sun,* New York: Abelard-Schuman, 1960.

Aston, W. B., "The Age of the Gods," *The Nihongi* (Chronicles of Japan From Earliest Times to A.D. 697), London: Geo. Allen & Unwin, 1906.

Baker, Robert H., *Astronomy,* Princeton, N.J.: Van Nostrand, 1959.

Baly, Denis, *The Geography of the Bible,* New York: Harper & Bros., 1957.

Bates, D. R., *The Planet Earth,* London: Pergamon Press, 1964.

Benagh, Christine L., *Meditations on the Book of Job,* Houston: St. Thomas Press, 1964.

The Bible   Amplified Version
              Berkeley Version
              King James Version

Burrows, *The Oracles of Jacob and Balaam,* London: Burns, Oates & Washbourne, 1938. Reprinted, Seattle: Pacific Meridian.

Ceram, C. W., *Gods, Graves and Scholars* (The Story of Archaeology), New York: Alfred A. Knopf, 1951.

Chapman, Sydney, *The Earth's Magnetism,* London: Methuen and Co., 1951.

Clark, Robert E. D., *Darwin: Before & After,* Exeter, Devon, England: Paternoster House, 1948.

Clark, Robert E. D., *Science & Christianity, A Partnership,* Mountain view Calif.: Pacific Press Publishing Assn., 1972.

Cook, Melvin A., *Prehistory and Earth Models,* London: Max Parrish, 1966.

Cook, Melvin A., *The Science of High Explosives,* Appendix III. Huntington N.Y., Robert E. Krieger Publishing Co., 1971.

Courville, Donovan A., *The Exodus Problem and Its Ramifications,* Loma Linda, Calif.: Challenge Books, 1971.

Cummings, Violet M., *Noah's Ark: Fact or Fable?* San Diego: Creation Science Research Center, 1972.

Custance, Arthur C., "Flood Traditions of the World," *Doorway Papers No. 18,* Brockville, Ontario, 1969.
Custance, Arthur C., *Without Form and Void,* Brockville, Ontario: Doorway Papers, 1970.
D'Aulaire, Ingri and Edgar Parin, *Book of Greek Myths,* New York: Doubleday, 1962.
Dake, Finis Jennings, *Dake's Annotated Reference Bible,* Atlanta: Dake Bible Sales, 1965.
Davidheiser, Bolton, *Evolution and the Christian Faith,* Nutley, N.J.: Craig Press, 1969.
Davidson, Martin, *The Gyroscope and Its Applications,* London: Hutchinson's Scientific and Technical Publications, 1946.
De Grazia, *The Velikovsky Affair,* New Hyde Park, N.Y.: University Books, 1965.
Dewar, Douglas, *The Transformist Illusion,* Murfreesboro, Tenn.: Dehoff Publishing Co., 1957.
Doig, Peter A., *A Concise History of Astronomy,* London: Chapman & Hall, 1950.
Enoch, The Book of, as translated by Richard Laurence, Seattle: Pacific Meridian, 1950.
Filby, Frederick A., *The Flood Reconsidered,* Grand Rapids: Zondervan Publishing House, 1970.
Forward, Robert L., "Pluto, Last Stop Before the Stars," *Science Digest,* August, 1962.
Gallant, Rene, *Bombarded Earth,* London: John Baker, 1964.
Garfinkel, Boris, Alan Jupp and Carol Williams, "A Recursive von Zeipel Algorithm for the Ideal Resonance Problem," *Astronomical Journal,* Vol. 76, March 1971, pp. 157-166.
Ginzberg, *The Legends of the Jews,* Volumes I to VII, Philadelphia: The Jewish Publication Society of America, 1913.
Glass, Billy P. and Bruce C. Heezen, "Tektites and Geomagnetic Reversals," *Scientific American,* July, 1967.
Gnevyshev, M. N., "On the 11-Years Cycle of Solar Activity," *Solar Physics,* Vol. 1, 1967, pp. 108-120.
Goldreich, P. and S. J. Peale, "Spin-orbit Coupling in the Solar System, I", *Astronomical Journal,* Vol. 71, 1966, pp. 425-438.
Goldreich, P. and S. J. Peale, "Spin-orbit Coupling in the Solar System, II", (The Resonant Rotation of Venus), *Astronomical Journal,* Vol. 72, 1967, pp. 662-668.
Golub, Jacob S., *In the Days of the First Temple,* Cincinnati: Union of American Hebrew Congregations, 1931.
Gray, Andrew, *Gyrostatics and Rotational Motion,* New York: Dover Publications, 1959.
Greenberg, R. J., C. C. Counselman III, and I. I. Shapiro, "Orbit-Orbit Resonance Capture in the Solar System," *Science,* November 17, 1972, pp. 747-749.
Griffin, G. Edward, "Cataclysm from Space 2800 B.C." filmstrip, Thousand Oaks, Calif.: American Media, 1971.

Halley, Henry H., *Henry H. Halley's Bible Handbook*, Grand Rapids: Zondervan Publishing House, 1965.
Hartshorne, Richard, *Perspective on the Nature of Geography*, Chicago: Rand McNally, 1959.
Hawkins, Gerald S. and John B. White, *Stonehenge Decoded*, New York: Delta Books, 1965.
Heirtzler, J. H., "Sea-floor Spreading," *Scientific American*, December 1968, pp. 60 ff.
Himmelfarb, Gertrude, *Darwin and the Darwinian Revolution*, New York: Doubleday & Co., 1959.
Hindley, Keith B., "The Quadrantid Meteor Stream, *Sky and Telescope*, March 1972, p. 162.
Homer, *Iliad* (The Iliad of Homer, Translated by Samuel Butler), Roslyn, N.Y.: Walter J. Black, 1942.
Hooker, Dolph Earl, *Those Astounding Ice Ages*, New York: Exposition Press, 1958.
Ions, Veronica, *Indian Mythology*, Toronto: Paul Hamlyn, 1967.
James, E. O., *The Ancient Gods*, New York: G. P. Putnam's Sons, 1960.
Jasher, The Book of, Mokelumne Hill, Calif.: Health Research, 1966.
Jensen, Kenneth L., *Wisdom, The Principal Thing*, Seattle, Pacific Meridian Publishing Co., 1971.
Juergens, Ralph, "Reconciling Celestial Mechanics and Velikovskian Catastrophism", *Pensee*, Fall 1972, p. 6.
Josephus, Flavius, *The Works of Flavius Josephus*, Bridgeport, Conn.: M. Sherman, 1828.
Jueneman, Fred B., "Velikovsky," *Industrial Research*, March, 1973, pp. 40 ff.
Katasev, L. A. and Kulikova, N. V., "On the Motion of the Tunguska Meteorite in the Earth's Atmosphere", *Solar System Research*, Vol. 1, No. 1, Jan.-Mar. 1967, p. 44.
Kaula, William M., *An Introduction to Planetary Physics*, New York: John Wiley & Sons, 1968.
Kortkov, R. and Dicke, R. H., Comparison Between Theory and Observation For the Outer Planets, *The Astronomical Journal*, June 1959, p. 157.
Kruska, Martin, Ralph Juergens, C.E.R. Bruce and Melvin A. Cook, "On Celestial Mechanics", *Pensee*, Winter, 1973, p. 51.
Kuiper, Gerard P. et al., *The Earth as a Planet*, Chicago: Univ. of Chicago Press, 1954.
Kuiper, Gerard P. et al., *Planets and Satellites*, Chicago: Univ. of Chicago Press, 1961.
Leith, T. H., "Galileo and the Church: Tensions With A Message for Today" *Journal of the American Scientific Affiliation*, Vol. 25, No. 1, March 1973, p. 21 and No. 2, June 1973, p 64.
Livius, Titus, *Livy* (Translated by I. W. Bieber), Philadelphia: David McKay, 1872.
Luce, J. V., *Lost Atlantis*, New York: McGraw Hill, 1969.

Marinatos, Spyridon, "Thera, Key to the Riddle of Minos," *National Geographic,* May 1972, pp. 702-726.

Mavor, James W. Jr., *Voyage to Atlantis,* New York: G. P. Putnam's Sons, 1969.

McDowell, Charles, "A History of Middle East Catastrophes, 1500-950 B.C.," *Unpublished Manuscript.* History Department, Cuyahoga Community College, Parma, Ohio.

Moorhead, Paul S. and Martin M. Kaplan, *Mathematical Challenges to the Neo-Darwinian Interpretation of Evolution,* Philadelphia: Wistar Institute Press, 1966.

Murray, Bruce C. and Michael C. Malin, "Polar Wandering on Mars?" *Science,* March 9, 1973, pp. 997-1000.

Nelson, Byron C., *The Deluge Story in Stone,* Minneapolis: Augsburg, 1931.

Newton, Isaac, *Observations Upon the Prophecies of Daniel and the Apocalypse of St. John,* London: Darby and Browne, 1733. Reprinted, Seattle: Pacific Meridian Publishing Co., 1966.

Ovid, *Metamorphoses* (Translated by Rolfe Humphries), Bloomington, Indiana: Indiana University Press, 1958.

Patten, Donald W., *The Biblical Flood and the Ice Epoch,* Seattle: Pacific Meridian Publishing Co., 1966.

Patten, Donald W., et al, *Symposium on Creation* I, II, III, IV, Grand Rapids: Baker Book House, 1968, 1970, 1971, 1972.

Pensee, A journal published by Student Academic Freedom Forum, Lewis & Clark College, Portland, Oregon, May 1972, Fall 1973, Winter 1973.

Pickering, James S., *1001 Questions Answered About Astronomy,* New York: Dodd, Mead, 1959.

Polano, H., *The Talmud,* London: Frederick Warne & Co., Ltd., (n.d.).

Proctor, Mary, *The Romance of Comets,* New York: Harper & Bros., 1926.

Rehwinkel, Alfred M., *The Flood,* St. Louis: Concordia, 1951.

Richardson, Robert S., *Exploring Mars,* New York: McGraw Hill, 1954.

Richardson, Robert S. and Chesley Bonestell, *Mars,* New York: Harcourt Brace & World, 1964.

Rushdoony, Rousas John, *The Mythology of Science,* Nutley, N.J.: Craig Press, 1967.

Sabin, Frances E., *Classical Myths Today,* New York: Silver Burdett Co., 1940.

Scheidegger, Adrian E., *Principles of Geodynamics,* Berlin: Springer-Verlag, 1963.

Schubart, Joachim, "Long-Period Effects in the Motion of Hilda-Type Planets," *Astronomical Journal,* March 1968, pp. 99 ff.

Schweizer, Francois, "Resonant Asteroids in the Kirkwood Gaps and Statistical Explanations of the Gaps," *Astronomical Journal,* August 1969, pp. 779 ff.

SELECTED BIBLIOGRAPHY

Shapiro, I. I., "Resonance Rotation of Venus," *Science*, Vol. 157, 1967, pp. 423-425.

Smith, A. E. Wilder, *Man's Origin, Man's Destiny*, Wheaton, Ill.: Harold Shaw Publ., 1968.

Steinhauer, Loren C., "Out of Whose Womb Came the Ice?" *Symposium on Creation IV*, Grand Rapids: Baker Book House, 1972.

Strong, James, *The Exhaustive Concordance of the Bible*, Nashville: Abingdon, 1890.

Struve, Otto and Velta Zebergs, *Astronomy of the 20th Century*, New York: MacMillan, 1962.

Swift, Jonathan, *Gulliver's Travels*, Cleveland: World Syndicate Publ., 1935.

Swift, Jonathan, *A Tale of a Tub*, London: J. M. Dent & Sons, 1953.

Takahashi, Kozo, "On the Relation Between the Solar Activity Cycle and the Solar Tidal Force Induce by Planets," *Solar Physics*, 1968, pp. 598-602.

Thiele, Edwin R., *The Mysterious Numbers of the Hebrew Kings*, Grand Rapids: Wm. B. Eerdmans Publishing Co., 1965.

Thom, A., *Megalithic Sites in Britain*, Oxford: Clarendon Press, 1967.

Velikovsky, Immanuel, *Ages in Chaos*, New York: Doubleday & Co., 1952.

Velikovsky, Immuel, *Earth in Upheaval*, New York: Doubleday & Co., 1955.

Velikovsky, Immanuel, *Oedipus and Akhnaton*, New York: Doubleday & Co., 1960.

Velikovsky, Immanuel, "On Decoding Hawkins' Stonehenge Decoded", *Pensee*, May 1972, p. 24.

Velikovsky Immanuel, *Worlds in Collision*, New York: Doubleday & Co., 1950.

Von Weizsacker, *The Relevance of Science* (Creation and Cosmogony), New York: Harper & Row, 1965.

Ward, William B., *Out of the Whirlwind*, Richmond, Va.: John Knox Press, 1958.

Watson, Fletcher G., *Between the Planets*, Philadelphia: Blakiston, 1941.

Watts, Raymond N. Jr., "Some Mariner 9 Observations of Mars," *Sky and Telescope*, April 1972, pp. 208 ff.

Weaver, Kenneth F., "Mariner 9 Journey to Mars," *National Geographic*, February 1973, pp. 231-263.

Whiston, William *Astronomical Principles of Religion*, London: J. Senex, 1717. Reprinted, Seattle: Pacific Meridian Publishing Co., 1966.

Whiston, William, *A New Theory of the Earth*, London: Benj. Tooke, 1969. Reprinted, Seattle: Pacific Meridian Publishing Co.

Williams, J. G. and G. S. Benson, "Resonances in the Neptune-Pluto System," *Astronomical Journal*, March 1971, pp. 167-177.

Index

Abraham, 5, 20, 22, 200, 201, 237, 255-260, 263, 267, 289, 309, 310
Aeolis, 18
Aeschylus, 84
Agamemnon, 94, 163
Age of Bronze (Ovid), 25, 270, 272, 281
Age of Gold (Ovid), 25, 270, 272
Age of Iron (Ovid), 271, 272, 281
Age of Silver (Ovid), 25, 270, 272, 281
Ahab (King), 53, 155, 158, 159
Ahaz (King), 47, 60, 98, 112, 123
Ajalon, Valley of, 180, 185
Albedo defined, 33
Alinda (asteroid), 75, 78, 83, 274, 279
Allan, R. R., 73
Alpers, Anthony, 30
Alpine-Himalayan Mtn. Cycle, 308, 312, 313
Amorites (see Hyksos), 191, 203, 204, 237
Amos, 4, 34, 39, 94, 130-145, 243
Ancilia, 16, 22
Aphelion of Earth, 69, 70
Aphelion of Jupiter, 73
Aphelion of Mars, 69, 70
Aphrodite, 10, 24, 27, 72, 86, 93, 94, 127, 163-165, 245, 281
Apollo, 10, 14, 77, 84, 86, 93, 94, 127, 163-165, 245, 281
Ararat Mt., 308, 313
Archangel, 50, 59, 234
Arcturus, 204, 205, 258
Ares (Aries), 2, 10, 36, 164, 165, 230, 245, 249, 292, 302, 303
Aristotle, 65, 190
Armilustrium, 17
Armitage, Angus, 188
Asimov, Isaac, 300, 302, 304
Ashtoreth (Astarte, Istar), 15, 29, 47, 54, 86, 94, 129, 141, 145, 157, 230, 237
Atlantis, 199, 215, 225, 238, 239, 245-248

Baal, Baal/Mars, Bel, Bel-Marduk, 29, 47, 53, 54, 141, 145, 153, 155-160, 163, 204, 230, 237, 238, 257, 263, 288
Bacon, Francis, 65
Balder, 12, 22
Behemoth, 206, 207, 244
Bellarmine, Roberto, 190, 197
Benagh, Christine L., 204
Benson, G. S., 65, 80
Bethhoron, 176, 179, 185, 192, 193
Bethlehem Star, 196
Bolsena (see Volsinium)
Bronshten, V. A., 93

Caesar, J., 14
Calendars, 15, 16, 23-28, 52, 98, 134, 228, 230, 349
Calchus, 94, 163
Caldera, 112, 239, 240, 242
Canals of Mars, 109, 110, 295
Carmel, Mt., 153, 157, 159
Case 1 catastrophe, 145, 150, 151, 170, 177, 198-202, 228, 249, 250, 251, 291
Case 2 catastrophe, 145, 150-153, 170-173, 177, 198, 201, 250, 283, 284, 291
Cassini Gap (Saturn's rings), 73, 105
Celtics, 15, 23-25, 230, 248, 266
Cephalus myth, 213, 215
Ceram, C. W., 287, 288
Chapman, Sydney, 104, 221
Chang, Ralph, 87
Charles, Robert H., 195, 256, 257, 283, 308
China asteroid, 78, 81, 83
Chronos, 10, 16, 28, 281, 282
Circum-Pacific cycle of mtn. uplifts, 308, 312, 313
Clark, Robert E. D., 8, 189, 198
Clematis asteroid, 78, 81, 83
Continental Drift Theory (see Wegener), 261, 262
Cook, Melvin A., 109

Copernicus, N., 186, 188, 190
Cosmogony defined, 203, 204
Cosmology defined, 203, 204
Courville, Donovan, 223
Crete, 18, 27, 139, 164, 165, 238-248
Critias (see Plato), 199, 246
Curie point, 109
Custance, Arthur G., 194

Dake, Finis J., 42, 143, 157, 202
Darwin, Sir Charles, 189, 280, 314, 318
D'Aulaire, Ingri and Edgar Parin, 180, 284, 285
David, 160-165, 175, 302
Davy, Sir Humphry, 291
Deborah, 169, 197
DeCeault, C. William, 123
Deimos (satellite of Mars), 33, 91, 96, 292-304
Deucalion, 243
Deux ex machina (hand of God), 280
Druids, 14, 15

Earth oblateness (bulge zone), 116, 117, 258
Edison, Thomas A., 318
Einstein, Albert, 171
Electra (former planet), 90, 91, 96, 128, 168, 225, 226, 194-296
Elijah, 32, 141, 153, 155-159
Enoch, Book of (see R. H. Charles), 50, 59, 234, 317
Etruscan (Tuscan), 16-19, 22, 92, 126
Ezekiel, 32, 64, 65, 141, 153, 155-159

First-born, 212, 213
Flamens, 16, 22
Frenkel, J., 305
Frigga (Freyia), 11, 12, 14
Frogs, 209, 210
Frost plates on Mars, 125, 126

Gabriel (celestial angel), 38, 128, 167
Galanopoulos, Dr., 246

Galileo, G., 190, 197, 293
Geomagnetic field (sheath), 33, 43, 44, 61, 67, 88, 96, 109, 113, 128, 262, 307, 308
Gibeon 55, 176, 180, 185, 191-193
Ginzberg, Louis, (Editor of Talmud and Talmudic commentaries), 20, 38, 87, 127, 128, 135-138, 157, 159, 176, 179, 180, 192, 237, 254, 255, 263, 269, 282, 287, 289, 316, 317
Glass, Billy P., 67
Golden calf (see bull of Apis), 235 235
Golub, Jacob S., 57
Grand cycle of catastrophism, 4, 87, 177, 178, 269, 270, 272, 278-282, 311
Greenhouse effect (canopy), 272, 311, 315
Griqua asteroid, 78, 81, 83
Gulliver, Capt. Lemuel, 292, 297-299
Gyroscope, 113-119, 182, 197

Habakkuk, 4, 34, 42-47, 57, 93, 94, 111
Hall, Asaph, 292-294, 297
Halley, Edmund, 298-301
Halley's Comet, 271
Halloween, 15, 24
Hamlet, 171
Hasta, 16, 27
Hawkins, Gerald S., 13, 164, 266, 286
Hecuba (Gk. deity), 84, 86
Hecuba Gap (Hecuba asteroids), 77, 78, 81-86, 105, 278
Heirtzler, J. H., 64, 67
Helios, 27, 86, 101, 180, 284
Hermes (Mercury), 10, 72, 127, 164, 279
Heroditus, 29, 287, 288
Herschel, Sir William, 298, 300
Herzian-Caledionian mtn. uplift cycle, 317
Hesiod, 302, 303
Hestia (Gk. diety), 77, 84

Hestia Gap (see Alinda), 73, 77, 78, 83, 84
Hezekiah (King), 23, 32, 34, 38-41, 46-48, 50-53, 63, 126, 128, 184, 193, 195, 230-232, 280
Hiezen, Bruce C., 67
Hobal (Hobaal), 29
Homer, 53, 84, 86, 93, 94, 163-165, 168, 169, 292, 302, 303
Horse latitudes (clim. zone) 233
Hudson, Liam, 267
Hutton, James, 8, 267, 318
Hyksos (see Amorites), 203, 204

Iliad, 86, 94, 153, 163, 164, 169, 245, 302
Indo-Aryan cosmology, 26, 27
Indra, 1, 27, 28, 90, 248
Inverse cube law, 103, 104, 221
Inverse square law, 103, 114, 221
Ipuwer, 215, 223, 232
Isostasy (see mtn. uplifts and rift valleys), 259

Jasher, Book of, 180, 183, 184, 201, 251, 282, 308, 310, 315, 317
Jensen, Kenneth L., 145
Jeremiah, 54, 64, 195, 196
Jeroboam II (King), 133-135, 136
Jerusalem Bolide, 49, 50, 57, 92, 96, 101, 127, 220
Joel, 94, 130, 131, 142-144
Jonah, 130, 131, 135, 136
Jordan (body of water), 175, 221
Josephus, Flavius, 131, 136, 137, 166, 167, 173, 176-178, 180, 199, 231, 251, 256, 257, 263, 269, 270, 283, 289, 298, 308, 309, 316
Jotham (King), 134, 138, 140
Jubilees, Book of, 195, 256, 257, 263, 283, 308, 309
Jupiter, 7, 10-17, 22, 24-26, 75, 77-83, 105, 108, 155, 165, 177, 204, 255, 258, 263, 270-272, 274, 275-282, 289, 290, 292, 295

Kaaba (stone), 167
Kant, Emmanuel, 6. 7, 189, 318

Katasev, L. A., 92, 93
Kepler, Johannes, 129, 298
Kirkwood Gaps (see Hecuba Gap, Hestia Gap), 73, 77
Knossos (see Crete), 239, 242
Koldewey, Robert, 287
Krakatoa, 61, 140, 210-212, 222, 225, 242-245
Krebbs, H. A., 249
Kulikova, N. V., 92, 93

Laminated terrain (on Mars), 125
Langmuir, Irving, 267
Lapides sileces, 17, 22, 27
Laputans, 297-303
Lehman, J. C., 305
Lengthened month, 23, 24
Leprosy, 137, 138
Leviathan, 38, 206, 207
Lichtenstein, G. C., 171
Line of apsides, 96, 274, 276, 279
Livy (Titus Livius,) 20
Lowell, Percival, 110
Luce, J. V., 215, 239, 242-244, 248
Lupus Martius, 22
Luther, Martin, 186, 188, 197
Lyell, Sir Charles, 8, 46, 280, 308, 314, 318

Malin, Michael C., 125, 126
Maoris (see New Zealand), 29, 30, 181
Marchesvan, 178, 179, 191, 228-231, 309
Marinatos, Spyridon, 239, 245, 246
Maruts (Mars-asteroids), 27
Maui (see Maori), 29-31, 181, 197
Mavor, James, 215, 225, 239, 242, 243, 245, 246, 248
Mazzaroth, 204, 205
McDowell, Charles, 86, 94, 153, 160, 203, 215, 228, 236, 303
Mecca, 65, 167, 168
Melanchton, Philip, 188
Menzilah, Lake, 221, 236, 243
Mercury (see Hermes), 10, 11, 12, 14, 22, 24, 72, 80, 127, 207, 258, 276, 308, 310, 311

INDEX 327

Merry-go-round 72, 80
Michael (archangel), 38
Milman, Henry Hart, 315
Minoans, 18, 27, 139, 239, 244
Model, 14, 81, 83, 84, 96, 104, 108, 110, 131, 227, 228, 254, 272, 278, 279, 290
Moments ("6 and 30", see Long Day of Joshua), 183
Moon's dimensions, 116
Moscow, 65, 135
Moses, 5, 32, 139, 164, 203, 204, 230-232, 236, 243, 244
Mountain uplift cycles (see also Alpine-Himalayan, Circum-Pacific and Herzian-Caledonian), 312-314, 317
Murray, Brad C., 125, 126

Nahum, 94, 130, 131, 143, 144
Nebular hypothesis (Kant), 6, 7
Neptune, 7, 80, 82, 128, 196, 258, 276, 278, 293
Newell, Norman, 280
Newton, Isaac, 6, 221, 298-301
New Zealand (see Maoris), 29, 30, 181
Nicholson, Seth, 294
Nile River (Delta), 209, 221, 224, 226, 242, 244
Ninevah, 33, 49, 135, 136, 144, 193
Noah, 5, 12, 32, 49, 55, 56, 139, 177, 194, 195, 243, 269, 308, 309, 310, 316, 317
North Pole, 123, 182, 185, 198, 350
Numa (Numa Pompilius, Roman king), 14, 22-24, 52, 126, 231, 232

Obelisk, 2, 60, 98, 123, 126, 223, 229
Odin (Teutonic deity), 11, 12, 14, 22
Ogyges, 243
Olympic, Olympus, 10, 13, 84, 163, 181, 272, 281
Orion, 204, 232, 258
Orpheus, 29
Ovid (Publius Ovidius Naso), 25, 31, 94, 177, 180, 270-272, 281
Ozone, 311

Peirce, Charles S., 169
Peleg, 259, 264, 290, 291, 309, 316
Pendulum, 78, 80, 82, 278
Perigee of Moon, 176
Perihelion of Asteroids, 82
Perihelion of Earth, 69, 70, 97, 99, 150
Perihelion of Jupiter, 73, 278
Perihelion of Mars, 69. 70, 97, 99, 150, 293
Perihelion of Saturn, 278
Perizim, Mt., 185
Phaethon (Gk. myth), 25, 30, 31, 45, 180, 181, 182, 184, 185, 197, 263, 285
Phobos (satellite of Mars), 33, 91, 96, 292-304
Phoenix bird myth, 263
Plato, 84, 199, 215, 238 ff.
Pliny (Gaius Plinius Secundus), 19, 93
Plutarch, 23, 126, 127, 279-281
Pluto, 7, 80, 82, 128, 196, 276, 278
Polyani, M., 150
Poseidon (Gk. diety), 10, 77, 84, 164, 168
Proctor, Mary, 271
Ptolemy (Claudius), 186, 190
Pyramid star charts, 127

Quirinus (see Chronos), 16, 281

Rabshakeh, 32, 34-36, 40, 51
Raguel (celestial angel), 59
Rahab (celestial dragon), 208
Ramael (celestial angel), 38
Raphael (It. painter), 209
Red Sea (Reed Sea, see Lake Menzilah), 209, 221, 236, 243
Resonance defined, 2, see p. 276
Rhea Silvia, 20, 21
Rheticus (G. J. von Lauchen), 188, 190
Richardson, Robert, 295, 299, 300, 302
Rift Valley (in Africa), 87, 208, 255, 258-262
Rift Valley (on Mars), 112, 113
Roche' Limit, 89, 116

Rome (Romans), 10, 11, 14, 16-26, 36, 77, 83, 93, 196, 271, 272, 281
Romulus, 17, 20-23, 280, 302
Roscher, Wilhelm Heinrich, 84
Russia, 64, 135

Samhain, 15, 24, 230
Sammael (celestial archangel), 59
Samuel, 166-168
Sanskrit, 1, 11, 26, 230
Saturn, 7, 10, 12, 13, 24, 25, 73, 81, 83, 91, 96, 104, 155, 177, 226, 230, 258, 274, 276-282, 290, 293
Schiaparelli, Giovanni, 109, 294, 295
Schliemann, Heinrich, 164, 168, 169, 245
Schubart, Joachim, 81
Schweizer, Francois, 81
Seneca, 93, 271
Sennacherib, 32-39, 42, 46, 48-51, 57, 192, 193, 195, 280
Shebna, 32, 34, 38-41, 47, 48, 51
Sibyl, 283
Sinai, Mt., 175, 224, 225, 236, 238, 245
Sinai (Peninsula), 40, 112, 199, 224, 225, 232-234, 242
Socrates, 10, 281
Solon, 246
Stanyukovich, K. P., 93
Steinhauer, Loren C., 87, 89, 314
Stonehenge, 13, 172, 264-266, 271, 286, 287, 290
St. Petersburg, 92
Swift, Jonathan, 8, 292, 297-303

Talmud, 2, 131, 136-138, 140, 157, 173, 176, 178, 180, 184, 199, 201, 203, 234, 251, 254, 263, 269, 288, 308, 315, 317
Teeter-totter, 75, 78, 80, 274, 278, 279
Tektites, 67
Teutons (Teutonic), 1, 2, 11-14, 16, 22-26, 83, 228

Theomagical approach, 189
Thera, 18, 238, 239, 242-246, 248
Thiele, Edwin R., 47, 134, 158, 160
Thor (see Jupiter), 11, 12, 14, 16, 22, 26
Tiamat (celestial dragon), 208
Timaeus (see Plato), 199, 246
Tishri (Tishri calendar), 230, 231, 308
Titans (Gk. deities), 139
Toro asteroid, 80
Transient decay curve, 311
Trojan asteroids, 80
Troy (Trojans), 112, 167, 245
Tubulistrium, 17
Tunguska Bolide, 92, 127, 179
Tyrrhenian Sea, 18

Uranus, 83, 258, 293, 298
Uzziah (King), 131, 134, 135, 137

Vedas, 175
Venus, 7, 10-12, 14, 15, 25, 29, 72, 86, 94, 129, 141, 145, 157, 164, 165, 204, 230, 237, 255, 258, 276, 289, 315
Velikovsky, Immanuel, 17, 19, 23, 28, 29, 37, 93, 110, 126, 209, 213, 215, 223, 232
Vesta (see Hestia), 77
Volsinium (Lake, meteoritic, see Bolsena), 18, 19, 92

Ward, William, 207, 208
Wegener, Alfred L. (see continental drift theory), 261, 262
Whiston, William, 131, 167, 176, 298-303
Williams, J. G., 80
Wolfe, Humbert, 318

Zeus (see Jupiter), 10, 11, 26, 27, 31, 72, 77, 84, 94, 163-165, 180, 181, 245, 281
Zoroaster, 196